T0211549

Beginning RPG Maker MV

Second Edition

Darrin Perez

Apress®

Beginning RPG Maker MV

Darrin Perez
San Lorenzo, Puerto Rico

ISBN-13 (pbk): 978-1-4842-1966-9   ISBN-13 (electronic): 978-1-4842-1967-6
DOI 10.1007/978-1-4842-1967-6

Library of Congress Control Number: 2016943554

Managing Director: Welmoed Spahr
Lead Editor: Ben Renow-Clarke
Development Editor: Matthew Moodie
Technical Reviewer: Robert Reed
Editorial Board: Steve Anglin, Pramila Balen, Louise Corrigan, Jim DeWolf, Jonathan Gennick, Robert Hutchinson, Celestin Suresh John, Nikhil Karkal, James Markham, Susan McDermott, Matthew Moodie, Ben Renow-Clarke, Gwenan Spearing
Coordinating Editor: Nancy Chen
Copy Editor: James Compton
Compositor: SPi Global
Indexer: SPi Global

Distributed to the book trade worldwide by Springer Science+Business Media New York, 233 Spring Street, 6th Floor, New York, NY 10013. Phone 1-800-SPRINGER, fax (201) 348-4505, e-mail orders-ny@springer-sbm.com, or visit www.springer.com. Apress Media, LLC is a California LLC and the sole member (owner) is Springer Science + Business Media Finance Inc (SSBM Finance Inc). SSBM Finance Inc is a Delaware corporation.

For information on translations, please e-mail rights@apress.com, or visit www.apress.com.

Apress and friends of ED books may be purchased in bulk for academic, corporate, or promotional use. eBook versions and licenses are also available for most titles. For more information, reference our Special Bulk Sales–eBook Licensing web page at www.apress.com/bulk-sales.

Any source code or other supplementary material referenced by the author in this text is available to readers at www.apress.com. For detailed information about how to locate your book's source code, go to www.apress.com/source-code/.

Printed on acid-free paper

This book is dedicated to the eternal pursuit of one's dreams
in the face of seemingly insurmountable adversity. Never stop fighting!

Contents at a Glance

Contents

About the Author

Darrin Perez (1988-) was born in Alexandria, Virginia and currently resides in Puerto Rico. His debut fantasy novel, *Whispers of Dawn*, was written as a self-imposed challenge in the spirit of NaNoWriMo (National November Writing Month). He has also written many articles on video games at *Hubpages* and published an ebook concerning RPG Maker VX Ace (a video game development engine) as well. His newest nonfiction book, *Beginning RPG Maker MV*, is the second edition of the *Beginning RPG Maker* Apress book series and the fourth book that the author has published with the company.

About the Technical Reviewer

Robert Reed first started using RPG Maker in his teenage years with RPG Maker 2000. With that experience, he pursued and obtained a Bachelor Degree in Game Design from Collins College in 2011. Through that time, he has followed each incremental release of the RPG Maker series and learned several programming and scripting languages, including C++, C#, Javascript, Java, ActionScript 3.0, and LUA. He resides in Phoenix, Arizona.

Acknowledgments

I would like to acknowledge the efforts of everyone in Apress who has worked with me, especially Ben Renow-Clarke, who approached me once again to write this second edition of the book, and Nancy Chen, who has served as this book's coordinating editor. It's her job to make sure that everything is flowing as it should during the book's development. Honorable mentions include Matthew Moodie (development editor) and Dhaneesh Kumar (formatting and composition). Without the efforts of those working in Apress, you would not be reading this book at this time.

Robert Reed served as this book's technical reviewer, and I would like to thank him for helping me make this book the best it can be. His diligent and measured approach to chapter reviews was key to making sure that the book's code was functioning as it should. However, I can't continue without acknowledging Michael Lin's technical review work in the first edition of this book. Had he not done the initial tech review, you might not be reading this second edition right now. Sometimes it's the smaller things that have the biggest impact; a butterfly effect, if you will.

I would like to thank the RPG Maker community as a whole for all that they have done to make exploring and using each new version of RPG Maker as easy as humanly possible. They have provided countless resources (in the form of tutorials and other essential assets such as sprites and music). Working with a game-development engine can be a daunting task, but they are always willing to lend a helping hand to anyone who needs it. There are far too many people to name, but I hold the community fondly in my heart (even if it has been forever since I've visited).

On a personal level, I have to thank my parents, Jose Perez and Victoria Diaz, who provided (and still provide) me with the support I needed to push through the barriers that one faces when writing a work such as this. It wasn't easy, but here we are, and we have survived!

I also have to thank my closest friends for being constant bulwarks of support and always listening to me rant about this or that.

Finally, I thank you, my dear reader. At the end of the day, all writers make sacrifices to get a solid book out to you and everyone else who desires to read about a certain subject. It is when I see the number of people who read my work that I can boldly say that the sacrifices were worth it. May you enjoy reading this book as much as I enjoyed writing it!

Introduction

It has been a long journey to reach this point. The story of what would eventually become this book started humbly, as a much smaller (self-published) offering titled *The RPG Maker VX Ace Help Guide for Beginners: Tips and Tricks You Can Use For Your Very Own RPG* (quite the mouthful, right?) that was released exclusively in e-book format for the Amazon Kindle. I was contacted by Ben Renow-Clarke in early June of 2014 about writing a RPG Maker book for Apress. He even specifically noted that we could expand on my e-book; a sentiment I promptly agreed on. Work on *Beginning RPG Maker VX Ace* started a few months later and was completed some time after. Of course, the industry doesn't stop moving, and it thus became necessary to update *Beginning RPG Maker* for MV, the newest version of Degica's video game creation software. Updating the book was a process that took the better part of three months and I'm rather proud of the final result. In reading this text, I am confident that you will understand why. This book is the manifestation of my desire to teach other people the things I have learned during my time using RPG Maker in general and MV specifically.

If you're reading this book, you are probably interested in learning about RPG Maker MV. If you've just started using RPG Maker MV, the amount of features it offers for your roleplaying game development may be confusing. That's what I'm here for. During the course of this book, I will give a basic overview of the engine, give tips and tricks that will help you start getting a foothold on understanding RPG Maker MV, and even give you some of the code I've personally used in my time using RPG Maker Ace and MV. So, take a deep breath, and let's go!

What is RPG Maker MV (RMMV)?

RMMV is the latest version of the roleplaying game development engine published by Degica and developed by Kadokawa Games. It was designed with ease of use in mind and allows a complete beginner to create a complete RPG without needing a single day of programming experience. It was released internationally October 23, 2015 and in Japan December 17, 2015 (marking an uncommon occurrence; a Japanese-created product that is released later in its country of origin than in other countries). As with earlier iterations of RPG Maker, games have already been developed with it. Here's a list of features that RMMV brings to the table:

- A powerful eventing system. Events are essentially precoded instances that allow you to do many of the most common RPG things, such as create a treasure chest, a shop, or an inn, force player movement, and create nonplayer characters (NPCs for short) that change what they say based on the player's actions.

- A fully developed turn-based battle system. Besides the classic forward-facing view of earlier RPG Makers, MV also provides support for side-view battles, if those are more your style. For the sake of differentiating this edition of *Beginning RPG Maker* a little more from the first edition, I'll be using the side-view battle system. If you want some other battle system altogether, then you can script one (or commission someone else to do the same). However, that is an advanced topic and I will not be touching upon it in the context of this book.

- A character generator. This generator allows you to create your very own characters by using and mixing predetermined art assets. It can create both the character sprite and the portrait.

- Modifiable skills and item damage formulas. If you want to change the default formula for the Attack command, you can. Likewise, you can change different skills and items so they damage or heal based on both the user's and the enemy stats.

- The ability to create and use multiple tile sets, and edit the passability and terrain tags of those tile sets. Terrain tags can be used with switches and variables to create damage floors, among other things.

- The ability to create enemy encounters and define the regions they spawn in, all with the help of the self-titled Region Tool.

- The ability to use events and JavaScript to give additional effects to items and skills above and beyond the already extensive functionality that RPG Maker MV provides out of the box.

What Is a Roleplaying Game (RPG)?

Chances are that, if you've picked up this book, you probably already know what an RPG is. Most likely you've played some of them by now. Sticklers would say that every game is technically a roleplaying game, given that you control a character or group of characters in your attempt to win the game. On that note, here's a list of criteria I consider essential for a game to be considered an RPG:

- A system that rewards character progression. The most common of these is the experience system. By gaining a certain amount of experience (commonly abbreviated to XP or EXP), the player's character gains a level. The higher the character's level, the stronger they are. Leveling up normally grants new abilities and perks for the character as well.

- A predetermined storyline. While most other genres of video games have a story, nowhere is it as important as in an RPG. It is, usually, the main reason people play RPGs.

- A player character (PC). This is the human player's persona within the in-game universe. The player experiences the game's story through the eyes of his character.

- Nonplayer characters (NPCs). Real life would be boring if you were the only one in it, right? In the same way, a video game would be fairly dull if you were in a completely blank slate devoid of all interaction. NPCs help give the RPG world life as well as serve the many roles required in virtual society. By definition, every character that the player cannot control is an NPC.

There are surely other criteria by which an RPG can be defined, but the ones just listed are, in my appraisal, the most important.

About this Book's Source Code

Given the sheer size of RPG Maker MV's audio and image project folders (they take up about 400 MB of space), I decided to remove them from each of the source code chapter folders. Otherwise, the source code download would be over 6 GB in size! The audio and img folders were respectively placed in a single Assets folder, bringing the size of the entire source code download to a much more manageable size (less than 500 MB). To run a chapter's MV project file correctly, you'll need to copy the audio and img folders within Assets to that chapter's folder. You can find a bit more information in the source code's readme if need be (including a pair of screenshots that will help you visualize what I mean).

■ **Caution** While my way of packing the source code saves you the trouble of *downloading* ~6 GB of content, do keep in mind that the book's source code folders will take up about that much disk space, should you have all 15 project chapter files on your drive at the same time with the associated assets folders pasted within.

PART 1

Creating a Solid Foundation

Everything worth doing starts with a single step. It is the same with creating your very own video game, whether with a development engine such as RPG Maker MV (RMMV) or utilizing your own programming skills. This part of the book will cover the following topics:

- Installing and starting up RMMV, as well as a short overview of story and game play in the role-playing genre of video games.

- The use of switches and variables to create quests and area exits, among other things.

- Adding maps to your project to encompass various typical RPG locales, such as towns and dungeons, manually and with RMMV's own Load function.

- A detailed overview of the RMMV database and how it pertains to player characters, enemies, collectible items such as weapons and potions, and other RPG essentials.

- Populating our first dungeon, complete with enemies, treasure chests, and a boss encounter.

I hope you're as excited as I am! Without further ado, let's begin!

CHAPTER 1

Starting Out with RPG Maker MV

This chapter will cover the following subjects:

- Installing RPG Maker MV (RMMV)
- A short overview of story and game play in roleplaying games (RPGs)
- Starting up RPG Maker and taking your first steps toward creating your very own game

---

Note This book will exclusively cover RPG Maker MV. If you have an earlier version of the engine (such as XP, VX, or VX Ace), you will have to upgrade to MV to follow along.

Before you can use RMMV, you must have it installed. First, I'll walk you through the process of getting and installing your own copy of RMMV.

Where Can I Get RMMV?

RMMV (and a slew of related products) can be purchased from the official site at www.rpgmakerweb.com. The exact link is http://www.rpgmakerweb.com/products/programs/rpg-maker-mv. Alternately, RMMV is also available from Steam.

Note If you're a Mac user, you'll need to grab the Steam version, as the standalone installer is Windows-only.

When it's not on sale, RMMV costs $79.99, but you can try it free for 20 days by grabbing the trial version if you're a Windows user. Unfortunately, Mac users have no trial version at this time; a situation we can only hope changes eventually.

You will be asked for your name and e-mail address when you download the RMMV trial.

Electronic supplementary material The online version of this chapter (doi:10.1007/978-1-4842-1967-6_1) contains supplementary material, which is available to authorized users.

So, I Downloaded a Copy of RMMV. What Next?

If you have a standalone version of RMMV, what follows next is finding the downloaded archive and running the Setup.exe located within it. Afterward, installing it is as easy as following the steps in the installer.

Once the installation is complete, loading it up for the first time will bring up a screen such as illustrated in Figure 1-1.

Figure 1-1. *The starting screen for trial versions of RMMV*

The screenshot is pretty self-explanatory. If you have purchased RMMV, you need only type in your product key as well as the email you provided at that time to activate the software by clicking on the Activate button. Otherwise, you can click on Buy Now to buy a copy of RMMV. If you would rather keep using the trial, you can just click Continue.

▪ **Note** If you're using the Steam version, that platform will automatically install RMMV for you once you purchase it and choose to download it. As it is a full version by default, you shouldn't have to worry about the activation screen just described.

So, I'm Done

Welcome to the world of video game development! I hope you enjoy your stay! Now that you have a functioning copy of RMMV, we can continue. Before we start using the application, it would be good to talk about RPG design in general. Let us begin with the most important aspect, the story.

░ **Note** The current version of RPG Maker MV at the time of this writing is version 1.1. If you have a newer version of the software, it may include extra features not discussed here.

Story

Perhaps the most important thing about an RPG is its story. Even in the days of old, when the first *Dragon Quest* (known as *Dragon Warrior* in the United States until the eighth entry in the series was released) and *Final Fantasy* games were in their prime and storage was an issue with the earliest consoles, RPG developers sought to invest their players into the simple plot that they managed to fit within the cartridge. Perhaps the most important thing I can point out is that not every story needs to be complex. Complexity helps, sure, *if you can make it work*. Sometimes, it's the little things that have the greatest impact. The basic facets of *any* basic RPG story are virtually identical to those used in your standard fantasy or sci-fi book with a heroic protagonist:

- *You have a protagonist*: In an RPG, this is the main character controlled by the player. The protagonist is a distinct entity, with goals, dreams, and desires.

- *You have a conflict*: The most typical fantasy conflict for both books and video games is a great evil that rises, and only the hero/chosen one/protagonist (whether alone or with help) can defeat them. With that said, don't limit yourself. If you come up with a great plot that involves a conflict between the protagonist and himself, for example, feel free to take that ball and run with it.

- *You have obstacles*: Think back to the last RPG you played or fantasy book you read. The protagonist did not start the adventure and defeat the main villain within ten minutes/pages (if they did, it was probably a fake-out and not an actual victory). The protagonist probably started from a position of relative weakness and set out into the world to defeat the antagonist, being deterred every so often by hostile forces (some aligned with evil, and some not) and hindrances such as a broken bridge or a collapsed mine shaft.

- *You have a climax and a resolution*: The protagonist, after countless tribulations, finally reaches the castle of the "Dark Lord." With a carefully calculated strike of his weapon of choice, he defeats his timeless foe. Or does he? Depending on the type of story you want to tell, perhaps your antagonist escapes to live another day. Perhaps he was merely subordinate to an even greater evil.

A great story can save an otherwise mediocre RPG, but a mediocre story can ruin even great RPGs. You must define what type of story your RPG will have. Following are some questions that should get you thinking along the right track:

- *Will it be a fantasy RPG?* If so, will magic be prominent? Will alternate forms of abilities, such as technology or something else altogether, take center stage?

- *Or will you have a sci-fi RPG?* That's neat, too. Will technology be prominent, or will the setting be a devastated future where everyone is basically surviving with sticks and stones?

- *When will the story take place?* You can have a modern-day story set in a high school, for example, or a historical spy thriller set during the cold war. Maybe you want your story to take place in prehistory!

- *Who is your protagonist?* Is he young? Old? Is your protagonist female? Define why your protagonist is doing what he/she is doing. A good backstory can set the stage for greater things during the actual story.

- *Who are your protagonist's allies?* Do they know each other at the time of the game's events, or will they meet one during the game? Define their backstories. Or perhaps you want a mysterious type in your party? Those are cool too, if you know how to create them.

- *What is your protagonist's quest?* Is he/she seeking an artifact to save the world? Or perhaps the end of the world will be brought about by a heinous villain. Of course, you could just do something else entirely and have your party go on a journey of self-discovery.

- *Who are some important nonplayer characters in the story?* Will they aid or hinder the party? Are any of them related to any of your party members?

All of those questions are good to consider for getting the ball rolling on a great story. It's important to take some time to think about the story you want for your game before you get too invested in trying to actually create it. Or maybe you don't want to make an RPG at all. Although this book is meant to teach you about the intricacies of RMMV via the creation of an RPG, there's nothing to prevent you from applying the knowledge you will gain from this book to create something completely different. You could use RMMV's framework to create a game that eschews battles and magic systems altogether! In fact, there have been many games created with earlier versions of RPG Maker that are not RPGs. Off the top of my head, I can offer *You Are Not the Hero* (YANTH, for short) for RPG Maker VX Ace, which is a quirky action-platformer with many minigames and a self-aware sense of humor. You could take it even further by creating, with the engine, an interactive novel in the same vein as *To the Moon (*created using RPG Maker XP*)*. At the end of the day, the only limits to your story are those you place on yourself.

Game Play

Of course, while the story of an RPG is important, you want your game play to be a bit more enticing than just going into a single 30-floor dungeon and killing things (although that *has* worked on more than one occasion as well, especially for action RPGs). Basically, ask yourself this question: Would I play this game from start to finish? If you can't answer yes to that question with a straight face, you have to re-evaluate your game, or have friends do it for you. A tried-and-true template for an RPG's game flow is the following:

- A town gives the player quests with objectives located at a nearby dungeon.

- The dungeon is filled with those objectives and a boss.

- After defeating the boss, the player unlocks the next area.

- This is a new town and a new dungeon.

- Repeat until the final dungeon with the final boss.

It may seem ridiculously simple and boring, but several famous RPG franchises (*Dragon Quest* and *Final Fantasy* come to mind) had plots for most of their earlier iterations that followed that general sequence. Of course, there's no problem with making the game a bit more nonlinear and allowing your players to branch off into areas they perhaps shouldn't be in yet (as long as there is an appropriate risk-to-reward ratio). Also evaluate whether you want to add vehicles to your game, such as airships, submarines, or horses. You might even make certain vehicles available only after lengthy side quests but reward the player for doing those quests by allowing the special vehicle to access otherwise inaccessible areas. Here are some other things to consider concerning your game's play:

- *What type of progression will you be using?* Will you have the conventional system of gaining experience via combat/quest completion and then grant skills/spells/abilities as your characters level up? Or maybe you will go for something a little less conventional, perhaps a system similar to *Final Fantasy 2* (the real *FF2*, not the one released in the West that is technically *Final Fantasy 4*), in which you get stats by doing, so that if you take hits, you gain health. If you cast a spell, you gain magic points, and so forth.

- *How difficult do you want the game to be?* Easier isn't always equal to boring, mind you. *Chrono Trigger* is one of the most renowned Japanese RPGs of all time, and I've always felt that the battle system and encounters were on the easier side for such a game. *Shin Megami Tensei*, on the other hand, is rather fair, if extremely challenging, for newer players. Fairness is ultimately more important than difficulty when it comes to RPG game play.

- *How many characters will the player's party have?* Is the protagonist an army of one, or does he/she have allies? I'll elaborate on the importance of this in the following paragraphs.

Balance is an important consideration when you are designing your game. A preceding bullet point asks about party size. There is a concept in video game theory, especially related to turn-based games, called action economy. Generally, each character gets only a certain number of actions in the period of time defined as a turn. The more characters you have, the more actions your party receives in total. For example, the original Dragon Quest had the player control a single hero. That meant effects that caused the player character to miss a turn (such as sleep) were particularly dangerous. It also created a trade-off whereby if you were close to defeating an enemy but your hero was near death, you had to decide whether to heal yourself or attack again. If you were making an RPG with a single playable character, you would have to keep such facts in mind.

On the flip side, if you have a party of three or four characters, you must design some of the party's potential enemies around that. Maybe the party will face off against venomous plants that can spew poison at the entire group. When you have multiple characters, you can be a little more liberal with effects that cause turn-skipping, as the player would still have other characters to defeat those effects or otherwise continue fighting. A game's balance is one of the hardest things to perfect but is, thankfully, something you can work toward with the feedback you receive from your game's players and your own play-testing.

Entire works have been written about video game design, and it is beyond the scope of this book to discuss the topic further at this time. Even so, I will touch upon a few other facets of RPG game design specifically in later chapters, as the need arises. Let us move on to a basic overview of RMMV itself. So, you've probably already started up RMMV and have taken a cursory look around. If you have just recently installed the software (and gotten past the Product Activation screen if you're using the standalone version of RMMV), you'll notice that you're dumped into a lifeless screen, like the one in Figure 1-2.

Figure 1-2. *The opening screen of RPG Maker MV*

- The first thing you'll want to do is go to the File menu at the top-left of the interface and select New Project. That will bring up a prompt asking for three things.

- *Name*: Whatever name you put in this field will also populate the Game Title field. As the field suggests, it is the name of the folder that will be created to store your RMMV data.

- *Game Title*: Self-explanatory. This gets auto-populated with whatever you write in the Folder Name, but you can change the contents of this field manually just by overwriting the text.

- *Location*: Where the RMMV Project folder will be saved. You can click the small button to the right labeled "Choose…" to change the destination.

Once you have worked out what you want your project to be called, click OK. I called mine "BRMMV" and saved it in the default location. The program will take some time to add the relevant default assets to your new project and will then dump you on a barebones map such as the one in Figure 1-3.

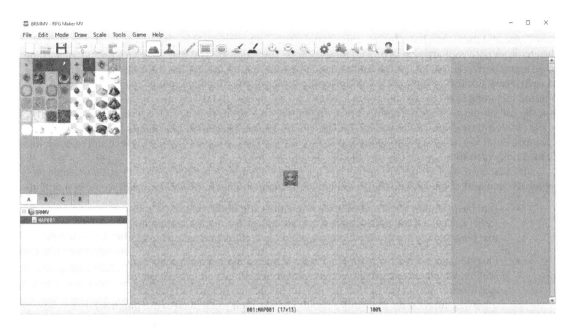

Figure 1-3. *Your first world*

Looks much better now, doesn't it? You should now be seeing a character with reddish-brown hair in the middle of an empty grassland. In the top-left part of the screen, you can see various graphics, each of a specific pixel size. Those graphics are called tiles and make up the pieces that you can use to create your own RPG locations. RMMV comes with a fairly robust Run-Time Package (RTP) that includes all sorts of things you will need for making your very own game. It will serve you well up to the moment you decide to use completely custom assets for your game development.

For now, let us mess around a bit. At the top of the screen, find the menu option named Game and click it. Then click Playtest. You will get a title screen with a nice song and the following options:

- New Game

- Continue: This should be grayed out, as there are no saved games to continue from.

- Options: Brings up a window with six gameplay-related options:

    - *Always Dash:* By default, the player character can dash at double speed during the game by holding the Shift key. With this option set to *on,* holding the key is not necessary.

    - *Command Remember:* This instructs the game to remember the last option selected in various game menus (such as the battle menu and the character status menu). It defaults to *off,* and turning it on is a matter of taste.

    - *BGM Volume:* Allows you to raise and lower the game's Background Music volume. Defaults to 100%.

    - *BGS Volume:* Allows you to control the game's Background Sound volume. Defaults to 100%.

    - *ME Volume:* Like the previous two options, but for Music Effects instead.

    - *SE Volume:* You get the idea, but this one is for Sound Effects.

9

Use your keyboard's arrow keys or your mouse (hooray for newly added mouse support in MV) to select New Game and then press Enter (or left-click if you're using the mouse). Now you should be able to control the character with your arrow keys or with mouse clicks. You'll quickly find that there's a whole lot of nothing to do in this barren grassland (you should also see that your main character has three other companions as well). Press X or Esc, or right-click with the mouse, to access the Character menu. You will see several options, including Save (which allows you to record your progress; RMMV defaults to Save Anywhere, but you can use simple eventing in combination with defined save points to have a save system similar to many of the *Final Fantasy* games, for example). Feel free to poke around in the various menus. (You can use the spacebar, Enter key, or left-click to select and X, Esc, or right-click to cancel/deselect.) Once you're done, hit Game End (which should probably be called End Game or Quit).

Now that we're back where we started, let's integrate everything I've talked about. First, let's change the name of Game End. If you click on the Tools item in the menu toolbar for RMMV, you will see several options

- Database (Hotkey F9): The Database is the meat and bones of RMMV in its stock form (and even if you make ample use of scripting). It contains a whopping 15 tabs that contain very nearly everything you could ever think of needing for an RPG.

- Plugin Manager (Hotkey F10): The Plugin Manager allows you to enable and disable plugins, which are essentially sequences of code created using JavaScript that can add functionality to your game. If you want to add new features to your game that are otherwise unavailable in RMMV's robust chassis, then you'll need to use plugins. I'll cover the use of this manager near the end of the book, when I cover basic scripting.

- Sound Test (Hotkey N/A): As the name suggests, you can listen to sounds contained within your project. The four different types of sounds are the following:

  - BGM—Background Music: Such things as the default title screen song are considered BGM.

  - BGS—Background Sounds: If you can hear something constant in an area, but it is not music, it is probably a BGS. Quake and Wind are two of the stock examples present within RMMV.

  - ME—Music Effects: Mini-songs, if you will, such as the tune played when you rest at an inn.

  - SE—Sound Effects: The simplest of sounds, yet so important as well. A slew of things are SE. The sounds of fire spells and sword attacks are but two of the types of SE present within RMMV's stock content.

- *Event Searcher (Hotkey N/A)*: A completely new menu option for this newest version of RPG Maker. I will cover it in greater detail in the next chapter once we start working on things that are relevant to the Event Searcher. Suffice to say that it can be really helpful when your game project gets bigger.

- *Character Generator (Hotkey N/A)*: Allows you to create new character (human-based) models by mixing and matching hair, eye, and skin color with many other customization options. If you'd rather, you can always click Randomize and see what pops up. New to MV is the ability to generate character models for side-view battles as well.

- *Resource Manager (Hotkey N/A):* Added back into MV for version 1.1, after an odd absence from MV 1.0. The Resource Manager allows you to preview, import, export, and delete assets from your RMMV project.

For this task, like most other things we'll do during the course of this book, we will want to go to the Database. Once there, you will see the 15 tabs I mentioned previously. To change the menu options, we click the Terms tab (which happens to be the last one). You'll see four major categories:

- Basic Statuses: A block containing full names and abbreviations for Level, HP, MP, TP, and EXP.

- Parameters: Contains the terms for what are also called stats (short for statistics) in RPGs. Examples include Defense and Luck.

- Commands: This section of the Terms tab contains names for menu options and item type names, among others.

- Messages: New to RPG Maker MV is the ability to change the contents of many messages that are displayed in gameplay.

The Commands section of the Terms tab is what we're looking for, as displayed in Figure 1-4.

Commands

Fight:	Escape:	Attack:	Guard:
Fight	Escape	Attack	Guard
Item:	**Skill:**	**Equip:**	**Status:**
Item	Skill	Equip	Status
Formation:	**Options:**	**Save:**	**Game End:**
Formation	Options	Save	Game End
Weapon:	**Armor:**	**Key Item:**	**Equip:**
Weapon	Armor	Key Item	Equip
Optimize:	**Clear:**	**Buy:**	**Sell:**
Optimize	Clear	Buy	Sell
New Game:	**Continue:**	**To Title:**	**Cancel:**
New Game	Continue	To Title	Cancel

Figure 1-4. *The Commands section of the Terms tab*

As you can see, from here we can change the name of any of those listed terms. So let's change "Game End" to "End Game." Click Apply to save the change and then OK to close the Database menu. Now, let's see if we can add some diversity to our player character's surroundings. Figure 1-5 shows my own efforts. Use the provided tiles to replicate it as best you can.

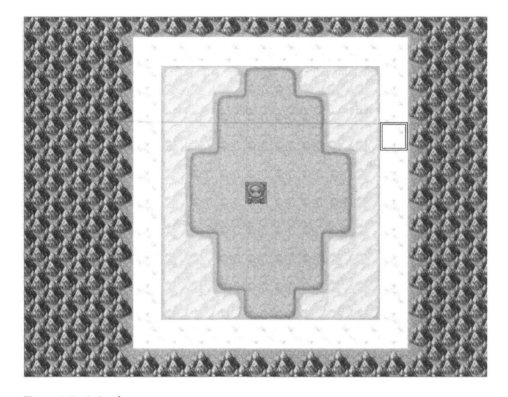

Figure 1-5. *A simple map*

From inner to outer layer, the tiles are

- Grass

- Desert

- Clouds

- Mountain (Dirt) on top of Wasteland

There are a few drawing tools that you can use (RMMV defaults to the pencil, which draws in tiles as you click/drag your mouse). They are located almost directly below the Help item of the menu toolbar. You can choose to draw rectangles or ellipses, or fill a large area with the same tile. I used the Fill tool to add the Wasteland tile and then the Mountain on top of the Wasteland.

■ **Tip** You can find the name of a tile by mousing over it. The tile name will be displayed in the lower-left corner of the application.

Once you have added the terrain to your map, load up the game again, and you should be able to move all the way to the clouds. The mountains will stop you from moving any further. Simple, isn't it?

Summary

This chapter has covered the installation and initialization of RPG Maker MV, as well as providing a short overview of game play and story design considerations and a first look at the game-development engine. However, there's not much of a game here yet. Let's move on to a topic that is important for creating video games of all genres, RPGs included—command variables and switches.

CHAPTER 2

Switches and Variables

If you have any programming experience, you're probably familiar with the use of switches and variables (especially the latter) in coding programs.

Switches? Variables? Pizza?

Yes, Yes, and with pepperoni, please. Seriously, though, let me explain. Switches and variables in RPG Maker MV (RMMV) are similar to boxes in real life. They both hold information you would want to use later on. They are ubiquitous in video games as well. Don't believe me? Here's a small list of things that, with the use of switches and variables, you can influence in any video game:

- The ability to keep track of the number of chests opened during the course of the game (variables).

- The ability to determine whether a boss has been defeated or not (switches).

- Preventing the player from accessing a certain area without a key or some other device (switches).

- Changing a quest reward based on the method the player used to complete the quest. For instance, you could give a 300-gold reward for killing a group of bandits, and give a reduced reward if the player drives them off, sparing them, instead (variables).

- Counting the number of enemies left on a certain screen (variables).

- Counting the steps your party has taken (variables). This has several applications, such as causing a nonstandard Game Over when the player exceeds a certain number of steps or granting the player an achievement or skill. You could use a variable to increase or decrease the power of a skill as well.

As you must have noticed, you cannot make a video game without switches and variables!

Switches and Variables Do the Same Thing, Then?

Mostly, but there are differences. For switches, think of a light switch that has an on and an off state. You can set conditionals that trigger only when a certain switch is on or off. Variables, on the other hand, can hold a number—any number that you can think of. Want to have -327 contained within a variable you call Bob? Sure, go right ahead! Basically, both switches and variables are used for storing relevant game information, but they are best used in different types of situations.

© Darrin Perez 2016
D. Perez, *Beginning RPG Maker MV*, DOI 10.1007/978-1-4842-1967-6_2

It is best to use a switch when you want to create a button/lever/switch in-game that is binary (that is, it has exactly two states). It is best to use a variable when you have a situation that cannot be covered with a simple on/off state. For example, if you wanted to count how many goblins a player has defeated, you would have to store that information in a variable. On the other hand, if someone gave your character a quest to slay five goblins, you could have a switch flip to the "on" state after the fifth goblin is defeated.

While switch and variable theory is nice and all, let's take some time to apply it.

Objectives:

- Add a button to the previously made map that creates an exit through which our intrepid hero can reach another map. After all, if I were him, I wouldn't want to be cooped up in a single 13×17 map for eternity!

- Create the exit itself.

So, how do we go about adding the necessary items to the map? We are finally going to start trying out the functionality that gives RMMV its reputation as a robust game-development engine that even a novice can use. If you look below and slightly to the right of the Game item on the menu toolbar, you'll notice a pair of icons (they are to the left of the drawing tool icons):

- The first icon, which should have a white square around it, if you haven't interacted with these icons previously, is Map mode, or as RMMV puts it, Map. As the name suggests, having Map selected allows you to add/remove tiles on your currently selected map. You can press F5 to switch to Map mode at any time.

- The second icon is the Event Editing mode (Event for short). (You can also press F6 to switch to that mode without having to click the icon.) Events form a large part of RMMV's stock functionality.

- An *event* is an object that occupies a single square on an RMMV map and carries out processing for pretty much all essential game functions. For example, we can create a shop run by a horse or a doorway that requires a key. Without events, you won't be able to do much, if anything, at all. All nonplayer characters (NPCs) are events, for example.

Click the Event icon (or press F6), and you'll notice that a grid appears on the map. If you right-click any square of the grid, you'll see a menu pop up, as in Figure 2-1.

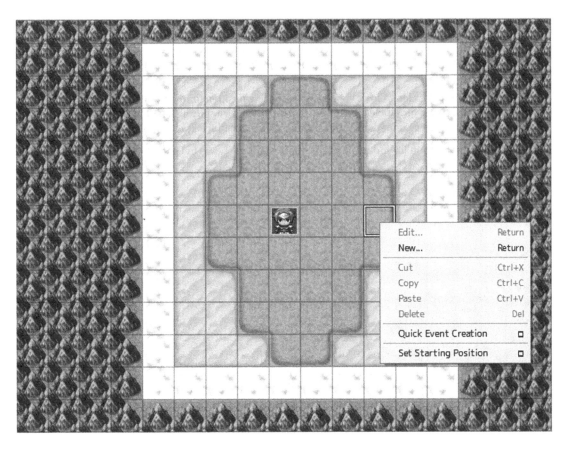

Figure 2-1. *The Event pop-up menu*

The available options are as follows:

- New: This allows you to place a new event on the map. We'll be using this frequently throughout this book.

- The editing tools (Cut/Copy/Paste/Delete) are grayed out because there is no event in the selected square.

- Quick Event Creation: RMMV comes with four quick events for things that are essential to any RPG experience:

  - **Transfer.** Creates an event that allows you to transfer a player from one place to another

  - **Door.** A situational type of transfer event, usually used for entrances to buildings

- **Treasure.** Creates an event that gives items or currency (default name "gold") to the player when he/she interacts with it

- **Inn.** Heals the player and his/her party (if applicable) for a predefined cost in currency

- Set Starting Position: Allows you to set the starting position for the player character and three types of vehicles (boat, ship, airship). Setting a starting position for the player character is mandatory, but starting vehicle locations are optional.

Click New Event and you'll wind up on a large blank slate, as shown in Figure 2-2.

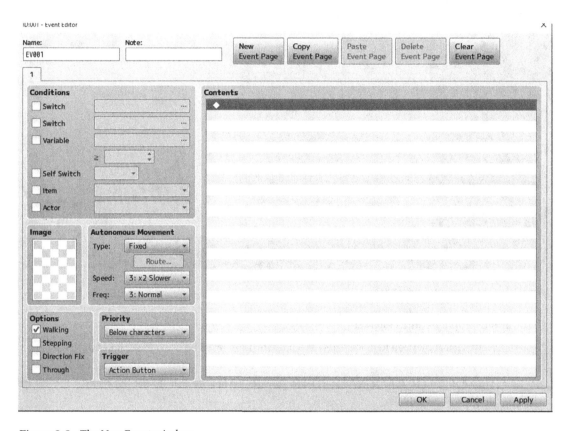

Figure 2-2. *The New Event window*

There are many aspects to the New Event screen, so let's break them down.

- In the upper-left corner, you have several Conditions. If you don't set any event conditions, the event in question will always be active.

- The checkerboard directly under Image can be double–left-clicked to display a list of graphics present within the project. You can then choose a graphic to represent the event. For example, you could use a graphic for a villager or a monster. We'll be using a button image later in the chapter.

- Below the checkerboard, you have a list of four Options:

    - **Walking.** Displays character movement. If you turn off Walking and have an NPC that moves, the character will appear to be sliding on the ground.

    - **Stepping.** When the check box is ticked, the NPC will walk in place. A neat use of Stepping is if you want to simulate gesturing during conversations.

    - **Direction Fix.** As the option name implies, when this check box is clicked the event will be unable to switch directions. You could use this for a shooting gallery type of mini-game, in which you want the player to face forward no matter what arrow key he/she presses.

    - **Through.** The player character can pass through an event that has this option toggled on. Logically, the event can also pass through the player character (in the case of a mobile event such as an NPC). This is cool for ghosts and other such apparitions.

- Autonomous Movement is divided into three functions:

    1. **Type.** Defines what kind of movement the event uses. There are four types of movement.

        - *Fixed*: An event with this type of movement will remain in its starting location. This is perfect for the many kinds of immobile things that you will need for your RPG.

        - *Random*: Events with a random movement type will wander wherever they like, with no rhyme or reason. I'd use this movement type sparingly, as it can cause some annoying situations if you have thin corridors in your game.

        - *Approach*: An event with this movement type will try to approach the player character. It is good for making a scene involving enemies chasing your players.

        - *Custom*: This allows the Move Route button to be clicked, which, in turn, lets you set a movement pattern for the event in question.

    2. **Speed.** This sets how quickly the event executes its movement pattern. The higher the speed, the quicker the event will step.

    3. **Freq.** Short for "Frequency." Sets how frequently the event executes its movement pattern. The higher the frequency, the more often the event takes a movement action.

- Priority defines what graphical layer an event is rendered on, relative to the player character:

    1. **Below characters.** Means that the event is located beneath the player character's feet. This is good for floor switches and staircases.

    2. **Same as characters.** Means that the event is located on the same graphical layer as the player character. This is perfect for NPCs and inanimate objects, such as cabinets and trees.

    3. **Above characters.** Means that the event is located over the player character's head. This is useful for chandeliers and ceilings, among other things.

- *Trigger* defines how the event can be activated.

    1. **Action Button.** An event that activates via the use of the Action Button (spacebar or Enter, by default) when appropriate. If the event has *Below characters* priority, the player character will have to stand on top of the event to activate it. If the event has *Same as characters* priority, the player character will have to stand next to the event while facing it to activate it. Last, if the event has *Above characters* priority, the player character will have to stand under the event to activate it.

    2. **Player Touch.** An event that activates when the player character touches the event by walking into it. It is affected by Priority much like the Action Button.

    3. **Event Touch.** An event that activates when it touches the player character. It is similarly affected by Priority as the previous two options. I prefer to use Player Touch, but you'll need Event Touch on the map, if you're trying to make moving projectiles that your players must dodge, for example.

■ **Note** An easy way to determine whether you need Player Touch or Event Touch is the following: for something that you want the player to trigger at his/her convenience, use Player Touch. For something that the player must avoid or is otherwise triggered outside his/her control, use Event Touch.

---

    4. **Auto run.** An event with the Autorun trigger is always on and will repeat its actions until interrupted somehow. This is probably the easiest way to crash your game when you're just starting out in RMMV. I generally only use it for cinematic sequences (such as events in which you have the game auto-control the player character in an in-game cut scene).

    5. **Parallel.** Similar to an Autorun trigger, a Parallel event is always on. However, it will not interrupt other game functions. This is the type of event you should use to handle large-scale area transitions, among several other things.

- The entire right half of the New Event screen contains its Contents. By right-clicking (and left-clicking New) or double-left-clicking anywhere inside the window boundaries, you'll find yourself looking at a long list of event commands. They represent the many things that we can do with RMMV without having an inkling of JavaScript knowledge. I will cover a few of these later in this chapter and many more throughout the book.

- At the very top of the page, you'll see five buttons involved in the creation and deletion of Event Pages. A single event can have up to 99 pages.

An Event Can Have 99 Event Pages!

Yes, seriously. I'm hard-pressed to think of any situation in which you'd have to make use of all 99 pages, but most events you create for your RPG will require more than one. Multiple event pages are how you can make NPCs change conversations as you progress within the game, to name but one thing you can do with them. As a matter of fact, the button event I will create shortly will have two pages.

Ready?

Let us begin. First of all, check Figure 2-3 for the end result.

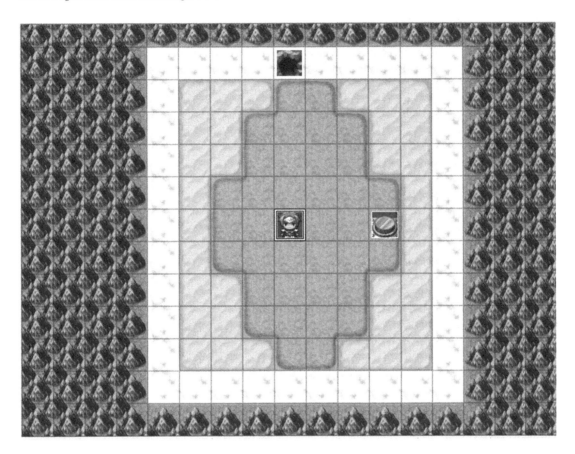

Figure 2-3. *The finished button and exit in place*

That's a green button located three steps to the player character's right and the exit five steps to the north. The button event is two pages, and the exit event is one page. Before I explain what commands to add, let's think about the situation critically. Our player starts the game and sees nothing of note, save a single button. You want the player to press the button and receive some sort of feedback after the fact, so that he/she knows he/she did. So, page 1 of the button event will have a graphic of the green button in a raised position, while page 2 of that event will have a graphic of the same button in a lowered position. We will inform the player via a text box that the button has been pressed, before we do that.

Pressing the button will reveal the exit to the north. You are starting to see how this will all work out. In essence

- We want a button that the player can press to reveal an exit.

- We do not want the exit to be revealed before the player presses the switch.

- We want the switch to reflect the fact that the player has pressed it.

How do we do that? With a switch! The final results for the pages are shown in Figures 2-4 to 2-6. We'll step through the required instructions for reaching this state next.

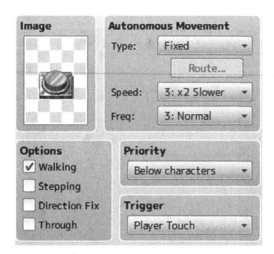

Figure 2-4. *The first page of our button*

```
♦Text : None, Window, Bottom
:      : You stepped on the switch!
♦Play SE : Jump1 (90, 100, 0)
♦Control Switches : #0001 Switch = ON
```

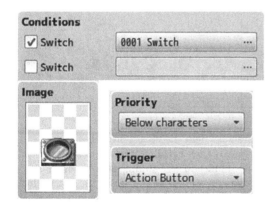

Figure 2-5. *The second page of our button*

```
♦Text : None, Window, Bottom
:      : You see a button pushed into the earth.
```

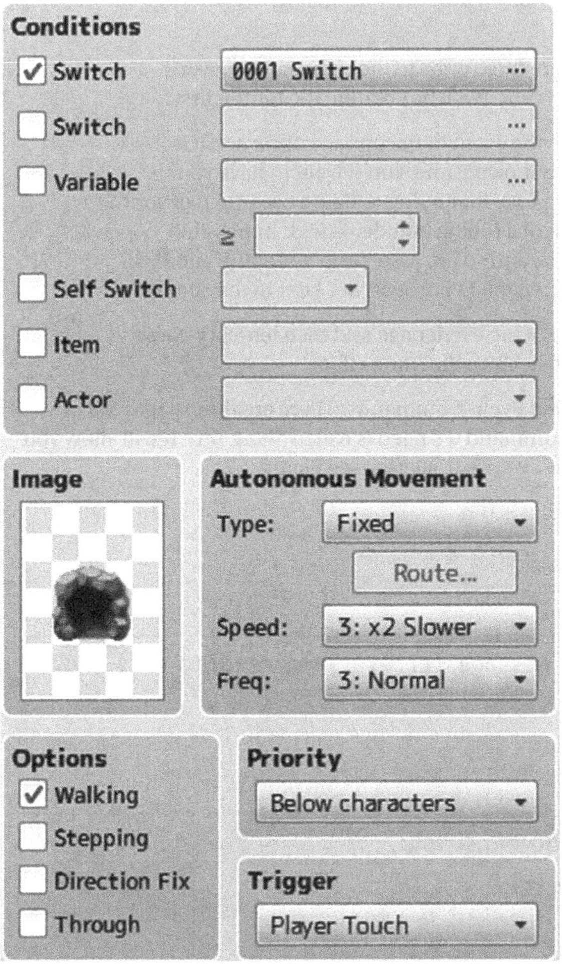

Figure 2-6. *Our exit event for transferring the player to the next map*

♦Transfer Player : MAP001 (0,0)

⬛ **Note** If an event has a single page with a condition that has yet to be met, it will be invisible in-game. Thus, the player will not be able to see the exit until the "Switch" Switch is on.

23

Creating the Events

- While in Event mode, right-click the square three grids to the right of the player's starting position and then left-click New Event. We'll be creating the button first.

- On the blank event page, you can rename the event in the upper-left corner. It is currently unimportant, but if you make your own game, you'll want to have your events properly identified. Trust me when I say that trying to figure out which of your 38 events on a map is supposed to represent a rolling boulder is nigh impossible when they're named EV001, EV002, EV003, and so on. Also, proper identification will be relevant to our interests when I talk about the Event Searcher later in the chapter.

- Right-click the ♦ sign in the Contents part of the event page and then left-click New. Alternatively, you can double–left-click to achieve the same effect.

Now you can see a long list of appropriately named Event Commands. There are three pages full of useful commands for your eventing needs. The first command we need is called *Show Text*. It will allow you to write in some text to be displayed in a box when the event is triggered; see Figure 2-7.

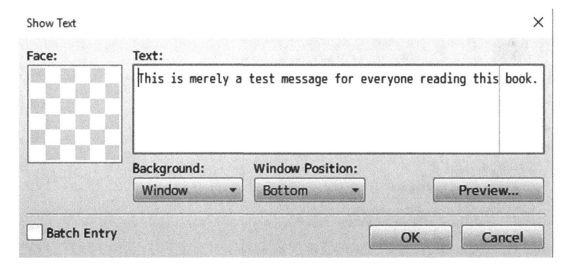

Figure 2-7. *The Show Text event window*

As you can see in Figure 2-7, there are a few things you can do with this command:

- You can add a character portrait to the text box. Keep in mind that doing so reduces the amount of text that you can fit in each line.

- On that note, you may have noticed the almost transparent line that divides the words "this" and "book." This gray line marks the amount of text that will be readable in-game. If you add a character portrait, the line shifts to the left, as the portrait takes up space that would otherwise be available for text. The text in Figure 2-7 would read roughly as follows in-game: "This is merely a test message for everyone reading this." Adding a portrait cuts the message down to, "This is merely a test message for everyone r." You can use Enter to break up your lines, so that they don't hit that limit. A text box can fit up to four lines of text.

- The Batch Entry option can be toggled to allow you to write more than four lines of text. (It adds a scrollbar to the right of the text box.) Additional Show Text commands will automatically be created after every fourth line of text that you have, once you select OK.

- Background affects the appearance of the text box itself. The default is Window, which will display the text box in the color set within RMMV. The default is -34 Red/0 Green/68 Blue and can be changed with the use of the Change Window Color event command. You can also set the text box to Dim and Transparent. Transparent can be quite useful if you have a scene in which you have blacked out the screen and just want to show the text, without the accompanying text box.

- Window Position is fairly self-explanatory. You can set the position of the text box on the screen when it is displayed. It defaults to Bottom and can also be set to Middle or Top, as desired.

  Let's write "You stepped on the switch!" and then click OK.

- The next step is not strictly required but adds a little atmosphere to the event. By using the Play SE command (available on the second page of the Event Command list), you can set a sound effect to be played after you step on the switch. I chose the Jump1 SE and left it at default volume, pitch and pan. You can play around with one or the other, to see how they affect the sound effect in question.

- Last, we toggle the switch! The Control Switches event command is on the first page of the Event Commands list.

When you click it, the command will display the screen shown in Figure 2-8. The Control Switches command is rather simple. You choose a single switch or a batch of switches to flip, and then you decide whether you want to set them on or off. You can click the button labeled "…" to change the switch you are affecting (as well as give the switch a proper name, as all switches and variables default to having a blank name). Here, I've given Switch #0001 the name of Switch, but you can rename it to something like "ButtonPress" or "ButtonSwitch." Once that is ready, all you have to do is set the other options, so that they match mine as shown following:

- Options
  - Toggle on Walking.
- Autonomous Movement
  - Type: Fixed
  - Speed: 3: ×2 Slower
  - Freq 3: Normal
- Priority: Below Characters
- Trigger: Player Touch

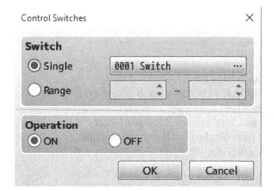

Figure 2-8. *The Control Switches window*

■ **Note** The green switch I used is from the tileset called !Switch1; it is the one in the top-left corner of the green buttons.

That concludes the first event page for the button. Now, what you need to do is choose New Event Page. You will see a new tab numbered 2 appear. Make sure to toggle the conditional, as I did, and set the relevant options, as shown following:

- Conditions: *Switch:* 0001 Switch

- Priority: Below characters

- Trigger: Action Button

I also added some text: "You see a button pushed into the earth." Once that is done, you can press OK, which will place you back at the map screen.

■ **Note** The green button graphic used in page 2 is the one in the lower-right corner of the group of relevant graphics in !Switch1.

Finally, right-click the square five steps to the north of the player's starting position and set the parameters for the Exit Event as I have done here:

- Conditions: Switch: 0001 Switch

- Options: Toggle on Walking

- Autonomous Movement

  - Type: Fixed

  - Speed: 3: ×2 Slower

  - Freq: 3: Normal

- Priority: Below characters

- Trigger: Player Touch

■ **Note** The graphic used for the exit can be found in the Tileset-B graphics group. It is two tiles down and one tile right from the upper-left corner.

As for the contents of the exit event, there are two ways to create a transfer event, as follows:

1. Create it manually. You should do so for the practice, but keep in mind option 2 for the future.

2. Use the Quick Event Creation ➤ Transfer option to achieve the same effect.

If you prefer to do it the long way, *Transfer Player* can be found on the second page of the Event Command List. Clicking Transfer Player in the event command menu will present an image similar to Figure 2-9.

Figure 2-9. *The Transfer Player event dialog*

For now, just leave the settings as displayed in Figure 2-9. We'll expand on this in the next section. Once all is said and done, you can play-test the game in its current state. Feel free to move around and interact with the button. If you have set up the map events correctly, all of the following should be true:

- Walking onto the button will cause the button event to trigger a text box pop-up, as well as the sound effect to play and the switch to sink into the ground.

- After the switch is pressed, you should see the exit reveal itself at the upper part of the screen.

- Pressing the spacebar or Enter key or left-clicking when you are on top of the pressed button will give you the relevant text, telling you that the button is already pressed.

- Walking into the exit will put you in the upper-left corner of the same map, unable to move as the mountain tiles used are impassable, as set within RMMV itself (passability can be changed in the Tilesets tab of the Database; I'll touch upon that in a later chapter).

■ **Note**   When an event has multiple pages, the *rightmost* page with valid conditions is executed. That is the reason we have the button event ordered as it is. If it were reversed, the event would keep repeating itself every time you stepped onto the square.

Creating Your Second Map

You may have noticed earlier that the destination for the map exit has been set to the same coordinates as the exit itself. What we need to do now is create a new map and change the Transfer event command to send us to that map. To do that, start by looking at the lower-left corner of the map screen, shown in Figure 2-10.

Figure 2-10. *This portion of the screen displays all of the maps in your game*

You should see something similar to the preceding screenshot. On your end, BRMMV will be whatever you decided to call your project. MAP001 is the default 13×17 map that is automatically inserted into every new project. Right-click MAP001 and you'll see the following options:

- *Edit (Hotkey: Space)*: Allows you to edit the currently selected map

- *New Map (Hotkey: Enter)*: Creates a new map

- *Load (Hotkey: N/A)*: RMVXA comes with a wide range of premade maps you can use to see how to lay out many areas typical of the standard RPG experience.

- *Copy/Paste/Delete*: These are the editing tools available when dealing with maps.

- *Shift (Hotkey: Ctrl+T)*: Allows you to move the map a certain number of squares in the direction you choose.

- *Generate Dungeon (Hotkey: Ctrl+D)*: Randomly generates a maze, based on the map size, whether you prefer to have a maze-type dungeon or a room-type dungeon, and a selection of wall and floor tiles. Additionally, you have a pair of options to further tweak your random creations:

  - *Add Margins*: In RPG Maker VX Ace, generating a dungeon would create a series of rooms surrounded by a border made up of wall tiles. This border was roughly 10×10, meaning that extremely small dungeons would have one room of similarly diminutive proportion. In MV, the border is now optional and controlled by this option.

  - *Wide Passages*: As the option name suggests, turning on Wide Passages will increase the size of any connecting corridors in the generated dungeon.

■ **Note**   The generated dungeon overwrites whatever is in the currently selected map. Be careful you don't accidentally mess up a created map when using this feature. It is best to create an entirely new map and right-click it to avoid any potential mess-ups.

- *Save as Image (Hotkey: None)*: New in MV is the ability to save any given map as an image (PNG format) to the directory of your choice. It is certainly a much easier way to get a screenshot of your maps for various purposes, at least one of which will be acted upon near the end of this book (teaser: It involves mini-maps).

For now, let's click New Map. You will land on the screen shown in Figure 2-11.

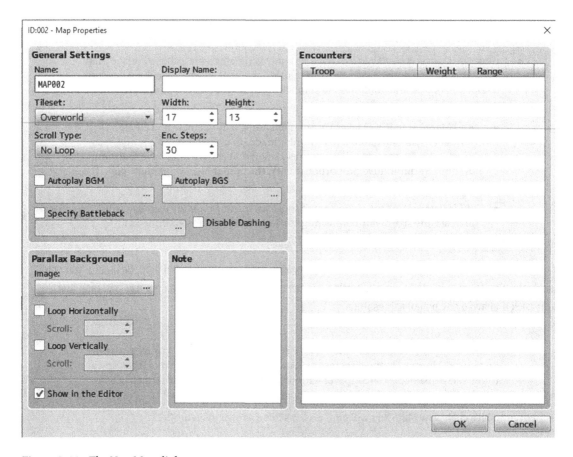

Figure 2-11. *The New Map dialog screen*

- *Name* is the internal name of your map, that is, the name the map has while you're working on your game in RMMV. This can be edited if desired. For example, MAP001 is the internal name of the default map included in all RMMV projects when they are created.

- *Display Name* is the name of the area as displayed in-game. When your player reaches an area that has a nonblank display name, the game will display the area name in a small box near the upper-left corner of the screen.

- *Tileset*: Each tileset is created with a distinct graphical goal in mind. The map properties default to Overworld, which is the tileset you would use for a world map.

- *Width and Height* control the map's size. In MV, there is no minimum map size although, as you can imagine, a 0×0 map is going to be pretty pointless.

- *Scroll Type* allows you to make a map that loops in on itself horizontally, vertically, or both. This is very good for a world styled much like our own planet.

- *Enc. Steps* determines the number of steps, on average, that the player must take before being attacked by a random encounter.

- *Specify Battleback* allows you to set a background that will be displayed during combat with enemies.

- *Autoplay BGM/BGS*: This pair of options allows you to change the background music and sounds when the player first enters the new map.

- *Disable Dashing*: Players can be moved in double time during game play by holding down the Shift button as they move. You can disable this functionality on a map by toggling this check box.

- *Parallax Background*: This can be used to make a dynamic background that moves when the player moves. It can be used for such things as simulating an elevator going up or down floors.

- The *Notes* field is pretty much self-explanatory. It can be used to write down things related to the map in question. If you want to write up a list of important events that occur on a certain map, this would be the perfect place to put it.

- Last, but definitely not least, we have the *Encounters* section on the right side of the screen. I will cover this in greater detail later in the book, but for now note that it concerns monsters and their appearance rates.

Those are the relevant options. Let us set them as follows:

- Name/Display Name: Second Area

- Tileset: Outside

- Width/Height: 30/30

- Auto-Change BGM: Field2

When you're ready, click OK. You will be greeted with a large checkerboard of nothing.

Why Is the Map Empty?

While MAP001 comes with grass tiles already set, subsequently created maps are completely blank (to be precise, that's the transparent tile). To answer the question posed by the section heading, it's just the way RMMV works. Worthy of note is the fact that a 30×30 map is large enough to require you to use the scrollbars (even if you've been following this book while using RMMV full-screen). Make sure your editing mode is set to Map Mode (click the relevant icon or press F5) and then draw a rectangle with the Meadow tile that starts at (0,0) and ends on (21,12), for a rectangle that's 22 × 13.

Tips

- As a reminder, the rectangle drawing tool for tiles is directly to the right of the pencil tool.

- You can find the specific coordinates for a certain square on your map by looking near the lower-right corner of the map screen while your cursor is over that square.

- You could mark the end location of your rectangle with the pencil tool to have a reference to where you want to drag to. This can be useful given the fact that the X and Y coordinates stop displaying while you are dragging a rectangle.

- I specified (21,12), as much of the map as I can see while RMMV is in a maximized form and not using the scrollbars. If you can see more or less of the map, you may have to drag, squish, or expand your program size to be able to use the rectangle as I intend. Additionally, a pair of buttons can be used to zoom in and out to help see the whole map. Because MV has larger tiles than Ace, this is a smaller area than the one I used for this same example in the first edition of the book.

As you can see, the tileset for Outside has different tiles than the Overworld tileset. Find (9,0) on the new map and the Dirt (Meadow) tile and draw a vertical line to (9,4). After that, take some time to add some terrain and play with the tileset.

Notes

- Adding certain types of terrain, such as ledges and walls, will cause small shadows to be rendered automatically. This is meant to simulate the effects of sunlight. You can use the Shadow Pen (the final drawing tool I have not mentioned yet) to remove those shadows or add some more of your own.

- Tilesets have multiple pages. The Outside tileset has three pages. Page A of a tileset is dedicated to major terrain, such as grass/dirt/snow, ledges, and structures. Other pages contain doodads to flesh out what would otherwise be a fairly dull map.

You can find my rendition of the 22×13 area in Figure 2-12. Make sure your road is in the right place (and I'd highly recommend having at least the ledges directly to the sides of that road as well). Once that is done, switch to Event Mode and right-click (9,0). It's time to create another transfer event.

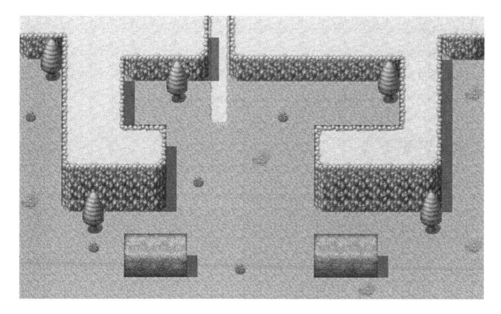

Figure 2-12. *My final map for the second area*

Don't forget to switch the event trigger to Player Touch; otherwise, the player will have to press spacebar or Enter or left-click to activate the event. Set the destination to one square south of the exit on MAP001. (You can left-click the map list within the Transfer Player menu to change which map you are looking at.) If you have followed the book up to now, that should be (8,2). Then left-click MAP001 in the main map screen to return to the first map. Right-click the Exit event and then left-click Edit. What you want to do is edit the Transfer Player command so that it points to the dirt road in our second map. For the sake of this tutorial, let's place the destination at (9,2). Right-click the Transfer Player command and choose Edit, to make the appropriate changes. What you *don't* want to do is place it right where you have the event to transfer to MAP001, as that has the potential to cause issues.

If you have done all of the above, you are now set. Play-test the game and see what happens.

■ **Note** If your character is going through the exit and facing north instead of south, it is because you must manually change the direction he/she faces after said transition. You can do this by changing the Direction setting in the Transfer Event dialog screen from Retain to Down.

Cool! Now, About Those Variables . . .

Okay fine, you're right. Let's apply the usage of variables before we end this chapter and move on to meatier subjects. Take a look at your second map. Place five trees (wherever you like, as long as you stay within that 22×13 area we populated with grass) around the area. If you managed to copy the map I created earlier, then the five trees you already have will be perfect.

■ **Note** For larger graphics (such as the trees we've used) that take up more than a single tile of space, you will have to place each individual tile accordingly. Trees have a top tile for foliage and a trunk as the bottom tile.

What we're going to do now is have each tree increase the value of a variable by one when the player interacts with it. We have to make sure that the player can't just interact with the same tree five times. In other words, each tree can only be counted once. So, how do we do this? There are several ways, but I'm going to take advantage of the fact that this is the switches and variables chapter to talk a little about self-switches.

Each event can contain up to four self-switches. While switches and variables have global scope (that is to say, the value of a switch or variable can be accessed from any other part of RMMV), self-switches are local in scope. The rest of your game's events care not if Event #441 on Map #72 has its self-switch B (self-switches go from A to D) set to the "on" state. It only holds importance to that one specific event itself.

So we need an event that does the following:

- Displays a text box telling the player a little about the tree.

- Increases the value of the Tree variable by 1, if it is the first time the player has interacted with that tree. Otherwise, do nothing.

With that said, if you like a challenge or have previous coding experience, I invite you to try to figure this one out by yourself. You'll need to keep in mind the following:

- The tree is a solid object, unlike the cave entrance/clearing we have used as our pair of exits so far during the book. That means the player will not be able to step on the event square.

- It is preferable that the player interact with the tree rather than having to run into it to trigger the event.

- You will need a new Event Command called *Conditional Branch* to check for the self-switch.

- On that note, you'll have to make use of *Control Variables* as well.

- You'll also need *Control Self Switch*. Otherwise, using the Conditional Branch command would be in vain.

- You're essentially using the same event five times.

Did you figure it out? If you think you have (or are stumped), let's resume. The crux of this particular exercise is in those new event commands that I have not explained yet. I wholeheartedly recommend experimentation throughout your use of RMMV. After all, video game design is basically one long sequence of problems to be solved. (The same can be said of programming.) With that in mind, let's take a look at the Conditional Branch command shown in Figure 2-13.

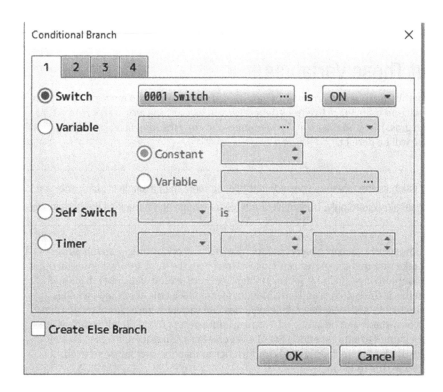

Figure 2-13. *The Conditional Branch event dialog*

■ **Note** In programming, a conditional is a statement that is true when a certain condition is met. In this case, we're talking about a simple if/else condition. For example, if I have more than three cats, I am a cat person; else, I am not.

The Conditional Branch command in RMMV automatically defaults to the switch option. Click the self-switch bubble and then set it so that the branch check for A is OFF. Near the bottom of the screen, you'll notice an option called Create Else Branch. It is turned off by default, but you can toggle it to add an Else branch to your conditional. In this book, I'll only be using Else branches when strictly necessary. It's a personal matter of taste. In any case, we won't need the Else that leaving that check box checked would create, as we don't want the event to execute anything within that branch if the self-switch is already on.

The second new event command we should look at is Control Variables. Figure 2-14 shows the Control Variables menu as seen when accessed.

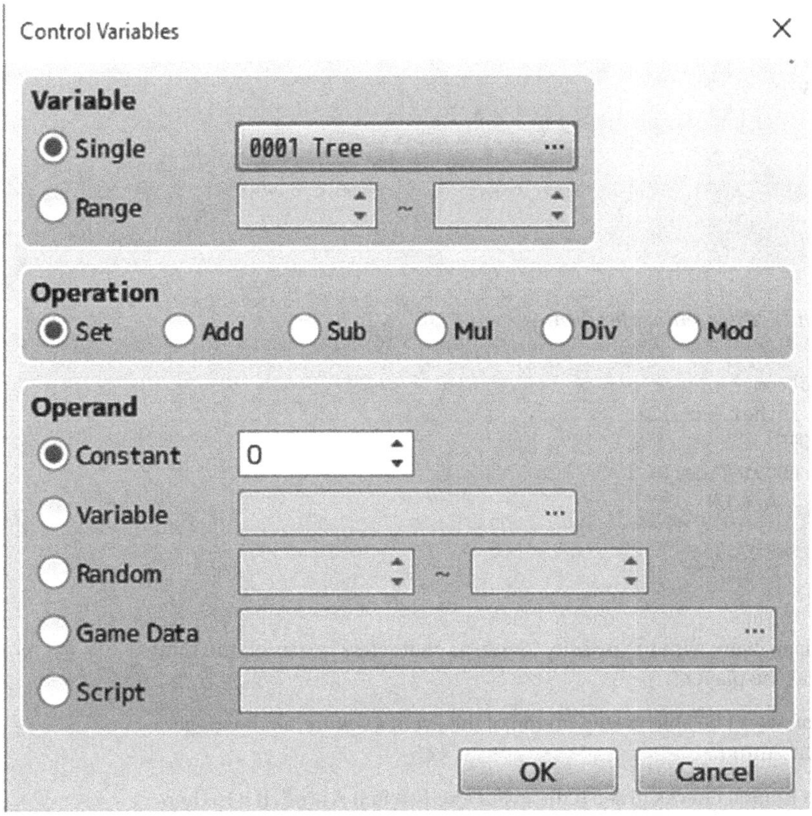

Figure 2-14. *The Control Variables event dialog*

Like Control Switches, Control Variables allows you to manipulate a single variable or a batch (group) of variables at the same time. However, variables enable you to do many more things than switches. This is mostly owing to the fact that a variable can hold any number (or character, for that matter, but that's only doable via scripting in RMMV), while a switch can only hold an *off* or an *on* state. In what may seem as a rather meta thing, a variable can be affected by the value of *another* variable. *Final Fantasy* uses variables in such a way to great effect. For example, a certain character's weapon in *Final Fantasy* IX causes greater damage the more dragons it has killed during the course of the game. While making a weapon stronger based on such a variable requires scripting in RMMV, you *can* create a skill that does much the same, and it does *not* require scripting.

For this exercise, all we have to do is name the variable in question (I called it Tree), change the operation to Add, and set the Operand to Constant with a value of 1. If you leave the operation on Set, it will give the variable the value of 1. You want the variable to gain 1, not stay at 1, when the player interacts with a tree. To summarize, when the player performs an action on the tree the first time, the variable "Tree" will be increased by 1.

Finally, we need to add a Control Self Switch event. Control Self Switch is a simple enough event command that I won't illustrate it. All you can do with that command is select one of the four self-switches and set its state to ON or OFF. Set self-switch A to ON, and there you have it.

In simpler terms, here's the solution. Figure 2-15 shows the necessary Priority and Trigger settings.

35

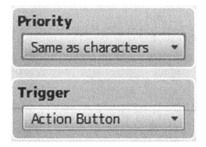

Figure 2-15. *The Priority and Trigger settings for the tree*

```
♦Text : None, Window, Bottom
:     : This tree looks rather peculiar.
♦If : Self Switch A is OFF
   ♦Control Variables : #0001 Tree += 1
   ♦Control Self Switch : A = ON
   ♦
: End
♦
```

- As noted earlier, an event with the priority "Same as characters" exists on the same graphical layer as the player.

- On that note, you won't be able to step on top of the event's square, so the trigger should be Action Button.

- The conditional branch checks to see if the event's self-switch A is off. If it is, then it adds one to the value of Tree and turns self-switch A on, preventing a single tree from adding more than one to the variable.

- Copy and paste this exact event to the four other trees you have placed on the map, and you're done. You can do this by right-clicking the event on the map editor and selecting *Copy*, then right-clicking the square you wish to paste the event to and selecting *Paste*. Alternatively, you can use the *Copy Event Page* button within the event properties.

What's the Point?

There is no greater honor than botany. No? Okay, fair enough. Let's add a final event that requires the Tree variable to be at 5. We'll make it a treasure chest, to show off the relevant Quick Event.

- First, find a nice unoccupied space on your second map.

- Right-click and select the Treasure event from Quick Event Creation.

- Because the quest involved trees, let's give the player something made with wood as a reward. Select the Bow from the list of weapons and then click OK.

- Now, right-click that event and click Edit. What we want to do is make it so the chest is invisible until the player has taken a look at all five of the trees. To do that, check the Variable condition on the first page of the event and set it to say "0001 Tree ≥ 5." Once that is ready, you're done!

Check Figure 2-16 to see how the relevant part of the second map looks for me. Except for the five trees and the road, your map will probably look different.

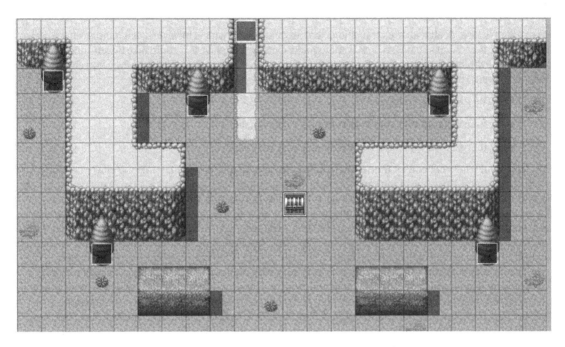

Figure 2-16. *The final second area map, showing the events*

Before we move on, I'd like to tweak something. During your play tests, you have probably seen that MV defaults to a party of four premade characters. What we're going to do is lower the party to just Harold, the first character in line. How? Here are some directions.

- Open the Database by finding the relevant option in the Tools item of MV's main menu and clicking it (or pressing F9).

- Once it is open, click the System tab.

- In the top-left corner of the System section, you should see the Starting Party block. Erase each of the other three party members by right-clicking their name and then clicking Delete (alternatively, left-click the name and press the Del key).

One character is much easier to work with than four, although the party will gain at least one member before this book is done.

■ **Note** Incidentally, Harold cannot equip the Bow in his current state. I'll cover how to allow him to do so in the next chapter.

Anyway, let's continue. Here's one final application of variables that will most likely be of great use as you work on your RMMV game.

Advanced Challenge: Using Variables to Handle an Area Transition!

Up to now, we have dealt with area transitions that are one square wide. However, what happens if we make an expansive area, such as a desert, and want to make exits for the player? It could take dozens of events to cover a single direction. Why spend 10–40 events for area transitions on a single map when you can cover them all in one? This exercise requires the use of the following:

- The Parallel event trigger

- A pair of variables to hold the character's coordinates

- Liberal use of the Conditional Branch event command

First, switch to Event editing mode. Then, find a nice spot in the second map that the player cannot reach. In my case, I'll use one of the squares on the mountaintop. Afterward, create a new event at that square. Set the event trigger to Parallel. Next, we'll have to check for the player's X,Y positions at all times. That is the reason we use Parallel. (Remember, Autorun is meant more for cinematic sequences. Trying to use it for an event such as this will only cause the game to hang.) The secret lies in the Control Variables command, specifically the Game Data category of operand. The Game Data category defaults to Map ID. Click the button labeled "…" on the far end of the bar, to change what type of data you want to assign to your variable.

Once you click the button, you'll notice a slew of possible things you can plug into a variable. What we're looking for is the player's position on the map (a.k.a. his/her x and y coordinates). Thus, we click the Character option, which defaults to Player's Map X. Exactly what we need! Select that, and then make sure you're saving the value to a new variable (I'm calling variable 2 X and variable 3 Y). Afterward, create a new Control Variable command and repeat the process up to the point where you are looking at the Player's Map X setting. Click the arrow on the drop-down menu for Map X, and it will reveal four more settings. The one we want, of course, is Map Y.

Here's where it gets interesting. I'm going to recommend that you lower the map size to 22×13 (the size of the grass rectangle we made in starting our second map). To be fair, it doesn't particularly matter for this exercise, but it'll help you visualize the boundaries in-game. Now what you have to do is figure out the boundaries of each side of the map on which you want to have area transitions. Let me use some Region numbering, shown in Figure 2-17, to help you visualize what I mean.

■ **Note**　I'll cover how to place and use regions in proper detail later in the book.

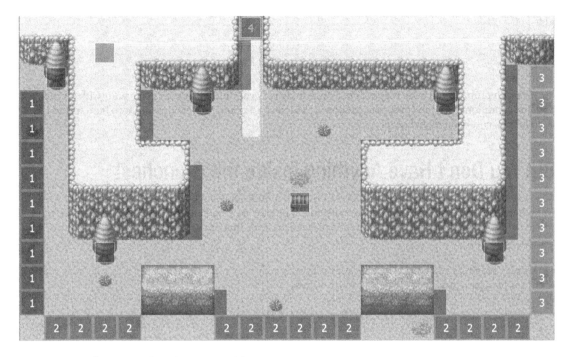

Figure 2-17. *The map Regions for our transitions*

We have a single transition marked by the number 4 to the north. Additionally, we have 9 squares on the left, 14 squares on the bottom, and 10 squares on the right. That would be 33 transition events, if we did them one by one. So let's not.

Let's Crunch Those Map Boundaries, Shall We?

The topmost square of the left boundary is (0,3), while the bottommost square of the left boundary is (0,11). The leftmost square of the bottom boundary is (1,12), while the rightmost square of the bottom boundary is (20,12). The topmost square of the right boundary is (21,2), while the bottommost square of the right boundary is (21,11).

What does this mean? Well, we can see some trends.

- When you trace a horizontal boundary, you will find that the value of Y stays the same.

- When you trace a vertical boundary, the value of X stays the same.

Thus, our conditional branches should read as follows:

```
♦Control Variables : #0002 X = Map X of Player
♦Control Variables : #0003 Y = Map Y of Player
♦If : X = 0
  ♦
: End
♦If : Y = 12
  ♦
: End
```

```
♦If : X = 21
  ♦
: End
♦
```

You can probably tell what is going on. Notice that every conditional branch event ends with an End. The first conditional branch covers the left border. The second branch covers the southern border, and the third branch covers the right border.

But You Don't Have Anything Inside the Branches!

Keen eye! Indeed, you would be correct. Feel free to put in transfer events, as you see fit, to wherever you want them to lead. The best use of such a transition in practice is to send the player to the world map (on which it doesn't particularly matter where the player exits, only that he or she exits the area map from a certain direction).

```
♦Control Variables : #0002 X = Map X of Player
♦Control Variables : #0003 Y = Map Y of Player
♦If : X = 0
  ♦Transfer Player : MAP001 (13,6) (Direction: Left)
  ♦
: End
♦If : Y = 12
  ♦Transfer Player : MAP001 (8,11) (Direction: Up)
  ♦
: End
♦If X = 21
  ♦Transfer Player : MAP001 (4,6) (Direction: Right)
  ♦
: End
♦
```

In the first edition of this book, this would have been the last section before the summary. However, there are two new features in MV that I want to cover before calling this chapter closed. First is the Event Searcher I mentioned in the previous chapter. So, without further ado…

The Event Searcher

The Event Searcher is a new utility in RMMV that can be used much as its name implies: to search for events. For what purpose? Well, it's of virtually nil use at this time, but imagine you have twenty events and need to find in how many of the events you called a certain variable or switch. That's where the Event Searcher can help. I won't be actively working with it in this book (because misplacing events and/or event commands shouldn't be a problem as long as you faithfully follow the text), but don't let that stop you from using it. To access the Event Searcher, you'll need to go to the Tools section of the main menu and click Event Searcher. Once there, you should see a screen such as the one in Figure 2-18.

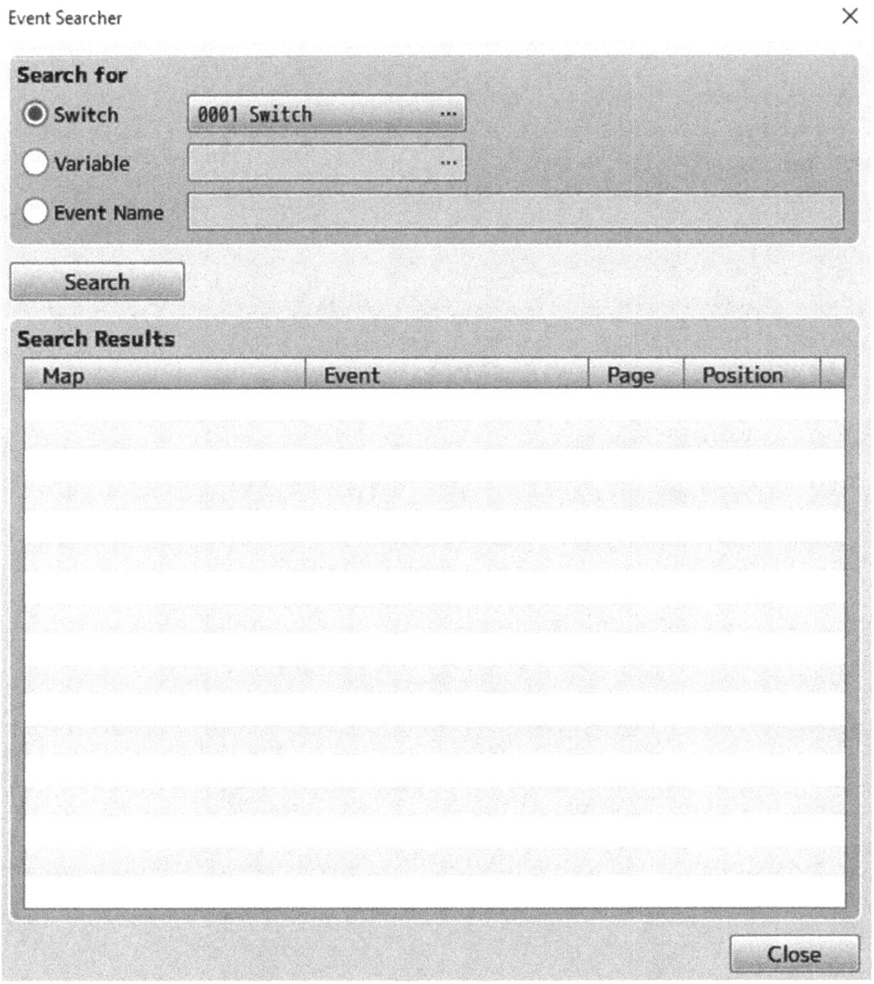

Figure 2-18. *The Event Manager*

To use our completed exercise as an example, suppose you wanted to make sure you have five events that add to Tree's value. In the *Search for* box, you would click the *Variable* bubble. As the very first variable in our project, Tree will appear by default. Otherwise, you would need to click the button displaying *0001 Tree* and select the correct variable. Make sure Tree is selected and click Search. You should see five results appear, as in Figure 2-19.

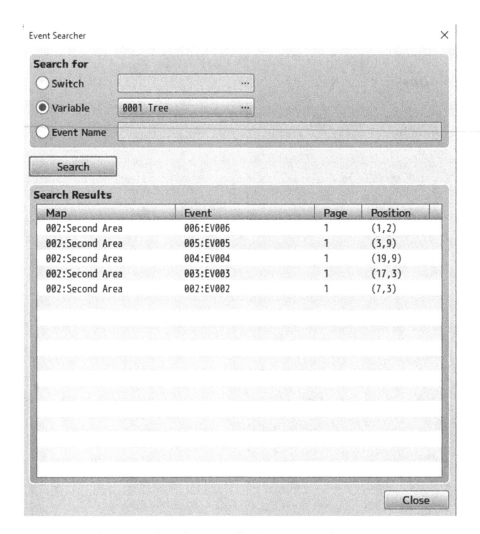

Figure 2-19. The five search results returned by the Event Searcher

You're even given the precise location of each relevant result. Awesome, isn't it? I'm sure you can see the possibilities for such a tool. It's really good for error-checking purposes. Now, on to the second new feature of RMMV, which is useful for similar reasons.

Test

If you're anything like me, you'll probably overlook the Test option while eventing. Although it's not a magic bullet that can solve all problems, Test is a neat new function in MV that allows you to check that your event commands are working as intended without having to load up a playtest. As a general note, Test is useful to check event sequences that are self-enclosed (that is, events that don't rely on other events to complete themselves). It won't do any good if you try to use it to test the validity of the Parallel event that we created earlier in the chapter, for example, as that relies on the player walking into certain squares to trigger the transfer event (you *can* use it to test the transfer events themselves, although that is of limited use if you want to know if the *whole event* is working fine or not). Go ahead and experiment a bit with it before you move on to the chapter summary (and thus, the end of the chapter).

■ **Tip** You can test multiple lines of code during a single test (the reason I talk about sequences in the paragraph above). To do so, you need only click on the first intended line of code, hold down Shift, and then click in the last line of code you intend to test. You should see the relevant event commands highlighted in blue. You can then right-click anywhere in the highlighted area and select the Test option (hotkey: Ctrl + R)

Well, I think it's time to finish this chapter. I have a whole slew of cool things for us to work on in the next chapter, so I hope you're as excited as I am!

Summary

That concludes this chapter on switches and variables. Here are three more exercises for you to stretch your mind with:

1. Using an event with Autorun, create a two-page event that greets the player with a text box upon arriving at the second area.

    - As with Parallel events, I recommend you place this event somewhere that the player cannot access.

    - Only the first page of the event should be Autorun. The second page should be blank, with a trigger that is not Autorun or Parallel. Flipping a self-switch on page 1 and using it as a conditional on page 2 would probably work best.

2. Using an event with Autorun, use the Fadeout and Fadein event commands to cause the screen to black out momentarily and then reveal the treasure chest, instead of it popping immediately into being.

    - The easiest way to accomplish this is by cheating a little. The chest is set to appear when Tree is equal to 5. Make it so that the chest appears when Tree is equal to 6. Then, with Fadeout, you can create an Autorun when Tree is equal to 5, add 1 to the value of Tree, and Fadein, in that order.

    - The use of a self-switch is also recommended for this event. An Autorun left unchecked *will* hang your game.

3. Tweak the five tree events so that they also display a text box that tells players how many trees they have looked at up to that point.

    - Tool tips are your friend here. Place your cursor over the text box in the Show Text event command and leave it there until the tool tip appears. You'll see a text option that allows you to print the value of a variable as text.

Next, let's talk about a large part of what makes RPGs what they are: characters and enemies!

CHAPTER 3

Of Friends and Foes

We spent the previous chapter talking about the use of switches and variables within RPG Maker MV (RMMV). What we discussed there is just the tip of the iceberg in terms of what you can do with them, but it's time to start populating our roleplaying game (RPG) world. One thing every video game needs is a character for the player to control. Even a game as simple as *Pong* has the player controlling a paddle and trying to get a ball past an opponent's own paddle. So far we have been controlling a party made up of RMMV's default characters (now reduced to just Harold). It's time to get to know Harold a little better. Make your way to the Database (by pressing F9 or finding it in the Tools item of the menu toolbar) and open the Actors tab. When you first install RMMV, your first foray into the Database will automatically lead you to the Actors tab, but recall that we have already poked our heads in there to change some of the game's terms. Take a look at Figure 3-1.

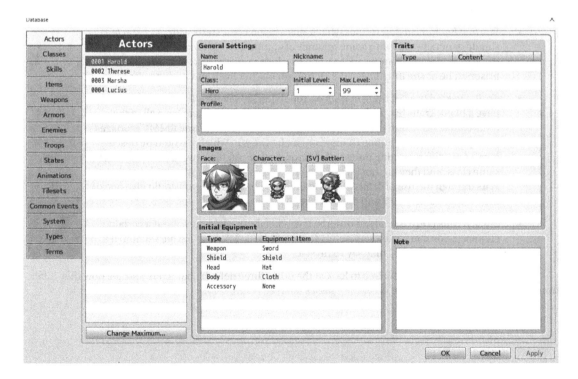

Figure 3-1. *The Actors tab in RMMV's Database*

© Darrin Perez 2016

D. Perez, *Beginning RPG Maker MV*, DOI 10.1007/978-1-4842-1967-6_3

In RMMV, player characters (those the player can mix and match in his/her party) are called *actors*. As you can see at the upper left of the preceding screenshot, the program comes with four premade actors. You can change the maximum number of characters and add some more of your own. You can edit or erase the premade actors as well. There are various things to cover here, so let's work our way through this part of the Database.

- *General Settings* cover an actor's basic information and are largely self-explanatory. Of note is *Class*, which will be discussed when we reach the appropriate tab of the Database. *Profile* is a character's biographic summary. "He searches the land for the chosen one" is an example of such a summary.

- You can tweak an actor's initial level, which will determine at what level he/she joins the party when placed in the game. You can also change an actor's max level as well, limiting his/her growth, if you have a reason to do so. It's common to limit a character's maximum level when you have a temporary party member. You can set his/her initial level equal to its maximum, and he/she will stay at the same level for the duration of their stay in the party.

- There is a set of three *Images*. The one on the left is the character's portrait, while the one in the middle is his/her sprite set, which covers appearance as well as movement patterns. New to MV is the rightmost graphic, called *[Sv] Battler*. Sv is short for Side view, a battle type that you are familiar with if you have played early *Final Fantasy* games. We'll be covering Side view in more detail during the course of this book. As it's the new battle type, we will be using it for our game's battles instead of the more traditional top-down view.

- *Starting Equipment* determines what items a given actor starts with. A character should generally start with some manner of equipment, although there are times when it would not be appropriate (such as when a protagonist starts the game as a prisoner; he or she might have the clothes on his/her back and nothing else).

- *Traits* are kind of a big thing in RMMV. You'll quickly see that the four actors each have a blank Traits list, and that's because the default characters have all of their traits contained within their classes and not themselves. The way RMMV manages this by default is fine, although there are niche cases in which it would be best to have some differentiating traits at the Actor level. If you have two characters of the same class, and they are not identical twins, you could differentiate some of their stats through the use of Traits at the Actor level. For example, you could give one of the characters HP * 80% and the other MP * 110%.

- Finally, *Note* is just a notepad of sorts. If you need to make notes about a certain character, you can write them here. Most parts of RMMV have a Note section. It's awfully convenient, if I may say so myself.

That covers the Actors tab. Feel free to look at the other three default characters and see how they differ from Harold. Afterward, let's move on to the Classes tab (see Figure 3-2).

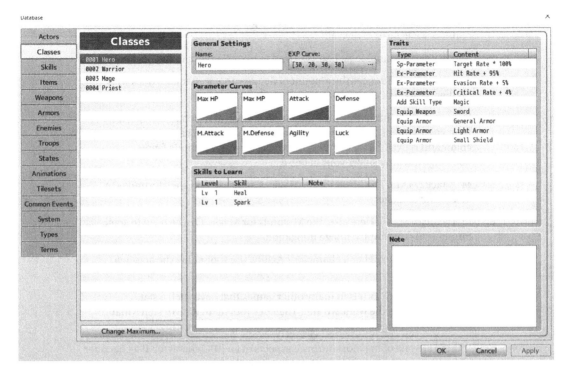

Figure 3-2. *The Classes tab in RMMV's Database*

The four actors each have their own class. Harold's class is Hero (which perhaps explains why he was the leader of the premade party). Take a look at each of the classes and note how its traits and skills differ (you won't see any difference in their parameter curves, but I'll address that in Chapter 5, after the party gains a new member worth differentiating). RMMV prefers to place character-defining traits within the Classes tab, as an actor's class highly defines him/her. As a case in point, look at everything that is governed strictly by class:

- *EXP Curve*: *EXP* is short for "Experience." If you click the button where the bracketed numbers are located, you'll see what those four values relate to and how you can use them to tinker with the rate of advancement. You can make levels easier or harder to get, via the use of this property. By default, the four premade classes all have the same experience curve. If you want actors to level up based on their class, you can tweak their curves here. To take a predominantly pen-and-paper example, *Advanced Dungeons & Dragons* (video game adaptations of that ruleset include *Dark Sun* and *Baldur's Gate*) had an experience system in which classes leveled up at a rate proportionate to their power. So the Spellcasters, who arguably had more power, took a longer time to gain a single level than the "weaker" classes, such as Thief, who leveled up faster to compensate for their lower overall power level.

- *Parameter Curves*: These affect the rate at which a given class gains its stats. You can edit a parameter by double-clicking it, which will bring up a graph. There are eight stats in RMMV.

1. Max HP (Maximum Hit Points). If these drop to 0, the character is dead and requires some form of revival.

2. Max MP (Maximum Magic Points). Used to cast all manner of magic spells.

3. Attack (ATK). Influences the amount of damage that a character does with his/her weapon of choice.

4. Defense (DEF). Influences the amount of damage that a character suffers from enemy attacks. The default damage formula for the basic Attack command is [ATK * 4 - DEF * 2]. Essentially, the basic formula favors boosting your attack over your defense.

5. M. Attack (MAT). The M stands for Magic. Can be used in spell formulas to determine damage.

6. M. Defense (MDF). Here also, the M stands for Magic. Can be used in spell formulas to determine damage mitigation.

7. Agility (AGI). The higher a character's Agility, the sooner he/she acts in a given battle turn.

8. Luck (LUK). Much as it is in many other games that have such a stat, Luck in RMMV is the wildcard stat. The Luck tool tip in RMMV states that Luck "affects things like the chance of status ailments occurring."

- *Skills*: These are one of the most intrinsic aspects of an RPG character. If a character did not have any skills, it would only be able to attack with its weapon, and that would probably get boring after a while. Some examples of skills include healing spells and power attacks. Harold starts with a healing spell and a spell that does Thunder damage. He does not learn any new skills during the course of the game.

- *Traits*: These define many miscellaneous, but important, aspects of a class. Let's break down the Hero class, trait by trait:

    1. *Target Rate* marks the rate at which a member of this class is targeted by enemies. The default rate is 100% and can be increased or decreased as desired. A particularly large warrior might warrant a higher Target Rate, while a smaller thief would probably warrant a lower Target Rate. Say you have a party of three: a large warrior with 200% Target Rate, a normal-sized guard with 100% Target Rate, and a small thief with 50% Target Rate. It is four times more likely that the warrior will be attacked than the thief. It is half as likely that the thief will be attacked as the guard.

    2. *Hit Rate* is what is more generically known in RPGs as *accuracy*. In RMMV, a character's total accuracy is equal to its Hit Rate plus any bonus Hit Rate it is gaining from its equipment. A character's ability to land its attacks and skills is negatively modified by any Evasion the enemy has. The stock functionality of RMMV is set up so that the game calculates first to see if an actor lands its attack and, if so, checks whether the enemy dodges the attack.

    3. *Critical Rate* is the chance a character has to land a critical hit for triple the normal damage. An actor's chance to land a critical hit is reduced based on the enemy's Critical Evasion Rate.

4. *Add Skill Type* is a trait that allows a chosen class to use a category of skills. In this case, Heroes can use Magic-type skills. By default, RMMV has two skill types: Special and Magic. A class requires access to a skill type to be able to use skills from that type.

5. *Equip Weapon* and *Equip Armor* are both fairly self-explanatory. They define what kinds of weapons and armor a given class can use. If you don't assign any Equip traits to a class, it will be unable to equip anything (which, to be fair, might be good for a completely unusual player character type, such as a wolf or a yeti).

From the Classes tab, let's move on to the Skills tab, which has a lot of information. The first time I laid eyes on that part of the Database, I nearly fainted. Rest assured that it is not as overwhelming as it initially seems. Let's break up this tab into two parts. Figure 3-3 shows the first half.

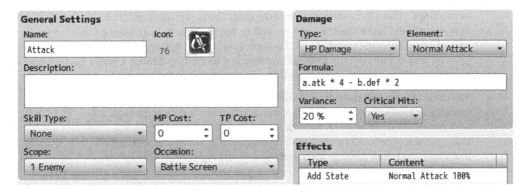

Figure 3-3. The upper half of the Skills tab in RMMV

We're looking at the very first skill in the list of 10 provided by default within RMMV. Skills 1 and 2 are internally important for RMMV, so take care not to edit them, unless you're sure of your changes. The first skill in RMMV is the basic attack:

- *General Settings* provide basic, yet essential, values to be tweaked. Skill Type denotes what type of skill category must be unlocked for a player to use that skill. As Attack is a generic basic attack, anyone can use it. Similarly, it has no MP or TP (Technique Points) cost. A character gains TP from taking damage and using skills, including Attack.

- *Scope* defines what is affected by the skill. The basic attack hits a single, targeted enemy.

- *Occasion* toggles when a skill can be used.

    1. Always. The skill can be used in and out of battle.

    2. Battle Screen. The skill can only be used in battle.

    3. Menu Screen. This is the character menu that we accessed back in Chapter 1.

    4. Never. Seems pointless, but it's actually useful for a skill that you only want to be used under highly specific circumstances. (You would probably want to create an event to trigger the skill, in that case.)

- *Damage*: Besides having a marginally misleading name (as you can use the formula for healing spells as well), this has a few intricacies of its own:

  1. *Type*. The type of effect you want this skill to have. To confuse the issue even more, you have HP and MP Recover as two of the seven possible options. The *None* type can be useful for skills that cause status effects but do not do any actual damage in causing them.

  2. *Element*. Determines the elemental typing of the skill. Normal Attack is its own special element, which leads me to believe that it is coded in that way so that Attack can benefit from the elemental properties of a character's weapon, to take one example.

  3. *Formula*. That little box you see there carries nearly infinite potential. Entire forum threads have been filled throughout the Internet on making unconventional damage formulas for seemingly anything you can think of in RMMV. Later I'll showcase some of the ones I've personally used. For now, you should know that the user of a skill is expressed by a (`a.atk` in the case of Attack) and the target of a skill is expressed by b (`b.def`, for this skill). Leaving your cursor over the formula box for a few seconds will cause a very helpful tool tip to appear, so I'll leave that as a short exercise for you.

  4. *Variance*. Determines the range of values a skill returns. Attack has a variance of 20(%). To give an example, a character able to do 100 damage with Attack would actually do anywhere between 80 and 120. I prefer my skill variance to be low, but then again, I also prefer my characters to have low stats rather than the high stats that the default characters come with in RMMV.

  5. *Critical Hits*. Determines whether a skill can land a critical hit or not.

- *Effects*: These are to skills what Traits are to actors (and, as we'll see later, enemies and other items as well). When used, Attack has a special effect to add a state named Normal Attack. I wouldn't tamper with that. You can add other effects to the basic attack if you're curious, though.

The Skill tab doesn't seem so intimidating now, does it? We're more than half done looking at it as well! Take a look at Figure 3-4 for the lower half of the Skills tab.

Figure 3-4. *The lower half of the Skills tab in RMMV*

- *Invocation*: This affects the use of the skill itself:

    1. **Speed.** This adjusts the user's Agility upward or downward when using the skill. (Speed can be a negative value.) You can make a skill that's guaranteed to strike first, by giving it high Speed. You can also make a skill that causes its user to act last, by giving it highly negative Speed.

    2. **Success.** The chance of the skill to actually connect. I tend to use a non-100% Success rate for skills that cause nasty status effects, such as instant death or petrification.

    3. **Repeats.** How many times the skill is triggered when used once. Most skills should only trigger once, but multi-hit skills work precisely by repeating.

    4. **TP Gain.** The amount of TP a character gains from skill use is governed by this value right here. So, you could easily make a skill with the sole purpose of boosting your character's TP to 100. (TP caps at 100, unlike MP, which can go all the way to 9999.) Likewise, you could create a skill that doesn't grant TP to its user.

    5. **Hit Type.** There are three possible hit types for any given skill:

- *Certain Hit*: A skill with this hit type ignores the user's accuracy and the target's evasion stats. The only determinant of whether a Certain Hit skill will work is its Success %.

- *Physical Attack*: A skill with this hit type connects based on the user's hit rate and is affected by the target's evasion rate, as well as its own Success %.

- *Magical Attack*: A skill with this hit type connects based on the target's magical evasion rate and the skill's Success %.

    6. **Animation.** What is displayed when you use the skill in battle.

- *Message*: This is fairly self-explanatory. The only thing I would note is that you need a single space before your skill message. Take a look at the message for the Attack skill and you'll see what I mean. Without the space, it will look in-game like "Characterattacks!" instead of "Character attacks!" when you use the skill.

- Below Message, there are three buttons: *casts *!, does *!,* and *uses *!.* The tool tip for the buttons is "Generate Message: Automatically makes the message." Clicking one of those buttons replaces the text in the *Message* text boxes with predetermined text. For Attack, the text would read "casts Attack!", "does Attack!", and "uses Attack!", respectively.

- *Required Weapon*: This is the last item in the Skills tab, and it does what it implies. You can adjust it so that a certain skill requires a certain weapon type (such as a rain of arrows ability requiring a bow or crossbow). You can be strict and leave it at one weapon type or relax the restriction a little and add a second weapon type. (A powerful swing of your weapon is a skill that can be done with both a sword and an axe, for example.)

You can see a screenshot of the Items tab in Figure 3-5, but you'll probably understand why I'm going to gloss over the details. It holds many similarities to the Skills tab. (Neat fact: Internally, Skills are also considered items, so this is merely a case of the stock functionality matching the code.) So there are only one or two new things to even mention:

- *Item Type*: These are subdivided into Regular Item (very nearly every type of item you could think of) and Key Items. Key Items are important things that the player acquires and should never get rid of (or is required to use for a specific purpose). A potion, food, and a smoke bomb are but three examples of Regular Items, while an ancient key or a royal missive are good examples of Key Items. In MV, Hidden Items (A and B) have been added as well. Hidden Items are only visible during events that involve selecting items. They're good for token-type items (like collectibles and keys) that you don't necessarily want the player to see in their inventory for any reason.

- *Price*: Items, weapons, and armor can have a set price (in in-game currency). Items with a value of 0 cannot be sold (but you can have an item that costs 0 for sale in a shop; I usually don't recommend that, mind you). Items sell for half of their value.

▪ **Note**   With very few exceptions, you should set the price of your Key Items to 0, so that they cannot be sold. You would think that Key Items have protection from being sold, but that is not the case in RMMV.

- *Effects*: Much as in the case of skills, your items can have a variety of effects. If you'd prefer, you can even use the damage formula for curative items or consumable damage items (think bombs and throwing stars).

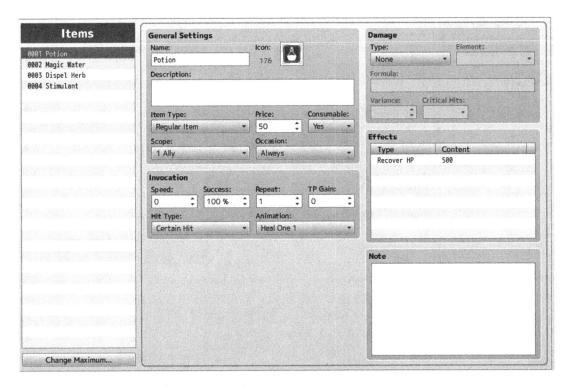

Figure 3-5. *The Items tab of the RMMV Database*

As you can see, the Items tab is pretty much identical to Skills. In any case, I will be elaborating on the Weapons tab and glossing over the Armors tab for the same reason that I skimmed over the Items tab. Refer to Figure 3-6 for a screenshot of the Weapons tab.

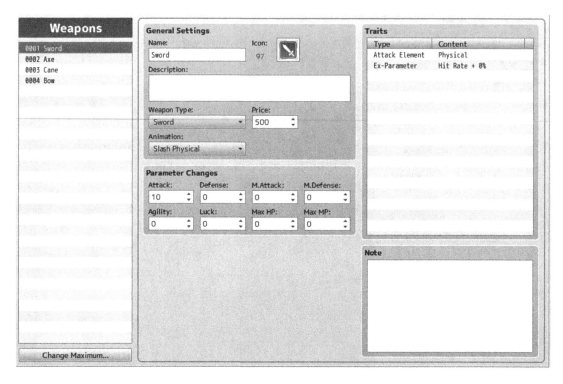

Figure 3-6. *The Weapons tab of the RMMV Database*

Just as items have two different types, you can define your weapon (and armor, for that matter) type as well. The Weapon Type drop-down menu will be populated with the terms listed in the Terms tab for that category. What makes weapons and armor different from items is their ability to be equipped by eligible actors. As equipment, they grant parameter changes (usually bonuses, but you could have cursed items that reduce stats as well) and have features that further add to their properties. In the case of weapons, you must also define their attack element. Most weapons do physical damage, but a flaming blade would do fire damage, while a bow of ice could inflict extreme cold or water damage.

■ **Note**   Unlike some other RPG systems, RMMV does not give weapons an inherent damage range. (For example, Greatswords in *Dungeons & Dragons* have a 2–12 damage range, modified by the wielder's Strength.) What you see in a weapon's Parameter Changes is what you get.

The Armors tab is essentially identical. (See Figure 3-7.)

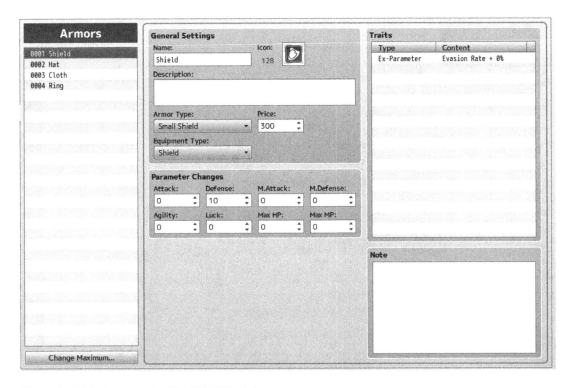

Figure 3-7. *The Armors tab of the RMMV Database*

The main difference is that the Armors tab also has an *Equipment Type*. As you can see, shields and accessories are also considered armor in RMMV (the former makes sense, but the latter is a bit odd).

Time for Enemies!

Yes, indeed. An RPG wouldn't be much of one if there weren't foes to serve as obstacles for the player and his/her companions. Check Figure 3-8 to see a screenshot of the Enemies tab.

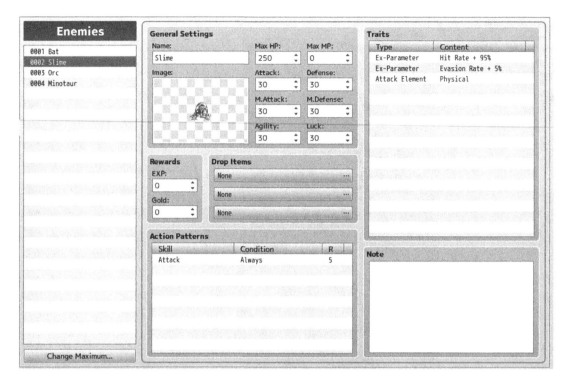

Figure 3-8. *The Enemies tab of the RMMV Database*

In this figure, we can see Slime, one of the Japanese RPG genre's weakest but most iconic monsters. The *Dragon Quest* series has cute slimes, while RMMV's rendition is creepier. Like actors, enemies have eight stats. They also confer rewards—in experience and gold—when defeated and can also potentially drop items for the player. You can set up to three items for an enemy to drop, with a probability of 1/X (where X can be any number from 1 to 1000). I personally don't recommend drop rates lower than 1/128, but that's mostly because I have not played an RPG in which most of the item drops are rarer than that (*Dragon Quest 8*, if I recall correctly, had a few 1/256 drops, but they were situational at best).

Action Patterns are what give an enemy most of its bite. The lowly Slime can only use the basic attack that we saw a few pages back. I'll be discussing *Ratings* in detail later in the chapter. Last, *Traits* are back and used for enemies in much the same way that they are for actor classes. Slime has a 5% chance of missing on its attacks (95% Hit Rate), as well as a 5% chance of dodging physical attacks (5% Evasion). Its attacks inflict physical damage. You can give enemies resistances and immunities to types of damage and status effects (defined with States in RMMV).

This discussion has been a bit long, so let's touch on one last section before applying all that we have talked about so far. Figure 3-9 shows the Troops tab. You could design a thousand monsters, but you must actually form them into a troop for them to initiate a valid encounter. The very first troop in the list is a pair of Bats. Let's talk a bit about each of the commands available.

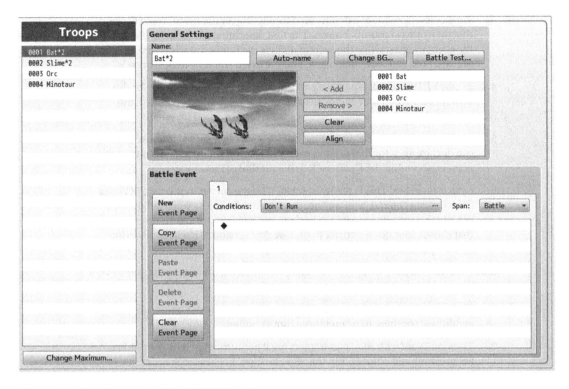

Figure 3-9. *The Troops tab of the RMMV Database*

- *Auto-name* names the troop based on the number and type of monsters contained within. The default troops are all named in the Auto-name style.

- *Change BG* allows you to change the background during battle testing. This has no effect on the Battlebacks in your game.

- *Battle Test* allows you to create a party of up to four actors equipped with items you choose to face off against the currently selected troop. During a Battle Test, the party gains 99 copies of every item in the Database.

- *Add* allows you to include a monster in a troop, while clicking an individual monster and pressing *Remove* clears it from the troop. If you want to *Clear* out the troop completely, that would be the option to click.

- Dragging on a monster placed in a troop allows you to change its in-battle position. This is merely for aesthetic purposes and has no effect on combat. You can use *Align* to return all monsters to their default positions.

- Events return with a vengeance in the Troops tab, in the form of *Battle Events*. They have six different conditionals, available from the drop-down menu:

  1. If you don't use *any* of the conditionals, the event will default to *Don't Run*. As implied, an event with Don't Run will never trigger.

  2. *Turn End*. An event with this conditional will trigger after all battlers (party members and enemies) have taken their turn.

3. *Turn*. Allows you to set a determined turn to trigger the event. You will see that there are two number boxes. The first determines the turn in which the event triggers, while the second defines the interval at which the event repeats. (You can leave that blank, and the event will only trigger once.)

4. *Enemy's HP*. You must specify a particular enemy within the troop for this conditional. When that enemy reaches the HP value you designated, the event will trigger.

5. *Actor's HP*. Same as the preceding, but for actors instead of enemies. You can declare an actor that doesn't even exist within your game (as long as the actor exists within the Database), so be mindful of that.

6. *Switch*. Switches! This is really useful for a boss monster in the style of Zoma from *Dragon Quest 3*, who was nearly unbeatable, unless you used the Orb of Light. You can flip a switch, based on any relevant conditions elsewhere, that causes your boss monster to be a weaker version of itself (by lowering its stats permanently, for example).

- Battle Events also have three types of Span, determining how many times the event triggers:

  1. *Battle*. An event with the Battle span triggers only once per battle, even if its conditions continue to be met throughout combat.

  2. *Turn*. An event with this span triggers once per turn, even if its conditions are met multiple times within the same turn.

  3. *Moment*. An event with this span triggers repeatedly, once conditions are met. I rarely use this type of span, as it has a fair chance of causing your game to hang in an infinite loop if you mess up.

Playing with the Database

There you have it. We have seen most of the Database by now, so let's integrate into an exercise all that we have learned. But first, let me point out something you may have noticed already. As it so happens, MV has a very bare-bones database by default. There are only four premade enemy types, and none of them have assigned experience or gold rewards. Additionally, they all have 30 in every stat except HP, which happens to be the only stat that changes between the enemy types. This trend of scarcity is fairly persistent across the various tabs (all premade weapons and armors cost exactly 500 Gold, for another example). RPG Maker VX Ace, by contrast, came with a very robust database (which I made ample use of in the first edition of this book, as my design philosophy here is to learn the engine). Creating a game with the engine just happens to be the most effective way to do so, in my opinion. So, all that said, what can we do? Create the Database entries ourselves, of course! It's a great opportunity for me to delve into basic RPG game design philosophy, so look forward to snippets of that throughout this book.

■ **Note** As it turns out, Kadokawa released a more robust Database file for MV some time after the software release. However, because it's not strictly included with the program (it exists as a separate download at the time of this writing), I'd rather just create my own assets and allow you to participate in the creative process.

Anyway, I believe we had an exercise pending...
Objectives:

- Change Harold so that he can use bows as well as swords.

- Increase the Skills tab maximum to 40 and create a skill in slot 11 that requires the use of a bow.

- Give Harold the skill that you have created.

- Increase the Items tab maximum to 40. Create a regular item that can be used to attack enemies and is consumed on use and a key item.

- Increase the Weapons tab maximum to 40 and create a bow for Harold to use.

- Increase the Enemies tab maximum to 40 and come up with a new enemy.

- Increase the Troops tab maximum to 40 and make a troop containing one Slime and one of the new enemy you create.

With the information already provided, the preceding should be fairly easy to accomplish. Take some time to read the various things in each tab, so that you can make a more measured decision in tweaking your creations, and it should be as easy as counting. RMMV is nothing if not intuitive. Let me write up the changes that I made.

- **Change Harold so that he can use bows as well as swords.** To do this, you can add the Equip Weapon (Bow) feature to Harold or his class, and it will have the same overall effect for our purposes. I chose to add it to his class.

- **Create a skill that requires the use of a bow.**

  1. I made a new skill that I named Spark Arrow. It is of the Magic skill type and costs 10 MP per use. It has a scope of 1 Enemy and can only be used in battle. Its hit type is Magical Attack, while its animation is Pierce Thunder. As intended, I set it to require the use of a bow.

  2. For my skill's damage formula, I used [(a.atk * 4 - b.def * 2) + (a.mat * 2 - b.mdf * 2)] (I spliced the Attack and Spark damage formulas together sans the 100 damage from Spark). It does Thunder HP Damage with a variance of 10 and can inflict Criticals. It has no special effects.

- **Give Harold the skill that you have created.**

  1. To add a skill to a class, double-left-click (or right-click and then select Edit) within the Skills list of that class. You can do the same on an already added skill, to edit or erase it.

  2. Because we want to add the new skill, let's add it to the blank slot directly below Spark. For this exercise, let's set the level at which to learn our bow skill at 1. That means Harold will have that bow skill from the start of the game.

- **Create a regular item that can be used to attack enemies and is consumed on use and a key item.**

  1. My regular item is a Bomb. It deals exactly 50 physical damage to all enemies when used (you can write in numbers into the damage formula). It is Consumed when used and costs 100 gold to purchase from a shop (which means that it sells for 50 gold). It has a Physical Hit Type and the Fire All 1 animation.

  2. My key item is an Old Key. It has no price, cannot be consumed, and has a scope of None and an occasion of Never. Such an item seems useless at first glance, but it can be used in conjunction with the Item conditional. It is mainly used for events involving locked doors/gates, to allow players to open them, if they have the appropriate key item.

- **Create a bow for Harold to use.**

  1. I created a new bow called Harold's Bow and gave it an attack value of 20.

  2. It has no value, so it cannot be sold, and it has the Pierce Physical animation.

  3. It has the following Traits:

     - Does physical damage

     - Grants a bonus of 5% Hit Rate to its wielder

     - Prevents shields from being used (via the use of the Seal Equip trait) at the same time as the bow

     - Grants a 5% bonus to the wielder's Critical Rate

■ **Note**   This is Harold's Bow. What stops another bow user from using this bow? Good question. It's clunky, but outside of scripting, the easiest way to create a weapon that only a certain character can use is to make a whole new weapon type for that character. You could call the new weapon type HBow (short for "Harold's Bow") and then allow Harold to use weapons of the HBow type. Anyway, let's resume.

- **Come up with a new enemy.**

  1. I made a new enemy called the War Orc. I used *Hue* (set to 190) to give the Orc graphic a bluish tinge. Using Hue is awesome for the shameless, but necessary, RPG convention of having recolored enemies. Rather than have to manually recolor the same sprite multiple times, you could just have a single sprite and tweak it with Hue within RMMV.

  2. It has 250 MHP, no MMP, 30 Attack ATK, 15 Defense, 15 M. Attack, 15 M. Defense, 25 Agility, and 25 Luck.

  3. The War Orc gives 33 EXP and 50 Gold when defeated and has a 1/8 chance of dropping a Bomb.

  4. For features, it has 95% Hit Rate, 5% Evasion, and physical damage for its normal attacks.

  5. Its attack pattern consists solely of attacking normally.

Notes

- There is a method to the seeming chaos of this monster definition. It will become clearer when we add other monsters to our game later in the book. For now, note that the War Orc represents a monster archetype; rather than having balanced stats, it has stronger Attack at the expense of its defensive stats.

- M. Attack is useless on enemies that don't use Magic. Similarly, if you ever make an enemy that only uses Magic, its Attack stat will serve equally little purpose.

I Want My Monster to Do More Than Just Attack with a Weapon!

A good wish—and easy to accomplish as well. Let's take a closer look at *Action Patterns*. As you have probably noticed by now, many lists in RMMV can be edited in the same way. That is, double-left-click or right-click and select Edit. When you do the same in the Action Patterns area of an enemy page, Figure 3-10 shows what comes up.

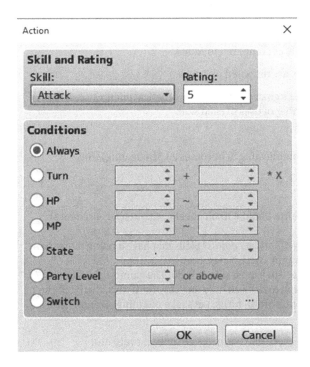

Figure 3-10. *The screen displayed by choosing to add or edit a skill to an enemy's Action Patterns*

- *Skill* is a drop-down menu that allows you to select the skill that you want the enemy to use.

- *Rating* is a value that does nothing in itself. However, when an enemy has multiple skills, it looks to their rating values to determine what to use. I've always felt that the official explanation for Rating in Ace was ridiculously clunky yet somehow managed to convey the intended message. If anything, the MV version of the Rating explanation is even clunkier. RMMV says: *"Priority of the action. Of all actions meeting the conditions, the one with the highest rating will be the standard, and the one within 2 rating points of the standard will be used. Actions 1 rating point away will be used 2/3 of the time and those 2 rating points away will be used 1/3 of the time."*

An Explanation of Ratings

Confusing, isn't it? I'll do my best to explain! Suppose we give our new enemy two new skills, Skill A and Skill B. So now, the enemy has Attack, Skill A, and Skill B in its action pattern list. If we leave Attack's rating at 5, give Skill A a rating of 4, and Skill B a rating of 3, here is how the probabilities work:

- Attack: The standard/baseline for the action pattern, as it has the highest rating

- Skill A: Will be used two-thirds of the time, as compared to Attack

- Skill B: Will be used one-third of the time, as compared to Attack

It doesn't seem like this explanation helps, but let's go deeper. If our hypothetical enemy uses a total of 100 actions, we can roughly expect the following number of uses of each skill:

- Attack: 50/100 uses

- Skill A: 50*2/100*3 = 100/300. When we simplify that, it becomes 33.3(repeating)/100. Let's call that 33/100.

- Skill B: 17/100 (to add up to 100 actions)

If we go back to the previous set of bullets, we realize that the math checks out. Attack is used most frequently, followed by Skill A, and last by Skill B.

Okay, what happens if the rating difference is more than two points? Skills that have a rating more than two points lower than the highest usable skill will never be used. Never, ever.

How about those conditions? Do they affect rating? They most certainly do. The game checks for *usable* skills. So, if you have a skill with rating 9 and a condition to be used only on every third turn, then it doesn't matter what rating any other skills have on the other, non-third, turns. Let's take our initial example and add a Skill C that relies on such a conditional:

- Skill C—Rating 9: 100% chance to use on every third turn; 0% chance on every non-third turn

- Attack—Rating 5: 50% chance to use on every non-third turn; no chance to use on every third turn

- Skill A—Rating 4: 33% chance to use on every non-third turn; no chance to use when Skill C's turn rolls around

- Skill B—Rating 3: 17% chance to use when Skill C is unavailable; nil on those chances when Skill C is usable

Feel free to test the rating system for yourself, by giving enemies extra skills and using Battle Test to see how often Slimes use each ability.

░ **Hint**   For that one skill to be used on every third turn, you would place a 3 in the second number box for the Turn No. conditional. You can determine the first time an enemy uses a skill, based on what turn number you put in the first box.

By skillful use of conditionals, you can create enemies that have predetermined patterns of attack. For example, here's a boss pattern I came up with when working on my own game. The pattern in Figure 3-11 is for an enemy that attacks on the first turn, skips a turn, and then uses a power attack (in this case, Triple Attack). That sequence is repeated until the player or the boss is defeated. The turn skip is a skill that has no effects save for displaying a message (in the case of MV's Wait: "<enemyname> waits.").

Action Patterns

Skill	Condition	R	
Attack	Turn 3+3*X	4	
Wait	Turn 1+3*X	5	
Triple Attack	Turn 2+3*X	5	
Attack	Turn 0	5	

Figure 3-11. *The action pattern for a boss I came up with when working on my game*

░ **Note**   Naturally, were you to implement such a pattern in your own game, you'd want the turn skip to display a warning message to the player so they'd know to Guard (as in the battle menu option to mitigate damage) or otherwise prepare for the power attack.

Let's finish this exercise!

- **Make a troop containing one Slime and one of the new enemy you create.**

  1. Highlight Slime on the list to the right of the troop graphic and click Add. Afterward, highlight your new enemy and repeat the action.

  2. You can manually name the troop or use Auto-name.

There you have it! Look at Figure 3-12 to see the finished troop. We now have several new things to make the game a bit more unique. Before we move on, make sure to edit the treasure chest on the second map so that it gives the player the new bow we created before, instead of the stock Bow.

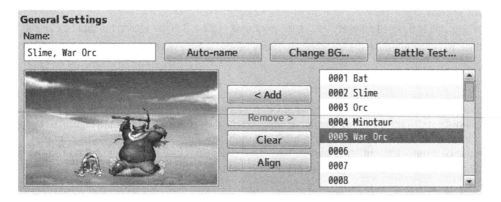

Figure 3-12. *The newly created troop*

With that done, let's add the new content to the map.

- To add the new troop to the map, you'll have to go to the second map's Properties by right-clicking its name in the map screen and selecting *Edit*. We have not covered map *Encounters* yet, but they are plug-and-play. Basically, if you interact (as usual, double left-click or right-click and then select Edit) with the currently empty list, you'll get the pop-up shown in Figure 3-13.

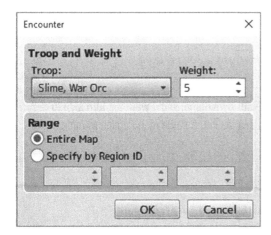

Figure 3-13. *Editing an encounter in a map's properties*

- *Troop* is a drop-down menu that lets you select which troop of enemies you wish to add to the encounter table. Scroll all the way down to the bottom and select the new troop you created.

- *Weight* determines how often the encounter appears. Because we have only one encounter, the actual value of Weight is unimportant. When you have multiple encounters, the chance of encountering any particular troop is equal to [Troop Weight ÷ Total Weight]. So, if we had three troops with the same weight, the chance to encounter each troop would be 1 in 3.

- *Range* specifies whether the troop can be encountered anywhere on the map or if its absence/presence is determined by a particular Region (I'll cover Regions in the next section). Let's make it so that our troop only has a chance to appear from Region 1. Click Specify by Region ID, and you'll see the three number boxes brighten. You can specify up to three regions in which that troop can be encountered on the current map. Let's just write in a 1 in the first box. You'll notice that the Range of the troop is 1. Had you set the range to Entire Map, it would indicate "Entire Map" instead.

░ **Reminder** Enc. Steps determines the average number of steps the player must take to encounter enemy troops within appropriate areas. The default is 30.

Regions

As already noted, Regions define where certain troops of enemies can be found. RMMV allows you to place up to 255 (!) distinct regions on a single map, although you'll be hard-pressed to use that many anywhere but on a larger world map (and maybe not even there; Ace's previous 63 regions were plenty enough to begin with). Ace used to have a dedicated Region Editor, accessible via the main menu of its interface. MV instead integrates its Region Mode into its tilesets (find the tileset labeled R). This means that you can paint Region tiles using Map editing mode (hurray for drawing Region rectangles!) Find a solitary corner of your map, switch to the R tileset, and make a small square or rectangle Region 1. Figure 3-14 shows my own map, for reference.

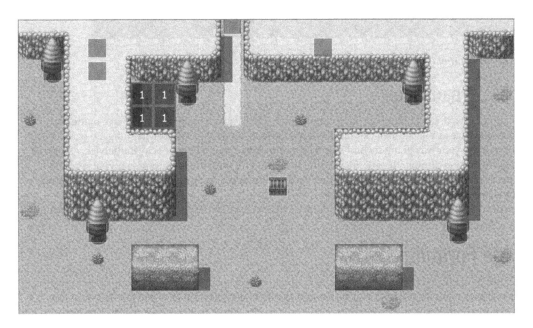

Figure 3-14. A map with Regions added

Let's play-test the game with the appropriate changes! If you did not set an appropriate battleback beforehand, the combat screen will look something like Figure 3-15.

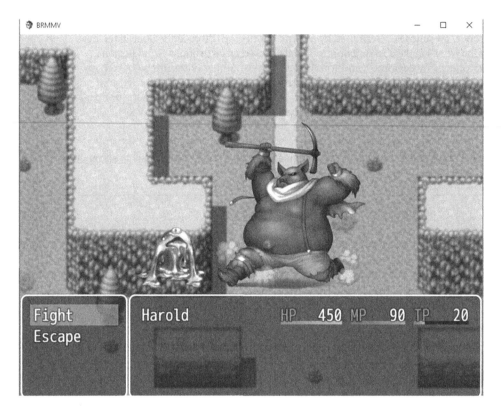

Figure 3-15. *The combat screen with the new troop created previously*

The Default Battleback

When you don't set a default battleback for a certain area, RMMV just displays a static image of the player's current surroundings as the battle background. As you can see, it's a bit . . . underwhelming. So close your play-test and make your way to the second map's properties once again. Find Specify Battleback, toggle the check box, and browse through the graphics. I used Grassland for both the foreground and background, but feel free to choose something different. When you encounter the troop once again, you'll see that the battleback is now an actual defined background.

We're nearing the end of this chapter, but I think it's time to have a little discussion about damage formulas.

Damage Formulas

Up to now, we have created one new skill, as well as one item that used the damage formula box. However, we have used the default formula. What if we wanted to use different formulas? If you take a look at the premade skills in RMMV, you'll see that not all skills are created equal. Following are some examples of different circumstances that can be covered by different damage formulas.

- *An attack that pierces the enemy's defense*: If you want to alter the basic formula, use [a.atk*4] instead of [a.atk*4 - b.def*2]. A skill that doesn't factor in an enemy's defense in the damage formula will do damage based on the user's attack. Likewise, you can make a spell in the format [a.mat], instead of [a.mat - b.mdf], to have a magic defense piercing skill.

- *An attack that does damage based on the target's HP*: You can plug MHP (Maximum HP) and HP (current HP) into formulas as well (Maximum MP and MP, too). What if you wanted to make a gravity attack in the vein of *Final Fantasy*'s Demi spells? Gravity skills, by definition, cannot kill their target. So, let's use HP. Writing [b. hp/4] would result in a skill that causes damage equal to a quarter of the enemy's remaining HP. If we were to switch HP with MHP, the same skill would do a quarter of its maximum HP in damage instead.

- *A skill that boosts the user's stats while damaging the enemy*: If you look at the stock functionality of RMMV, you'll notice that this is seemingly impossible. If you create an attack and use Effects to add states or buff/debuff stats, you'll see that the target will get them as well. But perhaps I want a skill that increases my Agility for two turns every time I connect with it. We can use .addBuff() to accomplish that (.addDebuff() lowers a stat instead). So a skill that boosts the user's Agility for two turns while damaging an enemy would look something like this: [a.addBuff(6,2); a.atk*4 - b.def*2].

What's with the numbers in the .addBuff parentheses? Perhaps I should explain. When you add buffs or debuffs via the damage formula box, you can declare the parameter (stat) to affect, as well as the turn duration. Parameter 6 is Agility, and the turn duration is 2.

Parameter Abbreviations

If you're curious to see the various parameter abbreviations in RPG Maker MV, let's take a short trip to JavaScript land (the first of many in this book).

- If you're using Windows, open Notepad and then make your way to the js folder of your game project. The JavaScript file we're interested in is called rpg_objects.js.

- If you're using Mac OS, any basic text processor will serve your purposes as well as Notepad. Find the rpg_objects.js file in the js folder of your game project.

- In either case, open the JavaScript file and make your way to Game_BattlerBase (use the Find function and search for that term). If you scroll down some after landing on the right part of the code, you'll find a JavaScript object (Object.defineProperties) that contains a list of parameters and their internal values. Given that the relevant MV code is over three pages long and the Ace equivalent a little under half of that, I provide the latter for the purpose of saving space. While the way the parameters are expressed and coded differs slightly between Ace's Ruby and MV's JavaScript, the values themselves match (for example, Maximum HP is 0 in both Ace and MV).

```
#--------------------------------------------------------------------------
# * Access Method by Parameter Abbreviations
#--------------------------------------------------------------------------
def mhp;  param(0);   end         # MHP   Maximum Hit Points
def mmp;  param(1);   end         # MMP   Maximum Magic Points
def atk;  param(2);   end         # ATK   ATtacK power
def def;  param(3);   end         # DEF   DEFense power
def mat;  param(4);   end         # MAT   Magic ATtack power
def mdf;  param(5);   end         # MDF   Magic DeFense power
def agi;  param(6);   end         # AGI   AGIlity
def luk;  param(7);   end         # LUK   LUcK
def hit;  xparam(0);  end         # HIT   HIT rate
```

```
def eva;  xparam(1);  end        # EVA  EVAsion rate
def cri;  xparam(2);  end        # CRI  CRItical rate
def cev;  xparam(3);  end        # CEV  Critical EVasion rate
def mev;  xparam(4);  end        # MEV  Magic EVasion rate
def mrf;  xparam(5);  end        # MRF  Magic ReFlection rate
def cnt;  xparam(6);  end        # CNT  CouNTer attack rate
def hrg;  xparam(7);  end        # HRG  Hp ReGeneration rate
def mrg;  xparam(8);  end        # MRG  Mp ReGeneration rate
def trg;  xparam(9);  end        # TRG  Tp ReGeneration rate
def tgr;  sparam(0);  end        # TGR  TarGet Rate
def grd;  sparam(1);  end        # GRD  GuaRD effect rate
def rec;  sparam(2);  end        # REC  RECovery effect rate
def pha;  sparam(3);  end        # PHA  PHArmacology
def mcr;  sparam(4);  end        # MCR  Mp Cost Rate
def tcr;  sparam(5);  end        # TCR  Tp Charge Rate
def pdr;  sparam(6);  end        # PDR  Physical Damage Rate
def mdr;  sparam(7);  end        # MDR  Magical Damage Rate
def fdr;  sparam(8);  end        # FDR  Floor Damage Rate
def exr;  sparam(9);  end        # EXR  EXperience Rate
```

Mind you, buffs and debuffs only apply for the first eight in the list (in other words, MHP through LUK).

So, States Work in the Same Way, Right?

Mostly. You can declare .addState(X), where X is the database entry for the state you wish to use. The number of turns a state will last is determined by the state's properties in the Database. So if we have the default list of states (of which there are 10), we can make an attack that poisons the user and damages the enemy as follows: a.addState(4); a.atk*4 - b.def*2.

It is good to note that you only really need to use the commands when you want to apply effects to both the user and the target. If you have a healing spell that also increases Agility, you can cover that just fine with a damage formula and the Add Buff Effect (or you could use a Recover HP effect for the healing part of the spell as well).

With all that said, let's take a peek at the States tab of the Database (Figure 3-16).

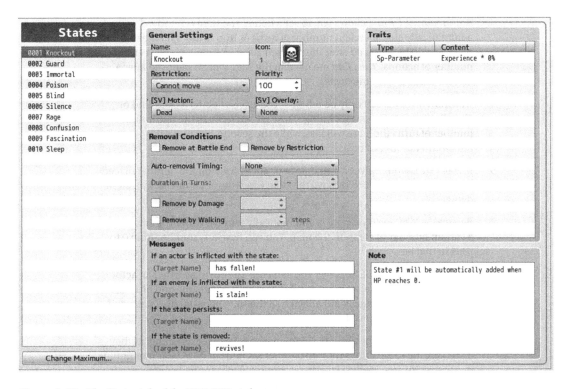

Figure 3-16. *The States tab of the RMMV Database*

As previously noted, using .addState requires that you set which state you want to add, and it looks at the database value to determine what to add. So, Knockout is 1, while Blind is 5, for example. States have one or two new things, but not much that we haven't seen in a similar form already.

- *Restriction* defines what happens to someone affected by the state. Most of the options are more forced actions than restrictions. In the case of Knockout, the actor or enemy *cannot move* (logically, as they are dead!). However, you also have *None*, *Attack an enemy*, *Attack anyone*, and *Attack an ally*.

- *Removal Conditions* define when a state is removed. This is more important for actors, given that enemies cease to be after you are done battling with them. If you don't define any removal conditions, the only way to remove the state would be to have an item or event that does just that.

  1. *Remove at Battle End* is self-explanatory. Once the battle ends, so does the state.

  2. *Remove by Restriction* used to have a somewhat inaccurate tool tip in the Ace era. Thankfully, it's a lot clearer now in MV. The RMMV tool tip says: "Will be replaced by a new state with a different action restriction". For example, you can have a Rage state that is affected by restrictions so that if your actor affected by Rage is stunned or otherwise hindered, he/she loses the state (MV actually has a stock Rage state, but it's not affected by restrictions by default).

3. *Auto-removal Timing* allows you to set whether the state is removed automatically after a certain number of turns or not. *Action End* means that the state will be removed after the affected actor or enemy takes a certain number of actions. *Turn End* means that the state will be removed after a certain number of battle turns.

4. *Duration in Turns* can only be edited if you have selected Action End or Turn End in Auto-removal Timing. The first box defines the minimum number of turns the state will last, while the second box notes the maximum number of turns.

5. *Remove by Damage* gives a percentage chance based on the number placed in the appropriate box to remove the state when the actor or enemy suffers damage.

6. *Remove by Walking*. The state is automatically removed after the actor takes a certain number of steps on the map. You can have any number from 0 to 9999 in that box.

7. There are four kinds of *Messages* you can edit. They display when an actor is inflicted with a state, an enemy is inflicted with a state, the end of a turn when an actor or enemy is still affected (if the state persists) by a state, and when the state is removed.

8. Last, *Traits* return once again but don't bear additional explaining, as they do mostly the same things they do in other sections. It does bear mentioning that state 0001 is a special state that is automatically applied whenever a character's HP reaches 0. By default, it is called Knockout.

Back to Damage Formulas?

Back to damage formulas! We already scratched the tip of the figurative iceberg by noting the existence of addBuff() and addState(). Incidentally, removeBuff() and removeState() exist as well. The remove methods only accept a single parameter within their parentheses. In the case of removeBuff, you declare which of the eight main stats you wish to remove a buff for. For removeState, you define which state is to be removed.

You may have noticed that, in my use of those mentioned methods, I used a semicolon to divide them from the damage formula. There is a little-known rule about damage formulas that is not mentioned within RMMV, but here it is: *In any formula, you must end the formula with a damage value (or healing, as the case applies).* The easiest way to prove or disprove that assertion is by editing the damage formula of your new bow skill and adding a semicolon after the damage with an addState or addBuff command (remember that "a" before the command denotes user, while "b" denotes target). If you did it correctly, you'll see that your skill now does nothing except apply the buff or state. Now, switch the two halves of the formula around, and you'll do damage again.

Here are some other neat things you can do with damage formulas:

1. *Making a skill that does more damage based on the target's active states*: Say you want an enemy that poisons the player's party and then tries to consume that poison to do massive damage to its victims. You could have a formula like so: if (b.isStateAffected(x)) { b.removeState(x); Winter.phys(1.0,a,b); } else {0}. isStateAffected is another method within RMMV. As the name might suggest, it checks whether the target has x state, where x is the number of the state in the Database.

2. If the target has x state, the skill removes the state and then applies a custom damage formula I came up with (that's the `Winter.phys` part). In Chapter 14 I'll cover how to add extensive damage formulas as code for you to call as in the preceding. In the meantime, if you wish to test the damage formula just shown for yourself, change `Winter.phys(1.0,a,b)` into any number of your choice.

■ **Tip** You'll also need another skill that inflicts a state that your new skill can then remove, if you wish to test the formula.

---

3. If the target does not have x state, then the skill does 0 damage.

Those of you with programming experience (especially in JavaScript, but even if not) will probably recognize the preceding formula as an `if` conditional branch. The damage formula box is fully robust. It will hold any amount of JavaScript you can fit in there (which, given that MV's damage box has no character limit, is pretty immense).

Additional Exercises

Okay, first let's list some extra exercises for you to do. Then, I will explain what that strange method up there involves.

1. Make a troop with a single monster that says some words before dying.

   - Death (applied automatically via the Knockout state when an enemy or actor is out of HP) is prioritized over any other consideration in battle, so you'll have to make the enemy immortal (there's a default state in RMMV that covers exactly that), have a conditional that triggers when the monster drops to 0% HP, have the monster say its words, and then remove the Immortal state, so that the death sequence can trigger.

   - This troop event can be done with two event pages. The first one should have a Turn 0 conditional and a Battle Span (as we only want this event to execute once per battle). You can use the Change Enemy State event command to set the monster's Immortal state.

   - The second event page for this exercise should have a Condition of Enemy HP <= 0% and a Battle Span. Because death is prioritized, the monster must say its words before you remove the state.

   - *You can find a completed example of this exercise in Troop #255 of the source code's Database.*

2. Create an enemy with three different skills (including the normal Attack skill). Have one skill require the enemy to be in a state to use, and have another of its skills grant that state.

   - *You can find the skill example in Skill slot #255 and the enemy example in Enemy slot #255.*

3. Create an enemy that uses a single skill on a three-turn countdown:

- Perhaps the best way to do so within the confines of RMMV is to create one "skill" for each countdown turn, much as I did for the boss attack pattern I showed you some time ago. If you look at the message box for a skill, you'll see it has two lines. On line 1, you can write "is charging up a massively powerful attack," and on line 2, you can write the appropriate number (3, 2, or 1).

- Remembering the whole thing about ratings and conditional uses of skills, you can also have the monster use a normal attack pattern that changes to the countdown when the monster is down to half HP or less.

- *You can find the new skill examples in Skill slots #251 to #254 and the enemy example in Enemy slot #254. You can find the enemy in an example Troop (slot #254).*

4. Create a damage formula that includes a variable:

- A variable has to be expressed in the form `$gameVariables.value(n)`, where n is the variable's ID.

- Remember that a variable is, after all considerations, a number. You can use the variable as an attack multiplier, for example.

- Variables default to a value of zero, so you may want to make a troop with your new enemy to give the variable a nonzero value and make sure that the damage formula is working correctly.

- *Skill #251 has the appropriate damage formula and Troop #254 (as in the previous exercise) contains the enemy that uses the relevant skill.*

About that Winter Up There...

You may be wondering the purpose of writing your formula somewhere else and calling it via code, instead of just typing it into the formula box. Well, back in the Ace era, the damage box had a 100 character limit. So, if you had a sufficiently large formula, you needed to do it this way or you couldn't do it at all. Although MV's formula box has no such limit, doing it this way has the advantage of neatness. Take a look at the formula that I used at one point in a game I was making using RMVXA:

```
a.atk>b.def ? a.atk*0.5*(1.0+(1.0-(b.def*1.0/a.atk*1.0))) : a.atk*0.5*(a.atk*1.0/b.def*1.0)
```

And that's *after* I applied some basic programming logic to shorten the expression. This formula is written as a ternary expression. In simpler terms, it's another way to write out an `if` conditional branch. It reads out as such:

- `If a.atk > b.def`

- `then a.atk*0.5*(1.0+(1.0-(b.def*1.0/a.atk*1.0))`

- `else (if a.atk < b.def) a.atk*0.5*(a.atk*1.0/b.def*1.0)`

The damage formula may seem alien, but the net effect it achieves is that a character can never deal more damage than its total Attack stat (which is the sum of a character's Attack and the Attack that it receives from its equipment). This formula favors lower stats a lot better than the default formula does. A similar formula is used for games in the *Dragon Quest* series (where the HP cap is 999 instead of 9999, as in *Final Fantasy*, and thus damage/healing has to be lower across the board).

Of course, as cool as the formula is, writing it out completely within the damage box took up very nearly every inch of space there was in Ace's damage box. So, I read up a bit and decided to create a module within RMVXA's Script Editor instead. As noted previously, I'll be leaving the discussion of how we would go about creating such a damage formula code in MV for Chapter 14, when other exercises I have lined up require the use of JavaScript. For now, here's a teaser in the form of the Ruby module I created in Ace for the purpose.

```ruby
module Winter
  module_function

  def phys(p, a, b, v = $game_variables)
    if a.atk > b.def
      return (a.atk*p*(1.00+(1.00-(b.def*1.00/a.atk*1.00)))))
    else
      return (a.atk*p*(a.atk*1.00/b.def*1.00))
  end
end

#Express in the form Winter.phys(p, a, b)
#p is the power multiplier for the ATK stat of the caster.

def sitva(bd, p, a, b, v = $game_variables)
  return ((bd + a.mat*p)*(a.mat*1.00/b.mdf*1.00))
end

#Express in the form Winter.sitva(bd, p, a, b)
#bd is the base damage of the Sitva
#p is the power multiplier for the MAT stat of the caster.

end
```

It's not much to look at, but it is basic-level Ruby programming at its finest. We'll be updating the code for JavaScript (and thus, MV), so look forward to that.

Summary

Over the course of this chapter, we covered a great part of the Database. The Database is required to create playable characters, enemies, and items for the player to collect. We created new items for our protagonist to use. In addition, we touched upon the Region tool and used it to create an area in which the player can engage a newly created troop. That concludes this chapter. In the next chapter, we will work on fleshing out our game a little more. How, you may wonder? We'll add more locations to the game!

CHAPTER 4

Fleshing Out Your World

Over the past two chapters, I've covered many basic but important aspects of RMMV. Now it is time to build on what you have learned, to start making our very own game. The first order of business is to add a few more maps, as we only have the two we created so far. To make sure that we are using the same content, and also to show off the relevant feature, let's use some premade maps.

Adding Content to Our Game World

Two RPG mainstays are towns and dungeons. Additionally, most RPGs have a world map that connects the various locations the player can visit during the game. So on that note, let's add three new maps from the premade selection that RMMV has available.

- From the main map screen, right-click your project's name in the lower-left corner and select Load.

You could have done the same thing by right-clicking MAP001 or your second map. That would have caused the new map to be placed under the previous map. Doing so is rather useful for organizing maps that share a similar purpose. Figure 4-1 shows an example of what I mean.

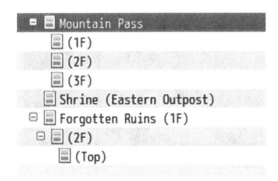

Figure 4-1. *A map list with nested locations*

■ **Note** In a sense, nesting related locations makes it easier to see what goes where on a meta level. This becomes more important as the size of the game increases. It is not actually necessary but can be a time-saver.

- After clicking Load, you'll see a wide variety of maps to use. First, let's choose our world map. I picked World 1, a world map with one rather large landmass cut roughly in two by a mountain range and various smaller continents and islands. Set World 1's BGM to Field2 and choose Disable Dashing on the world map.

- Next, let's add a town map. Right-click World 1 and select Load. Given that the world map has plenty of water, let's use the Fishing Village for our very first town. Set the Fishing Village's BGM to Town1.

- Last, let's add a dungeon. Right-click World 1 again and load up the sample map list. The Stone Cave is a nice and simple dungeon layout, so let's select Stone Cave. Set the Stone Cave's BGM to Dungeon1.

Now, what if I told you that I want you to place two of the same Stone Cave maps within a single map? Sounds like a cue to painstakingly spend a few hours drawing the second copy of the Stone Cave, right? Wrong! It took me longer than I care to admit to realize that you can copy-paste terrain as easily as you can an event. How do we do this?

1. First, right-click the existing Stone Cave map and use Load to add the second Stone Cave to your project. Note that it is a 41×30 map.

2. Next, let's prepare the first Stone Cave to receive its twin. Go to the first Stone Cave's map properties and increase its width by 51 (Stone Cave's width plus 10 more squares, to effectively split the two maps). You'll see transparent tiles fill the extra space.

3. Now, switch over to the second Stone Cave and zoom out until you can see the entire map on the screen (in my case, that is 42%; you can see your zoom level at the bottom of MV's interface, to the right of the current map name, as in Figure 4-2).

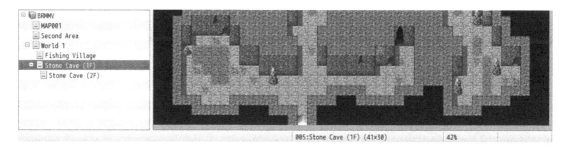

Figure 4-2. *Screenshot of the zoom level, with some of the MV interface included for visual reference of position*

■ **Tip** You can find the Zoom buttons, as well as a third button that sets the zoom level back to the default of 100%, to the right of the map-drawing tools.

1. After making sure that you're in Map editing mode and using the Pencil tool, right-click the upper-left corner of the second Stone Cave and drag the cursor all the way to the lower-right corner. If you do this correctly, your cursor should now be moving around a huge white square.

2. Switch back to the first Stone Cave and scroll to the part of the map filled with transparent tiles. Once you have the square in a good spot, left-click once. Like magic, you'll see the extra Stone Cave appear. You can fill in the transparent tiles with the Darkness tile from tileset A, or just leave them as they are (transparent tiles show up black in-game). Your Stone Cave map should look like Figure 4-3. (This screenshot was taken at 25% zoom level.)

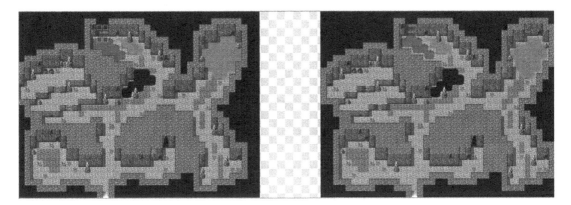

Figure 4-3. *Both instances of the Stone Cave placed on a single map*

Before we move on, make sure you delete the extra Stone Cave map (the one that has a single cave instead of the edited one that now has two).

Populating the World Map

Now we are ready to start populating our game world. Let's make our way to World 1. RMMV's premade maps come with already defined terrain but none of the other trappings that make a world map what it is. What we're going to do is place appropriate graphics for our newly created town and dungeon and our previously created map. I'm placing the three doodads on the southern end of a certain landmass. See Figure 4-4 for a zoomed-out look at the general area of the world our game will start in and then Figure 4-5 for the zoomed-in version. All of the graphics are on the B tab of the Overworld tileset.

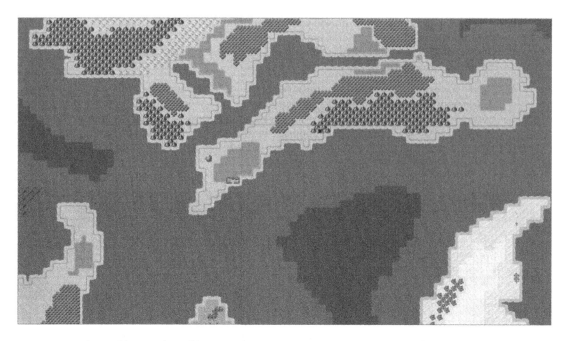

Figure 4-4. *The world map after adding appropriate graphics for each currently created area (zoomed-out)*

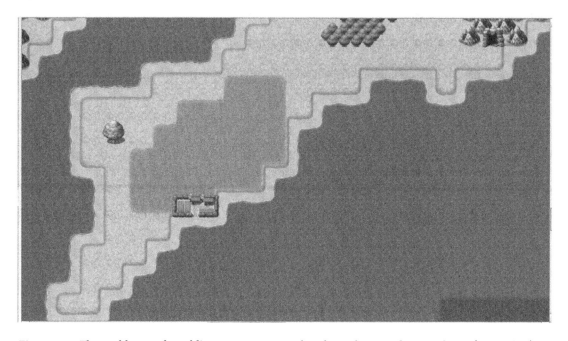

Figure 4-5. *The world map after adding appropriate graphics for each currently created area (zoomed-in)*

The giant tree to the northwest of the port town is the location from where our protagonist will exit the second area. I placed the dungeon entrance in a conveniently sized hole to the northeast of the port town and the giant tree. Note the slight edits to the mountain range to better accommodate the dungeon entrance. Of course, as cool as they look placed as they are on the map, we must still create transfer events that actually take us to our new locations. If there was ever a place to use the Parallel event I mentioned back in Chapter 2 to cut down on overall event use, the world map is definitely it. Think back to your last RPG and how many locations you could reach from its world map. You can copy-paste the relevant event from the second map and tweak it for the world map. We want the giant tree to take the player to the Second Area map, the town graphic to take the player to the Fishing Village, and the cave graphic to take him/her to the Stone Cave. It should look something like this:

```
♦Control Variables : #0002 X = Map X of Player
♦Control Variables : #0003 Y = Map Y of Player
♦If : X = 52
   ♦If : Y = 92
      ♦Transfer Player : Second Area (10,10) (Direction : Up)
      ♦
   :  End
   ♦
:  End
♦If : X ≥ 55
   ♦If : X ≤ 56
      ♦If : Y = 95
         ♦Transfer Player : Fishing Village (6,4) (Direction : Down)
         ♦
      :  End
      ♦
   :  End
   ♦
:  End
♦If : X = 68
   ♦If : Y = 88
      ♦Transfer Player : Stone Cave (15,27) (Direction : Up)
      ♦
   :  End
   ♦
:  End
♦
```

Once you have done that, you can fix the Transfer event in the second map to allow the player to reach the world map. I will leave those tasks as exercises for you. Let's move on to the fishing village. It's time to populate it! (Take a look at Figure 4-6 to see a picture of RMMV's premade fishing village.)

Figure 4-6. *The Fishing Village sample map in RMMV*

Populating the Fishing Village

As you can see in Figure 4-6, the fishing village has five buildings. We will be creating a shop and an inn, and three houses as well. RMMV has templates for all of those, which will be extremely helpful in this endeavor.

How do I plan to lay out the maps for the building interiors? Generally, I prefer to use a single map for town interiors, as they tend to have the greatest number of locations. For dungeons, I usually have one map per floor (with the obvious exception of the Stone Cave, but I did that to illustrate the concept of having multiple locations in one map).

■ **Note**   RMMV has a rather generous map limit of 999, which you probably won't hit unless you make a particularly large game. However, the preceding discussion is good to keep in mind, if you decide to make the next 50-hour epic RPG.

So, let's create a new map a whopping 256×256 in size (the maximum map size allowed in RMMV) that uses the Interior tileset. Using premade maps and copy-paste, we're going to add all of the following to our map:

- Both floors of the inn connected together with a passage

- A general shop

- Three houses

■ **Note**   RMMV also has stock graphics and sample maps for a more modern type of game. While our game will be in the more classical style of fantasy RPGs, feel free to look at some of the modern sample maps and see what they're about.

- Keep in mind that you'll want to separate each individual building by roughly 10 spaces; otherwise, the player will be able to see the different buildings present on the same map if he/she strays too far to the left or right. What I usually do to make sure the gap between two buildings is exactly 10 squares wide is draw a line of distinct terrain to the right of the first building. Then you place the new building adjacent to the end of the line. Once you're done placing your buildings, you can erase the lines you made.

Anyway, let's begin. See Figure 4-7 for the inn that we will be using in the Fishing Village (created by merging the Inn 1F and Inn 2F sample maps together with a connecting corridor).

Figure 4-7. *A screenshot of the merged inn*

Note that Inn 1F is to the right of Inn 2F. I added a few doodads in the connecting passage so that it would appear less sparse in-game. Next, let's move on to the general shop. For the general shop, I took the premade item shop and tweaked it a little to show off armor and weapons. I then placed a second seat for the armor and weapons vendor (see Figure 4-8.)

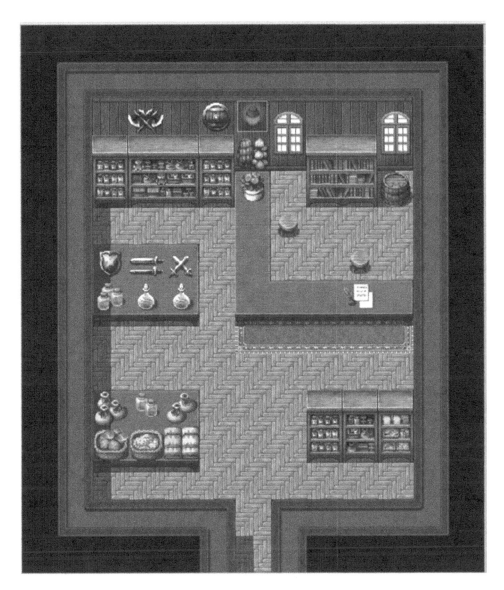

Figure 4-8. *The general shop map based on the item shop sample map*

For the three houses, there are several premades you can use. I'm going to use House 1, House 2, and Village House 1F. In the case of the Village House, I removed the staircase meant to lead up to a second floor and walled off that area. Once you're done, you can reduce the size of the map. Because I lined up all my buildings in one row, I went from 256×256 to 176×48. Figure 4-9 is a 10% zoom level screenshot.

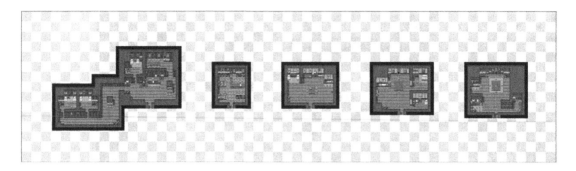

Figure 4-9. *The interior map for the fishing village's buildings*

Now let's get to work populating the fishing village! We're going to want nonplayer characters (NPCs) for each of the buildings. For the inn, you need the innkeeper. For the general shop, you'll need two shopkeepers. This is as good a time as any to use the character generator that RMMV provides, so make your way to the Tools tab of the menu toolbar and click the Character Generator.

Creating Characters to Populate Seaside

This section will take you through the process of creating an NPC and placing him/her in the game world. You should be looking at the Character Generator at the moment (see Figure 4-10).

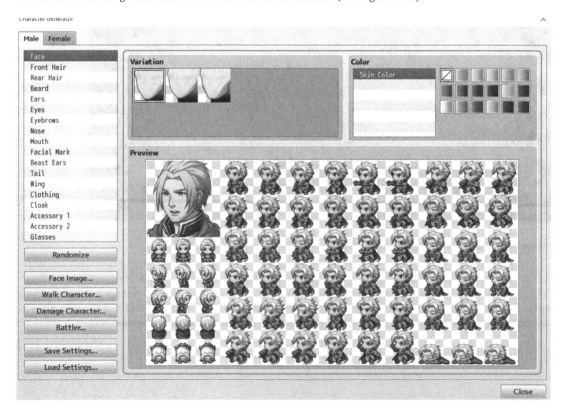

Figure 4-10. *The Character Generator*

As mentioned earlier in the book, the Character Generator is awesome for making a diverse range of characters without any graphical know-how. Mess around with the settings for a bit and note how each feature change affects the character's face and sprite. Once you're done, you can save the character sprites by clicking first Walk Character and then Export on the next screen, and writing a file name in the prompt that appears. I don't usually have character faces for my less important characters, but you can save your character's face via Face Image, if you wish.

░ **Note** Damage Character and Battler sprites are used for side-view battle mode. Incidentally, I'll be touching upon this new (for MV) battle mode later in the chapter, when we add appropriate enemy encounters to our little section of the world map.

Make a total of seven characters. Once you're done, placing a character on a map is as easy as switching to Event mode, creating a new event, and adding your freshly made character sprite to the event. Here is where we're going to place the character events:

- Place one character on the stool behind the counter at the inn. That character will be your innkeeper. Place a second character on one of the stools at the table behind the inn's counter.

- Place a character on each of the two stools at the general shop. These will be the item and equipment shopkeepers, respectively.

- Place one character at each of the three houses. One of the houses will contain a second character, but more on her later (we'll be using a stock graphic for her).

After all that is done, we have to link the buildings to the fishing village exterior. Use a Parallel event, as we have already done, and plug in the relevant Transfer events. With that done, make your way to the fishing village map. We have some tweaking to do! First of all, we have to add doors to each of the village's five buildings that have an entrance. Doors, as noted in Chapter 2, are a type of transfer event used for buildings. Add a door event to each of the buildings, making sure to link it to the correct destination on the other map. Figure 4-11 is an example of where the player should land after being transferred to the port town's inn interior.

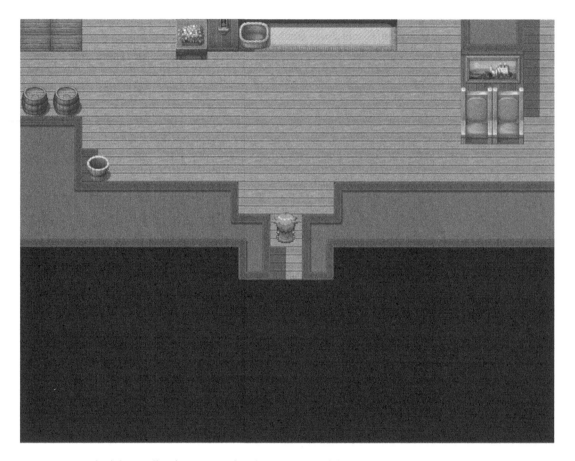

Figure 4-11. *The fishing village's inn. Note the player character's location*

As you can see, there is one square below the player in the inn. We can use that square in the Parallel event on that map to serve as the inn's exit.

■ **Note** Don't forget to link Seaside to the world map! Otherwise, the player won't be able to leave after entering the fishing village.

Make three more characters using the Character Generator and place them as so:

- Place one by the dock at the southern end of the village pier.
- Place one at 17, 26 (that's the square under the stump and adjacent to the brown rug).
- Place the last one looking over the well near the north end of town.

So, we've done a lot of character placing throughout the exterior and interior of the fishing village. But what are the NPCs doing there? What should they say to the player when he/she talks to them? Here's some setting info you can use to flavor what they could be talking about:

Harold awakes from an age-old slumber, finding himself within a ring of mountains that has only one exit. He appears within a small glen and finds his trusty bow after noticing some peculiar trees. Afterward, he finds himself to the northwest of a fishing village and makes his way there. The people of Seaside are frustrated with the current situation: ships have not docked there for the better part of a decade, crippling trade between Seaside and the rest of the world. Only the efforts of farmers living on the far end of the continent have kept them alive and well. Now, monsters from a cave to the northeast are attacking the farms and stealing their food. The people of the continent need a hero.

The only things I'll require are the following:

- The innkeeper informs the player of the threat of monsters from the nearby cave, explaining that they are threatening the town's livelihood. Set a switch to ON after the initial conversation and then have the innkeeper talk about something else, if the player speaks to him/her again. You can use Show Text events for the greater part of the conversation and Show Choices when you want the player to weigh in with a response.

- Marsha is the third premade actor in RMMV. Use her graphic as an event placed in the third house of the fishing village (the one created from the Village House 1F sample map). If the player has already talked to the innkeeper (the relevant switch is ON), have Marsha join Harold's party. If the player has not, Marsha should recommend that they speak to the various townsfolk, to get a feel for what's going on. This should be a three-page event, with the third page removing the Marsha event from the screen after she is added to the party. You can use the Change Party Member event command to have Marsha join the player's party.

If you're unclear on how to tackle those two character events, I will explain them in detail later in the chapter. With that said, I should take some time to cover *how* to make the various NPCs that will be running the inn and the shop. If you check the third page of the Event Commands list, you'll find a command called *Shop Processing*. Clicking it brings up a relatively simple window (as shown in Figure 4-12).

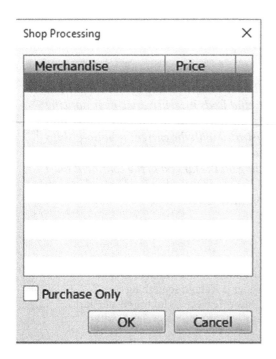

Figure 4-12. *The window that appears when Shop Processing is selected*

Essentially, Shop Processing allows you to create a list of items that the shopkeeper will then sell in-game. Double-left-click to add a new item. You can also set the item price here, if you want it to differ from the standard. The check box at the bottom allows you to create a shop that disallows selling. Here's a simple example of how the item shop NPC event could look:

```
♦Text : None, Window, Bottom
:     : What can I do for you, sir?
♦Shop Processing : Potion
:                : Magic Water
:                : Bomb
:                : Dispel Herb
:                : Stimulant
♦
```

In the same way, you can use a similar event for the equipment shop NPC. As for the innkeeper, there's no Inn Processing equivalent in the event command list, but Inns *are* a Quick Event. Clicking the Inn Quick Event will bring up the window shown in Figure 4-13.

Figure 4-13. *The Inn Quick Event*

Rather unassuming, isn't it? Select the character graphic that you designated to be your innkeeper, change the cost of staying the night if you wish, and then click OK. Next, take a look at the event that was created. Quite a few things in there, aren't there? The most important thing to note is the pair of screen fade commands. When the player pays the innkeeper for the room, the screen fades out, music is played, and then the screen fades back in. You could use a similar fade-out/fade-in coupling to add Marsha to the player's party without showing the event disappearing simultaneously (as that would look clunky, at best). So, let me explain how I laid out the events I required.

- The innkeeper

    1. Edit the default innkeeper event we have just created.

    2. Create a conversation between Harold and the innkeeper whereby a switch is turned on after the player accepts the quest.

Following is the conversation that I created, complete with an old RPG trope: the false choice:

```
♦Text : None, Window, Bottom
:     : Hello there, young one. What brings you to fair
:     : Seaside?
♦Text : None, Window, Bottom
:     : Harold explains what has happened recently.
♦Show Balloon Icon : This Event, Exclamation (Wait)
♦Text : None, Window, Bottom
:     : Could it be?
♦Text : Actor1(0), Window, Bottom
:     : What is it?
♦Text :  None, Window, Bottom
:     : Legends speak of a hero that was sealed within a
:     : glen in times long past.
♦Text : None, Window, Bottom
:     : We have dire need of a hero, lad. This port town is
:     : in danger, you see. Monsters have taken up residence
```

```
:       : at the cave to the northeast and are affecting our
:       : livelihood. Farmers live on the far end of this
◆Text : None, Window, Bottom
:       : continent and provide for our many food-related
:       : needs. Traders have not visited Seaside for nearly
:       : a decade. Ships that we send out do not return.
:       : Please aid us, hero!
◆Label : Repeat
◆Text : None, Window, Bottom
:       : What say you?
◆Show Choices : Yes, No (Window, Right, #1, #2)
: When Yes
   ◆Text : None, Window, Bottom
   :       : Thank you very much, lad! Please find Marsha. She
   :       : should be staying at her friend's house here in the
   :       : village. You can't miss it. The house has a small
   :       : crop garden. Marsha will aid you in your quest.
   ◆Control Switches : #0002 PlotAdvance = ON
   ◆
: When No
   ◆Text : None, Window, Bottom
   :       : But thou must!
   ◆Jump to Label : Repeat
   ◆
: End
```

As usual, I took the time to add a few new things for us to look at.

- *Show Balloon Icon* is a neat little event command that places a balloon over someone's head. (You can choose between the player, the current event, or another event on the same map.) In this case, the innkeeper gets an exclamation point, for reasons that make themselves obvious a few lines of text later. Wait for Completion means that the game will wait until that event command has resolved to continue event processing. If you don't toggle that option, the conversation will continue as the balloon appears.

- *Label* and *Jump to Label* are a pair of event commands that let you control event processing. Normally, events work much like regular computer programs. That is, they start resolving from the top of the code and end at the bottom. However, there are many situations in which we don't want this to be the case. For example, here we want the player to accept the quest given. Of course, it wouldn't be much of a game if he/she decided to say no. So, we invoke one of RPG's most classic tropes and pull a literal "But thou must!" on them if they do say no. The Jump to Label command then finds the designated label (in this case, called *Repeat*) and rewinds back to that point.

- *Show Choices* is what allows us to set the yes/no question in the first place. This event command can hold up to four choices and allows you to decide what to do when the player tries to opt out of the choice branch (with the Esc key, for example). You can set the choice branch so that the player cannot opt out of it, designate the choice to be picked if the player opts out, or create another branch when the player tries to opt out of the first one.

With that done, let's add Marsha to the game! First, make your way to the Actors tab in the database and increase Marsha's starting level to 5. Next, go to the fishing village building map that you created and make your way to the village house. At the stool closest to the fireplace, add a new event with a total of three pages.

Page 1 should look like this:

```
♦If : Self Switch A is OFF
   ♦Text : Actor3(7), Window, Bottom
   :     : What brings you to this humble village,
   :     : traveler?
   ♦Wait : 60 frames
   ♦Show Balloon Icon : This Event, Exclamation (Wait)
   ♦Text : Actor1(0), Window, Bottom
   :     : Everything all right?
   ♦Text : Actor3(7), Window, Bottom
   :     : Yes, you looked like somebody familiar.
   :     : That is all.
   ♦Control Self Switch : A = ON
   ♦
:  End
♦If : Self Switch A is ON
   ♦Text :  Actor3(7), Window, Bottom
   :     : If you'll be staying with us, you might
   :     : wish to speak with the innkeep at the
   :     : inn. He has eyes and ears all over the
   :     : continent.
   ♦
:  End♦
```

Remember to set Marsha's character graphic, as well as keep the event trigger as Action Button. As the preceding event page displays, there is a *Wait* event command that can be used when you want to force the game to pause for a certain amount of time. Sixty frames are equal to a single second for Wait's purposes.

For page 2, you'll want to set a conditional for PlotAdvance to be ON (the switch I used during the conversation with the innkeeper). Then, once you have done that, take a look at the next page to see what you should add:

```
♦Text : Actor3(7), Normal, Bottom
:     : I can see it in your eyes. The innkeep
:     : has told you of our problem. I would see
:     : the monsters felled as soon as possible.
:     : When do we leave?
♦Play ME : Fanfare1 (90, 100, 0)
♦Text : None, Window, Bottom
:     : Marsha has joined your party!
♦Fadeout Screen
♦Wait : 120 frames
♦Change Party Member : Add Marsha
♦Control Self Switch : B = ON
♦Fadein Screen
♦
```

The first half of the event, leading up to Fadeout Screen, is pretty self-explanatory. What the second half does is create a transition that allows Marsha to join the player's party without making it obvious that you're removing the event version of her. The screen fades out with a two-second delay, and Marsha is added to the party via the use of the *Change Party Member* event command (which, incidentally, can also be used to remove party members, should the need arise). After that, we switch on the B Self Switch and have the screen fade back in. However, if we leave the event at that, you will have two Marshas. The third event page will have a conditional of Self Switch B and nothing else, not even a character graphic. Once Marsha has joined your party, the related event will, as far as the player knows, cease to exist. Internally, though, it still does.

Now that we are done with that, head over to the System tab of the Database for a moment and untoggle the Show Player Followers option. This will make it so that Marsha does not appear behind Harold when she joins the party. While being able to see your entire party on the screen is rather cool, I've found that it opens the door to potential problems (as your companions are affected by collision detection as well) with certain types of events. Also, while you're here, toggle the Use Side-View Battle option. As mentioned earlier in the book, we are going to use the side-view battle mode (mostly to showcase it, as battles play out identically in both types of battle view) for this project. So, there you have it.

Having done the above, it's time for a necessary intermission. Let's take some time to talk about the basics of game design (and add some new assets and change others while we're at it).

A Basic Discussion of Game Design

As noted in the previous chapter, MV's relatively bare-bones Database will require us to create manually the various things that our game requires to be more than a mere skeleton, so to speak. This section is all about that. Let's start with items, as they are most immediately relevant to this chapter.

Items

Think back to the last RPG you played, and you will realize that items played a very important part in them. Try to imagine what a game without curative items would be like! Broadly speaking, items can be used for a staggering number of things. Here are a few, off the top of my head:

- As mentioned, you can have items that cure. All four of MV's premade Items have curative properties. The *Potion* restores HP, the *Magic Water* restores MP, the *Dispel Herb* removes most negative status effects, and the *Stimulant* can revive dead allies.

- On the flip side of the previous bullet, you can have items that harm. The Bomb we created in the last chapter is but one example of such an item. Poison bottles that apply the same-named status effect when used on enemies are another.

- Not all items are meant to be consumed in a single use. Perhaps the player finds an artifact that allows them to see through clouds of magical darkness. Or, even more simply, there are countless examples of magical keys in RPGs that fit into any number of doors and never break or expire on use.

What we generally want to do when designing items for an RPG is address needs the player may have during the course of the game. Key Items are generally easier to design, as you typically use their absence to prevent access to areas until they have been obtained (you might need a fire wand to melt a wall of ice, for example). So, what regular items should we add to our game? That will become clearer when we figure out what types of enemies and skills we want to have, as the need for most consumables arises from battling foes and suffering from their attacks and status effects (or alternately, from facing an enemy that requires a specific type of damage to defeat). Even so, let's go ahead and add a few that are RPG staples. All of the items in Table 4-1 are variations of the four premade items included in all RMMV projects.

■ **Note**   The new items start in the slot after the Old Key we added to the Database in the previous chapter. The premade items will not be replaced.

Table 4-1. *Three New Items to Add to Our Project's Database*

Name	Effects	Price
Antidote	Cures Poison	25
Eye Drops	Cures Blind	25
Energy Potion	Restores 500 HP and 200 MP	200

MV's Dispel Herb is rather good as a catch-all remedy for negative status effects. However, it's a bit expensive. What generally happens in RPGs is that cheaper items are available to cure one or two status effects. Then, you can choose to carry the more expensive remedies if you want to make sure you can cure any status effect in case of emergencies. So for that purpose, I have created the Antidote and Eye Drops items. Note their price relative to the Dispel Herb. The third item is a fusion of the Potion and Magic Water premade items. Since it is action-efficient in battle to use an Energy Potion instead of one each of the other two items, you'll probably want to make it more expensive than both of the other items combined, as I did. Space would also be a concern in RPGs with limited inventory space, but that consideration doesn't apply to games created with MV.

Now that we have some new items for our game, let's move on to equipment.

Equipment

While items are important in RPGs, that doesn't mean we can just gloss over weapons and armors. Try to imagine an RPG where the intrepid hero is limited to a single weapon and suit of armor for the entire game. One of the main attractions of an RPG is the sense of progression, which is why many systems for character progression have been created throughout the years. Experience is a classic method of character progression, and so is equipment. You want to have various tiers of equipment in your game so that the player always feels like they are improving their gear. Much as you do with items, you'll want to consider the types of enemies that you include in your game when creating your game's equipment. We'll be tweaking the first three premade monsters in the Database in the last section of this intermission, but here are two tables. Table 4-2 will provide a list of new weapons to add to the Database while Table 4-3 will do the same for armor.

■ **Note**   The new weapons start at slot 6 of the Weapons tab (as Harold's bow is in slot 5), while the armors start in slot 5 of the Armors tab. The premades won't be replaced.

Table 4-2. *A List of New Weapons to Be Added to Our Project's Database*

Name	Stat Bonuses	Price
Dagger	+5 Attack	100
Short Sword	+10 Attack	250
Long Sword	+15 Attack	750
Wand	+2 Attack, +5 M. Attack	200
Oak Wand	+5 Attack, +10 M. Attack	500
Short Bow	+7 Attack	180
Long Bow	+14 Attack	700

Table 4-3. *New Armors to Be Added to Our Project's Database*

Name	Stat Bonuses	Price
Cloth Shirt	+5 Defense, +1 M. Defense	100
Leather Armor	+10 Defense, +2 M. Defense	250
Studded Leather	+15 Defense, +3 M. Defense	750
Cloth Robe	+3 Defense, +3 M. Defense	100
Silk Robe	+6 Defense, +6 M. Defense	250
Cloth Cap	+2 Defense	50
Leather Cap	+5 Defense	200
Buckler	+2 Defense	50
Small Shield	+5 Defense	200
Power Ring	+10 Attack	500
Magic Ring	+10 Magic Attack	500

Contrary to logic, you'll want the Dagger's Weapon Type to be Sword instead so that Harold can equip it (not that there's much point, given that his bow is four times stronger than the Dagger). The wands should be of the Cane type, as there is no proper Wand Weapon Type by default in MV (feel free to edit the Cane Term in the relevant Database tab if this bugs you).

Of particular note are the last two entries in Table 4-3, which are actually accessories. Accessories in MV are also located in the Armors tab of the Database (to put it another way, there is no separate Accessory tab within the software). The Cloth Shirt, Cloth Cap, and the pair of Rings should have the General Armor Type, the two Robes belong to the Magic Armor Type, the Leather equipment should be of the Light Armor Type, and the Buckler and Small Shield are of the Small Shield Type. With that set and done, let's move on to a discussion about enemies wherein we can tie everything we have talked about together.

Enemies and Player Progression Considerations

In my opinion, designing enemies is both the easiest and hardest part of RPG game design. It's easy because you can let your imagination fly and come up with all sorts of viable concepts for your game. It's hard because if you want to maintain good game balance, you have to consider the following:

- The size of the player's party: Our game's party will be two characters. The more characters in the party, the more actions the player gets to use per turn to fight enemies. As a result, any given group of enemies becomes functionally weaker when facing off against a larger group of player characters. Similarly, a given group of enemies will be more dangerous if you have fewer party members.

- The experience levels of the player's party: Because levels determine stats in MV (and in most other RPGs as well), they are also important when determining how strong an area's enemies should be. You want the enemies in a given area to be an adequate challenge for the player, given their current character level.

- The player character's equipment: As levels influence character stats, so too does equipment. There's an important interplay at work between player stats and enemy stats. If the player characters have vastly superior stats to their enemies, they will win battles effortlessly. Likewise, if the enemy has vastly superior stats as compared to the player's party, they will be nigh-unbeatable.

- The player's progress in the game: Enemies should become stronger throughout the course of the game. This should be reflected in stats, but also in the attacks that are used on the player's characters. Status effects should become more commonly used as the player reaches the end of the game.

In a nutshell, you want your enemies to have a good balance relative to your game's player characters. On that note, here are some calculations for various values of player character Attack and enemy Defense. Note that Table 4-4 assumes the default MV attack formula of [a.atk*4 – b.def*2].

Table 4-4. *Effects of Various Attack and Defense Values on Damage Dealt*

Player's Attack	Enemy's Defense	Damage to Enemy
10	10	20
20	10	60
30	10	100
30	20	80
30	30	60

Generally speaking, this will help us determine the stats we should give to our enemies. A rather basic baseline is that a regular enemy should be weaker than a player character. Here are some guidelines I use when designing enemies:

- At the start of the game, we can only assume that the player character has the equipment they started the game with. Enemies in the first area should be balanced accordingly.

- Enemies in an area after an equipment shop or dungeon should be balanced assuming that the player has acquired new weapons and armor. In the case of equipment shops, you need to figure out roughly how much gold the player would reasonably have access to. For dungeons, I assume the player has grabbed all obvious chests and none of the hidden chests. That seems to generally coincide with what happens in a player's first play-through of a game.

- In addition, we have to consider experience and gold gains from enemies as well. For experience, I generally have the player character gain a level after defeating ten level-appropriate enemies. Thus, if you're fighting weaker enemies, you'll level up slower than if you're fighting stronger enemies. Gold is a bit trickier, as you need it for both better equipment and consumable items. The price of equipment should generally correlate with the amount of stats it gives. For the purposes of this book, let's strive to make it so that the player will be able to get a new area-appropriate weapon or armor for roughly every ten level-appropriate enemies defeated. This won't be an exact science, but then again, it doesn't have to be. The beauty of creating a game is that you can keep balancing until the day you decide to stop working on the game altogether (although it's obviously good form to make sure your overall game balance is at least adequate before a formal game release, if you're looking to go commercial, or even if you're just making games casually).

- As mentioned before, you must consider the stats of each player character and how they grow with experience. For reference, Harold's Attack for the first five levels of his development is 16, 18, 19, 20, and 21. Note that a Level 1 Harold equipped with his special bow will have a total of 36 Attack. His Defense gain for those five levels is identical. As you can probably see, equipment will be a greater indicator of what a player character can defeat in our game than raw character stats. Incidentally, this is how many RPGs do it.

To close out this section, Table 4-5 lists the first three enemies in the Database, tweaked to give the player experience and gold, and with differing stats for variety.

Table 4-5. *The Stats of the Three First Enemy Entries in the Database, Tweaked for Our Game's Purposes*

Name	HP	MP	ATK	DEF	MAT	MDF	AGI	LUK	EXP	G
Bat	100	0	15	15	15	15	15	15	5	10
Slime	200	0	20	20	20	20	20	20	11	15
Orc	300	0	25	25	25	25	25	25	20	25

For our game's first area, enemies will have balanced stats. In subsequent areas, I will introduce a little more stat diversity, based on several popular monster archetypes (as I already did in the previous chapter with the War Orc, who has relatively high Attack, but lower defensive stats). My intent for the first area is to have the equipment that costs 250 gold be the intended top-end equipment the player can purchase just by spending a little time fighting enemies outside the first dungeon. The next tier of equipment, which costs 750 gold, will become relevant when we work on the aforementioned dungeon. As such, Orcs (being the strongest enemy in the region) give exactly one tenth of the gold needed to purchase one piece of that equipment. Each enemy grants experience based on the character level they're intended to be battled at (such that defeating ten of that enemy grants a level-up). Bats are Level 1, Slimes are Level 2, and Orcs are Level 3.

I hope you have enjoyed this intermission. It's always good to take some time to think about *why* we do things in game design, instead of just doing them by rote. Anyway, let's get back to our regularly scheduled text. I believe we were about to create the two shops with their respective inventories.

Populating Seaside's Shops

I will list the items I have placed for sale from each of the shop NPCs (Figure 4-14). The leftmost list is the weapon shop, the center list is the armor shop, and the list on the right is the item shop.

Figure 4-14. The three shops of Seaside

What happened to the equipment shop? Recall that we have two NPCs. One will sell items while the other sells weapons and armors. There are two ways to tackle the equipment shop.

- The easier way is just melding the weapon and armor shop lists together for the equipment NPC.

- The harder way is using the Show Choices event command to have the shopkeeper ask whether the player wishes to buy weapons or armor. Then, depending on the player's response, you would process the appropriate shop list.

░ **Note** You can check the equipment shop NPC in the source code if you'd like to see eventing for what I'm talking about in the second bullet.

That's about it for the fishing village. We will revisit it later in the book, when we discuss side quests.

Creating Random Encounters for the World Map

Next, let's add some random encounters to the part of the world map to which we currently have access. For this, we can use Regions (see Figure 4-15).

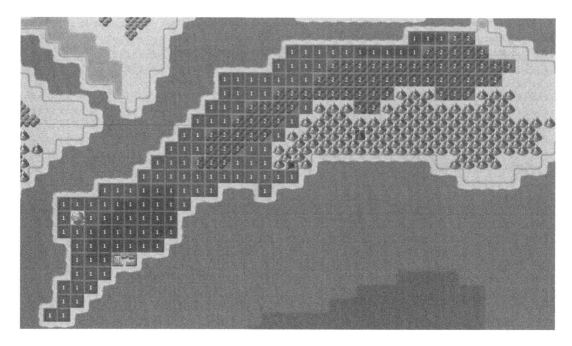

Figure 4-15. *The world map. Regions have been added*

Region 1 encompasses the entirety of the area's grasslands, while Region 2 is used for the forests. Let's add some encounters to each region. In this case, I numbered the areas based on encounter difficulty, which is a good way to go, so that you can remember what you want appearing in a certain area. Let's use the first three premade monster types that we tweaked back in our design discussion. See Figure 4-16 for a list of encounters that I set for the world map as of now.

Troop	Weight	Range
Bat	25	1
Bat*2	20	1
Slime	20	1, 2
Slime*2	10	1, 2
Orc	15	2
Orc*2	10	2

Figure 4-16. *The encounters table for the world map*

As you can see, I made the total weight of the encounters 100, although that is not strictly true. For example, there are only four total encounters available in Region 1, with a total weight of 75. That means that you have a 25/75 chance of meeting one Bat, a 20/75 chance of seeing two Bats, a 20/75 chance of engaging one Slime, and a 10/75 chance of facing off against two Slimes. Slimes also appear in Region 2 alongside Orcs, which don't appear at all in Region 1. Orcs, being the strongest enemy type, appear less frequently than Slimes.

▓ **Note**   You'll need to create the troops listed in Figure 4-16 that don't exist by default. Specifically, those would be the single Bat, single Slime, and Orc*2 troops.

As promised early in the chapter, here's a little aside for the side-view battle mode.

Battles in Side-View

We now have some nice random encounters for our world map, so it's the perfect time to show off the new battle mode introduced in RPG Maker MV. A picture is worth a thousand words, as the saying goes, so take a look at Figure 4-17.

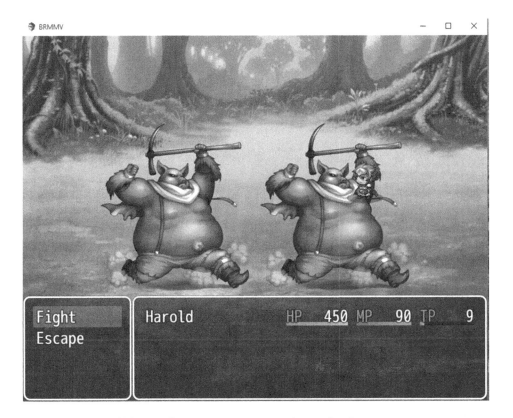

Figure 4-17. *Harold facing off against two Orcs in a side-view battle*

The first thing you may have noticed is that Harold is awfully close to that second Orc. We'll have to manually move the enemies in each troop so that they're aligned on the left side of the screen. The Align command in the Troops tab doesn't help, as it tries to line them up horizontally (which is good for top-down battle mode, but not so good for side-view, as you can see) instead of vertically. Go ahead and take a little time to do that before moving on. There's not much more to tell about this type of battle mode, as the only changes are cosmetic. You'll be able to see your characters react to being at low health and/or affected by status effects, but not much else changes between the modes. The neatest minor thing you may miss is that the enemy sprites are flipped to face right in the Database when you turn on side-view mode; if you revert to top-down, you'll see them face left once again. Before we head off to the next section, take a look at Figure 4-18, which shows off the Orc*2 encounter properly aligned for side-view.

Figure 4-18. *Harold facing off against two properly aligned Orcs in a side-view battle*

Now, we need to speak more about battlebacks.

A Discussion on Battlebacks

Up to now, we've had a single area with a single encounter. When you have a map that has uniform terrain (much like most dungeons), you can just set the area's battleback in the map properties. However, the world map is a conglomeration of various types of terrain (a cursory peek at World 1 reveals snow and desert areas). It would be rather odd to have a forest battleback for a brawl in the snow, wouldn't you say? So, what we can do is apply past knowledge in a neat little exercise.

▨ **Objective** Create an event that allows the battleback to change, based on the region the player is in when an encounter occurs.

How do we go about this? If you think back to Chapter 2, we used a Parallel event that wrote the values of the player's X and Y to variables to determine map boundaries for area transitions. Here, we can use the Get Location Info event command in conjunction with *Control Variables*, conditional branching, and Change Battleback within a Parallel event to make sure the battle background is always appropriate to the area in question. As Change Battleback is pretty much equivalent to just setting a default area battleback in a map's properties, let me speak a little more of Get Location Info. Figure 4-19 is a screenshot of that event command.

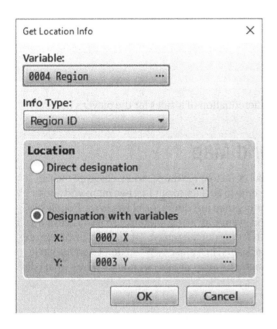

Figure 4-19. *The Get Location Info event command*

As you can see, *Get Location Info* first asks for the variable in which you wish to store your relevant information. I created a new variable named Region just for this occasion. Next, use the second drop-down menu to define what information you wish to write to that variable. Region ID is preselected here, but it is the last item on the *Info Type* list. The others are

1. **Terrain Tag.** If you go to the Tilesets tab in the Database, you'll notice a series of buttons on the right side of the screen that range from Passage at the top to Terrain Tag itself at the bottom. Terrain tags are a minor, but useful, way to define different areas, without the use of regions. All tiles default to 0 and can go up to 7. A little more on this (and more general terrain considerations) later.

2. **Event ID.** If the player is currently on top of an event square, using this option will write the specific Event ID to your variable of choice.

3. **Tile ID (Layers 1–3)** are the final three items before Region ID. This refers to the tile's ID internally. I'll leave it as an exercise to you to figure out uses for this particular command. (I prefer terrain tags, to be honest.)

Last, we want to select *Designation with Variables*, as we want the event to poll the player's position on a continuous basis.

As for the rest of the event, you can use conditional branches to check for the player's current region and change the battlebacks accordingly, like so:

```
♦Control Variables : #0002 X = Map X of Player
♦Control Variables : #0003 Y = Map Y of Player
♦Get Location Info : #0004, Region ID, ({X},{Y})
♦If : Region = 1
  ♦Change Battle Back : Grassland & Grassland
  ♦
: End
♦If : Region = 2
  ♦Change Battle Back : Grassland & Forest
  ♦
: End
♦
```

The preceding battlebacks should give some form of differentiation of locales for the player's benefit.

Adding Transfer Events to the World Map

While you're on the world map, you should add another Parallel event for area transfers as well, given that we have three locations on this map already. Now, let's take some time to go back to our first two maps and add to them. We want to give the game a coherent direction in plot, rather than just dump the player in the middle of a map unceremoniously. So on the first map, let's add an Autorun event with no conditionals, so it will activate as soon as the player enters the game. The first order of business is fading out the screen. Then, use transparent text boxes aligned with the center of the screen to give a relevant backstory. Just make sure you don't start the game with an overly long text dump, as most players hate that. A paragraph or two should be enough. Here's what I did:

```
♦Fadeout Screen
♦Text : None, Transparent, Middle
:     : A young man awakens from his slumber. He knows only
:     : that his name is Harold. He knows not where he is, nor
:     : why. What adventures await him? It is time to find
:     : out!
♦Wait : 60 frames
♦Control Self Switch : A = ON
♦Fadein Screen
♦
```

Make sure you create a second page within the event that is empty and only active once that self-switch has been turned on, or your game will loop that event page forever. On the second map, add an NPC blocking the road that speaks of the five trees that block access to Harold's Bow and then disappears. Here's what I did:

```
♦Text : Actor1(0), Window, Bottom
:     : Who are you?
♦Text : None, Window, Bottom
:     : Me? I am but a man who used to be a king, in ages
:     : long past. Your bow has been sealed within this
:     : glade for as long as you. Examine the five trees
```

```
:      : and claim your birthright. Fare thee well.
♦Text : Actor1(0), Window, Bottom
:      : Wait, what are you-
♦Fadeout Screen
♦Text : None, Window, Bottom
:      : Before Harold can finish his sentence, the enigmatic
:      : figure disappears.
♦Control Self Switch : A = ON
♦Fadein Screen
♦
```

As in the previous event, have a second blank page after this one. We need to do two more things. First, to the Treasure Chest event, add a new switch that is set to ON once Harold opens the treasure chest revealed by the trees. Have a text box appear telling the player to head to Seaside once he/she receives the bow. Second, add a conditional to the Parallel event on this map that requires this switch to be turned on. This prevents the player from leaving before taking the chest's contents. Once all is said and done, the player will know that he/she is a mysterious being awoken from a deep slumber and has a first objective in the game world.

Our next task will be to populate our very first dungeon, but that is a subject best left to its own chapter. Before ending this chapter, however, let's talk a little more about tilesets and terrain tags, as promised previously.

A Little More on Terrain Tags and Tilesets!

To talk about *terrain tags* is to talk about tilesets, as they are intrinsically linked. As mentioned previously, each tile can have a Terrain tag value between 0 and 7. Off the top of my head, here are a few of the cool things that terrain tags allow you to do:

- You can have a Parallel event running that turns all floor tiles with a certain terrain tag into damage floor tiles.

- You can have a minigame, in which the player must step on tiles in a certain order, just by setting the terrain tags of each set of tiles to a different number.

- You can have skills that have differing effects, based on the current terrain tag, similar to *Geomancy* from some of the *Final Fantasy* games. A skill could do more damage in the grasslands but have a chance to freeze victims in the snow.

For a little number, terrain tags sure can do a lot, eh? Of course, the Tilesets part of the Database is as robust as any other. Given that we have not looked at it yet, let's take some time to do so (Figure 4-20).

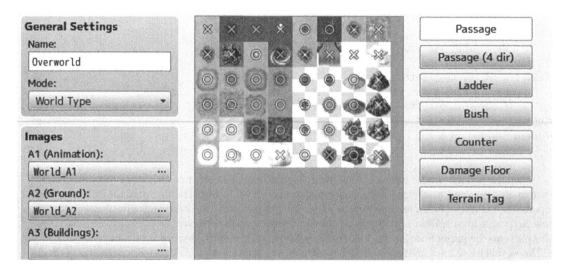

Figure 4-20. *The Tilesets tab in the RMMV Database*

While *Name* in *General Settings* is self-explanatory, *Mode* is far from it. I leave it as an exercise to you to read up on Resource Specifications in the Help file, as RMMV itself recommends in the Mode tool tip. Most of that will be of little interest to you, unless you want to add your own custom tilesets (whether created by yourself or purchased from a graphic designer) to RMMV. What is most relevant to beginner-level RMMV users is the set of buttons I mentioned when talking about terrain tags. Let's start from the top.

- *Passage* determines whether or not a player character can walk over the specific tile.

- *Passage (4 dir)* is for specific tiles. On tiles that allow the use of this property, you can control from which directions the player is allowed to enter that square of terrain. This is really useful for maps such as desert areas with rapidly moving sand that only allow movement in certain ways.

- *Ladder*, as the name implies, is used for ladder-type graphics. Basically, whenever you want the character to climb, you use the ladder property.

- *Bush* makes it so that the bottom part of the character is obscured when passing through a tile with that property.

- *Counter* is of particular interest. You probably noticed that we have placed several NPCs behind counters at the port town. If you have been doing some experimentation on your own, you will know that you must be standing adjacent to an event to trigger it via the use of Action Button/Player Touch/Event Touch. However, if your event is separated from the player by a tile considered a counter, you can still interact with him/her. It allows us to have NPCs like the innkeeper, who are otherwise trapped, but permits interaction with the player nonetheless.

- While you can use terrain tags for the same effect, there is a specific terrain property for *Damage Floors*. Designate a tile as a damage floor, and it will damage players who pass over it for 10 damage.

A Discussion of Floor Damage

How do I know how much damage such tiles cause? Well, it's all contained within a few lines of code in the rpg_objects.js JavaScript file we've already looked at once before. These lines are contained within Game_Actor.

```
Game_Actor.prototype.basicFloorDamage = function() {
    return 10;
};
```

You'll probably be interested to know that you can have variable floor damage, depending on the type of floor. Let me illustrate with some code that I hammered out in about a minute.

■ **Note**   It's not the best idea to edit code directly, as this opens up the possibility of messing something up that RMMV needs for proper functioning. That said, once you gain some experience with the engine, you'll get a feel for what's safe to edit and what's not. In any case, plugins can be used for much the same effect, as I'll illustrate near the end of the book.

```
Game_Actor.prototype.basicFloorDamage = function() {
    switch ($gameVariables.value(4)) {
        case 0:
        default:
            return 10;
        case 1:
            return 20;
        case 2:
            return 35;
        case 3:
            return 60;
    }
};
```

■ **Note**   default is a catch-all parameter that covers what happens within the switch statement if $gameVariables.value(4) is equal to something other than specified by one of the explicit cases.

Instead of a single global value for floor damage, we can have multiple values, as set by a particular variable. In this case, I chose to use $gameVariables.value(4) (where 4 is the variable ID in the Database), signifying the variable containing the Region ID. You could consider leaving a simple return value (like the default number) for damage floors set within the Tileset tab and then have other damage floors marked by regions or terrain tags.

Additional Exercises

Here are some final exercises for you to close out this chapter with a bang!

1. Expand the innkeeper so that you can choose to wake up in the morning or nighttime.

   - Having night in your game is as simple as applying a filter on the graphics. The *Tint Screen* command is perfect for this and, in fact, even has a specific color setting for nighttime. However, if you want nighttime to influence random encounters, that is quite a bit harder. It takes a small amount of scripting, and a fair amount of eventing, to have different encounters based on the time of day. Even so, you can stop the player character from leaving town and have certain events happen only at night.

   - I recommend having a `Daytime` switch and a `Nighttime` switch, if you're going to do this. Then, you can differentiate what events trigger when using the relevant conditionals. Just make sure you set one of the switches to on at the very start of the game. (Switches default to off and variables to 0 when a new game is created.) You can find a basic example for this exercise in the map titled Ch.4 Extra Ex. 1,3,4. You can test it out by setting the player's starting location on that map and then starting a New Game. The example covers resting at an inn until evening or morning, but nothing else. The other possibilities mentioned above are left as a challenge to the reader seeking something a bit more complex.

2. Have some NPCs in Seaside give the player items when they're talked to.

   - You have already used *Change Party Member* to add Marsha to the player's party in Seaside. However, there are four other event commands in the Party category, and they can be used to grant items, weapons, gold, or armor to the player. Treasure chest events actually use those event commands to give items.

   - A common mistake is to give players an item and not tell them that they received it. Make good use of the *Show Text* command!

3. Make it so that the player cannot access the dungeon until Marsha has joined the party.

   - This is as easy as adding a conditional branch to the relevant transfer event. If Marsha is in the player's party, then they are transferred to the dungeon. Otherwise, they take a step back from the dungeon entrance on the world map and say that they would rather find help first.

4. Make it so that the player cannot even see the dungeon until Marsha has joined the party.

   - Event slot conservation be darned; at this point you'll probably want to eliminate the dungeon transfer part from the main Parallel event. Then make a two-page event at the dungeon location where the *first* page is blank, and then the *second* page has the relevant graphic and only appears when Marsha is in your player's party. The second page would be Below characters, with a Player Touch trigger taking them to the dungeon as normal.

▨ **Note**   You can find example events for the third and fourth exercises on the same map where I placed the example eventing for the first one. The western house contains the event for the third exercise, while the eastern house contains the event for the fourth exercise.

Summary

This chapter took us from a two-map prototype to the beginnings of an actual RPG. We added a fishing village and the foundation of our first dungeon to the game. We populated the fishing village with shops, a plot hook for our player to grab, and a new companion. In the next chapter, we will be populating our first dungeon with treasure chests and enemies.

CHAPTER 5

Your First Dungeon

In the previous chapter, we fleshed out our small game, adding many features to make it feel more like an actual game and less like a disjointed mess. Our player now has an idea of what he or she should be doing. So in this chapter, we will tackle the task of populating the dungeon that we created (or, rather, copy-pasted) in the previous one. That said, before we start on the chapter's main subject matter, it's time to take another necessary intermission to explore game design concepts. This time, the topic at hand is skills and differentiation between character classes.

A Basic Discussion of Game Design: Skills and Class Differentiation

Now that our party consists of two characters, it's a good time to differentiate them a bit. As it stands, Harold has only three skills (the two default premades the Hero class starts with and the bow skill we created back in Chapter 3). However, Marsha, a Mage by class, has only one skill! Now, what kind of Mage is that? Let's create some new skills for Marsha. The first order of business is to figure out what types of magic we want her to be using. Since the default classes in MV seem to suggest an homage to *Dragon Quest* (originally *Dragon Warrior* in the West), let's run with the idea to flesh out our classes. Mages in *Dragon Quest* traditionally use fire, ice, and explosive magic. To keep the skill list a bit more lean, let's just go with fire and ice magic. Marsha already has the Fire spell, so it's as easy as just creating an Ice spell to match the existing spell. Of course, we want Marsha's prowess as a Mage to improve as she advances in levels, so she'll need better versions of those spells. So we'll make three tiers (this, incidentally, is a popular convention with *Final Fantasy* damage spells) of Fire and Ice. That puts Marsha's spell count at 6. Now, let's come up with four more to make it a neat 10:

- For two of those four, we could have single-target and all-party versions of an agility-boosting spell. Higher agility means that you act sooner. Faster is better.

- For the other two, we could have single-target and all-enemies versions of a defense-reducing spell. While Marsha's spells target an enemy's Magic Defense, such a spell would be of use to allow Harold's physical attacks to do more damage.

Okay, so technically that's two pairs of spells rather than four individual spells, but they'll do the job nicely. Table 5-1 breaks down each skill's most important details so that you can add them to your project's Database.

© Darrin Perez 2016
D. Perez, *Beginning RPG Maker MV*, DOI 10.1007/978-1-4842-1967-6_5

Table 5-1. *The List of New Skills for Marsha to Be Added to the Database*

Name	Scope	MP Cost	Damage Formula / Effects	Animation
Ice	1 Enemy	5	100 + a.mat * 2 - b.mdf * 2	Ice One 1
Firebolt	1 Enemy	10	200 + a.mat * 3 - b.mdf * 2	Fire One 1
Icebolt	1 Enemy	10	200 + a.mat * 3 - b.mdf * 2	Ice One 1
Fireblast	All Enemies	20	300 + a.mat * 4 – b.mdf * 2	Fire All 1
Iceblast	All Enemies	20	300 + a.mat * 4 – b.mdf * 2	Ice All 1
Haste	1 Ally	5	Increases Agility by 50% for four turns (applied by setting the skill's Add Buff: Agility effect twice).	Powerup 1
Mass Haste	All Allies	10	Increases Agility by 50% for four turns.	Powerup 1
Shatter	1 Enemy	5	Decreases Defense by 50% for four turns (applied by setting the skill's Add Debuff: Defense effect twice).	Powerdown 3
Mass Shatter	All Enemies	10	Decreases Defense by 50% for four turns.	Powerdown 3

■ **Tip** Each individual Add Buff or Add Debuff effect causes a 25% shift in the affected stat. That's why we have the relevant skills in Table 5-1 set the effect twice.

With that done, we need to add the skills to Marsha's class skill list. Because we want her to grow into her skills, we'll have her start with only Fire and Ice. She will learn Haste and Shatter at 5 (which effectively means that she'll start with those two as well, given her starting level), Firebolt and Icebolt at 10, Mass Haste and Mass Shatter at 15, and Fireblast and Iceblast at 20. We'll want to edit her stats to differentiate her from Harold as well, but first let's work on Harold's skill list. Heroes in *Dragon Quest* (to continue the theme), unlike Mages, have been many things throughout the series. For example, in *Dragon Quest 3*, they were jacks-of-all-trades that could use most weapons and armors, and could use various spells from both the Cleric and Mage spell lists. That said, one of the most emblematic features of *Dragon Quest* Heroes is their exclusive ability to use lightning magic. We have three skills for Harold already, so let's create five more for Harold. As a jack-of-all-trades, he'll also borrow a spell or two from Marsha to finish fleshing him out.

- An easy choice is making a stronger version of the Spark spell that Harold knows from the start of the game. Naturally, it should cost more and do more damage.

- If we model Harold after the DQ3 Hero, he should probably have access to beneficial magic normally reserved for cleric-types. This will help to contrast a bit with the offensive prowess of Marsha's Mage class. However, since he's *not* a Cleric, he should only get access to the single-target versions of such spells. We'll give him a spell to boost Defense and another to boost Attack.

- We have two slots left. Keeping with the theme of beneficial magic (and to balance the offensive magic we'll be giving him), one should go to a spell version of the Antidote item, while the last one should contain a spell that cures Sleep and Confusion.

See Table 5-2 for a list of the new skills created just for Harold. Then I'll discuss a few extra skills that we'll be adding to his list (from the premades and from Marsha's own list).

Table 5-2. A List of New Skills for Harold to be Added to the Database

Name	Scope	MP Cost	Damage Formula / Effects	Animation
Spark Storm	All Enemies	15	350 + a.mat*2 – b.mdf	Thunder All 1
Fortify	1 Ally	5	Increases Defense by 50% for four turns.	Powerup 3
Empower	1 Ally	5	Increases Attack by 50% for four turns.	Powerup 2
Purge	1 Ally	5	Removes Poison from the target ally.	Cure One 1
Rouse	1 Ally	5	Removes Sleep and Confusion from the target ally.	Cure One 2

■ **Note**   Now is probably a good time to add descriptions to every skill and item the player will be able to use. No such precaution is necessary for skills that only enemies will use. For that matter, weapons and armors only need a description if they give a bonus that doesn't appear in-game (anything in the Traits section of the weapon/armor); you would inform the player of the extra bonuses via the description. We as designers know what each skill and item does, but other people playing our game would not, except through trial and error, if they lack descriptions.

Now that we've given Harold a good mix of unique skills, it's time to set at what levels he will learn his unique skills as well as those he borrows from Marsha and from the premade Database. Leave Harold's three starting spells as they are. Then give him Purge and Fortify at 5, Empower, Rouse, and Dual Attack at 10, Firebolt and Icebolt at 15, and Spark Storm and Triple Attack at 20. Before moving on, set the Add Skill Type: Special trait to the Hero class. Then go to the Skill tab and set Dual Attack and Triple Attack's skill type to Special. Set Dual Attack's TP cost to 20 and Triple Attack's TP cost to 50. With all that done, we're finished with Harold!

It's time for the last part of this intermission: tweaking Marsha's stats so that she's differentiated from Harold. To do that, we first need to know what the base stats for any premade character are. See Table 5-3 for a helpful breakdown.

Table 5-3. The Base Stats Shared by All Premade MV Classes

Stat Name	Stat Value at Level 1	Stat Value at Level 99
Max HP	450	5350
Max MP	90	1070
Attack	16	138
Defense	16	138
Magic Attack	16	138
Magic Defense	16	138
Agility	32	277
Luck	32	277

Let's keep Harold's stats as listed here. If we follow along with the initial premise that our Hero is a jack-of-all-trades, it should then follow that Marsha would have stronger Magic stats (but weaker Attack and Defense) than Harold. Likewise, you would expect a dedicated spellcaster to have more MP and less HP than a generalist character. To be fair, that has to do more with the classic stereotype that caster-types are frail, sacrificing their own endurance and physical condition to become superior users of magic. Even so, we've already borrowed plenty from classic RPGs, so let's go with it. While Mages in Dragon Quest tend to be slow, let's keep Marsha's Agility at default. Anyway, what does this all mean for the Mage class? See Table 5-4 for a breakdown of how Marsha's class should look after the proposed changes.

Table 5-4. *The Mage Class Stats After Adjusting Parameters as Intended*

Stat Name	Stat Value at Level 1	Stat Value at Level 99
Max HP	225	2675
Max MP	180	2140
Attack	8	69
Defense	8	69
Magic Attack	32	277
Magic Defense	32	277
Agility	32	277
Luck	32	277

Now Marsha is a magical powerhouse who is relatively frail, especially when confronted with physical attacks. All of this theory is awesome, you may say, but how would we go about actually changing her stats? Recall that in Chapter 3 we discussed Parameter Curves in the Class tab. You can tweak Marsha's stats by doing the following (for the purposes of this tutorial, let's use Max HP):

- Double-click on the Max HP curve for the Mage class.

- Find the Generate Curve button and click it.

- Replace the default endpoint values with the ones provided in Table 5-4.

That's all there is to it! Go ahead and do the same for every other stat that requires it (all but Agility and Luck). Then let's take a moment to change the party characters' initial equipment to some of the stuff that we designed in the previous chapter. Equip Harold with the Dagger, Buckler, Cloth Cap, and Cloth Shirt (no accessory). Equip Marsha with the Wand, Cloth Cap, and Cloth Robe (no shield or accessory).

With our characters differentiated, we can move on to the chapter matter at hand—creating the dungeon. If you think back to when we initially created our two-level Stone Cave, you'll realize that we actually didn't do anything with it in terms of tweaking terrain. It's time to change that fact! Figure 5-1 shows a screenshot of the first floor of our expanded Stone Cave, after my tweaks. Do the best you can to change your dungeon area accordingly.

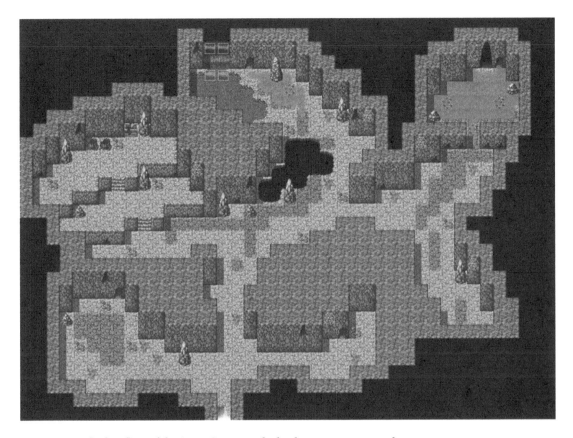

Figure 5-1. *The first floor of the Stone Cave, tweaked to better serve our needs*

Among the most important changes are these:

- The two-space entrance has been moved from the area directly to the east of the entrance to the upper-right corner of the map.

- The lower-right corner of the map has been closed off a bit.

- The passage leading into the upper-right corner of the map has been reduced to a single square of space.

Now, take a look at Figure 5-2. Whereas the first floor of the dungeon changed only minimally, the second floor has undergone some bigger changes.

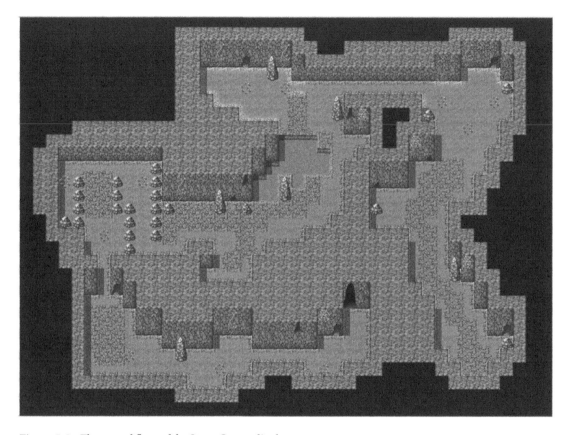

Figure 5-2. *The second floor of the Stone Cave, edited to serve our purposes*

As you can see, I edited the second floor rather more drastically. I had to remove the dungeon entrance, as this is a second floor. Note how I placed moss upon most of the rocky ground, giving more of a grassy feeling to the second floor. The second level is almost completely linear. Besides a small opportunity to go left instead of right after the pool of water, the player has no choice but to loop around the dungeon floor until they reach its lower-right corner. Take some time to tweak your second floor appropriately and then read on. The next order of business is to determine how you want your enemies to appear in the dungeon.

Random or Static?

The heading poses a very important question without an easy answer.

Random

By default, RMMV has a random encounter system in place that allows the user to cause enemies to attack the player after a certain average number of steps (determined by Enc. Steps).

Static

The alternative is to do as games such as *Final Fantasy: Mystic Quest* have done. That is, place enemy troops directly on the map. In RMMV, you can do this much as you would any other event.

Really, it all depends on the type of game you want. There's nothing wrong with having a game in which every single enemy is placed on the map already (as is the case with *Final Fantasy: Mystic Quest*). In any case, even if you use a random encounter system, you'll still want to place bosses accordingly.

Creating Static Encounters

For the sake of completeness, let's have both types of encounters within our dungeon. As we have not placed a static encounter before, let's start with those. To place a static enemy, create an event, choose an appropriate graphic, and find the *Battle Processing* event command. When you click it, you'll get the menu displayed in Figure 5-3.

Figure 5-3. *The Battle Processing event command*

- The *Troop* section allows you to decide what encounter to place within the event. It defaults to *Direct designation*, which is the option I most frequently use. However, you can also use *Designation with a variable*, in which case the encounter you get is based on the troop ID in the Database. Or, you can just have Battle Processing act like a random encounter and roll the dice on the encounters table in that map's properties.

- *Can Escape* can be toggled if you want to have an encounter that you can run away from. For most boss battles, I would leave this one off. For everything else, you can turn this on.

- *Can Lose* is self-explanatory. This is good for those battles in which you want the player to lose to advance the plot or for an optional battle with a nonplayer character (NPC) that ostensibly wouldn't kill the player if it wins (such as a sensei who trains the character).

The one trick with static encounters is that you must place them in spots that the player must pass through, or else they might as well not be there. If we take a look at the first floor of our dungeon, you'll realize that there are only a few spots where this is true. After deciding where we want our enemies, we can add Battle Processing events that look like this:

```
♦Battle Processing : Slime, Hill Orc
: If Win
   ♦Control Self Switch : A = ON
   ♦
: If Escape
   ♦
:  End
♦
```

For the sake of this example, I have the troop we created in Chapter 3 here. Because these are non-boss fights, we can toggle Can Escape. However, we do not want the players "cheating" the encounters, as it were. That is, we have to make sure that they defeat the encounter before being allowed to pass. So, we make it so that the encounter disappears only if self-switch A is turned on (via the use of a second blank event page with the appropriate conditional). A new area necessitates new enemies, so take a look at Table 5-5 to see the three enemy types for this dungeon.

Table 5-5. *List of Enemies Populating the Stone Cave*

Name	HP	MP	ATK	DEF	MAT	MDF	AGI	LUK	EXP	G
Minotaur	450	25	25	40	25	40	30	35	89	75
War Orc	350	0	40	20	20	20	40	40	89	75
Snake	250	0	40	10	10	10	60	30	67	60

⬛ **Note** The War Orc in Table 5-5 is the same one we created in Chapter 3 to practice editing the Database. Thanks to our previous balance considerations, it is necessary to tweak him to better fit this stage of the game. Additionally, the Minotaur is the premade enemy, also tweaked to fit the area the player finds him in.

The Minotaur and Snake enemies each represent an example of a new archetype. The Minotaur, in contrast to the War Orc, has high defensive attributes but low Attack. The Snake is an example of an enemy that is more annoying than strictly dangerous. At 60 Agility, it is highly likely that the Snake will attack first in any given turn. At 10 Defense (and M. Defense) and 250 HP, it's also highly likely that the player will be able to slay any annoying Snakes within the first turn with a well-placed spell or physical attack. Each of our three enemies will have an additional feature; in the case of both the Minotaur and the War Orc, this feature comes in the form of an extra skill besides the basic Attack. The Snake will have the Attack State trait to inflict Poison 25% of the time it lands an attack on its target. See Figure 5-4 for the action patterns for the Minotaur and War Orc enemies.

Skill	Condition	R	Skill	Condition	R
Attack	Always	5	Attack	Always	5
Fortify	Turn 2+4*X	8	Eye Gouge	Always	4

Figure 5-4. *Action patterns for the Minotaur (left) and War Orc (right) enemies*

To aid the Minotaur's archetype of "defensive champion," I gave him the Fortify spell (that was the reason I gave the Minotaur 25 MP) to cast every fourth turn starting on turn 2. I gave the War Orc an entirely new skill (Eye Gouge) that inflicts Blind 25% of the time it hits its target. Its Attack Element is Physical, with an HP Damage type and [a.atk*3 – b.def] as its damage formula. Its Animation is Pierce Effect. Once you have finished adding those values, make four troops, like so:

- Three troops that contain a single unit of Minotaur, War Orc, and Snake respectively. The Minotaur troop should already be created if you didn't erase the premade troops (to be precise, it's in troop slot 4).

- A fourth troop that contains two Snakes.

With our Database set for the rest of this chapter's material, let's move on. I placed five static encounter events and circled them on the screen shown in Figure 5-5.

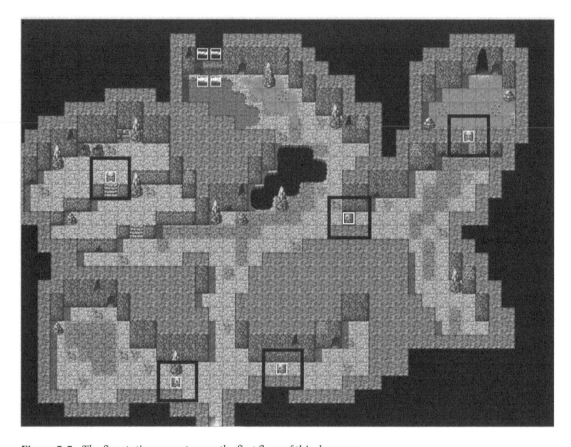

Figure 5-5. *The five static encounters on the first floor of this dungeon*

Each of those five static encounters is against a single War Orc. Next, I will add five treasure chests to that floor as well. Can you guess where I'm going to place them? A good rule of game design is that the player should feel rewarded for going out of his/her way to explore a dungeon in its entirety (see Figure 5-6).

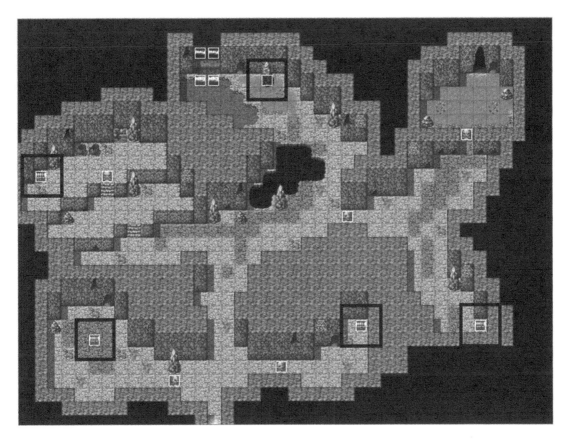

Figure 5-6. *The first floor of the dungeon, now with added treasure chests!*

I placed five treasure chests on the map (four of them are visible, while the fifth is a blank graphic placed atop the rock near the northern end of the floor). That hidden chest rewards players who interact with their surroundings. Here's a little teaser concerning the rest of the encounters for this dungeon: We're going to have the Minotaurs be static encounters for the second floor, while the Snakes will be random encounters on both floors. Give the single Snake troop a Weight of 2 in the map properties and the Snake*2 troop a Weight of 1 (this way, it's twice as likely to encounter one Snake randomly as two). Now, what happens if we wanted to make it so that Snakes only appear in the second floor of the Stone Cave without the use of Regions? Take a gander at the next section.

The Change Encounter Event Command

Given that I've covered a fair number of the event commands already, you have probably seen Change Encounter under the System Settings section of the event command list. This simple command defaults to Enable. If you set it to Disable, you will encounter no enemies until it is set back to Enable, even if the map in question has listed encounters. In this dungeon, it's as easy as setting up the Parallel transfer event, as we have done several times before, and then just adding the Change Encounter command before the transition.

■ **Note**   Keep in mind that your own entrances and exits will not coincide with mine unless you have created a copy identical to my own map (or grab the map from the source code). Make sure to replace the following X and Y coordinates with your own map transitions if that is the case, or the event will not work!

```
◆Control Variables : #0002 X = Map X of Player
◆Control Variables : #0003 Y = Map Y of Player
◆If : X = 35
   ◆If : Y = 3
      ◆Comment : This exit leads to the second floor.
      ◆Change Encounter : Enable
      ◆Transfer Player : Stone Cave (76,22), (Direction: Down)
      ◆
   : End
   ◆
: End
◆If : X = 15
   ◆If : Y = 29
      ◆Comment : This exit leads to the world map.
      ◆Change Encounter : Enable
      ◆Transfer Player : World 1 (68,89) (Direction: Down)
      ◆
   : End
   ◆
: End
◆If : X = 76
   ◆If : Y = 21
      ◆Comment : This exit leads to the first floor.
      ◆Change Encounter : Disable
      ◆Transfer Player : Stone Cave (35,4) (Direction: Down)
      ◆
   : End
   ◆
: End
◆
```

■ **Note**   Although I won't be disabling random encounters on either floor of this dungeon, you can do so if you wish. If you go this route, you'll want to tweak the relevant world map transfer event to disable encounters when you enter this dungeon as well.

Once you've set up the transfer events, the static encounters, and the first floor treasure chests, we have only the following to do:

1. Add some static encounters to the second floor. For the sake of consistency, we'll add five.

2. Add a few chests to the basement. We'll add three.

3. Add the dungeon boss.

See Figure 5-7 for a view of the second floor with the added events.

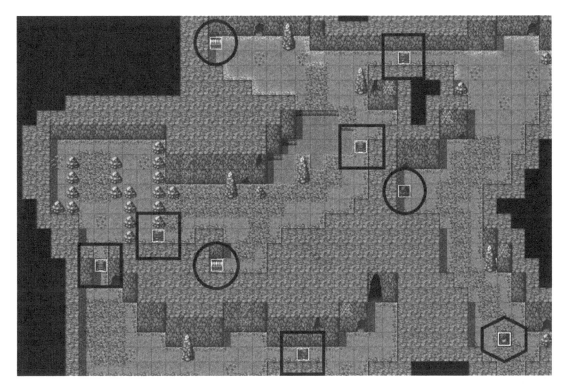

Figure 5-7. *The second floor of the dungeon with added enemies (squares), treasure chests (circles), and the boss encounter (hexagon)*

As you can see, we have two visible chests and an invisible chest near the dungeon's boss. The player enters the map through a cave in the lower middle area and has to make his/her way to the boss at the lower-right corner. Once the player speaks with the boss, he/she will be forced to fight him.

Our First Boss

An RPG would be rather boring if all of the enemies had similar levels of power. That is one of the main reasons why bosses exist. As the name implies, a boss is the strongest enemy in a given area. If the area in question is plot-relevant, then the boss must usually be defeated, to progress in the game's story. See Figure 5-8 for the relevant data on our first boss, Augustus.

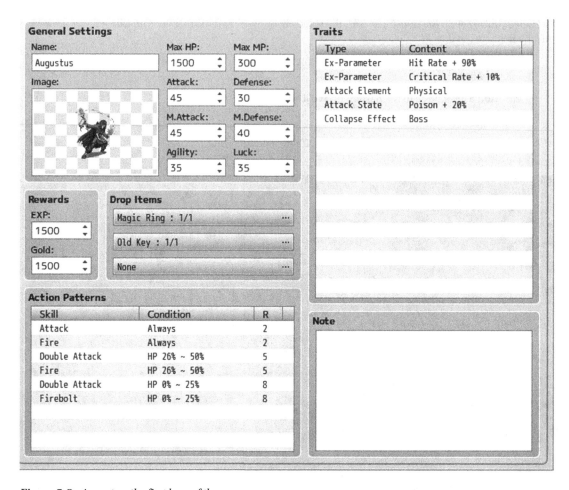

Figure 5-8. *Augustus, the first boss of the game*

For the first 50% of his health, Augustus will use normal attacks and the Fire spell. Once he is hurt, he will start to attack twice. At the last quarter of his health, he will swap out Fire for the stronger Firebolt. When defeated, he is guaranteed to drop a Magic Ring and the Key Item we created back at Chapter 3. (See, I didn't forget about it; now's the perfect time to give it to the player, though.) Read on to see the boss event itself in all of its glory.

```
♦Text : Evil(3), Window, Bottom
:     : It has been far too long...niece.
♦Text : Actor3(7), Window, Bottom
:     : Uncle Augustus?
♦Text : Evil(3), Window, Bottom
:     : Yes, my niece. I have heard of your
:     : companion. Harold, is it not? The hero of
:     : old. My dark master has requested this
:     : boy's head.
```

```
♦Text : Actor1(0), Window, Bottom
:      : I am not a boy, and you may not have it!
♦Text : Evil(3), Window, Bottom
:      : Heh, do you think you can surpass the power
:      : that has been granted to me? Prepare to
:      : suffer!
♦Change Battle BGM : Battle2 (90, 100, 0)
♦Battle Processing : Augustus
♦
```

Page 1 of the boss event has an Action Button trigger, so the player has to walk up to the boss before it will act. Note that we change the battle background music to something else before the fight. Feel free to replace the one I used with another of your choosing.

```
♦Change Battle BGM : Battle1 (90, 100, 0)
♦Text : Evil(3), Window, Bottom
:      : Impossible. So, this is the power that the
:      : chosen one holds…
♦Text : Actor3(7), Window, Bottom
:      : Farewell, uncle. May you find peace in the
:      : afterlife.
♦Fadeout Screen
♦Control Self Switch : A = ON
♦Wait : 120 frames
♦Fadein Screen
```

Page 2 is an Autorun trigger with a switch conditional (BossDefeated). That switch, as you will see in a moment, will be toggled when Augustus is defeated by the player and before he dies. The last page has a conditional of Self Switch A and is otherwise completely blank with an Action Button trigger. Finally, here is the troop event for our first boss:

- Page 1 of 3
- Condition: Enemy HP (1) <= 50%
- Span: Battle

```
♦Text : Evil(3), Window, Bottom
:      : The little brat and my foolish niece
:      : show their teeth. Very well. Two can
:      : play at that game.
♦Change Enemy State : Entire Troop, + Immortal
♦
```

- Page 2 of 3
- Condition: Enemy HP (1) <= 25%
- Span: Battle

```
♦Text : Evil(3), Window, Bottom
:      : No! This is NOT where I fall! Feel my
:      : unending wrath!
♦
```

- Page 3 of 3

- Condition: Enemy HP (1) <= 0%

- Span: Battle

```
♦Text : Evil(3), Window, Bottom
:    : This is not over. My master will avenge me!
♦Text : Actor1(0), Window, Bottom
:    : We will stop your master as well!
♦Control Switches : #0004 BossDefeated = ON
♦Change Enemy State : Entire Troop, - Immortal
♦
```

I use the Immortal state to great effect here, to make sure that the boss does not die before giving his final speech. We add the Immortal state before he reaches 0% HP and then take it away once he's done speaking at 0% HP. We also make it so that the BossDefeated switch is turned on when he is defeated, which plays into the boss event mentioned on the previous pages.

That just about finishes our very first dungeon. Play-test the game and see if it is balanced or not. If you find that some of the enemies are too strong or too weak, feel free to increase or decrease their stats accordingly. Constant play-testing is most important when dealing with enemies, given that you may over- or underestimate their numbers. What seemed like a particularly difficult enemy troop on paper may be trivial for the player's party by the time it reaches the relevant area.

You'll want to add appropriate weapons and armor for Harold and Marsha to become stronger. Among the chests of our first dungeon, I placed a Leather Armor, an Oak Wand, and a Silk Robe.

Additional Exercises

Here are some more exercises to make your dungeon a little more interactive.

1. Create some interparty banter between Harold and Marsha, if they are both present.

We can cheat a little with this, given that Harold will always be in the party and given the layout of this dungeon's second floor. Thus, we only need conditionals to check for Marsha's presence and can use a single variable that is increased in value by 1 for each event triggered. This is one of those things that will make more sense if I show you, so check the following code.

```
♦If : X = 63
  ♦If : Y = 26
    ♦If : Marsha is in the Party
      ♦If Dungeon1Talk = 0
        ♦Control Variables : #0005 Dungeon1Talk += 1
        ♦Text : Actor3(7) Window, Bottom
        :    : …
        ♦Text : Actor1(0), Window, Bottom
        :    : Are you well, Marsha?
        ♦Text : Actor3(7), Window, Bottom
        :    : I have a strange feeling at the pit of
        :    : my stomach.
        ♦Text : Actor1(0), Window, Bottom
        :    : You haven't eaten for a while.
```

```
        ♦Text : Actor3(7), Window, Bottom
        :     : Hah! No, it's not that. Let's move on.
        ♦
      : End
      ♦
    : End
    ♦
  : End
  ♦
: End
♦
```

This event triggers at the marked location shown in Figure 5-9.

Figure 5-9. *The location where the previously mentioned event will trigger (the black square below the rock)*

There are a whopping *four* conditional branches up there, but the first two are just location-checking, in the way we have usually done for our Parallel events so far. The third branch checks for Marsha's presence, while the fourth makes sure that the relevant variable is set to 0. If everything checks out, the variable value is increased by one, and we get a short conversation between our two party members.

■ **Note**   Unless you use Jump Label, an event will always resolve from top to bottom once it has been triggered. Thus, it doesn't matter if you increase the value of the variable directly after the branches or at the end of the conversation, as long as you do so after the event is triggered and before the end of the whole event.

You can add more of those conversations throughout the dungeon as the player gets closer and closer to the boss location. It's a nice little way to add some atmosphere to what would otherwise be a rather unassuming affair.

2. Expand the boss event so that the square it occupies becomes a one-way exit from the dungeon after its defeat.

- My favorite graphics to use from RMMV's default set for this task are the crystals (!Crystal).

- Add the graphic of your choosing; use the Action Button trigger for the last page of the boss event; toggle Direction Fix; and then add the following content.

```
♦Text : None, Window, Bottom
:     : A strange crystal stands on the spot that Augustus
:     : was slain. It appears that it will send you
:     : back to this dungeon's entrance. Touch it?
♦Show Choices : Yes, No (Window, Right, #1, #2)
: When Yes
   ♦Text : None, Window, Bottom
   :     : You feel yourself being whisked away!
   ♦Transfer Player : World 1 (68,89) (Direction: Down)
   ♦
: When No
   ♦Text : None, Window, Bottom
   :     : You decide against touching the crystal.
   ♦
: End
♦
```

Summary

In this chapter, we took a little time to flesh out our two party members with skills and appropriate starting equipment and differentiated Marsha's stats from Harold's. Then we created our very first dungeon and populated it with treasure chests and enemy encounters, of both the static and random types. Additionally, we created our game's first boss to oppose the player. In the next chapter, we will work on our game's second dungeon, which will be somewhat more exciting than this one.

PART 2

Increasing the Complexity

Up to now, we have created a bare-bones game with a single town (with one map for the exterior, and another for the interior), a single dungeon, and a pair of starting area maps all connected by a world map. That puts our MV project at six maps. During this part of the book we will explore the following topics:

- Adding a second dungeon to the game that requires the key item we created in Chapter 2 to be opened.

- Adding an arena that makes ample use of eventing and allows the player to fight predetermined enemy encounters for fame and glory.

- Adding a treasure hunt system to the game with a Compass item that tells the player their X,Y coordinates and hiding treasure in certain parts of the world.

- And more!

We have just scratched the tip of the iceberg of RMMV so far. When I said at the start that RMMV is robust, I meant it! So let's keep on going!

▓ ▓ ▓

CHAPTER 6

Your Second Dungeon

When we left off our RPG story, Harold and Marsha defeated the latter's uncle in (not-so) gruesome combat. What follows next? Well, as a long-time RPG player and overall gamer, my first reaction would be to return to Seaside and see what (if anything) has changed and then decide on my alter-ego's next course of action. That is the initial topic for this chapter. The first order of business is to update the Seaside nonplayer characters (NPCs) to reflect recent events.

Updating Our NPCs

In true RPG convention, our intrepid hero and his mysterious companion will find that news of their endeavors travels faster than they do. To update any NPC, all you need to do is make a new event page for it that requires the BossDefeated switch we created last chapter. Let's have the innkeeper tell the player of the new tidings. Here's a short setting blurb that you can use to tweak the innkeeper's conversation:

> *Ever since Harold and Marsha's defeat of Augustus, the locals claim to hear a disturbing humming sound that fills the night air at Seaside. One of the locals believes that the strange sounds are coming from the ancient tower at the far end of the continent. The ancient tower, they are quick to add, has been sealed for the better part of a century and seemingly has no path of entry. The people of Seaside worry that perhaps the sounds portend some greater calamity . . .*

As in any good RPG story, we had previous events lead the player into new ones. In this case, and as you'll recall, Augustus gave away a plot hook after being defeated by Harold and Marsha. He spoke of the dark master that would "avenge him." What better place to house a dark master than in another dungeon? Now you may be wondering why I would have two dungeons in a row. Well, I finished Part 1 with a dungeon, so it felt appropriate to start Part 2 with the same. It is also a good chance to show off some more advanced eventing than we've seen up to now. As a minor teaser, think about the following situation:

> *You have a majestic dragon statue that you want the player to look at (and possibly even interact with). The easiest way to set up the events is to have a single Same As Characters/ Action Button event for every square that the statue occupies. However, that is highly wasteful of event slots. What if I told you that there was a way to have two events that could cover a theoretically infinite number of, places?*

Do the possibilities boggle the mind? Well then, let us hurry toward that exercise. First, however, we must create our dungeon maps. This time, we'll have three levels to our dungeon, and each map will occupy its own slot (if only to vary a bit from what we designed for the first one).

© Darrin Perez 2016

D. Perez, *Beginning RPG Maker MV*, DOI 10.1007/978-1-4842-1967-6_6

The First Two Floors of Our Second Dungeon

The map we're using is Tower 1F, with quite a few changes. First, I closed off the starting area with blocking events, allowing the player to advance no farther unless he/she has the Old Key with which to open the tower's doors. Players that fancy themselves explorers can see and enter the tower ahead of time but will be unable to get past that first room. If they do have the relevant item, they can open the doors, which grant access to the tower proper. Holes in the ground block easy access to the staircase up, which leads to the dungeon boss on the small third floor. Instead, the player must make their way to the upper-right corner of the tower, which has an entrance to a cave (which is our second floor) that eventually connects back to the upper-left corner of this first level. Take a look at Figure 6-1 to see the ground floor.

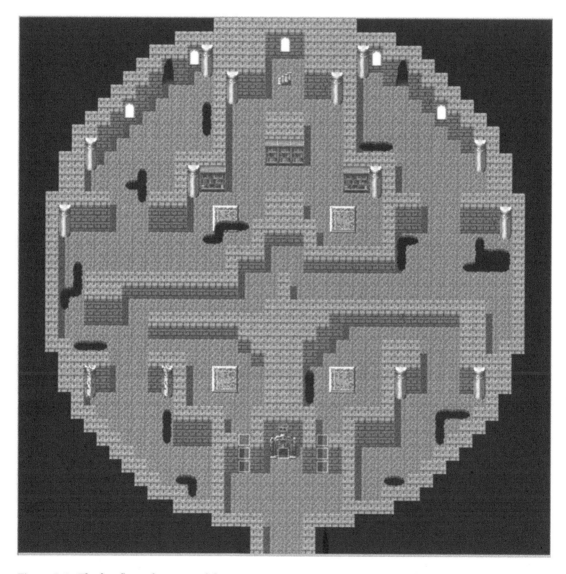

Figure 6-1. *The first floor of our second dungeon*

Note   Let's use the Dungeon2 BGM for all levels of this dungeon. Set it to 70% Pitch.

Of particular note is the stone directly north of the entrance to the tower. This stone contains the event that will allow the player to use the Old Key to enter the tower and turn them away until they do. Here's what the event looks like:

- Page 1 of 2

    - Image: None

    - Priority: Same as characters

    - Trigger: Action Button

```
♦Text : None, Window, Bottom
:      : You see a well-worn keyhole.
♦If : Party has Old Key
  ♦Text : None, Window, Bottom
  :      : You insert the Old Key.
  ♦Play SE : Transceiver (90, 100, 0)
  ♦Fadeout Screen
  ♦Text : None, Window, Bottom
  :      : A rumbling sound covers the area.
  ♦Play SE : Earth4 (90, 100, 0)
  ♦Control Switches: #0005: TowerOpen = ON
  ♦Fadein Screen
  ♦Text : Actor3(7), Window, Bottom
  :      : The doors are open. Now we can move on!
  ♦
 : Else
  ♦Text : Actor1(0), Window, Bottom
  :      : Hmm. Looks like I need a key of some sort.
  ♦
 : End
♦
```

- Page 2 of 2

- Condition: Switch 0005 TowerOpen

- Priority: Same as characters

- Trigger: Action Button

```
♦Text : None, Window, Bottom
:      : You see a well-worn keyhole.
♦Text : None, Window, Bottom
:      : You have no further use for this keyhole.
♦
```

Then, at both sides of the stone, I placed three door graphics that have two event pages. The first page has a priority of Same As Characters and a trigger of Action Button, and it displays a text box stating that "You see an ancient door with no keyhole." The second page requires the TowerOpen switch to be on and has no image or event commands, a priority of Below characters, and a trigger of Action Button. See Figure 6-2 for a zoomed-in screenshot of the tower entrance.

Figure 6-2. *The tower entrance, with added events*

As you may have already inferred, the bookcases added right before the staircase to the top floor are going to be relevant later in the chapter. Take some time to edit the dungeon floor appropriately and then right-click on your Tower1 map and Load up the Lava Cave map that will serve as our second dungeon's second level. As it turns out, there will be little editing of this area (this also happens to be true for the third floor, which is essentially one screen in size, but more on that in a bit). In fact, the entirety of the changes to the Lava Cave can be summarized in two bullets:

- We need to add a bridge to allow the player to cross the lava river past the large staircase.

- We're going to add the dragon statue teased in the start of the chapter, along with appropriate cobblestone tiles.

See Figure 6-3 for a visual representation of the former and Figure 6-4 for the latter.

Figure 6-3. *The bridge (using Stone Bridge (H) tiles) spanning the lava lake*

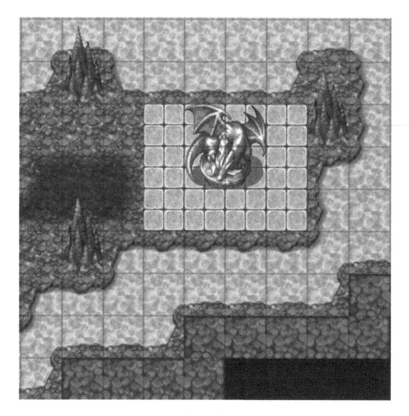

Figure 6-4. The dragon statue added to the Lava Cave

Not much else to say about Figure 6-3, save for the general observation that RPG Maker MV has preset events in many of their sample maps (you can see some in the screenshot). They're usually used for little doodads like lamps or, as in this case, to have certain parts of flowing terrain move faster than others.

I tweaked the terrain a bit around the statue and added some Cobblestone tiles, but that's about it. Since the Lava tiles are damage floors, the player will be taking damage for just about every step they take in the area. That's a fairly cool gimmick for a dungeon, but let's tone it down so that the brighter tiles don't do any damage. Make your way to the Tilesets tab, and then select the Dungeon tileset. Once there, select the Damage Floor option. You'll see that a few of the tiles are now marked with a pair of gray triangles that resemble spikes. The bright lava is the first tile of the fifth row of tab A of the Dungeon tileset. Click the tile once and you'll see the triangles disappear. Now, if you play-test the game, the player should not take damage as long as they stick to the brighter lava tiles. Figure 6-5 shows how the map looks now with the minor edits.

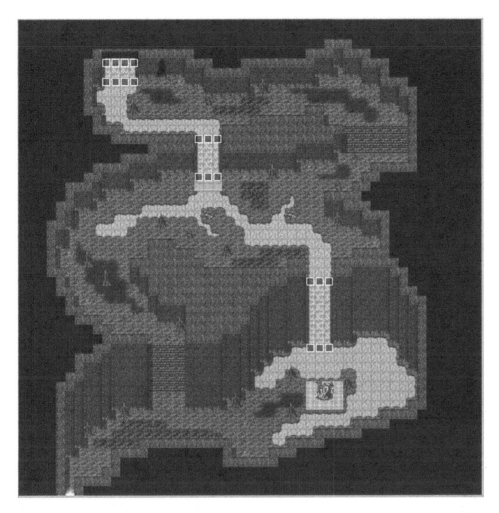

Figure 6-5. *The Lava Lake after the minor edits described in the text*

This dungeon will have a total of seven treasure chests scattered throughout its first two floors. I'll leave precise placement of those chests to you, the reader, although you are more than welcome to peek at the source code folder to see where I decided to place mine. That said, you may want to wait until we add some new items to our Database later in the chapter first, as I'll give you a list of equipment you should include in the possible chest rewards. It's time to use that dragon statue we placed in the Lava Cave. It is to be fuel for our latest eventing exercise.

Interacting with the Dragon Statue

We want to make it so that the player can interact with the dragon statue from every adjacent square, using only two events. Doing this the wasteful way would spend two extra events (four in total). The larger the object in question, the more efficient these pairs of events will be, compared to having one event per square. As I tend to note, eventing is just like programming, which is all about problem-solving. We have a problem and want to solve it.

- We need an event to keep track of the player's position while he/she is around the dragon statue.

- We need the other event to act as the interaction event (this is the one that will be the Same As Characters/Action Button).

- We must make sure that the player is actually looking at the statue. It wouldn't do for the player to be looking in the opposite direction and getting the dragon statue information when he/she presses the Action Button.

We actually have all that is called for in the preceding three bullet points, even if it does not appear to be so. We've used the first event several times already, but for transfer events. All we will do is change what we're going to use it for.

Drawing a Perimeter

Our first order of business is noting which squares are around the dragon statue. That will be our perimeter, if you will. Take a look at Figure 6-6.

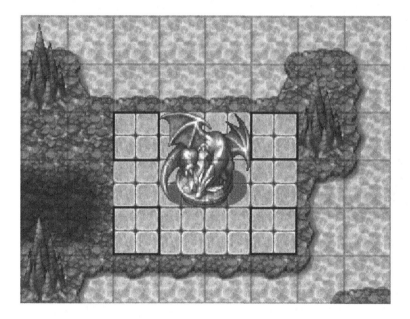

Figure 6-6. *A zoomed-in view of the dragon statue on this floor of the dungeon*

Figure 6-6 is a highly zoomed-in screenshot of the dragon statue and its surrounding squares. You'll want the X and Y values to draw the effective perimeter. Check the following code to see what I did for that first part.

```
◆Control Variables : #0002 X = Map X of Player
◆Control Variables : #0003 Y = Map Y of Player
◆If : X ≥ 31
   ◆If : X ≤ 34
      ◆If : Y ≥ 38
         ◆If : Y ≤ 40
```

```
    ♦Jump to Label : Step 2
        ♦
    :  End
   ♦
  :  End
 ♦
:  End
♦
:  End
```

As usual, we write the player's position into a pair of variables and then check against the current map coordinates to see if they are in the dragon statue's perimeter. If they aren't, nothing happens. If they are, we have a label called Step 2 that continues the event. Here's the next part of the event:

```
♦If : #0078 ≥ 999
  ♦Label : Step 2
  ♦If : X = 31
    ♦If : Y ≥ 38
      ♦If : Y ≤ 39
        ♦Control Variables : #0002 X += 1
        ♦Set Event Location : DragonTopic, Variable ({X},{Y})
        ♦Jump to Label : Done
          ♦
        :  End
       ♦
      :  End
     ♦
    :  End
   ♦
  :  End
♦
:  End
```

Moving Our Interaction Event

Two new things in the perimeter-establishing event are of interest:

- First, we have a dummy variable (which has a set value of 0), and we have the system try to resolve the branch if that variable is greater than or equal to 999. Because we are not writing anything there, this branch will never be true. So, why have it at all? Remember: Events execute from top to bottom, unless prevented from doing so. We have this dummy branch here so that the rest of the event will only execute when we use the Jump to Label command to jump to Step 2 inside the branch itself.

- Second, we have the engine of what will make this whole event work in the first place. In this portion of the event, we're checking to see if the player is standing on the two squares to the left of the dragon statue. If he/she is, we add one to the value of X and use a new event command. *Set Event Location* allows you to change the position of any event (including the triggering event itself, for any reason) on the map. What we want to do is have the Action Button event used for the dragon statue move to meet the player's movement. It's a sneaky little trick that gets the job done in this case. See Figure 6-7 for a screenshot of what the command entails.

Figure 6-7. *The Set Event Location event command*

From here, you can select which event to move. Then you can choose to designate a specific location for the event, use variables to determine the location, or exchange it with another event's location. In the case of events with graphics, you can also determine whether they retain their former facing or change to a different direction. You can probably already tell what that +1 to X is about. Because the player is standing one space to the left of the statue, we have to move the event one space to the player's right, so that he/she can interact with it while facing eastward. Now that you understand the logic behind this event, can you figure out how to do the other two? The northern squares are blocked off by lava, so you don't have to take them into consideration for this exercise. To clarify, you need to account for the player being below the statue and to its right. If you think you have it (or otherwise need the help), here's the final part of the Parallel event:

```
◆If : Y = 40
   ◆If : X ≥ 32
      ◆If : X ≤ 33
         ◆Control Variables : #0003 Y -= 1
         ◆Set Event Location : DragonTopic, Variable ({X},{Y})
         ◆Jump to Label : Done
         ◆
      :  End
      ◆
   :  End
   ◆
:  End
```

```
♦If : X = 34
    ♦If : Y ≥ 38
        ♦If : Y ≤ 39
            ♦Control Variables : #0002 X -= 1
            ♦Set Event Location : DragonTopic, Variable ({X},{Y})
            ♦Jump to Label : Done
            ♦
        :  End
        ♦
    :  End
    ♦
:  End
♦Label : Done
♦
```

The first set of branches is called when the player is below the statue, and the second set is used when he/she is to its right. You'll also see the Jump to Label that triggers once a single branch has been executed. It is there merely as an extra precaution to make sure nothing strange happens when the event runs. We're done with half of this exercise; now we need the event that will actually trigger when the player attempts to interact with the statue. First, right-click any one of the squares that make up the dragon statue and create the event. Looking back at the zoomed picture, you'll note the following:

- The player may only interact with the top-left and top-right squares by facing right and left, respectively.

- For the lower two squares, the player has two possible facing directions.

Checking Our Player's Directional Facing

We need a way to make sure that the player is facing the right way. Enter the Conditional Branch once again. Up to now, we have been using conditional branches almost exclusively to check against variable and switch values. However, there are *three more pages* of things you can check against. If you click page 3 of the conditional branch command, you will find the Character X is Facing Y conditional. X defaults to the player but can also check for every single event on the current map, and Y is the direction the player or event in question is facing. Here's the relevant event:

```
♦If : Player is facing Right
    ♦If : X = 32
        ♦Jump to Label : Text
        ♦
    :  End
    ♦
:  End
♦If : Player is facing Up
    ♦If : Y = 39
        ♦Jump to Label : Text
        ♦
    :  End
    ♦
:  End
```

```
♦If : Player is facing Left
   ♦If : X = 33
      ♦Jump to Label : Text
      ♦
   : End
   ♦
 : End
♦Label : Text
♦Text : None, Window, Bottom
:     : You see a majestic dragon statue. It hums with power.
♦Text : Actor3(7), Normal, Bottom
:     : I sense immense power emanating from this
:     : statue. Be mindful. It would be best to
:     : return at a later time.
♦Text : None, Window, Bottom
:     : Touch the statue?
♦Show Choices : Yes, No (Window, Right, #1, #2)
: When Yes
   ♦
: When No
   ♦
 : End
♦
```

We set up a series of conditional branches to ensure that the player is facing the right way, depending on their current location. Afterward, we make sure that the value of X or Y (as the case may be) is within the dragon statue graphic. If both conditions check out, we display the relevant text and give the player a choice. As you can see, I have left both possible answers empty. We'll revisit this one much later in the book, as we put the finishing touches on our game. Anyway, take a look at Figure 6-8 for the third floor of our second dungeon. The base sample map used was Hall of Transference.

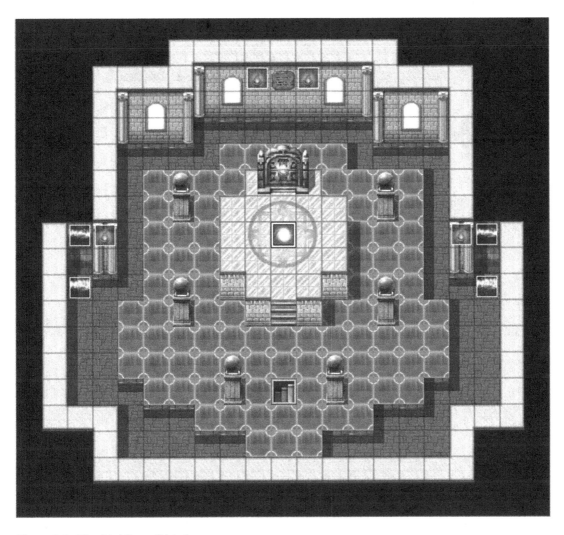

Figure 6-8. *The third floor of this dungeon*

Much like the Lava Cave before it, the Hall of Transference needs practically zero alterations. All I really did was remove the exit at the southern end of the map, replacing it with an appropriate staircase. The event in the middle of the sigil on the ground will be replaced by a graphic of this dungeon's boss. On that note, let's create this dungeon's boss. The General_m battle sprite looks like a fairly foreboding enemy that could easily be a boss.

Our Second Boss

Take a look at Figure 6-9 for our Dark General's stats. Of note is the Dark General's weakness to Light. Cleave and Ruin are new skills that will be listed later in the chapter when we create our new dungeon's enemies and their associated skills. Similarly, the Dragonscale Leather is a special armor drop that will also be listed later on. In contrast to Augustus, this boss is more of a physical powerhouse, which allows the player to use Harold's Fortify spell to great effect.

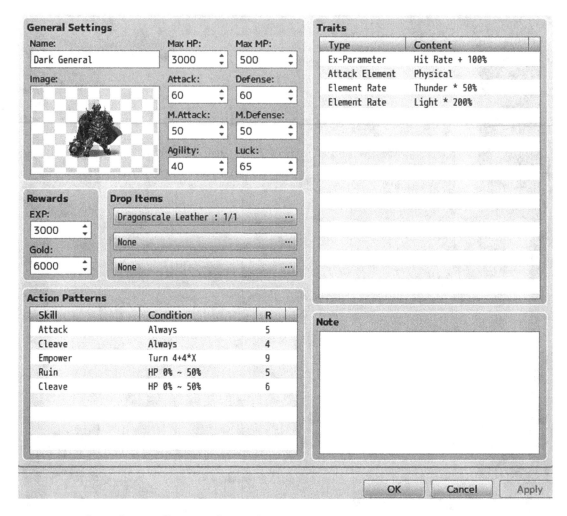

Figure 6-9. *The Dark General's entry in the Database*

Creating a Bookcase Interaction Event

Let's give Marsha an item that allows her to capitalize on the Dark General's weakness to Light. There are several bookcases in the final section of the first floor, and we want the central bookcase in the set of three in the middle to grant the book. Here's the relevant bookcase event.

```
◆Text : None, Window, Bottom
:      : You see an ancient bookcase filled with old books.
◆If : X = 15
  ◆If : Self Switch A is OFF
    ◆Text : None, Window, Bottom
    :      : Marsha appears to be lost in thought as she runs a
    :      : hand through the bookcase.
```

```
♦Text : Actor3(7), Window, Bottom
:     : I feel warm power coming from one of
:     : these books.
♦Text : None, Window, Bottom
:     : Marsha passes a finger over each book, eventually
:     : landing on an otherwise unassuming red book.
♦Text : Actor3(7), Window, Bottom
:     : I'll be taking this book. It feels like
:     : we'll have a need for it soon.
♦Play SE : 'Item3', 80, 100
♦Change Armors : Book of Light + 1
♦Text : None, Window, Bottom
:     : Obtained \C[2]Book of Light\C[0]!
♦Control Self Switch : A = ON
```

Not noted: branch ends that are ultimately irrelevant to the event. First, I added the Book of Light to the Database under the Armors tab. It is of the Magic Armor type and equips to the Accessory slot. While Marsha has the Book of Light equipped, it gives her 10 Defense and the ability to cast Light, a new Magic skill that costs 10 MP and deals [150 + a.mat * 2 – b.mdf] Light damage (with a variance of 10%) to its target. Of course, because we don't want this sequence of events to repeat more than once, we have the relevant self-switch flip on, so that the event skips through the self-switch conditional on subsequent interactions.

Creating Our Second Boss Event

Once we have created the bookcase event and the Book of Light item, all we have to do is create the boss event on the top floor and set up the area's random encounters. Because we already created an Action Button boss event, let's make this one rely on Autorun.

What we'll need:

- A Parallel event (You can use the transfer event for this, and you want to check for the player's X and Y coordinates in any case.)

- An Autorun event that activates when a particular switch is flipped on. This switch would be toggled when the player walks near the boss.

- A graphic that represents the boss itself, to be used in a third event

Here are the commands for the Parallel event.

```
♦If : X = 10
  ♦If : Y = 11
    ♦If : Self Switch A is OFF
      ♦Control Self Switch : A = ON
      ♦Control Switches : #0006 Boss2Encounter = ON
```

As with the bookcase event, we only want this snippet to trigger once, so we set an extra conditional that only allows the branch to be executed if self-switch A is off and then turn it on. We then flip the aptly named *Boss2Encounter* switch.

Creating the Boss Encounter

Our second event is an Autorun that triggers only if that switch is on. It contains most of the meat of the boss encounter; hence the descriptive heading. Page 1 of this event looks like this:

```
♦Tint Screen : (-68,-68,0,68), 60 frames (Wait)
♦Fadeout BGM : 3 sec.
♦Wait : 60 frames
♦Text : Actor1(0), Window, Bottom
:     : What's going on?
♦Wait : 60 frames
♦Text : Evil(5), Window, Bottom
:     : So, you are the two who defeated my
:     : servant.
♦Text : Evil(5), Window, Bottom
:     : Welcome humans. I am glad to make your
:     : acquaintance. I would have you join my
:     : cause.
♦Text : Actor1(0), Normal, Bottom
:     : No.
♦Set Movement Route : SecondBoss (Wait)
:                   : ◊Move Down
:                   : ◊Move Down
♦Text : Evil(5), Window, Bottom
:     : Heh. Was worth a try.
♦Control Self Switch : A = ON
♦Change Battle BGM : Battle2, (90, 100, 0)
♦Battle Processing : Dark General
♦
```

The Autorun starts with the screen being tinted using the Night filter. Afterward, the background music fades out over the next three seconds. A one-second pause precedes Harold wondering what's happening, and another one-second pause is triggered afterward. Then, we have our boss talk to the player. After an unsuccessful attempt to turn the heroes of good to the path of evil, the event that represents the boss moves two squares down (so that it is directly in front of the player), self-switch A turns on, the battle music is changed, and the boss fight is started. Page 2 of the Autorun event has the self-switch A equals on conditional and is completely blank. (Make sure that the trigger for page 2 is *not* Autorun.)

The Aftermath of the Boss Encounter

Page 3 of our second boss encounter event has a conditional that uses a switch toggled when the boss is defeated (I called that particular switch Boss2Defeated) and is another Autorun page.

■ **Reminder**   Make sure to set up an appropriate troop event for the Dark General that turns on the Boss2Defeated switch, or this next part of the Autorun event won't trigger!

```
♦Text : Evil(5), Window, Bottom
:     : Tch. You two are messing with forces
:     : beyond your ken. I am but one of many
:     : pledged to the will of the All Master.
♦Text : Evil(5), Window, Bottom
:     : Push farther then, fools. One of the
:     : Three awaits at a castle far to the
:     : north of here. Defeat him and see the
:     : truth of this world!
♦Fadeout Screen
♦Tint Screen : (0,0,0,0), 5 frames
♦Change Battle BGM : Battle1 (90, 100, 0)
♦Control Switches : #0008 PlotAdvance2 = ON
♦Control Self Switch : B = ON
♦Wait : 60 frames
♦Fadein Screen
```

Once the boss has finished speaking, we fade out the screen, remove the screen tint, restore the battle music to its default, and flip on two switches before finally fading the screen back in. Note that we don't play a BGM for the area after the boss has been defeated. This means that no music will be played until the player leaves the Hall of Transference. The first switch we will use to make the boss graphic event disappear, and the second one allows us to create the fourth and last page for this event. The last page will require self-switch B to be on and will be completely empty, with an Action Button trigger (much as page 2 was). The third and final event is the boss graphic and is two pages long. The first page has the boss graphic and no conditional. The second page has no graphic and requires PlotAdvance2 to be switched on.

Summary of Our Second Boss Event

That will conclude our most recent boss event. To summarize, we used three events:

1. **A Parallel Process event to determine when the player walks into the boss' domain.** It used a self-switch conditional to make sure that it cannot trigger multiple times (really important when dealing with a Parallel event).

2. **An Autorun event that made up the meaty portion of this exercise.** It spans four pages, with the first one activating thanks to the switch flipped in the Parallel event. The second page has a conditional that is met right before the boss attacks the party, while the third requires that the boss be defeated to be automatically executed. Last, the fourth page is the one that remains after the boss is defeated.

3. **A simple event meant to hold the boss graphic and nothing else.** This exists until the boss has finished talking after the battle and then disappears.

■ **Note**   It would be a good idea to create a warp point so that the player doesn't have to backtrack through the entire dungeon. I placed an event on the glowing stone behind the sigil on the ground.

There are three more things to cover before I end the chapter. The first is that we must create and set the random encounters (and associated skills for our new enemies and boss as well) for our second dungeon. We want the game's encounters to become progressively more difficult, so let's bump up the bar compared to the previous dungeon. Second, we'll need to add new equipment and items to our game's Database (and take a little time to update Seaside's shops appropriately). Last, we need to add this new dungeon to the world map and create a relevant transfer event.

The Second Dungeon's Random Encounters

Naturally, before we can set up the second dungeon's random encounters, we need to create enemies to fill the encounter table. See Table 6-1 for details on each enemy's stats.

Table 6-1. *The List of New Enemies to be Added to the Database*

Name	HP	MP	ATK	DEF	MAT	MDF	AGI	LUK	EXP	G
Assailant	600	0	50	50	50	50	50	50	114	150
Jellyfish	500	0	36	24	36	24	36	36	127	180
Lava Ogre	1200	0	90	10	10	10	10	10	270	300
Arcanist	400	100	20	25	65	55	40	40	157	225

The second dungeon has three floors, but since the third floor is basically one screen, let's have random encounters only on the first two floors.

- Assailants are just a standard balanced enemy that will appear on both floors, albeit with a 15% Evasion Rate instead of the standard 5%. They have a ¼ chance to drop a Bomb when defeated and a 1/20 chance to drop a Big Bomb (you'll see this new item listed in the relevant table of the next section of this chapter). This enemy has a weakness to Thunder (200%) and resistance to Fire (50%). Assailants use the Assassin battler graphic.

- Jellyfish are more interesting. Note their relatively low stats. They compensate by the fact that their basic attacks hit twice (via the Attack Times Trait; set to + 1). Additionally, they have a skill that also hits twice and has a 20% chance per hit to induce Sleep in its victim. This enemy resists Ice (50%) but takes slightly more damage from both Fire and Thunder (125%). It has a 1/5 chance to drop Coffee (a new item that removes Sleep from its target). Jellyfishes appear only on the first floor and use their self-named battler graphic.

- Lava Ogres are part of a particularly interesting monster archetype in Japanese RPGs; that of the inaccurate, but potentially lethal, berserker. The Lava Ogre's stats are abysmal, to put it lightly. That is, except for that 90 Attack and 1200 HP. Lava Ogres only have a 50% Hit Rate, but also have a 50% Critical Rate. Statistically speaking, a Lava Ogre should land a critical hit every fourth turn. They have a Cleave that hits all enemies as well as the basic Attack that targets a single foe. This enemy has no weaknesses or resistances and has a 1/10 chance to drop a Power Ring when defeated. I used Hue: 140 to give the Ogre graphic an appropriately reddish tone. Lava Ogres will only appear on the second floor and use the Ogre battler graphic.

- Arcanists are the last enemy of the dungeon and the first regular spellcaster of the game. They forsake having the Attack skill in exchange for using both Fire and Firebolt. This enemy has no weaknesses or resistances, and it drops Magic Water at a 1/5 chance and Magic Potion (a stronger version of Magic Water) at a 1/15 chance. Arcanists use the Mage battler graphic and appear on both floors of the dungeon.

Note You can set resistances and weaknesses to certain elements via the use of the Element Rate trait. Percentages over 100% indicate a weakness to an element, while percentages under 100% indicate resistance.

See Table 6-2 for a list of the new skills for the enemies of this chapter (including Ruin, the darkness spell used by the Dark General boss enemy). Then take a look at Figure 6-10 for the action patterns for each new enemy (except the Dark General, already covered in his own section).

Table 6-2. *A List of New Skills Created for This Chapter's Enemies*

Name	Scope	MP Cost	Damage Formula/Effects	Animation
Sleep Sting	1 Enemy	0	a.atk*5 – b.def*3 5% Variance, 20% Sleep, Repeat: 2	Pierce Effect
Cleave	All Enemies	0	a.atk*4 – b.def*2	Normal Attack
Ruin	1 Enemy	16	300 + a.mat*2 – b.mdf*4 10% Variance, 20% Poison, 15% Blind, 12% Sleep, Attack Element: Darkness	Darkness One 1

Skill	Condition	R	Skill	Condition	R
Attack	Always	5	Attack	Always	5
			Sleep Sting	Always	5

Skill	Condition	R	Skill	Condition	R
Fire	Always	5	Attack	Always	5
Firebolt	Turn 1+3*X	9	Cleave	Always	3

Figure 6-10. *The list of action patterns for each new enemy. Clockwise from the top-left: Assailant, Jellyfish, Lava Ogre, Arcanist*

Now we have four new enemies that we can place in the tower's random encounter lists. See Figure 6-11 for the lists for both floors.

Troop	Weight	Range	Troop	Weight	Range
Assailant	20	Entire Map	Assailant	15	Entire Map
Assailant*2	10	Entire Map	Assailant*2	10	Entire Map
Jellyfish	15	Entire Map	Lava Ogre	20	Entire Map
Jellyfish*2	15	Entire Map	Arcanist	10	Entire Map
Arcanist	10	Entire Map	Arcanist*2	5	Entire Map
Arcanist*2	10	Entire Map			

Figure 6-11. *The encounters list for the first (left) and second (right) floors of the second dungeon*

Of particular note is the fact that we have no Lava Ogre*2 troop. Given the battler graphic's sheer size, it would be hard to put two units of the Ogre graphic in a side-view format and not have one of them look weird or out of place. As mentioned before, we want to keep Harold and Marsha progressing nicely in terms of gear. That will be the focus of our next section.

New Equipment and Items for the Database

It would be an odd RPG that has a single shop in the entire game that also happens to never get any new equipment, no matter the player's progress. So, while our game is going to have a second town added later on in the book, we'll first improve our existing shop. For now, take a look at Tables 6-3 and 6-4 see the new weapons and armors to be added to our Database.

Table 6-3. *A List of New Weapons to be Added to the Database*

Name	Stat Bonuses / Traits	Price
Broadsword	+20 Attack	1500
Greatsword	+25 Attack	3000
Two-Handed Sword	+35 Attack / Seal Equip Shield	6000
Bronze Bow	+21 Attack / Seal Equip Shield	1400
Silver Bow	+28 Attack / Seal Equip Shield	3000
Magic Wand	+10 Attack, +25 M. Attack	6000
Dragontooth Blade	+7 Attack / Attack Element: Fire, Attack Times + 1	0

Table 6-4. *A list of New Armors and Accessories to be Added to the Database*

Name	Stat Bonuses/Traits	Price
Chain Mail	+20 Defense, +4 M. Defense	1500
Scale Mail	+25 Defense, +5 M. Defense	3000
Magic Robe	+15 Defense, +15 M. Defense / +5% Evasion	3000
Silk Cap	+3 Defense, +3 M. Defense	200
Magic Turban	+5 Defense, +5 M. Defense / +5% Evasion	1000
Defense Ring	+10 Defense	1000
Antimagic Ring	+10 M. Defense	1000
Iron Helm	+12 Defense	1700
Large Shield	+12 Defense	1700
Dragonscale Leather	+20 Defense, +15 M. Defense / Element Rate: Fire * 50%	0

Notes

- Although it was not explicitly mentioned back in Chapter 4 when we created our first batch of equipment, you'll want bows to have the Seal Equip: Shield trait so that Harold cannot equip with both a bow and a shield.

- The Dragontooth Blade doesn't interact with Harold's attack-based Special skills (Dual Attack and Triple Attack), given that the Attack Times trait only works with the Attack command. Using either of those skills will just have the player attack twice or three times whatever is standard for the skills in question. This means that the player must decide whether to use this special sword and just attack regularly. or use any other weapon for best results with the Special skills—a classic trade-off, if you will.

The final entries of both tables correspond to special dungeon artifacts. The Dragonscale Leather is dropped by the Dark General upon being defeated, while I placed the Dragontooth Blade in a special gold chest near the dragon statue. Besides the special Blade, I added a Chain Mail and Defense Ring among the seven treasure chests of this dungeon. You don't have to make every treasure chest item an upgrade, mind you. Here's a breakdown of the various armor types added to the Database during this chapter:

- *General Armor*: Dragonscale Leather, Defense Ring, Antimagic Ring

- *Light Armor*: Chain Mail, Scale Mail, Iron Helm

- *Magic Armor*: Magic Robe, Silk Cap, Magic Turban

- *Small Shield*: Large Shield

▪ **Note**   That last bullet is a literal oxymoron. To fix that, take a brief break, head over to the Types tab, erase Large Shield from Armor Types, and rename the Small Shield type to Shield.

Now, take a look at Table 6-5 for a list of the new items to add to the Database, all of which have been teased already.

Table 6-5. *A List of New Items to be Added to the Database*

Name	Effects	Price
Life Potion	Restores 1500 HP.	250
Magic Potion	Restores 500 MP.	500
Big Bomb	Inflicts 500 damage to all enemies.	1000
Coffee	Removes Sleep.	25

The most important thing to note is that while the Big Bomb has a sell value, it will not be available in any shop. Since each Big Bomb does 500 damage, it would be easy to just bombard every major enemy and trivialize the game's difficulty that way. So drops from certain enemies will be the only way for the player to get his/her hands on the high-grade explosives. Head over to Seaside and add a new page to both of the shopkeepers that requires PlotAdvance2 to be on. Then, in that new page, allow the shopkeepers to sell both the older items and the newer ones we have just created.

■ **Note**   It's also a convenient time to break off for a bit and update some of Seaside's NPCs. What would they have to say about the defeat of the Dark General? I leave that as an exercise to the reader.

We're almost done with the chapter, so let's keep going!

Placing the Second Dungeon on the World Map

All of the work that has been done in this chapter is for naught if we don't actually allow the player to visit the dungeon, right? So, I'm going to add an appropriate tower graphic (the leftmost Tower in tab B of the Field tileset) on the map. I'll place the base of the tower at 93, 83. See Figure 6-12 for a screenshot of how it should look once placed.

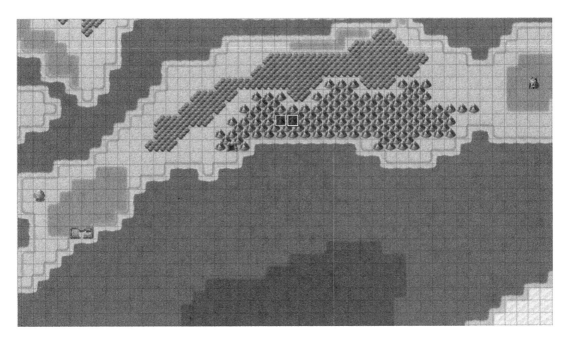

Figure 6-12. *The world map, now with the tower graphic added at the eastern end*

Once that is done, all that is left to do is create the transfer event, like so:

```
◆If : X = 93
  ◆If : Y = 83
    ◆Transfer Player : Tower 1F (20,37) (Direction: Up)
    ◆
  : End
  ◆
: End
```

Place that code within your existing Parallel event and make sure to add an appropriate transfer event within the dungeon to allow the player to leave. With this section out of the way, we can bid adieu to this chapter!

Summary

This chapter covered the creation and population of our game's second dungeon. We used RMMV's Sample Maps to great effect once again to create a ruined tower that connected with a lava cave. At the top of the tower awaited a dark general that our player needed to defeat. The dragon statue was the host of a particularly neat application of Parallel events to allow a single Action Button event to be used for interaction purposes. Last, we added more content to our Database to keep the game experience fresh. In the next chapter, we will have some fun with arenas and other such minigames!

CHAPTER 7

Arenas and Other Minigames

Harold and Marsha's adventures in our world have been relatively gloom-and-doom up to now. While they're merely player-characters and don't mind their status as such, their alter egos (the players themselves) would probably appreciate a change of pace. Minigames are a classic video game tradition. To take a somewhat recent example, *Grinsia* (which had a mobile release and a recent rerelease on the Nintendo 3DS) has a shooting gallery minigame. Sometimes the player just wants to explore off the beaten path and do something unrelated to the main plot at hand. Sidequests are a good way to do that, and I'll be talking about them in Chapter 8. This chapter, however, is all about having fun within the fun that is a game. Meta, isn't it?

Why an Arena Game?

Although they are nominally less of a minigame than most other concepts (given that arenas usually involve battling, which you already do in most RPGs), arena games require a decent amount of eventing and afford the opportunity to introduce features we haven't talked about before. Besides, you get to beat up assorted baddies for fame, glory, and special prizes! What's not to like?

What If I Want Another Minigame?

I have another idea lined up for this chapter, which involves using eventing to come up with a similar treasure chest game as the one in *The Legend of Zelda*. Near the end of the chapter, I'll also give you ideas for two more minigames! For now, though, let's press on with the arena.

Arena Overview

Just the mere mention of the word *arena* evokes gladiatorial combat, as in the times of ancient Rome. In an RPG, arena games can be loosely divided into two categories:

- One in which the player and/or his/her allies fight against predetermined encounters.
- One in which the player watches a group of combatants face each other and bets on the outcome.

© Darrin Perez 2016
D. Perez, *Beginning RPG Maker MV*, DOI 10.1007/978-1-4842-1967-6_7

The first type is much more common than the second, especially nowadays. You can look to *Dragon Warrior 3* for an example of the second. Here's a list of the things we'll need to have or know:

- A map in which we can host our arena. You can have both parts of the arena on one map, but we'll split them into two, to make things a little less cluttered.

- A nonplayer character (NPC) that allows the player to sign up for arena events.

- Another NPC that allows the player to trade in his/her hard-earned arena currency for rare prizes.

- A list of ranks to aspire to and battles to be fought, as well as the amount of special currency to award for each victory in a rank.

- Whether the player will have to fight alone or with the companions he/she has recruited during his/her quest.

Outlining Our Arena

This is one of those bigger projects for which it is better to write down everything you can before you sit down and start trying to event it. Let's lay this out one step at a time:

1. Number of Arena Ranks: 4 (D, C, B, A)

2. Cost to participate in a given rank: (D = 100, C = 500, B = 1000, A = 2500)

3. Number of battles per rank: 3

4. Currency awarded for clearing a rank: (D = 2, C = 4, B = 8, A = 16)

5. Rank D Battles

   - Bat*2

   - Slime*2

   - Orc*2

6. Rank C Battles

   - Snake*2

   - Assailant

   - Jellyfish*2

That's the outline for the things we want to include within our arena. Rank B Battles and Rank A Battles will need to be defined at the end of the chapter when we have more enemy encounters to work with.

Note   As currently presented, this arena minigame will reuse troops already created for our game's other content. As such, they will award experience and Gold when defeated. If you wish to prevent this, you'll need to make new versions of each enemy that award 0 EXP and Gold, along with troops to hold those altered enemies.

Creating the Arena Exterior

How do we go about setting up the arena itself? First, we have to create the first map for the arena. This is where the player will land upon accessing the location from the world map. Take a look at Figure 7-1 to see the layout of the first arena area. It is a 25×25 map with the Inside Tileset and the Battle1 BGM at 60% pitch.

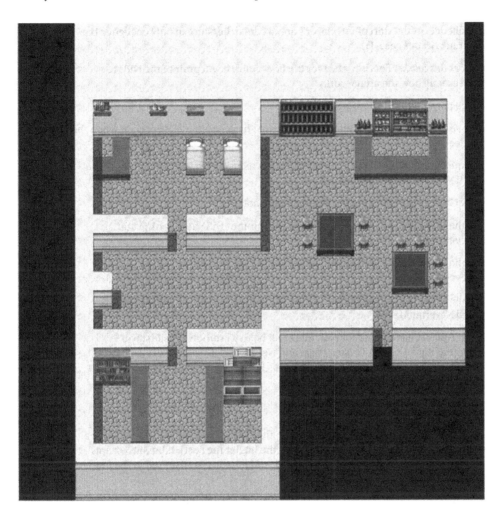

Figure 7-1. *The building that contains the arena*

The player enters the area from that opening near the southeastern end of the map. In front of him/her is the lobby, which could be home to other arena fighters. The northwest corner of the map has an inn, if the player needs to recover from wounds, while the southwest holds the arena sign-up NPC (left) and the arena exchange NPC (right). Feel free to use this basic map idea and flesh it out to your heart's content. Be forewarned that creating the arena as I did was a task requiring many long hours of trial and error. As we work through this, you'll quickly see why.

Overview of the Arena Sign-up Event

The arena sign-up NPC (and the exchange NPC, for that matter) will have an Action Button trigger. The NPC will greet the player, welcoming him/her to the arena, and then ask what it can do for him/her. I use a Show Choices event command with three choices at this point. The choices are

- *Arena Battle*: As the choice suggests, this will bring up a list of ranks that the player can challenge. At the start of the player's arena career, he/she can only challenge the lowest rank (in this case, D).

- *How does this work?*: This is perfect for the first-timer; it will prompt the NPC to explain exactly how the arena works.

- *Bye*: The player ends the conversation.

The preceding seems rather unassuming, but here's what happens in the event code when the player chooses Arena Battle:

- The game determines, via the analysis of various related switches, what ranks of the arena (if any) the player has cleared.

- A Show Choices prompt appears, based on that analysis:

    1. If the player has not cleared any ranks, the prompt will show Rank D and Nevermind.

    2. If the player has cleared Rank D, the prompt will show Rank D, Rank C, and Nevermind.

    3. If the player has cleared Rank C, the prompt will show Rank D, Rank C, Rank B, and Nevermind.

    4. If the player has cleared Rank B, there will be two prompts. The first will contain Rank D, Rank C, Next Page, and Nevermind. Clicking Next Page will reveal the second prompt, which contains Previous Page, Rank B, Rank A, and Nevermind.

    5. Rank A is the highest rank, so clearing it doesn't change anything.

- When the player chooses a rank to challenge, the arena NPC will charge the player a certain amount of Gold (the higher the rank, the higher the cost). If he/she accepts the cost, it is deducted from the player's Gold, and he/she is transferred to the proper arena map.

And that's only what's on the first map. There is an Autorun event that triggers, based on each separate rank, once the player reaches the second map, which serves out the relevant fights. If the player wins all three matches or is defeated, he/she is sent back to the first map, to speak with the arena NPC once again, which will either congratulate the player and give him/her a reward (in the case of a win) or urge him/her to do better next time (in the case of a loss).

Creating the Arena Sign-up

I'm going to make this slightly simpler than the version I came up with and disregard party members. Harold and Marsha will be able to both participate in the arena at the same time. Even then, I have to note that a total of ten switches are used for this event. (You would need one more switch on top of that for every character you want to remove temporarily from the player's party.) Here's the first stage of our arena event:

```
♦Text : None, Window, Bottom
:     : Welcome to the Arena, where battlers from all over
:     : existence come to do battle!
♦Label : MainMenu
♦Text : None, Window, Normal, Bottom
:     : What can I do for you?
♦Show Choices : Arena Battle, How does this work?, Bye (Window, Right, #1, #3)
: When Arena Battle
    ♦
: When How does this work?
    ♦Text : None, Window, Normal, Bottom
    :     : I'm glad you asked, wanderer.
    ♦Text : None, Window, Normal, Bottom
    :     : Essentially, you start at the bottom of the ladder,
    :     : at Rank D. Win three matches in Rank D and you
    :     : will unlock Rank C, and so on. It costs Gold to
    :     : compete in each rank, so mind your pocket.
    ♦Text : None, Window, Bottom
    :     : The top rank is Rank A, but none have ever
    :     : completed the three bouts at that level.
    ♦Text : None, Window, Bottom
    :     : You are completely healed at the end of each match,
    :     :  and you can use items as need be. However, be careful
    :     : as we do not refund the cost of items used in the
    :     : Arena. Use them only if they will secure your victory
    ♦Text : None, Window, Bottom
    :     : in battle.
    ♦Jump to Label : MainMenu
    ♦
: When Bye
    ♦Text : None, Window, Bottom
    :     : Later.
    ♦
: End
♦Label : EndPage
♦
```

The good news is that we're on our way. The bad news is that this is the simplest this event will ever be. Oh, boy, is it going to get extensive! We're going to want conditionals for each and every possibility. As already noted, a fresh player will have cleared no ranks. Each rank clear will be stored in a single appropriately named switch. We need to have a switch for each possible challenge as well. Last, we need a switch to flip when the player wins his/her matches and another to flip when the player loses his/her matches. What follows are a large series of conditional branches that will make perfect sense in hindsight. First, we have the conditional branch for when the player has not cleared Rank D. As you can see in the following code listing, we have a universal sentence that will show up before the event starts determining which branch will be executed; it asks the player what rank he/she would like to challenge. Because Rank D has not been cleared, the resulting prompt will only have two choices. Rank D has a cost of 100 Gold for the player, and if the player doesn't have the money, the game will return an error message and send him/her back to the initial three choices. If the player *does* have the Gold, it will be deducted, and the RankDChallenge switch will be flipped.

```
: When Arena Battle
   ◆Text : None, Window, Bottom
   :     : What rank would you like to challenge?
   ◆If : RankDClear is OFF
      ◆Show Choices : Rank D, Nevermind (Window, Right, #1, #2)
      : When Rank D
         ◆Label : RankDChallenge
         ◆Text : None, Window, Bottom
         :     : This will cost you 100 Gold. Are you sure?\$
         ◆Show Choices : Yes, No (Window, Right, #1, #2)
         : When Yes
            ◆If : Gold ≥ 100
               ◆Change Gold : -100
               ◆Text : None, Window, Bottom
               :     : Good luck!
               ◆Fadeout Screen
               ◆Play SE : Move1 (90, 100, 0)
               ◆Control Switches : #0015 RankDChallenge = ON
               ◆Transfer Player : Arena Grounds (8,8) (Direction : Up)
               ◆Jump to Label : EndPage
               ◆
            : Else
               ◆Text : None, Window, Bottom
               :     : You don't have enough Gold!
               ◆Jump to Label : MainMenu
               ◆
            : End
         ◆
      : When No
         ◆Jump to Label : MainMenu
         ◆
   : Branch End
```

You may notice the strange lack of Fadein Screen on this event. As we transfer the player to the other map, we use Fadein over there instead.

Creating the Arena Battle Event

Once the player has signed up to participate in the arena, he/she is transferred to the arena grounds. This section will walk you through creating the battle event that the player will have to face in the arena. Before talking about the event in question, take a look at Figure 7-2 for a screenshot of the arena grounds (a 17×17 Inside map with the Battle1 BGM playing at normal pitch).

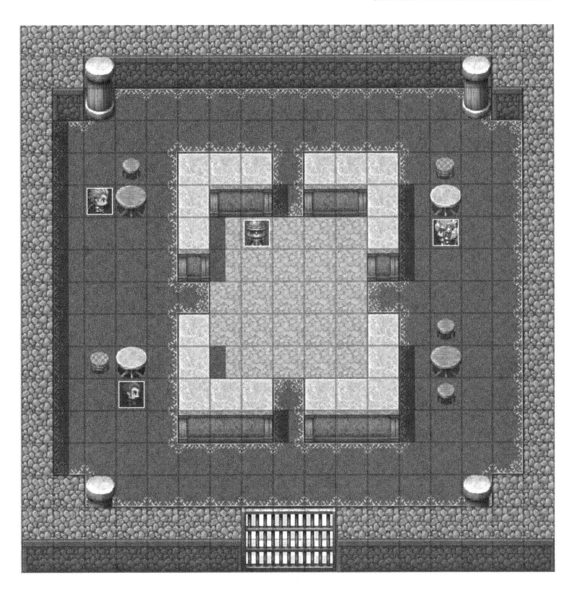

Figure 7-2. *The interior part of the arena, where the player battles assorted baddies for fame and glory*

We transfer the player to the center of that map, a few squares to the south of the armored NPC that we're using as the arena announcer. An RPG arena just isn't much of one if someone isn't announcing challengers and such. We can kill two birds with one stone by making that NPC our Autorun event as well. He will have a total of four event pages. Each page has a conditional for each particular rank challenge switch. Thus, page 1 requires RankDChallenge to be turned on, page 2 requires RankCChallenge to be on, and so on. The general format of the arena challenges is as follows:

- A short announcement of the player's party is made.

- A Battle Processing event begins, in which the player can continue the game if he/she happens to lose the battle.

- If the player wins, the game loads up the second fight. If the player loses, he/she is sent back to the first map.

- The same process is repeated until the player wins three fights or loses.

- Take a look here for a large part of the Rank D Challenge Autorun event:

```
◆Fadein Screen
◆Wait : 60 frames
◆Text : None, Window, Bottom
:     : Welcome to the Rank D Arena Challenge!
:     : Are the challengers ready?
◆Text : Actor1(0), Normal, Bottom
:     : I am.
◆Text : Actor3(7), Normal, Bottom
:     : As am I.
◆Text : None, Window, Bottom
:     : Let the games begin!
◆Battle Processing : Bat*2
: If Win
   ◆Recover All : Entire Party
   ◆Text : None, Window, Bottom
   :     : Our challengers have won Round 1!
   ◆Play SE : Applause1 (90, 100, 0)
   ◆Text : None, Window, Bottom
   :     : However, there are still two more rounds left!
   :     : Will our challengers rise to the challenge?!
   ◆Text : None, Window, Bottom
   :     : Round 2 is now!
   ◆Battle Processing : Slime*2
   : If Win
      ◆Recover All : Entire Party
      ◆Text : None, Window, Bottom
      :     : The challengers take the second win of the day
      :     : in Rank D!
      ◆Play SE : Applause1 (90, 100, 0)
      ◆Text : None, Window, Bottom
      :     : This is the moment of truth! Will our aspiring
      :     : challengers take the title? Or will the final
      :     : challenge of Rank D prove too much to handle?!
      ◆Text : None, Window, Bottom
      :     : Let loose the monsters of war!!
      ◆Battle Processing : Orc*2
      : If Win
         ◆Recover All : Entire Party
         ◆Text : None, Window, Bottom
         :     : They have done it!
         ◆Control Switches : #0014 ArenaWin = ON
         ◆Jump to Label : Return
         ◆
```

```
: If Lose
   ♦Recover All : Entire Party
   ♦Control Switches : #0013 ArenaLoss = ON
   ♦Jump to Label : Defeat
   ♦
 : End
```

As noted before, the Autorun event on the second map starts with a Fadein Screen (if we didn't do this, the screen would stay black). When you toggle the Can Lose check box, the Battle Processing event command as displayed splits into If Win and If Lose. Note the different switches that are flipped depending on whether the player wins or loses. We heal the player's party after every battle, win or lose. Here is the rest of the event:

```
 ♦
 : If Lose
    ♦Recover All : Entire Party
    ♦Control Switches : #0013 ArenaLoss = ON
    ♦Jump to Label : Defeat
    ♦
 : End
 ♦
: If Lose
   ♦Recover All : Entire Party
   ♦Control Switches : #0013 ArenaLoss = ON
   ♦Jump to Label : Defeat
   ♦
: End
♦Label : Defeat
♦Text : None, Window, Bottom
:     : The challengers have been defeated! Better luck next
:     : time!
♦Label : Return
♦Fadeout Screen
♦Transfer Player : Arena Exterior (7,20) (Direction: Left)
♦
```

Here you can see where all of those Jump to Label commands lead. As in several other cases previously, I used these solely as a precaution, given that there's no way for unwanted events to execute. The screen is faded out before we transfer the player back to the first map. The other three rank challenge events can be added to our announcer in the same way. All you have to change between each one are the chosen encounters and, if you desire, some of the text shown to the player when they win or lose.

Creating the Arena Result Event

Back at the first map, we need an Autorun event (I placed a blank graphic event behind the arena sign-up NPC) to handle the post-arena results. Because we have four possible challenges, and two possible outcomes for those challenges, this event will have eight total pages. Don't be daunted, as the pages are simple enough:

- Page 1 requires RankDChallenge and ArenaWin to be on.

- Page 2 requires RankDChallenge and ArenaLoss to be on.

- Every pair of pages after that will represent a different ranked challenge when the player wins and when the player loses.

```
♦Fadein Screen
♦Wait : 60 frames
♦If : RankDClear is OFF
   ♦Text : None, Window, Bottom
   :     : Congratulations on clearing Rank D!
   :     : Greater challenges await you in Rank C, whenever you
   :     : are ready to face them!

   ♦Control Switches : #0009 RankDClear = ON
   ♦Jump to Label : Done
   ♦
: End
♦If : RankDClear is ON
   ♦Text : None, Window, Bottom
   :     : Way to beat Rank D there!
   :     : However, you've done this already, right? Come on,
   :     : take a risk or two and take a harder challenge,
   :     : would you?!

   ♦Jump to Label : Done
   ♦
: End
♦Label : Done
♦Recover All : Entire Party
♦Play SE : Item3 (90, 100, 0)
♦Text : None, Window, Bottom
:     : You have earned 2 Arena Tokens!
♦Change Items : Arena Token + 2
♦Control Switches : #0015 RankDChallenge = OFF
♦Control Switches : #0014 ArenaWin = OFF
♦
```

This is the first half of the pair of events for Rank D challenges. As the pair of conditional branches and their contained text will imply, this is the page that requires that the player clear his/her challenge. We start with a Fadein (as the event on the other map ended with a Fadeout) and a one-second wait time after the screen fades in. Afterward, what executes next depends on whether the player has cleared Rank D before. If he/she has not, the first branch triggers, the player is congratulated on the first-time win, and the RankDClear switch is flipped on. Then we jump to the Done Label, where the player's party is healed, they are awarded two Arena Tokens (a Key Item that cannot be consumed, used, or sold from the player's inventory) and, because the player is through competing for the moment, we turn off the pair of switches that have been turned on (in this case, RankDChallenge and ArenaWin). That Jump to Label is *not* superfluous. Because the player now has RankDClear switched on, the next branch will execute automatically, unless we skip it via a label jump. That branch, incidentally, is what executes when the player has already beaten Rank D before and is just repeating the challenge. After a minor berating by the NPC, the event continues as before, with the player earning his/her reward, and the two relevant switches flipping off. On the other hand, here's the loss event for Rank D challenges:

```
◆Fadein Screen
◆Wait : 60 frames
◆Text : None, Window, Bottom
:     : Don't sweat it. It happens to the best of us. Get a
:     : bit stronger and come back fighting!
◆Recover All : Entire Party
◆Control Switches : #0015 RankDChallenge = OFF
◆Control Switches : #0013 ArenaLoss = OFF
◆
```

As you can see, it's pretty much a little fluff; then the party is healed, and then the challenge and arena loss switches are flipped off. Rather simple compared to the win event, isn't it? Now, win or lose, we're back at our starting location. The player can choose to attempt another challenge (including taking the Rank C challenge, if he/she beats Rank D on his/her first attempt) or go do something else.

Miscellaneous Arena Considerations

There are only two things left to cover for the arena game. First, let's include the code of the Arena Battle event when the player has beaten Rank D.

```
◆If : RankDClear is ON
  ◆If : RankCClear is OFF
    ◆Show Choices : Rank D, Rank C, Nevermind (Window, Right, #1, #3)
    : When Rank D
      ◆Jump to Label : RankDChallenge
      ◆
    : When Rank C
      ◆Label : RankCChallenge
      ◆Text : None, Window, Bottom
      :     : This will cost you 500 Gold. Are you sure?\$
      ◆Show Choices : Yes, No (Window, Right, #1, #2)
      : When Yes
        ◆If : Gold ≥ 500
          ◆Change Gold : -500
          ◆Text : None, Window, Bottom
          :     : Good luck!
          ◆Fadeout Screen
          ◆Play SE : Move1 (90,100,0)
          ◆Control Switches : #0016 RankCChallenge = ON
          ◆Transfer Player : Arena Grounds (8,8) (Direction : Up)
          ◆Jump to Label : EndPage
```

```
         ◆
      : Else
         ◆Text : None, Window, Bottom
         :     : You don't have enough Gold!
         ◆Jump to Label : MainMenu
         ◆
      :  End
      ◆
   : When No
      ◆Jump to Label : MainMenu
      ◆
   :  End
```

What we see here will be consistent in every conditional branch from here to the end of the arena sign-up event. We check to see if the previous rank in the list was cleared. If so, we make sure that the next one has not been cleared yet. If it has, we'd be skipping to the next branch in the line. In this case, as the player has only beaten Rank D, he/she should be challenging Rank C next. Note the Jump to Label if the player picks Rank D. Redundancy is fine for some fields of work, but in game design, you usually only want to write the same code once, if possible. Then you call back to that code when you need it. I'll be touching upon common events in a later chapter, to tidy up some of our previous code. For now, it will suffice to know that we have already written out the Rank D challenge in a previous conditional branch, so we just jump back to it, instead of repeating the same code a second time.

I'll leave the rest of the eventing of these already mentioned events up to you, as it is pretty much identical to what we have done so far. What you would need to fill out follows:

- *Pages 2 to 4 of the announcer Autorun event*: As already mentioned, each page will have a conditional based on the rank that is being challenged. You would have to create Ranks C through A.

- *Pages 3 to 8 of the post-challenge Autorun event placed behind the arena sign-up NPC*: Remember to have one page for a win and another for a loss, in each particular rank.

- *The remaining conditional branches in the arena sign-up event*: We need one when the player has beaten Rank C and another when the player has beaten Rank B.

Creating Our Arena Shop

Now we have most of the events set up; however, we have not done anything with the NPC that will exchange tokens for items. Let's remedy that. There are two ways to set up a token shop:

1. You award special key items that serve as currency. Then, you set up a special shop that, in reality, is a series of Show Choices that each costs a different amount of tokens.

2. You award arena currency by adding value to a variable. Then, by clever use of currency swapping, you make it so that you can use the default shop with the currency you have earned.

I'll show both possibilities, but the second is definitely easier than the first. Of course, to have a proper arena shop, we need goodies to sell in it. Take a look at Table 7-1 for a list of five items for the arena shop.

Table 7-1. *A List of New Items and Accessories to be Added to the Database*

Name	Effects	Cost in Arena Tokens (Price in Gold)
Elixir	Restores all HP and removes all negative status effects.	5 (1000)
Manawell Ring	+5 M. Attack, +5 M. Defense, +2% MP Regeneration	15 (3000)
Troll's Bracelet	+5 Attack, +5 Defense, +2% HP Regeneration	15 (3000)
Stone Ring	Element Rate: Physical * 50%, Element Rate: Fire, Ice, Thunder * 125%	25 (5000)
Heal Orb	Restores [200 + a.mat] HP on all allies when used. Key Item that is *not* consumed on use.	50 (10000)

In this table, you can see a previously mentioned game design concept applied in a different way. Back when we were working on the Stone Cave dungeon, I said that the player should be rewarded if they go out of their way to explore the entirety of an area. Similarly, the player should be rewarded for taking time to partake in otherwise optional content. The Elixir is a consumable item that combines the effects of the Dispel Herb with maximum HP restoration. Naturally, it cannot be purchased anywhere else. The same is true of the three accessories (which should have the General Armor type so that both Harold and Marsha can use them) and the final item as well. Take a moment to observe how each item is flavored (in particular, how the Stone Ring grants disadvantages as well as advantages when worn). Another consideration when working on an arena shop is the valuation of its currency. In other words: How much is an arena token worth? In the case of my items, each token has an effective value of 200 Gold (100 Gold if an item bought with the tokens is sold; items in MV sell for half of their buy price, by default). In your own game, you may consider increasing or decreasing the value of arena tokens. Generally, if you don't want the player to make a profit (in Gold) in the arena game, the items the player can get in the game need to be worth less than the cost of getting the tokens. Conversely, if you don't mind the player making bank on your game's arena minigame, then you can make it so that the effective value of arena tokens is higher than the cost of entry.

Following, you'll find a listing of part of the first arena shop possibility.

```
♦Text : None, Window, Bottom
:      : Hello there! This is the Arena Exchange! I can trade
:      : you special items for any tokens you may have
:      : earned from your Arena participation.
♦Text : None, Window, Bottom
:      : Here's what I have available.
♦Control Variables : #0006 ArenaCurrency = The number of Arena Token
♦Show Choices : Elixir, Manawell Ring, Troll's Bracelet, Stone Ring, Heal Orb, Nevermind
(Window, Right, #1, #6)
: When Elixir
   ♦Text : None, Window, Bottom
   :      : An Elixir will cost you 5 Tokens.
   ♦Text : None, Window, Bottom
   :      : You currently have \V[6] Arena Tokens. Will you
   :      : purchase an Elixir?
   ♦Show Choices : Yes, No (Window, Right, #1, #2)
   : When Yes
```

```
      ◆If : ArenaCurrency ≥ 5
         ◆Change Items : Elixir + 1
         ◆Change Items : Arena Token - 5
         ◆Text : None, Window, Bottom
         :       : Enjoy!
         ◆
         : Else
         ◆Text : None, Window, Bottom
         :       : You don't have enough Tokens!
         ◆
         : End
      ◆
    : When No
      ◆Text : None, Window, Bottom
      :       : Okay. See you later!
      ◆
    : End
```

We have the NPC greet the player, as is usual. Then we have a new variable to hold the number of Arena Tokens that the player has in his/her inventory. A Show Choices prompt appears, with the five possible item purchases and Nevermind as the last option. When the player clicks an item choice, the NPC confirms the cost, tells the player how many Arena Tokens he/she currently has, and asks if he/she wishes to purchase the item, bringing up a Yes/No choice prompt. We make sure that the player has the Arena Tokens to purchase the item in question. If the player doesn't, we return an error message; otherwise, we add the item to the player's inventory and remove the appropriate number of tokens. Now that you have the gist of the event, I'll leave the rest of this shop event up to you. Populating the rest of the item shop choices is as easy as copy-pasting the already completed part of the event, and changing the amount of tokens needed (and later taken away as payment), changing the item granted and any relevant text references. Last but not least, you'll want to add a short farewell to the Nevermind choice if the player decides not to buy any items at the first Show Choices junction.

⬛ **Note** You can see the complete event in action by talking to the top Arena Shop NPC in the source code project file.

This type of arena shop, as you can see, is simple enough, if a bit clunky. Unfortunately, it becomes less and less useful the more items you want to add to the shop. The Show Choices event command can only hold a total of six choices, so you would be required to add options merely to switch between Choice branches.

The second way is much easier and has only one quirk that will require scripting to address. However, as the quirk is graphical in nature, it doesn't affect the event's functionality, so have at it! Take a look at the following:

```
◆Text : None, Window, Bottom
:       : Hello there! This is the Arena Exchange! I can trade
:       : you special items for any tokens you may have
:       : earned from your Arena participation.
◆Text : None, Window, Bottom
:       : Here's what I have available.
```

```
♦Control Variables : #0007 PartyGold = Gold
♦Change Gold : - 9999999
♦Control Variables : #0006 ArenaCurrency = The number of Arena Token
♦Change Gold : + {ArenaCurrency}
♦Shop Processing : Elixir
:                 : Manawell Ring
:                 : Troll's Bracelet
:                 : Stone Ring
:                 : Heal Orb
♦Control Variables : #0006 ArenaCurrency = Gold
♦Change Items : Arena Token - 9999
♦Change Items : Arena Token + {ArenaCurrency}
♦Change Gold : -9999999
♦Change Gold : + {PartyGold}
♦
```

In the second type of arena shop, we save the player's Gold in a variable appropriately named PartyGold. Then we zero out the player's Gold and add his/her arena currency to his/her Gold value. We make sure that the *Purchase Only* check box is toggled and then add any items we wish the player to be able to purchase. Set the price of Elixirs to 5, the price of Manawell Rings and Troll's Bracelets to 15, the price of Stone Rings to 25, and the price of Heal Orbs to 50. After the player closes the shop, we restore his/her Gold and arena currency to their original places. Figure 7-3 shows the arena shop in all of its glory.

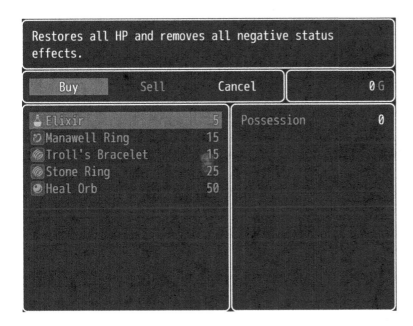

Figure 7-3. *The arena shop*

As you can see, despite the fact that we switched from Gold to arena currency, our shop is still using G (to represent Gold). A small amount of scripting can be used to change the currency symbol, as desired. In fact, you need only add two one-line Script commands. The first will switch the currency symbol to AT (short for Arena Tokens) in preparation for opening the shop screen, and the second will switch the currency symbol back to G after the player is done buying. Here's a snippet of the event, with Script events added in relevant locations:

```
♦Change Gold : + {ArenaCurrency}
♦Script : $dataSystem.currencyUnit = "AT"
♦Shop Processing : Elixir
:                 : Manawell Ring
:                 : Troll's Bracelet
:                 : Stone Ring
:                 : Heal Orb
♦Script : $dataSystem.currencyUnit = "G"
♦Control Variables : #0006 ArenaCurrency = Gold
```

Go ahead and test the event once again (this is a perfect time to use the Test option; recall that you need to shift-click to select the entire event before you click Test), and you should quickly see the difference. With that done, we have finally completed this part of Chapter 7! Here are some exercises to do before we move on to another minigame.

1. Add extra rewards that are earned by the player the first time he/she clears a certain rank.

2. Use Battle Processing: Same As Encounter in tandem with an encounter table on the map, to add some random possibilities to arena battles at Rank A. You can find an example event in the map named Ch.7 Arena Exercise 2. I set the arena host's trigger to Action Button, so you'll need to interact with him to start the arena event off.

As the player doesn't move while on the second map, you could leave the default Range on the possible encounters. Just to be safe, you could make it so that random encounters only appear on that map within a specific Region.

The Treasure Chest Game

This is a game in which the player opens a certain number of chests in the designated playing area. Will the player receive riches or scraps? In this section, I'll be creating a seven-chest game. Take a look at Figure 7-4 to see what the area looks like when complete.

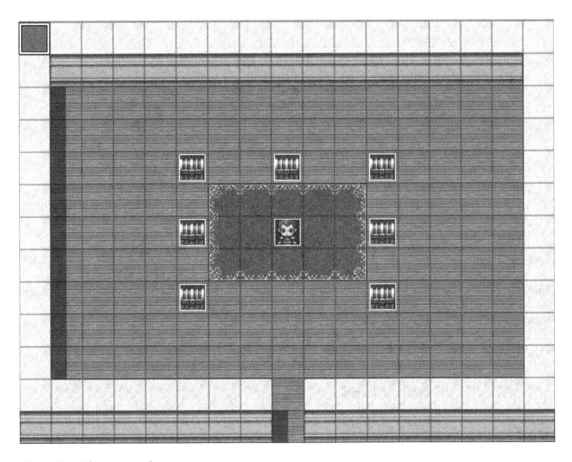

Figure 7-4. *The treasure chest room*

We have the game host in the center of the map, surrounded by his seven chests. Here's what we need to do to make our treasure chest game:

- Come up with a list of rewards that can be obtained. I'll list my seven, but feel free to come up with your own.

    1. Potion

    2. 1 Gold

    3. Elixir

    4. 1 Gold (Yes, the player has two chances to get 1 Gold.)

    5. Life Potion

    6. 200 Gold

    7. 500 Gold

- Add a variable that will store the current "seed" for the treasure chests. We want to make it so that the contents of a particular chest are one of those seven, on a random basis. Otherwise, the player can just open the same chest and get the same reward consistently. A chest's contents will change, based upon the seed value.

- Add a switch that will be flipped on while the minigame is in progress and turned off once it is completed.

- Make it so that, once opened, a chest disappears for the duration of the minigame and reappears afterward.

- Have a variable that decreases every time the player opens a chest. We'll set this to 2 at the start of the minigame, meaning that the player can open two of the seven chests present.

- Once two chests have been opened, announce that the game is over and reset the initial starting conditions, so that the player can play again, if he/she so chooses.

To pull this off with eventing, we'll have to set up each treasure chest individually, as well as create the NPC and the Parallel event that triggers when the game is over. I'm going to start with the chest in the upper-left corner. Let's call that chest the master, as the rewards listed previously will be placed into the event in the same order. Because the chests will be present even while the game is not active, we have to make sure that the player cannot open them. Each chest will be a two-page event, in which page 1 has a treasure chest graphic and Direction Fix has been toggled. (This makes it so that the chest does not appear to open slightly if the player interacts with it from certain angles.) If the player tries to interact with the chest, the event will show a text box declaring that it is locked. Page 2 has the TreasureChestStart switch conditional, meaning that it will not trigger unless the minigame is currently active. Like page 1, this page will have an Action Button trigger.

```
♦Set Movement Route : This Event (Wait)
:                   : ◊Direction Fix OFF
:                   : ◊Turn Left
:                   : ◊Wait: 3 frames
:                   : ◊Turn Right
:                   : ◊Wait: 3 frames
♦If : TreasureChestSeed = 1
   ♦Change Items : Potion + 1
   ♦Text : None, Window, Bottom
   :     : Got a Potion!
   ♦
:  End
♦If : TreasureChestSeed = 2
   ♦Change Gold : + 1
   ♦Text : None, Window, Bottom
   :     : Got a single Gold piece!
   ♦
:  End
♦If : TreasureChestSeed = 3
   ♦Change Items : Elixir + 1
   ♦Text : None, Window, Bottom
   :     : Got an Elixir!
   ♦
:  End
♦If : TreasureChestSeed = 4
   ♦Change Gold : + 1
   ♦Text : None, Window, Bottom
   :     : Got a single Gold piece!
   ♦
:  End
```

```
♦If : TreasureChestSeed = 5
   ♦Change Items : Life Potion + 1
   ♦Text : None, Window, Bottom
   :     : Got a Life Potion!
   ♦
: End
♦If : TreasureChestSeed = 6
   ♦Change Gold : + 200
   ♦Text : None, Window, Bottom
   :     : Got 200 Gold!
   ♦
: End
♦If : TreasureChestSeed = 7
   ♦Change Gold : + 500
   ♦Text : None, Window, Bottom
   :     : Got 500 Gold!
   ♦
: End
♦Wait : 30 frames
♦Control Variables : #0009 ChestsToOpen -= 1
♦Erase Event
♦
```

The first part of the event was copy-pasted from RMMV's Treasure quick event. It displays the animation that the player sees when opening a treasure chest. Afterward, we have the seven possible chest contents, based on the value of the TreasureChestSeed variable. The player will earn the appropriate item and be apprised of the fact via text box, and after a half-second pause, the value of ChestsToOpen will drop by 1, informing the game that the player has opened a chest. Erase Event is an event command I have not covered up to now, but it is as simple as can be. When an event processes Erase Event, it effectively ceases to exist until the player leaves the map. As you might have inferred, this could cause problems in the execution of the minigame. This will definitely be addressed in the Parallel event, when we get to it.

Populating the Chests of the Treasure Chest Game

If we want to have randomized results and have all seven rewards represented with every seed, each chest has to give different items for the same seed value. For example, if the chest in the upper-left corner gives a Potion when the seed is 1, another chest could give the single Gold piece in that case. Think of the list of items in a numerical sense. That first chest has its items in the order 1234567. The second chest (the one to the right; let's go in a clockwise rotation) has the items in the order 6412753. When the seed is 1, the player will receive 200 Gold, if he/she opens the second chest. The idea is that two chests not give the same item (except in the case of the pair of 1 Gold chests). This is rather hard to figure out mentally, given the large number of possibilities (many of which don't apply, as they would cause two or more chests to give the same item). I personally used random.org's list shuffler (www.random.org/lists). I wrote down 1234567 and then let the site do its work. A lot of the shuffled lists will not be valid, but it will give you a good idea of what item combinations you need, especially as you get closer to the last chest. Check Table 7-2 to see the seven-number lists I came up with.

Table 7-2. *The Seven-Number Lists That Determine What Chest Has What Item in the Treasure Chest Game*

1	6	2	7	4	3	5
2	4	7	3	5	1	6
3	1	6	2	7	5	4
4	2	1	5	6	7	3
5	7	4	1	3	6	2
6	5	3	4	1	2	7
7	3	5	6	2	4	1

As you can see, our master list is the leftmost column. Each column corresponds to a different chest from top to bottom. Take a moment to look at the numbers and note that no numbers repeat when reading from left to right. For example, the first row is 1627435, which has no numerical repeats. If your rows aren't repeating, chances are that the slot in question is fine. To prove the point, if the minigame rolls a 1 for the seed, here's what you can expect from each chest:

1. Potion

2. 200 Gold

3. 1 Gold

4. 500 Gold

5. 1 Gold

6. Elixir

7. Hi-Potion

Pretty neat, isn't it? As crunching permutations is rather secondary to the point of this book, feel free to use the grid that I came up with for your own chests. What you can do is copy-paste page 2 of the master chest event. Then, depending on the chest number, you move around the various items in the event page, so that the item order matches the ordered list that you want. Once you have done that, you renumber the conditional branches such that they go from 1 to 7, as in the master chest: same items, different seed order. For additional context, check the eventing of the second treasure chest on the following page, so that you can get a visual idea of what I mean. I'll leave the rest of the chests to you; they involve more of the same, as already noted.

```
♦Set Movement Route : This Event (Wait)
:                   : ◊Direction Fix OFF
:                   : ◊Turn Left
:                   : ◊Wait: 3 frame(s)
:                   : ◊Turn Right
:                   : ◊Wait: 3 frame(s)
♦If : TreasureChestSeed = 1
   ♦Change Gold : + 200
   ♦Text : None, Window, Bottom
   :     : Got 200 Gold!
   ♦
: End
```

```
♦If : TreasureChestSeed = 2
  ♦Change Gold : + 1
  ♦Text : None, Window, Bottom
  :      : Got a single Gold piece!
  ♦
: End
♦If : TreasureChestSeed = 3
  ♦Change Items : Potion + 1
  ♦Text : None, Window, Bottom
  :      : Got a Potion!
  ♦
: End
♦If : TreasureChestSeed = 4
  ♦Change Gold : + 1
  ♦Text : None, Window, Bottom
  :      : Got a single Gold piece!
  ♦
: End
♦If : TreasureChestSeed = 5
  ♦Change Gold : + 500
  ♦Text : None, Window, Bottom
  :      : Got 500 Gold!
  ♦
: End
♦If : TreasureChestSeed = 6
  ♦Change Items : Life Potion + 1
  ♦Text : None, Window, Bottom
  :      : Got a Life Potion!
  ♦
: End
♦If : TreasureChestSeed = 7
  ♦Change Items : Elixir + 1
  ♦Text : None, Window, Bottom
  :      : Got an Elixir!
  ♦
: End
♦Wait : 30 frames
♦Control Variables : #0009 ChestsToOpen -= 1
♦Erase Event
♦
```

That is a large part of the treasure chest minigame.

Creating the Treasure Chest Game NPC

Next, let's create the NPC. He's going to get straight to the point and begin with the all-important question: Want to play the Treasure Chest game? The player will get three choices at that time. He/She can answer Yes, at which point the NPC will note that it costs 500 Gold to play and ask the player to confirm. We have the usual processing to make sure that the player can't play if he or she doesn't have the Gold and have the NPC say good-bye if he/she says no. The second choice is humorously named "Huh?" and prompts the NPC to explain what the game is actually about. The last choice allows the player to say No from the first question and not have to initially say Yes. If the player says Yes and has the Gold to play, the NPC will deduct 500 Gold from the player, say a little line, and the screen will fade out. After the fade-out, we set the value of ChestsToOpen to 2, set the value of TreasureChestSeed to a random value between 1 and 7, and flip the TreasureChestStart to the on state. One second later, the screen fades back in, and the fun can begin. We add a simple second page to the NPC that gives him a witty one-liner urging the player to "Get to opening!" the chests, as it were, but only when TreasureChestStart is on. A listing of the first page of the NPC event follows.

```
◆Label : Main
◆Text : None, Window, Bottom
:      : Want to play the Treasure Chest game?
◆Show Choices : Yes, Huh?, No (Window, Right, #1, #3)
: When Yes
   ◆Text : None, Window, Bottom
   :      : That will be 500 Gold, if you will.\$
   ◆Show Choices : Yes, No (Window, Right, #1, #2)
   : When Yes
      ◆If : Gold ≥ 500
         ◆Change Gold : - 500
         ◆Text : None, Window, Bottom
         :      : Let the game begin!
         ◆Fadeout Screen
         ◆Wait : 60 frames
         ◆Control Variables : #0009 ChestsToOpen = 2
         ◆Control Variables : #0009 TreasureChestSeed = Random 1..7
         ◆Control Switches : #0019 TreasureChestStart = ON
         ◆Fadein Screen
         ◆
      : Else
         ◆Text : None, Window, Bottom
         :      : Come back when you have enough Gold!
         ◆
      : End
      ◆
   : When No
      ◆Text : None, Window, Bottom
      :      : See you later, then.
      ◆
   :  End
   ◆
: When Huh?
   ◆Text : None, Window, Bottom
   :      : Guess I should explain. These seven chests around
   :      : me contain either an item, some Gold, or a single
   :      : gold piece. The catch, of course, is that you may
   :      : only open two of them.
   ◆Text : None, Window, Bottom
   :      : Oh, and it costs you 500 Gold to play.
   ◆Jump to Label : Main
   ◆
```

```
: When No
    ◆Text : None, Window, Bottom
    :       : See you later, then.
    ◆
    : End
◆
```

> ▨ **Note**   It's as good a time as any to mention that \$ causes the game to display the party's current Gold when used within a text box. We've used it several times already for precisely that purpose.

Completing the Treasure Chest Game

Last, but definitely not least, we have the Parallel event. We have to make sure that we end the game right when the player has opened the second chest, lest he/she get greedy and open all seven of them. Also, we have to make it so that the player is temporarily removed from the map, so that the chosen chests can reappear for future play-throughs of the minigame. We can do this via the clever use of a switch that I'll call Intermission. The Parallel event is one page long and needs to have a condition of TreasureChestStart (otherwise, the player will loop infinitely between the two maps). The Parallel Process event starts with a conditional branch that requires ChestsToOpen to be equal to 0. Then it checks for Intermission to be off (which it should be). The NPC will say "That's it!" and the screen will fade out. The player will be transferred to a nearly blank map that contains a small Autorun event that flips on the Intermission switch and sends the player back to the Treasure Chest game map (specifically, one square to the south of the NPC and facing the player).

Back at the game map, the Parallel event has a second conditional branch that triggers only when Intermission has been turned on. We take a one-second pause and turn off the TreasureChestStart and Intermission switches, effectively resetting the minigame state so that the player can play again. Here's the Parallel event:

```
◆If : ChestsToOpen = 0
    ◆If : Intermission is OFF
        ◆Text : None, Window, Bottom
        :       : That's it!
        ◆Fadeout Screen
        ◆Transfer Player : Intermission (7,6) (Fade: None)
        ◆
    : End
    ◆
: End
 ◆If : Intermission is ON
    ◆Wait : 60 frames
    ◆Control Switches : #0019 TreasureChestStart = OFF
    ◆Control Switches : #0020 Intermission = OFF
    ◆Fadein Screen
    ◆
: End
```

The Autorun event on the intermission map is made up of two little lines:

```
♦Control Switches : #0020 Intermission = ON
♦Transfer Player : TreasureChestGame (8,7) (Direction: Up, Fade: None)
```

Related Exercises

With that done, you have just completed your very own treasure chest game in the vein of some of the *Zelda* games. Here are some neat exercises for you to try out that are related to this minigame.

■ **Note**   You can find an example of all three of the following exercises integrated into pages 3 and 4 of the upper-left chest of the Treasure Chest Game map in the source code project. You can change the Item conditional on page 3 from Heal Orb to something easier to obtain if you wish to test it out in-game.

---

1. Using the "Item" conditional of an event, make it so that the player can see the item that a particular minigame chest contains.

    -   The inspiration for this one comes from *Ocarina of Time*. In that *Zelda* entry, the player can see the contents of chests in a minigame, by using an item found at the bottom of a well.

    -   You could duplicate page 2 of each of your chests for this purpose and have a text box that allows the player to decide whether or not to open the chest, based on what it contains. Just make sure that it's page 3 and not 2; otherwise, it will never trigger. (Never forget that events attempt to execute from right to left; the rightmost page will always be executed, if possible.)

2. Make it so that an opened chest remains visible until the minigame ends.

    -   It's as simple as having for each chest one switch (you could name them TreasureChest1, TreasureChest2, and so forth) that is flipped on when its related chest is opened and including another event page that requires that switch to be flipped on and has a graphic of the open treasure chest.

    -   You'll have to toggle off those switches to reset the minigame conditions. Incidentally, that's the reason I don't use self-switches for the same purpose. A self-switch can only be affected at a local level, which means that if you flip Chest 5's A switch, for example, you would have to flip it off via Chest 5's event specifically.

3. Have items that can only be received once per play-through.

    -   Say you wanted to have a rare medallion as one of the seven possible rewards. What you could do is use a switch that flips on when the player finds the item for the first time, and then have a conditional branch that changes the item found in a chest in subsequent minigames.

    -   It might be tempting to use an *Item* conditional branch here, but that will only work if the rare item in question cannot be obtained elsewhere. Otherwise, weird things will happen. Mainly, the player will not be able to obtain the item if he/she already has it (even if the player has never gotten one from the minigame) and can get it multiple times if it has a sell price (by selling the one he/she has before replaying the minigame).

Other Minigames

A great minigame is one that makes the player want to play it even more than the actual game. I'm a personal fan of card games and have to admit that the Final Fantasy IX and *Xenosaga Episode 1* have card games that hooked me for dozens of hours. That's not bad for what is supposed to be a diversion from the main plot. Following, I'll list some other ideas for minigames and offer tips and tricks on how I would start tackling them within RMMV.

1. A sequence where the player has limited time to escape a certain area:

   - For example, let's say the player is in a space station that is being overrun by baddies. If the player does not reach the escape pod within 1000 steps, he/she gets a game-over.

   - There's no direct way to determine via eventing when a player has taken a step in RMMV. The easiest workaround is to use three variables. One variable checks the player's total steps at the start of the escape minigame. The second saves the player's current steps every time he/she moves, and the last variable is the difference between the first and second variables. We'll need a Parallel event to cover those interactions.

   - The Parallel event would have a conditional branch that requires the difference between the two variables to be 1000 or more. Once that is met, you employ the Game Over command for its sole use.

   - Of course, if the player makes it out in time, all is well.

   - To add to the tension of the situation, you can make it so that certain doors and elevators become inoperable at certain step milestones (such as 700 steps left, 300 steps left, and so on).

2. A matching-pair memory game involving NPCs or symbols:

   - Each pair of identical events should have its own variable. There should also be a variable equal to the number of total pairs at the start of the game.

   - Another variable should be set to 2 and drop each time the player selects a spot. When a member of a pair is spotted, its variable should be increased by 1.

   - When two spots have been uncovered, the counting variable will be at 0. The game should check to see if any pair variables are at 2. If they are, we remove them and award the player a point.

   - We can have another variable for Lives. The player loses a life every time he or she fails to match a pair. If the player is out of lives, the minigame ends prematurely, and we reward him/her based on points received.

   - If a pair has not been matched, we hide the two uncovered spots. If a pair has been matched, we use Erase Event on it.

Adding the Minigame Areas to Our World Map

That just about concludes our chapter, but for two more things. First, we haven't added our new locations to the world map! Take a look at Figure 7-5.

Figure 7-5. *Another part of our world map that has been populated with locations*

The tent is the arena and is located at (68, 73). The treasure chest game is located at the small building at (71, 64). The bridge to the east of the new locations appears when the player beats the tower's boss (we accomplish this by giving the event a *PlotAdvance2* switch condition) and has a Priority of Below Characters (this allows the player to pass over the bridge to the other side). Note that, by default, that strip of land is one tile east of its current location in Figure 7-5, so you'll need to shift it accordingly so that the bridge lines up nicely with the new part of the world map we want the player to explore. Make sure to take a moment to update the Transfer Parallel event (and, for that matter, don't forget to connect the Arena and Treasure Chest Game areas to the world map) accordingly before you move on.

The other thing we need to address is creating a few new enemies for our new part of the map, along with the regions where they will appear (incidentally, it's also a good time to fill in the tiles surrounding the tower, which we didn't actually do in the previous chapter).

New Enemies and Region Placements

You know the drill by now: We have a new area, and the new area needs some enemies. Table 7-3 lists the three enemies I created to populate Region 4 of our world map.

Table 7-3. *A List of the New Enemies for This Section of Our Project*

Name	HP	MP	ATK	DEF	MAT	MDF	AGI	LUK	EXP	G
Forest Rat	300	0	50	20	20	20	60	60	92	133
Troll	1000	0	70	75	40	40	35	50	412	550
Ruffian	850	0	60	60	60	60	60	60	242	375

As is also standard by now, here's a more detailed breakdown of each enemy type:

- Forest Rats are the weakest enemies of the new area. Given their relatively paltry experience and Gold rewards, you may wonder why I created them at all. Up to now, we have only had troops of one or two enemies. The newly created Rats fit yet another monster archetype: that of the *swarm*. A swarm is a large group of individually weak enemies that are threatening because of their numbers. Attacks that hit multiple enemies will make short work of swarms. Thus, the Forest Rat groups will be 3 and 5 units in size. I used a Hue of 115 to give the Forest Rat a greenish tone. Forest Rats drop Potions at a 1/5 chance and Dispel Herbs at a 1/20 chance. Forest Rats only use the Attack skill.

- Trolls are our newest Ogre variant, painted green with Hue: 275. Whereas Lava Ogres were all about the offense to the exclusion of everything else, Trolls are more about outlasting their enemies. They have high physical defense to thwart most of Harold's strongest attacks, and the Ex-Parameter: HP Regeneration + 4% Trait to recover 40 HP per turn. Magic attacks will be useful to bring down a Troll quickly. Besides the aforementioned HP Regeneration Trait, the Trolls I created have a few more traits worth mentioning:

  - I set the Troll's Hit Rate to 70%. While not as inaccurate as the Lava Ogres back at the Lava Cave, they will still be missing about 3 in 10 attacks.

  - Critical Rate of 20%. They will be landing some deadly blows, but at a lower average rate than their reddish cousins (14% of the time vs. the Lava Ogre's 25% of the time).

  - Attack State: Confusion + 25%. Sometimes the Troll just lands a blow that leaves its victim confused and struggling to figure out what just happened.

- Trolls use Attack and Cleave at all times (both skills have a Rating of 5). They have a 1/10 chance to drop a Big Bomb and a 1/10 chance to drop a Life Potion.

- Ruffians are this area's balanced enemy. As a result, there's not much to say about them. The Swordsman graphic is used for this enemy. They have three skills with a condition of Always. Attack and Eye Gouge have a Rating of 5 and Dual Attack has a Rating of 4. Lastly, they have a 1/15 chance to drop a Greatsword and a 1/15 chance to drop Chain Mail.

Now, we only need set the Regions and encounter tables for each new enemy type. But first, let's set up Region 3, where enemies appropriate to the area surrounding the tower will spawn, That way, our revised world map random encounters can cover both Region 3 and the regions to be used for the northern area. Take a look at Figure 7-6 for a look at how the area around the tower looks with Regions added.

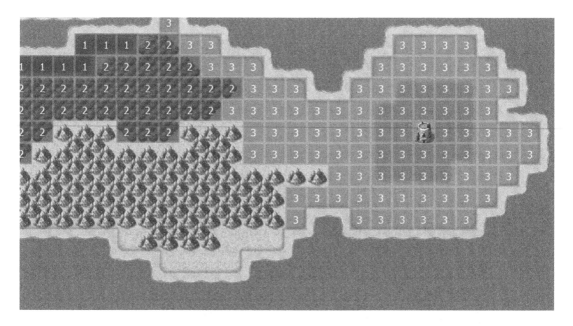

Figure 7-6. *The area surrounding the game's second dungeon, now with Regions added*

Note how Region 3 starts after the end of the long forest area that covers most of the middle of our game's initial continent. Now, take a look at Figure 7-7 for region placements in our newest area.

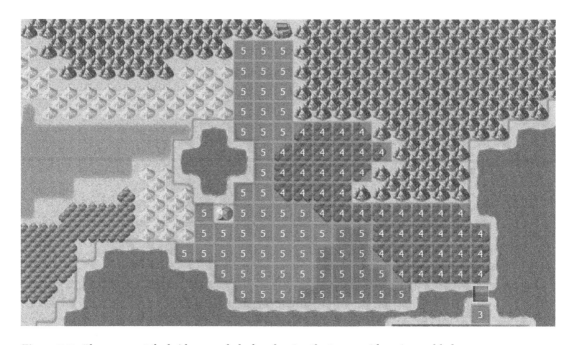

Figure 7-7. *The area past the bridge revealed after clearing the tower, with regions added*

Notice how I tweaked the terrain a bit by adding hills to better constrain Region 5, which is made up of grasslands. Now, take a look at Figure 7-8, showing the newly added encounters for our world map, based on our newly added regions.

War Orc	5	3
Minotaur	5	3
Snake*2	10	3
Forest Rat*3	10	4
Forest Rat*5	10	4
Troll	5	4, 5
Ruffian	5	4, 5
Ruffian*2	5	4, 5

Figure 7-8. *The encounters added to our world map's encounter table*

For Region 3, we reuse three out of four regular enemy encounters from the Stone Cave dungeon. Region 4 is the forest area immediately past the bridge and is where the player will have a chance to encounter the Forest Rat swarms. The other two enemy types will appear in both Regions 4 and 5. While we're technically done with the chapter's material, now's the perfect time for a bit of wrapping up.

Wrapping Up the Chapter

Recall at the start of the chapter that I mentioned that we would need to return to Ranks B and A of the Arena once we've added more enemy types to our game. In the following sections we'll do that and then update our Battleback event.

Adding Battles for Ranks B and A of the Arena

Rank B of the Arena should have the following battles for the player to overcome:

- Lava Ogre
- Arcanist*2
- Forest Rat*3

And, here are the three battles for Rank A:

- Forest Rat*5
- Troll
- Ruffian*2

Rank A is perhaps a bit too easy (or, more properly phrased, it isn't harder than Rank B by enough), but you can easily remedy that problem later on with some of the enemy types we'll be adding to our project.

New World Map Battlebacks

Now that we have three new regions in our game, it's a good a time as any to update our Battleback Parallel event to reflect the added areas. Here's a bullet list of what battleback should be displayed in each new region.

- **Region 3:** Grassland & Grassland (the same as Region 1)

- **Region 4:** Dirt2 & Forest

- **Region 5:** Dirt2 & Grassland

There you have it! We can stick a fork in this chapter, because it's done!

Summary

This chapter covered how to create an arena game in which the player can battle predetermined enemies to earn points toward rare and special items. I then showed how to make a treasure chest game in the spirit of some of the *Legend of Zelda* games and gave ideas for other possible minigames. Finally, I updated the world map with new regions and enemies and assigned those enemies as battles for the player to overcome in Ranks B and A of the Arena. In the next chapter, you will learn about optional quests (also called *sidequests*).

CHAPTER 8

Sidequests

In the previous chapter, we took a break from working on our game's main narrative. In this chapter, we're going to extend that break some more! Sidequests are similar in purpose to minigames, in that they allow the player to walk off the beaten path and receive rewards for things that do not directly advance the narrative. We can loosely classify sidequests into two major categories:

- **Permanent.** These sidequests become available at a certain point of the game and can be completed at any time before the player beats the final boss. Is the player one step away from entering the final dungeon? He or she can go kill the giant boar terrorizing a village halfway across the world.

- **Time-sensitive.** A sidequest that is active only for a certain part of the game. While it's not a sidequest, Excalibur in *Final Fantasy* 9 is a perfect example of a time-sensitive quest. Excalibur is a sword located within a chest in a late-game dungeon. The catch? You must reach the chest within 24 hours of starting the game. It's basically an extra reward for players trying to speed-run (beat the game as fast as possible). However, perhaps there's an old man sick with a horrible disease. A sidequest could be to go get the cure. If you keep advancing in the game while disregarding that sidequest, the old man may perish.

During the course of this chapter, we'll be making a sidequest of each type.

Let's Create a Permanent Sidequest!

The first quest we're going to create will be a permanent sidequest that can be done at any time, once it is unlocked. We'll make it so that the nonplayer character (NPC) appears after the player completes the first dungeon. As to where the NPC will be, there's only one place it could realistically be! Figure 8-1 shows a certain part of our fishing village.

© Darrin Perez 2016

D. Perez, *Beginning RPG Maker MV*, DOI 10.1007/978-1-4842-1967-6_8

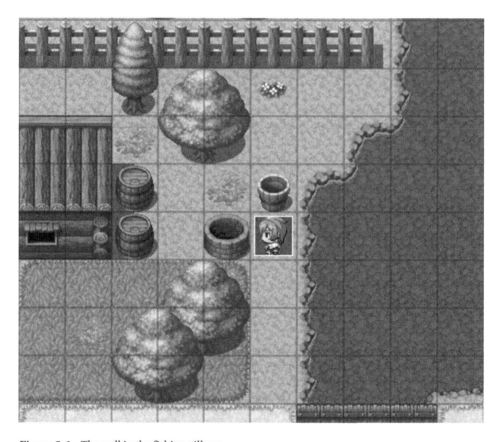

Figure 8-1. *The well in the fishing village*

We're going to have a sidequest involving the well, because quests involving a well are an RPG classic. For this exercise, we'll need the following things:

- An NPC that will be the quest-giver (in this case, one of the three NPCs created for the fishing village exterior back in Chapter 4). The quest will be available after the player has defeated Augustus at the first dungeon. On page 2 of its event (page 1 covers what is said before the player defeats Augustus), the NPC will mention strange sounds coming from within the well. Marsha will ask Harold if they should investigate, which prompts a yes/no choice. If the player says no, Harold will say that "It is too dangerous" and end the event. If the player says yes, the sidequest switch will be flipped.

- Page 3 of the quest NPC will be processed if the sidequest start switch is on and causes the NPC to warn the player to be careful. If the player has completed the sidequest, page 4 of the NPC's event will be triggered. The player will be able to talk to the NPC, who will ask what was inside of the well. Upon receiving an answer, the NPC will leave the area (via the use of a Fadeout screen and flipping self-switch A; we then require self-switch A to be flipped on for the fifth and last blank page).

- A Same As Characters/Action Button blank graphic event placed on the well. The first page will have no conditional and will display "You see Seaside's well." The second page will require that the sidequest switch be flipped on and will display the message but then continue to a choice asking if the player wishes to enter the well.

- A map of the well area that the player will enter upon climbing in.

- Some enemies to populate the well's innards.

- A boss to fight at the end, along with a special drop.

Creating the Sidequest NPC

Let's go in order. First, let's create the sidequest giver. Here are the sidequest giver's event pages:

- Page 1 (before Augustus is defeated): No event conditional.

```
♦Text : None, Window, Bottom
:     : Wells are such a fascinating thing, aren't they?
:     : It may not mean much here in Seaside, but imagine
:     : living in the middle of a desert. A well could be
:     : the only way to get any water.
```

- Page 2: Switch BossDefeated must be on.

```
♦Comment : Page 1 of the Sidequest Event
♦Text : None, Window, Bottom
:     : Hello there. I've been hearing strange sounds
:     : coming from the well.
♦Text : None, Window, Bottom
:     : Marsha looks at Harold.
♦Text : Actor3(7), Window, Bottom
:     : Should we investigate?
♦Show Choices : Yes, No (Window, Right, #1, #2)
: When Yes
   ♦Text : Actor1(0), Window, Bottom
   :     : Let's do it!
   ♦Text : Actor3(7), Window, Bottom
   :     : Indeed. Let us investigate.
   ♦Control Switches : #0022 SQ1Start = ON
   ♦
: When No
   ♦Text : Actor1(0), Window, Bottom
   :     : Sounds too dangerous.
   ♦
: End
♦
```

- Page 3: Switch SQ1Start must be on.

```
♦Comment : Page 2 of the Sidequest Event
♦Text : None, Window, Bottom
:     : Be careful, sir!
```

- Page 4: Switch SQ1Completed (flipped when the sidequest boss has been defeated) must be on.

```
♦Comment : Page 3 of the Sidequest Event
♦Text : None, Window, Bottom
:      : What was down there?
♦Text : Actor1(0), Window, Bottom
:      : Some monsters. They won't be making noise
:      : anymore.
♦Fadeout Screen
♦Wait : 60 frames
♦Text : None, Window, Bottom
:      : The villager nods, waves goodbye, and walks off into
:      : the distance.
♦Control Self Switch : B = ON
♦Fadein Screen
♦
```

- Page 5: Self-switch B must be on. It is a blank page with no NPC graphic.

Creating the Well (Event)

Of course, this won't be much of a sidequest if the player can't interact with the well. So, have a well event.

- Page 1: Has no conditions. Blank graphic with Same As Characters priority.

```
♦Text : None, Window, Bottom
:      : You see Seaside's well.
```

- Page 2: Requires SQ1Start to be on.

```
♦Text : None, Window, Bottom
:      : You see Seaside's well. Do you wish to climb in?
♦Show Choices : Yes, No (Window, Right, #1, #2)
: When Yes
   ♦Transfer Player : Inside the Well (8,5) (Direction: Down)
   ♦
: When No
   ♦
:  End
♦
```

That's the extent of our sidequest eventing on top.

Creating the Area Below the Well

Now, let us make our way into the bowels of the earth and continue. Take a look at Figure 8-2 for the well map that I created.

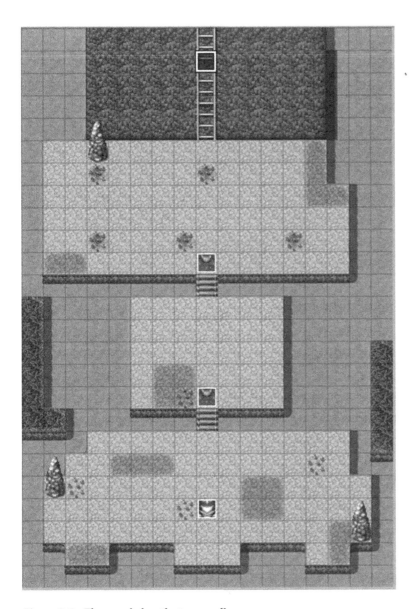

***Figure 8-2.** The area below the town well*

The player appears at the bottom of the ladder. The transfer event that leads back to the surface is four squares to the north of that position. The area, instead of having random encounters, has three static encounters. The first two are against two Dire Bats, stronger versions of the normal Bat that have the following parameters: 400 HP, 0 MP, 42 Attack, 30 Defense, 42 M. Attack, 30 M. Defense, 40 Agility, 40 Luck. They have 100% Hit Rate, 10% Evasion Rate, and the Attack Times + 1 trait. Finally, they grant 152 experience and 200 gold when defeated. The third encounter is against an Iron Giant. Discerning eyes will notice that the Iron Giant event is displaying only a head. Some of RMMV's largest stock monsters have 2×2 sprites contained in the $BigMonster1 graphic set or 3×3 sprites in $BigMonster2. The Iron Giant is one of them. So, while it appears that way in the editor, here's how it looks in-game (Figure 8-3).

Figure 8-3. *An in-game picture of the Iron Giant sprite*

I placed a Player Touch event one square below the second bridge, which will cause the player to fight the Iron Giant. For large enemies represented on the game map, I prefer to do it that way, as their sprites act weird if forced to move (with good reason: large enemies have only a forward-facing sprite). Thus, the Iron Giant itself is a two-page event with a page 1 that has a graphic and a page 2 that does not (page 2 requires that SQ1Completed be on). The trigger event, on the other hand, has a little more meat to it.

- Page 1: Has no conditionals. Has a Below Characters Priority and a Player Touch Trigger.

```
◆Text : Actor1(0), Window, Bottom
:     : What is THAT thing?
◆Text : None, Window, Bottom
:     : Harold points to a nearby giant.
◆Text : Actor3(7), Window, Bottom
:     : That appears to be a giant construct of
:     : some sort.
◆Text : None, Window, Bottom
:     : A rumbling sound makes itself heard.
◆Text : Actor3(7), Window, Bottom
:     : It appears to know we're here.
:     : Ready yourself, Harold!
◆Change Battle BGM : Battle2 (90, 100, 0)
◆Battle Processing : Iron Giant
◆
```

As is standard for boss fights, we change the Battle BGM to reflect the fact that the player is facing a particularly strong foe. You can see the Iron Giant's stats in Figure 8-4.

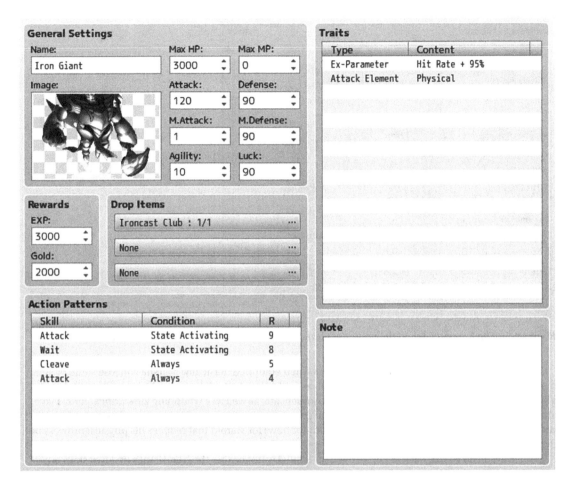

General Settings

Name: Iron Giant

Max HP: 3000 Max MP: 0

Image:

Attack: 120 Defense: 90

M.Attack: 1 M.Defense: 90

Agility: 10 Luck: 90

Rewards

EXP: 3000

Gold: 2000

Drop Items

Ironcast Club : 1/1

None

None

Traits

Type	Content
Ex-Parameter	Hit Rate + 95%
Attack Element	Physical

Action Patterns

Skill	Condition	R
Attack	State Activating	9
Wait	State Activating	8
Cleave	Always	5
Attack	Always	4

Note

Figure 8-4. *Tweaked stats for the Iron Giant enemy*

The Ironcast Club is a weapon that Marsha can equip, and it changes her playstyle a bit. If you've ever wanted your Mage to smack enemies with a stick, the Ironcast Club is your best bet! Figure 8-5 shows the details on this new weapon.

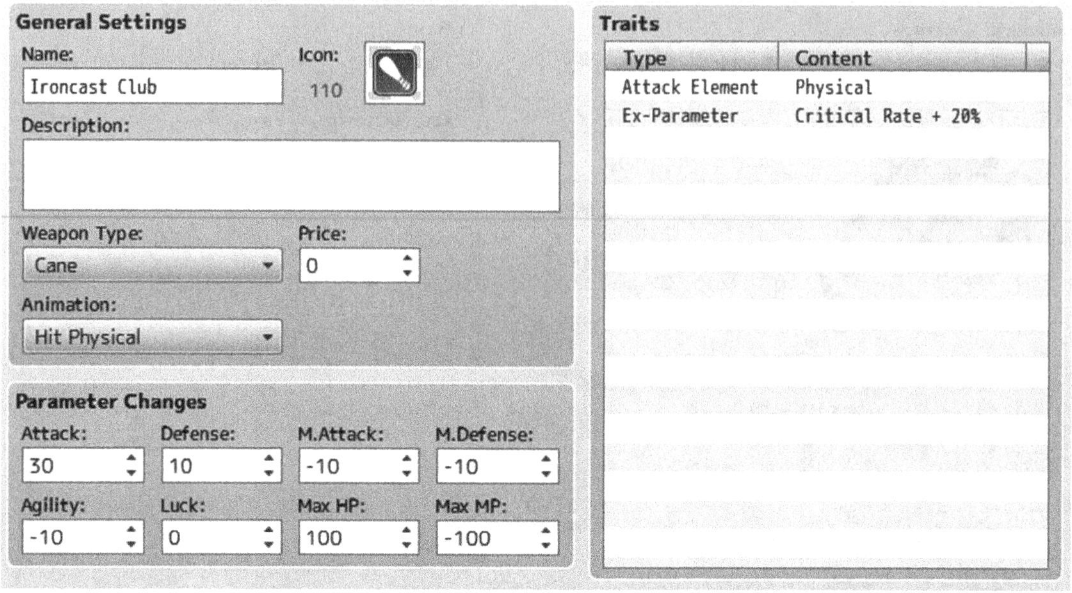

Figure 8-5. *The Ironcast Club in the project's Database*

This new weapon causes drastic stat changes when equipped. Basically, Marsha will lose some of her magical damage (and magical defense) potential, as well as become a bit slower. However, she will gain a sizeable 30 Attack, 10 Defense, and 100 HP to compensate, as well as a whopping 20% Critical Rate. I've always felt that a good RPG can benefit from such gimmick weapons by making certain characters more versatile. In a similar vein, we could create a sword (or bow) for Harold that reduces his physical prowess but massively improves his magical potential.

Anyway, if you glance back at Figure 8-4, you'll quickly notice that the Iron Giant's first two skills are used only while it is in the Activating State. This particular enemy represents the "slow starter" archetype. In essence, a slow starter begins combat with weakened stats, which eventually increase to a higher maximum. This gives the player a time limit of sorts before they start getting hit with stronger attacks and/or the enemy becomes more resistant to attack. So, what is that state all about? Take a peek at Figure 8-6 to find out!

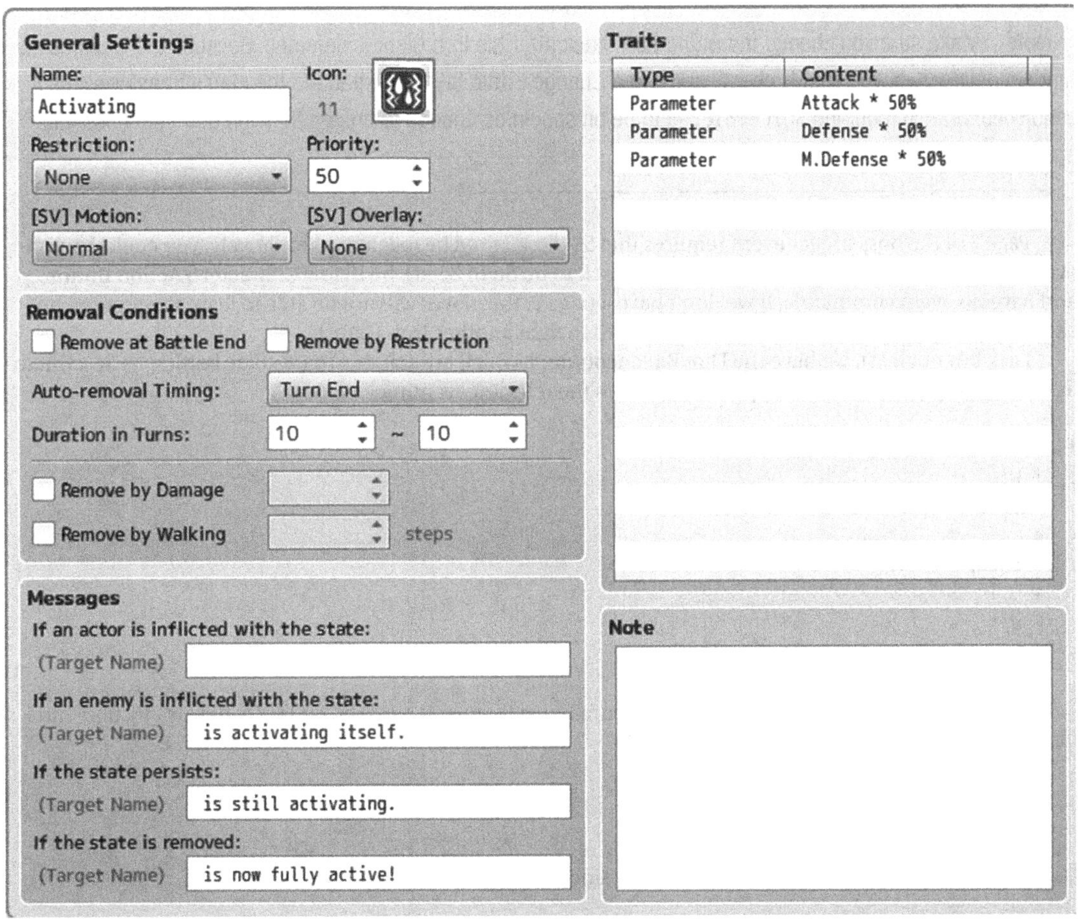

General Settings

Name: Activating
Icon: 11

Restriction: None
Priority: 50

[SV] Motion: Normal
[SV] Overlay: None

Traits

Type	Content
Parameter	Attack * 50%
Parameter	Defense * 50%
Parameter	M.Defense * 50%

Removal Conditions

☐ Remove at Battle End ☐ Remove by Restriction

Auto-removal Timing: Turn End

Duration in Turns: 10 ~ 10

☐ Remove by Damage
☐ Remove by Walking ___ steps

Messages

If an actor is inflicted with the state:
(Target Name)

If an enemy is inflicted with the state:
(Target Name) is activating itself.

If the state persists:
(Target Name) is still activating.

If the state is removed:
(Target Name) is now fully active!

Note

Figure 8-6. *A screenshot of the Activating State*

Since we want the Iron Giant to be at partial potential at the start of the battle, we can use a troop event to apply this state on the enemy on Turn 0. This state lasts a whopping ten turns, during which time the player is expected to bring down this foreboding foe (or at least weaken it to the point where victory is imminent by the time the state wears off).

■ **Tip** Since the player cannot escape from the Iron Giant battle, you can flip the SQ1Completed switch as soon as the battle begins, too. There is no need to make the Iron Giant Immortal, as we did with Augustus, unless you want to have the party (or the boss) talk at the end of the fight.

191

▪ **Note**   Make sure you change the Battle BGM back after the Iron Giant is defeated. Because the well has no random encounters, you could "cheat" and add a Change Battle BGM command to the map's transfer event. A conditional branch requiring SQ1Completed to be on should be enough to ensure that you don't get boss music against the Sahagins.

Page 2 of the boss trigger event requires that SQ1Completed be toggled (alternatively, you could have the event flip a self-switch and then require that switch to be on instead), be Below Characters/Action Button, and have no event commands. If we don't have a page 2, the player will not be able to leave the area (as he/she would keep getting turned around and forced to fight another Iron Giant).

Last, but not least, we have the Dire Bat encounters, which are standard-fare static battles, as described in Chapter 5. For the sake of completeness, here's the relevant eventing:

```
◆Battle Processing : Dire Bat*2
: If Win
   ◆Control Self Switch : A = ON
   ◆
: If Escape
   ◆
:  End
◆
```

There you have it! The player now has an extra quest that he/she can go on that is not strictly tied into the main plot.

Additional Exercises

Here are some exercises for you to flesh out this sidequest.

1.   Suppose we did want to tie this to the main plot. After the Iron Giant has been defeated, have Harold and Marsha talk about the possible connection between the Iron Giant's appearance and the sounds the villagers have been hearing ever since Augustus was defeated.

   •   You can use an Autorun event that requires SQ1Completed to be on. Just make sure the event has a page 2 that does *not* Autorun.

   •   For greater consistency, you could have a switch flip on when the player talks to a villager who mentions the strange nighttime sounds. Then, the party should only speak about the connection *if* they have heard about the happenings. Otherwise, you could just skip the chat altogether.

   •   On the topic of consistency, once the player has defeated the Dark General in the tower, the previous switch should have no way of being flipped on if it's still off at that time (as the villagers stop complaining about the noise after that part of the game).

2. Change the Iron Giant encounter so that the player has to withstand the monster's assault for a few turns. At the end of the final turn, the SQ1Completed switch is flipped, and the Iron Giant leaves the battle of its own volition, with the Escape skill.

   - The easiest way to make sure that a certain level of damage output is kept up is to have a completely static attack pattern. That way, the boss fight doesn't have random elements, such as the enemy using its strongest attack four times in a row. You can find an example of the altered Iron Giant and its associated troop in the Database. The altered Iron Giant is in Enemy slot #253, while its troop is in Troop slot #253.

3. Have Seaside's shopkeepers give the player a permanent discount for defeating the Iron Giant.

   - This is as simple as having a conditional branch in each of the town's shops. If SQ1Completed is on, then you charge a lesser price for every item in the shop. (You'll have to specify the lower price of each item manually.)

We have completed one of the sidequests we set out to make. Now, on to the second one!

Let's Create a Time-Sensitive Quest!

We have already created a quest that can be completed whenever the player chooses. However, time-sensitive quests are useful for giving the player a sense of the world moving on its own. So, let's make a second quest that is active from the start of the game *until* Augustus has been defeated. The quest will involve a man who wants five bat wings and is willing to give the player a monetary reward for getting them for him. We want this quest to have three possible outcomes:

1. Quest forfeited. Occurs if the player doesn't talk to the NPC at all until Augustus has been defeated. The man will reference the work of a third party to get him his bat wings and drop a hint that the player missed a possible quest.

2. Quest failed. Occurs if the player starts the quest but does not finish it before defeating Augustus. The NPC will chastise the player for not delivering on his/her word, while mentioning that another person came through for him.

3. Quest successful. The player accepted the quest and got the five bat wings, as requested, receiving a reward for his/her troubles.

This quest only needs some troop eventing and the quest-giving NPC event. First, let's place the quest-giver event (Figure 8-7).

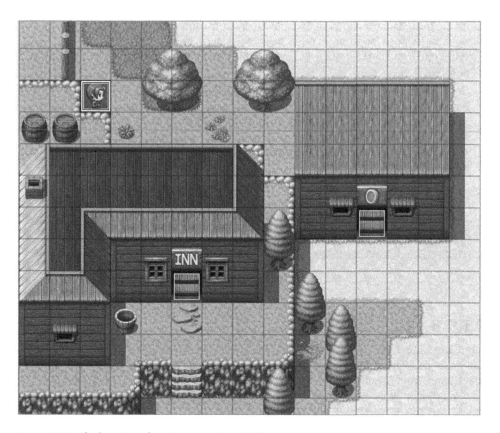

Figure 8-7.   *The location of our time-sensitive NPC*

There's a nice section of space right behind the inn that allows the NPC to be hidden and shady.

Creating the Sidequest NPC

For once, I'm going to work backward with this NPC. Create a total of five event pages for our quest-giver's event. We are going to fill them out from 5 to 1. Why? Recall that we want to have three possible outcomes. Pages 3 through 5 will contain those outcomes. On page 5, we'll require that SQ2Completed be on and have the NPC say some words of thanks for the player's earlier help.

```
♦Text : None, Window, Bottom
:     : Thank you for the help, lad!
♦
```

Page 4 will contain the quest failed message. This requires both `BossDefeated` and `SQ2Start` to be turned on. The player has taken too long to turn in the bat wings (or didn't even bother to do anything after accepting the quest). Here's what the NPC has to say about that:

```
♦Text : None, Window, Bottom
:     : Oh, hello there...
♦Text : None, Window, Bottom
:     : Guess you didn't want the gold so badly. I got an
:     : ambitious lass to do me the favor. Next time, don't
:     : say you'll do something and then not do it.
♦
```

Harsh, eh? Serves the player right for not bending to an NPC's will! Page 3 will require that `BossDefeated` is on (`SQ2Start` must be off). This will be the quest forfeited message. That is, the player didn't speak to the NPC at all before going on to defeat Augustus. The player didn't even know about the quest, so the NPC makes reference to it.

```
♦Text : None, Window, Bottom
:     : Hello lad. I just recently procured some Bat Wings
:     : to make my special potion. Shame you didn't talk
:     : to me earlier. I paid a lass 500 Gold for her
:     : efforts.
♦
```

That leaves only the first two pages. Page 1 will have no conditionals and consist of the NPC attempting to task the player with the quest that he/she can accept or refuse.

```
♦Text : None, Window, Bottom
:     : Hello there, lad. Could I interest you in a business
:     : proposition?
♦Show Choices : Yes, No (Window, Right, #1, #2)
: When Yes
   ♦Text : None, Window, Bottom
   :     : Awesome! I need 5 Bat Wings. I'm not particularly
   :     : picky about the bats you get them from.
   ♦Text : Actor1(0), Window, Bottom
   :     : What do you need them for?
   ♦Text : None, Window, Bottom
   :     : It's for a special brew I make this time every year.
   :     : You needn't concern yourself with the details.
   ♦Text : None, Window, Bottom
   :     : Come talk to me again when you have all five.
   ♦Control Switches : #0026 SQ2Start = ON
   ♦
: When No
   ♦Text : None, Window, Bottom
   :     : A shame, that. I'll be here waiting if you change
   :     : your mind. I can only wait so long, though, so don't
   :     : tarry overmuch.
   ♦
: End
♦
```

Accepting the quest will flip SQ2Start, allowing page 2 to be processed, so long as the player has not defeated Augustus or completed the quest already. Here's page 2:

```
◆If : BatWings < 5
   ◆Text : None, Window, Bottom
   :     : Do you have my Bat Wings, lad?
   ◆Text : Actor1(0), Window, Bottom
   :     : I'm working on it.
   ◆Text : None, Window, Bottom
   :     : Ah. Fair enough. Do deliver them as soon as you can.
   ◆
 : End
◆If : BatWings ≥ 5
   ◆Text : None, Window, Bottom
   :     : Do you have my Bat Wings, lad?
   ◆Text : Actor1(0), Window, Bottom
   :     : Here they are.
   ◆Text : None, Window, Bottom
   :     : The man counts them.
   ◆Wait : 60 frames
   ◆Text : None, Window, Bottom
   :     : ...and 5. That'll do it, lad. Much obliged.
   ◆Change Gold : + 500
   ◆Text : None, Window, Bottom
   :     : Got 500 Gold!
   ◆Text : None, Window, Bottom
   :     : This should tide me over for the rest of the year.
   ◆Text : Actor1(0), Window, Bottom
   :     : Glad I could help!
   ◆Control Switches : #0025 SQ2Complete = ON
   ◆
 : End
◆
```

Page 2 has a pair of conditional branches that trigger depending on whether the player has five bat wings or not. If he/she doesn't, the NPC will ask if the player has the bat wings, and the player will say that he/she is working on it. If the player does have five bat wings, the man will count them and give the player 500 Gold. Last, SQ2Complete will be flipped.

Of Bats and Their Wings

Now, you may be wondering how to make the bats drop their wings on defeat (death). That's as simple as some troop eventing. Make your way to the Troops tab in the Database and find the Bat troop. You can have the bat wings be a literal item or a variable that is increased. In the case of the former, I would have the bat wing be an item that can be sold for a little gold, and then make it so that a bat will drop one at a 1/1 or 1/2 chance. I've always found it silly in RPGs when a monster doesn't drop a relevant body part when you can see it on their graphic! With that said, let's use the variable approach for our batty friends. Given that we want a bat to drop its wing on death, recall that death in RMMV is prioritized over every other possible event.

If we don't use the Immortal approach, the last bat to fall in a fight will never drop its wing. Of course, if we're using a variable to keep track of their wings, we only want Immortal to be added to the enemies while we're doing the quest. Here's page 1 of the Bat troop:

- Condition: Turn 0

- Span: Battle

```
♦If : SQ2Start is ON
   ♦If : SQ2Complete is OFF
      ♦Change Enemy State : Entire Troop, + Immortal
      ♦
   : End
   ♦
: End
```

Turn 0 is the very start of a battle, before anyone has acted. We only want the event to trigger once per battle, and we only want it to trigger at all if the player has accepted the subquest and not yet completed it. In addition to what is displayed in the preceding code, you could add another conditional branch to that nest that requires BossDefeated to be off as well (remember that the player fails the quest if he or she defeats Augustus before turning in the bat wings). Following, I'll give the code for page 2. Once you're done with the Bat troop, you'll want to tweak the Bat*2 troop as well, keeping in mind that you want to make sure that each bat has its own event page, such as the one following:

- Condition: Enemy HP (1) <= 0%

- Span: Battle

```
♦If : SQ2Start is ON
   ♦If : BatWings < 5
      ♦Control Variables : #0010 BatWings += 1
      ♦Text : None, Window, Bottom
      :     : You got a Bat's Wing!
      ♦
   : End
   ♦
: End
♦Change Enemy State : #1 Bat, - Immortal
```

When the bat's HP drops to 0% or below, we check to see if the player is currently on this subquest. If he/she is, we check to see if he/she has five bat wings already. If he/she doesn't, we add one to the value of the BatWings variable and inform the player that he/she received a bat wing. At the very bottom of the battle event, we remove the bat's immortality.

■ **Note** It doesn't matter much either way, but if you want a little more efficiency, you can have a conditional branch that checks first to see if the bat has the Immortal state, rather than attempting to remove a state it might not even have.

▪ **Caution**   To be clear, when working on the Bat*2 troop, there should be a page 3 involving #2 Bat. Make sure you're removing Immortal status from the right bat!

There you have it! And it only took us four pages to create this quest as well.

Additional Exercises

Here are some extra exercises with which to flex your mental muscles.

1. Have an Autorun event on the world map that triggers when the player has five bat wings and forces them to fight a stronger bat (a sort of Bat King, if you will).

    -   As with every Autorun, make sure you have some way of escaping the page, or your game will loop it endlessly. Flipping a self-switch is as good a solution as any.

    -   I would make it so that the player cannot escape that fight.

2. Allow the NPC to sell his special brew to the player.

    -   It could be a special potion that both restores HP and removes some negative status effects. The man could sell the potion to the player via Shop Processing.

    -   Alternatively, it could be a one-time gift that boosts the stats of the character who drinks it.

Other Sidequest Ideas

As promised, we have come up with one sidequest that the player can go on at any time, once it is active, and another that has to be completed before a certain point in the game. Here are some other cool ideas that you can add to your own game.

1. A chest that works like *Final Fantasy* 9's Excalibur.

    -   Steps Taken and Play Time both work equally well for this. You could have a conditional branch for the treasure chest that requires Steps Taken or Play Time to be below a certain value. If the branch is true, then the chest will open; otherwise, a cryptic message will tell the player that the chest is sealed until the end of time.

2. A multistaged time-sensitive quest.

    -   The *Tales* series of RPGs (developed by Namco Bandai) are notorious for this. You have a quest that has five stages, but you have to finish the first stage before you beat the first boss and the second stage before you set sail to a new continent. On the new continent, you can start stage 3. Stage 4 requires that you not have uncovered the artifact of doom, while the last stage is permanently unlocked once you're on your way to the final dungeon.

    -   I'm not a huge fan of such types of quests, but they're not much harder to event than a regular time-sensitive quest. You just have to have each subsequent stage of the multi-quest check for the completion of the previous stage. If the player ever skips/misses a stage, he/she cannot reach the quest's conclusion.

3. A permanent sidequest that allows progression throughout the entire game.

- For this particular idea, I'm thinking about *Dragon Quest*'s Tiny Medals and *Grinsia*'s Old Glass Bottles. An NPC with a particular obsession wants you to collect all of the items of a certain type in the world. Each time you reach a milestone of items collected, it will give you a special item as a reward. It's something neat to do and look out for while traveling the world, and you can turn in the last collectible right before you end the game (or otherwise reach a point of no return).

In Chapter 10, I will be touching on a cool idea that could qualify as #3. But given the eventing involved and what you can do with it, I think it deserves a whole chapter's worth of material. The next chapter will be dedicated to the functionality that will make it possible.

Summary

In this chapter, I covered the concept of sidequests in RPGs, and we added a permanent sidequest to our game that could be done at any time, as well as a time-sensitive quest that must be completed before the player defeats Augustus. In the next chapter, we will discuss common events.

CHAPTER 9

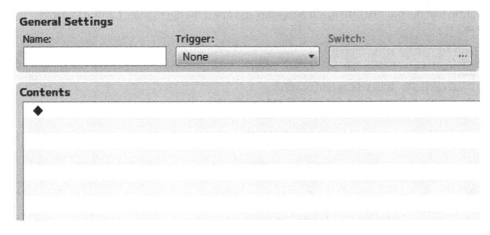

All About Common Events

This chapter is going to cover common events. You have probably seen the relevant tab within the RMMV Database already and are wondering what it's about. Well, here's the summary:

- A common event can be called using the *Common Event* command from any other event.

- It is useful for eventing things that you will repeat many times during your game. You can probably already think of two or three occasions on which this is true in the game we've been building throughout this book.

- A common event can have an Autorun or Parallel trigger, contingent on a certain conditional switch being on, as defined in the Common Events tab.

- Common events have a limit of one page—no more, no less.

- Common events are the only way to trigger events on item and skill use.

The final point is the most important to what we want to do in the next chapter. Of course, this is as good a time as any to show off the Common Events tab (Figure 9-1).

General Settings

Name:

Trigger:

None

Switch:

...

Contents

◆

Figure 9-1. *The Common Events tab of the RMMV Database*

© Darrin Perez 2016

D. Perez, *Beginning RPG Maker MV*, DOI 10.1007/978-1-4842-1967-6_9

Not much to it, literally. That should not come as a surprise, given that common events are just another type of event. A common event can have a trigger of None (in which case it will always trigger when called), Autorun, or Parallel. In the latter two cases, the conditional switch has to be on for the common event to trigger. We could have a two-line common event that contains the two Control Variable commands we use for our Parallel transfer events. There's a particularly neat item concept I learned how to event some time ago that I'm going to share in this chapter. Do you want to *Escape* from a dungeon automatically?

The Exit Item/Skill

Envision this scenario: The player has gotten through a particularly long dungeon and defeated the boss at the end. His/Her resources were sorely diminished, and he/she needs to get back to town. Most RPGs include a skill that automatically returns the player to the entrance to the dungeon, thereby bypassing the trip back.

To create an item or skill that will allow the player to exit a dungeon automatically, we'll need the following:

- A common event that checks to see which dungeon the player is currently in. If the player is not inside a dungeon, the event will return an error message. (You can also make it so that you can't escape from certain dungeons.)

- We have to update the world map's transfer event, so that it writes the dungeon location to a variable.

- We have to update our dungeons' relevant transfer events, so that if the player exits to the world map manually, the dungeon location variable is set to its default value.

- Last, we must actually create the item or skill that will hold this event.

Updating Our Transfer Events

First of all, we currently have two dungeons. (Given that the subquest well is right in town, let's not count it for the sake of this exercise.) The dungeon where the player finds Augustus will be 1, and the tower will be 2. I'm going to call the variable in question DungeonLocation, for the sake of clarity. In the world map's transfer events, you'll want to find the two that lead to our dungeons and insert the appropriate Control Variable command, like so:

```
◆If : X = 68
   ◆If : Y = 88
      ◆Control Variables : #0011 DungeonLocation = 1
      ◆Transfer Player : Stone Cave (15,27) (Direction: Up)
      ◆
   : End
   ◆
: End
◆If : X = 93
   ◆If : Y = 83
      ◆Control Variables : #0011 DungeonLocation = 2
      ◆Transfer Player : Tower 1F (20,37) (Direction: Up)
      ◆
   : End
   ◆
```

Then, in both of the dungeons, we find the transfer event that leads the player to the world map and have DungeonLocation set itself to 0 in those.

Creating the Exit Scroll

Next, let's create the item that will call the common event we want to make. Take a look at Figure 9-2 for details.

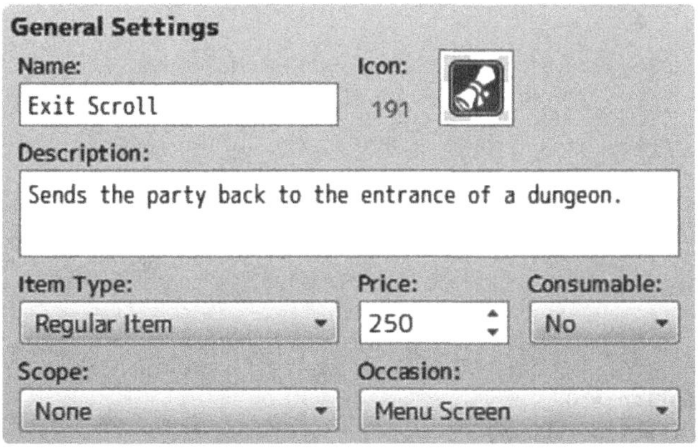

General Settings

Name: Exit Scroll

Icon: 191

Description: Sends the party back to the entrance of a dungeon.

Item Type: Regular Item

Price: 250

Consumable: No

Scope: None

Occasion: Menu Screen

Figure 9-2. *The Exit Scroll's general settings*

We have the Exit Scroll set so that it can only be used from the menu and is not consumed when used. Why? It's easier to handle item consumption within the event itself. Instead of just having the item consume itself, it will prompt a choice when used. It asks the player if he/she wants to leave the dungeon. If the player says no, then the item is left intact. On the other hand, when the player says yes, the event determines what dungeon the player is currently in and transfers the player to its entrance, consuming one Exit Scroll in the process.

Creating the Exit Event Logic with Common Events

I use two common events for the exit event logic. Here's the first common event:

- Name: ExitEvent

- Trigger: None

```
♦Text : None, Window, Bottom
:      : Would you like to leave the dungeon?
♦Show Choices : Yes, No (Window, Right, #1, #2)
: When Yes
   ♦Common Event : ExitEventBranches
   ♦
: When No
   ♦
:  End
```

It's nice and simple. We ask the player if he/she would like to leave the dungeon. If the player says no, we exit out of the event. If the player says yes, we call the second common event. Doing it this way reduces the clutter within one event. You could have a chain of common events, each calling the next one. The rest of the current common event is executed as applicable. For example, if you were to add a Control Variables command directly below the common event call, it would be processed before switching events. If you're using Autorun or Parallel events, you have to be particularly careful of chaining common events in that way, as it could get messy really fast. Here's the second common event called by the first:

```
♦If : DungeonLocation = 0
   ♦Text : None, Window, Bottom
   :      : You cannot use that here!
   ♦
: End
♦If : DungeonLocation = 1
   ♦Change Items : Exit Scroll - 1
   ♦Control Variables : #0011 DungeonLocation = 0
   ♦Transfer Player : World 1 (68,89) (Direction: Down)
   ♦
 : End
♦If : DungeonLocation = 2
   ♦Change Items : Exit Scroll - 1
   ♦Control Variables : #0011 DungeonLocation = 0
   ♦Transfer Player : World 1 (93,84) (Direction: Down)
   ♦
 : End
♦
```

DungeonLocation is equal to 0 at any time that the player is not within an applicable dungeon. If that is the case, the player will get an error message, and the event will end without consuming an item. When DungeonLocation has a value, the player is transferred to the entrance of the dungeon equal to that value, but not before consuming an Exit Scroll and setting DungeonLocation to 0. What if we wanted an item to allow the player to return to the last-visited town? We could have another variable to store the value of the last town visited by the player and then transport him/her directly inside when the item is used. You could even combine the DungeonLocation and TownLocation variables to make it so that you can only teleport to town if you are not inside a dungeon. That pretty much covers the use of common events, but this wouldn't be much of a chapter if I ended it this quickly, right? Instead, I'm going to write up some other ideas that I've created over time that involve the use of common events. But first, look at the skill version of Exit (Figure 9-3).

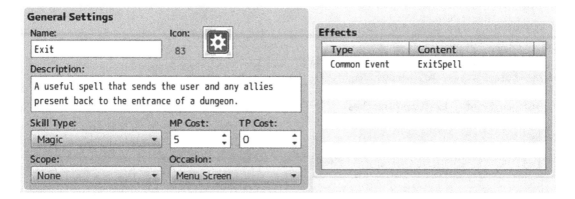

Figure 9-3. *The Exit skill uses the same common event as the Exit item*

Creating an Enemy with a Shifting Anti-element Barrier

Some of the most classic RPG battles involve a boss that has the ability to become immune to a certain element. That is as easy as creating a skill that grants an appropriate state. However, what happens if we want a *shifting* barrier? That's where common eventing comes in. Here's what we'll need:

- *Creating the skill*: It will have no other effects besides executing a common event.

- *A monster to use the skill*: We'll want it to begin battle with an anti-element barrier already, as the shifting skill *changes* the barrier that the user already has.

- *Three states that represent the elemental barriers*: Taking a look at the player's party, we see that they have relatively easy access to Fire, Ice, and Thunder magic, so let's have states for a barrier for each of those types.

- *The common event to govern the skill itself*

- *A small troop event for the monster that will use the barrier change skill*

I have future plans for the monster we're creating. (They'll be added as an encounter in Chapter 10.) For now, let's complete this exercise. Check Figure 9-4, to see our Barrier Change skill.

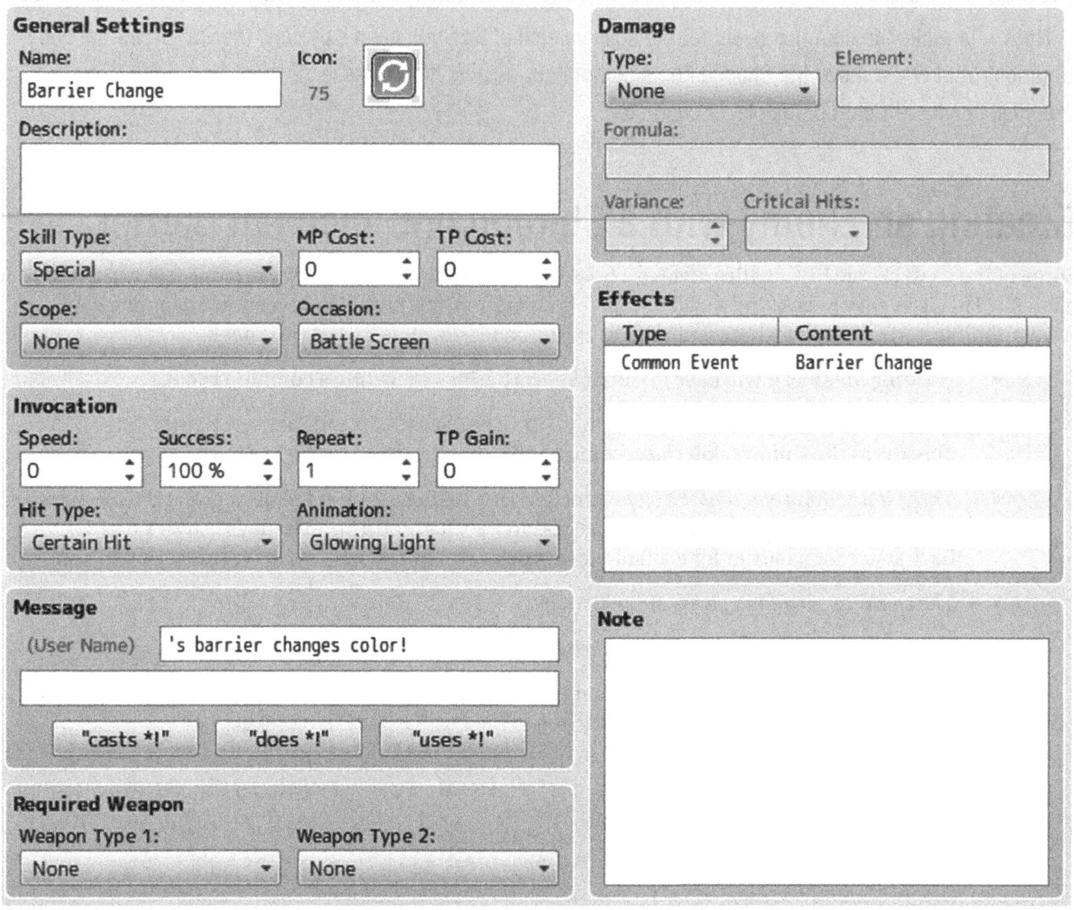

Figure 9-4. *The Barrier Change skill details*

Note the Scope of None in the Barrier Change skill. If we set the Scope to anything else, the game will return a message saying: "There was no effect on Spirit Essence!" every time Barrier Change is used. This occurs because the skill has no other effects besides displaying a simple message when someone uses the skill and calling the Barrier Change common event. Check Figure 9-5 to see the monster that will use the Barrier Change skill.

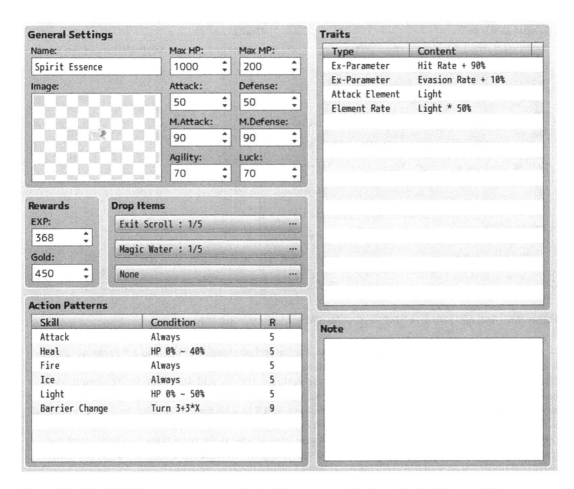

Figure 9-5. *The Spirit Essence, a new enemy that will use our associated new Barrier Change skill*

As you can see, we have it so that the Spirit Essence will use Barrier Change starting on turn 3 and will recast it every third turn after that. Heal is used when the monster is at 40% HP or less, and Light will be used when it is at 50% HP or lower. Next, let's create the appropriate states for our Barrier Change skill. I'll show off the first one and leave the other two to you. Figure 9-6 shows the first state.

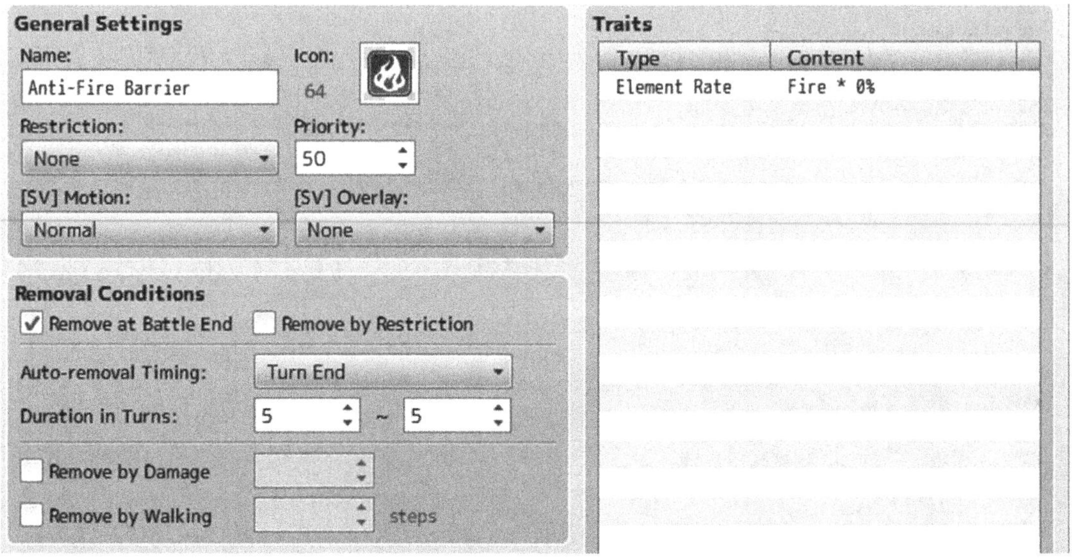

Figure 9-6. *Anti-Fire Barrier, one of three states affected by Barrier Change*

The Anti-Fire barrier is automatically removed at the end of a battle but will also auto-remove itself if five turns have passed. As its name suggests, someone affected by this state will sustain no damage from Fire-based attacks. You can copy this state to do the same for Anti-Ice and Anti-Thunder. The common event isn't much more of a hassle, to be honest. We want the skill, when used, to change the monster's active barrier, as previously noted. The relevant listing follows. You'll quickly notice the Jump to Label command used to great effect. A cursory look at the common event will show that Anti-Thunder Barrier would be up pretty much permanently, if we did not have those label jumps, as the conditions for each branch are met in the branch preceding it. The blank 1 in Change Enemy State represents the first enemy placed in a particular troop. For ease of use, we'll have our Spirit Essence be an army of one.

```
◆If : #1 is affected by Anti-Fire Barrier
    ◆Change Enemy State : #1, - Anti-Fire Barrier
    ◆Change Enemy State : #1, + Anti-Ice Barrier
    ◆Jump to Label : Done
    ◆
 : End
◆If : #1 is affected by Anti-Ice Barrier
    ◆Change Enemy State : #1, - Anti-Ice Barrier
    ◆Change Enemy State : #1, + Anti-Thunder Barrier
    ◆Jump to Label : Done
    ◆
◆If : #1 is affected by Anti-Thunder Barrier
    ◆Change Enemy State : #1, - Anti-Thunder Barrier
    ◆Change Enemy State : #1, + Anti-Fire Barrier
    ◆Jump to Label : Done
    ◆
 : End
◆Label : Done
```

Last, let's create a troop containing a single Spirit Essence and then add the following troop event:

Condition: Turn 0
Span: Battle
♦Change Enemy State : #1 Spirit Essence, + Anti-Thunder Barrier
♦Force Action : #1 Spirit Essence, Barrier Change, Random
♦

We want the initial barrier to be Anti-Fire. However, if we apply the state without using the Barrier Change skill, we won't get the skill use message. So we intentionally start one step away at Anti-Thunder and then force the Spirit Essence to use Barrier Change as the battle starts, setting it to the correct state. You can Battle Test this new troop with Harold and Marsha and then use the elemental spells to make sure that the monster is shifting barriers correctly.

■ **Note**   You can see which of the three barriers the enemy has at any time thanks to the fact that MV shows the states that are currently affecting any given battler in combat. Should you wish to prevent the player from seeing that information, you need only remove the relevant state icons from the three barrier states.

It's time for something a little more complicated.

Sneaky Like Ninjas: Creating the Smoke Bomb

I once wanted to create an item that allows the player to escape combat without fail. My initial attempts were functional but overly complex. After getting quite a bit of help, I learned of a solution that requires only a tiny bit of scripting. Suffice it to say that using the Escape effect available for items and skills is actually a bad idea. It will allow the player to flee *any* battle. Fighting the final boss? I'd rather not. Let's just Smoke Bomb out of there like ninjas. As you can see, that's a terrible idea. We want the player to be able to use the Smoke Bomb at any time he/she would be able to select the normal Escape command in the battle menu. As already noted, if you give an item the special Escape effect (you'll want to give the item itself a scope of User), the player will be able to retreat from any battle. To counter that, we need a way to make sure that the player is allowed to escape the battle. Make your way to the rpg_managers.js file, open it with your text editor of choice, and search for "BattleManager." You're looking for the start of the class (you'll know it when you find it, as there's a description of the class right above the first lines of code.) A few lines in, you'll see a variable named _canEscape. That variable shows up within the canEscape method in BattleManager and determines whether the player can escape from a particular battle. By default, the player can escape from every randomly generated battle and all event-created (Battle Processing) battles that have the Can Escape check box toggled. Conversely, escape from an event battle with Can Escape untoggled is impossible.

Now, let's create the common event that will handle the Smoke Bomb logic. Of particular note is the fact that you can use script code within conditional branches to the same effect as the more standard uses I have covered up to now. To call a method using a script, you use the format Class.method. That's why we have BattleManager.canEscape() in the following code:

```
♦If : Script : BattleManager.canEscape()
  ♦Comment : Escape = TRUE
  ♦Change Items : Smoke Bomb - 1
  ♦Text : None, Window, Bottom
  :     : You distract the enemy with the Smoke Bomb and
  :     : escape!
```

```
    ♦Abort Battle
    ♦
: Else
    ♦Comment : Escape = FALSE
    ♦Text : None, Window, Bottom
    :      : You can't escape from this fight!
    ♦
: End
♦
```

When the player uses a Smoke Bomb, we check to see if he/she can escape the fight in question. If canEscape returns true, the player can escape. In that case, we consume one Smoke Bomb, display a message, and abort the battle. If the player cannot, he/she will receive an error message saying as much, and the item will not be consumed. I'll leave the creation of the item up to you. Now, there are two more things to discuss before the end of this chapter. Here's the first . . .

Making Specific Random Battles Inescapable

We have created an item that can be used to escape from a battle with no fail rate, as long as the player is allowed to escape it normally. That brings up an interesting question: What happens if we want to make certain random battles inescapable? It's as easy as creating a new method within the BattleManager class:

```
BattleManager.setEscape = function(bool) {
    this._canEscape = bool;
};
```

Note I'll discuss plugins in Chapter 14. Much like the floor damage snippet given in Chapter 4, the snippet of code shown here would be better served packed into a plugin. Incidentally, we'll be packing both of those snippets into the same plugin, but more on that once it becomes relevant.

The preceding method is a simple one-liner. The bool inside the parentheses is a function parameter. Basically, we would express the new method in the form BattleManager.setEscape(bool), where bool should be true or false, as that is how canEscape is meant to be expressed (an assertion that you can verify by seeing how it is used within BattleManager). How do you use that new method? The easiest way is to have a troop event that triggers on Turn 0 and uses a script call for the new method. So, if you want to make it so that the player cannot escape from Slimes (for whatever reason), all you have to do is structure the troop event as follows:

```
Condition: Turn 0
Span: Battle
♦Script : BattleManager.setEscape(false)
```

Once the battle begins, you'll notice that it is impossible to escape, whether via the Escape command or the use of Smoke Bombs. In this way, it is possible to make troops that prevent the player from escaping when encountered.

> ■ **Note** Before moving on to the additional exercises, go ahead and add the Exit Scroll and Smoke Bomb items to Seaside's expanded shop (page 2 of the item shop that activates after the tower is cleared).

Additional Exercises

Before we end this chapter, I'll leave some more exercises for you to tackle concerning common events.

1. Create a note that someone would write before embarking on a long journey. Leave it on a table for the player to find and add to his/her inventory.

   - You can have the note display its text when the player grabs it. Then make it a Key Item that cannot be consumed and have the common event, if the player ever wants to read its text again. You can see an example of the note event in the second house of Seaside (the event is named Mysterious Note). The Mysterious Note Item is in Item Slot #20 and the Mysterious Note common event is in Common Event Slot #6.

2. Make a troop with three enemies, in which one enemy gives a random anti-elemental barrier to itself *and* its allies.

   - You can cover random with a variable similar to the seed we used for the treasure chest minigame. Just have the variable roll from 1 to 3.

   - Create one skill for each type of anti-elemental barrier.

   - The common event would have conditional branches for the three possible results. When the enemy with the skill uses it, the common event will trigger. The type of barrier will depend on the value of the variable and will be applied by means of Force Action. (Make sure you're applying Force Action to the skill user; it will be best if you only have one enemy that can use this skill.) Following is some sample code:

```
◆Control Variables : #0012 BarrierUp = Random 1..3
◆If : BarrierUp = 1
   ◆Force Action : #1, Anti-Fire Barrier, Last Target
   ◆
: End
◆If : BarrierUp = 2
   ◆Force Action : #1, Anti-Ice Barrier, Last Target
   ◆
: End
◆If : BarrierUp = 3
   ◆Force Action : #1, Anti-Thunder Barrier, Last Target
   ◆
: End
◆
```

You can find an example of this exercise in action in troop slot #252. The new skills are located in skill slots #247-#250, and the enemy that uses barrier-type skills on its party is in enemy slot #252.

Summary

In this chapter, I covered common events and several applications related to them. Among these applications are creating a Smoke Bomb item that allows guaranteed escape from nonforced encounters and a shifting-barrier skill. In the next chapter, I will cover all sorts of hidden things, such as treasures and passages.

CHAPTER 10

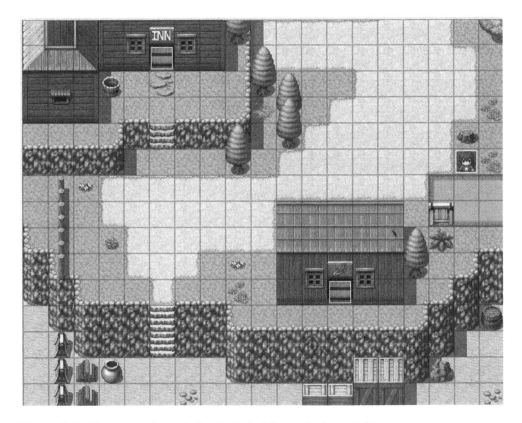

Hunting for Treasure and Other Hidden Things

Who doesn't like finding hidden things and ancient treasure? This chapter will be all about finding hidden treasure with the help of special items provided by NPCs or found in different locations. We'll apply what you have learned in the previous chapter to come up with all sorts of relevant things for the aspiring explorer and treasure hunter. First of all, we have to create a new establishment in Seaside. A treasure hunter is coming to town! You can see the treasure hunter's shop in Figure 10-1.

Figure 10-1. *The treasure hunter's shop is the building at the lower-right*

© Darrin Perez 2016

D. Perez, *Beginning RPG Maker MV*, DOI 10.1007/978-1-4842-1967-6_10

I reworked one of the buildings that lacked an entrance to create the treasure hunter's shop. The interior map is a tweaked premade Item Shop. We want the door to remain locked until Augustus has been defeated. Inside, behind the counter, we have the treasure hunter, who urges the player to pick up the sack at the nearby table when spoken to. The sack will contain this chapter's first item: the Compass.

⬛ **Note** I'll add the Treasure Hunter's Shop to the game as its own map. Alternatively, you could extend the Village Interiors map we created back in Chapter 4 to fit the new interior map.

The Compass

This item will be used to determine the player's current location, as well as enable the player to find hidden treasure chests in dungeons. The former can be accomplished with a three-line common event, while the latter will rely on the hidden chest events to require that the player possess the Compass (the Item Exists conditional). You can see the Compass item in Figure 10-2 and its associated common event immediately thereafter.

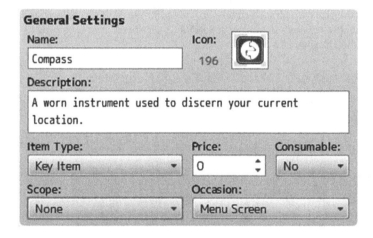

Figure 10-2. *The Compass Key Item to be used for treasure hunts*

- Name: Compass
- Trigger: None

```
◆Control Variables : #0002 X = Map X of Player
◆Control Variables : #0003 Y = Map Y of Player
◆Text : None, Window, Bottom
:    : Your current position is \V[2], \V[3].
◆
```

When the player uses the Compass from the menu, the game will poll the player's current X and Y position and display it in a text box. How will the player know where those chests are? The simplest way, and the one I'll be covering, is to have treasure notes that give the exact location of hidden chests, which makes it so that the player only needs to use the Compass to find them. That, of course, leaves the question of how the player will find those treasure notes. We can have the treasure hunter sell them! As already established in Chapter 7, eventing a shop with Show Choices is a pain, at best. Yet, we know that we want the treasure hunter to sell treasure notes that will lead the player to special loot. I have an alternate solution to our little quandary. We're going to use an event command we have not touched up to now: *Input Number*. First, let's come up with five hidden treasure locations (Figure 10-3).

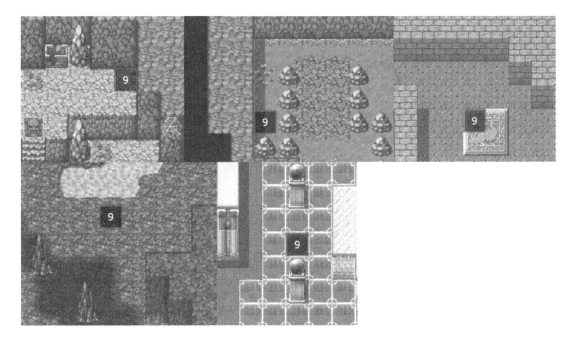

Figure 10-3. *The locations for the hidden treasure we will add to our game*

The ones listed in Figure 10-3 will do. I have marked the precise treasure locations with Region #9. From top left to bottom right, they are as follows:

- (11, 9) at the Stone Cave's first floor

- (54, 14) at the Stone Cave's second floor

- (15, 26) at Tower 1F

- (10, 23) at the Lava Cave

- (6, 9) at the Hall of Transference

How to Change Whether a Map Displays Its Name

For the sake of this exercise, it's time to give our dungeons proper names, so I'll call the first dungeon the Dark Cave. The second dungeon will be the Ruined Spire. Unoriginal, I know, but it serves our purposes. You can make it so that the game displays a location's name once and then no more (good for the first time a player reaches a new location). Displaying it is as easy as giving the location a name (by default, an RMMV game will display a location's name every time the player arrives at the area). I'll leave this as an exercise for you; however, if you decide to go through with this, you'll need switches for each location you would like to do this for. Additionally, you will have to have conditionals to make sure that the map name display is disabled on subsequent visits. Here's the example eventing for the first dungeon:

```
♦If : X = 68
   ♦If : Y = 88
      ♦Control Variables : #0011 DungeonLocation = 1
      ♦If : Dungeon1Visit is ON
         ♦Change Map Name Display : OFF
         ♦
      : End
      ♦If : Dungeon1Visit is OFF
         ♦Control Switches : #0027 Dungeon1Visit = ON
         ♦
      : End
      ♦Transfer Player : Stone Cave (15,27) (Direction: Up)
      ♦
   : End
   ♦
: End
```

I expanded the relevant transfer event to include the new content. If Dungeon1Visit is on, we disable the map name display. If Dungeon1Visit is off, we flip it on. This allows the dungeon's name to be displayed once. You'll want to make sure you have a Change Map Name Display : ON command for any transfer events leading out of that dungeon. Personally, I find this more of a hassle than it is worth and would rather either leave the map name blank or just let it display, no matter what. In any case, now you know, and learning is why you're here!

Creating Hidden Treasure Chests That Require the Compass to Be Found

We want to make hidden treasure chests that require the player to have the Compass. Once the player has the Compass, he/she can click the Action Button while standing directly over the spot in question and uncover hidden loot! I'll write out how the actual event should look like shortly, but I'll summarize it first.

- We can start from the Quick Treasure Event template. From there, remove the chest graphic from page 1 of the event. We want to fade out the screen, give the player a message that he/she is digging, and then have the player take a step back. That last part is arguably the most important. If you don't move the player's character out of the chest's square, he or she will be on top of the chest when it spawns.

- Before we fade the screen back in, use Set Movement Route to change the chest graphic from None to our desired sprite set. I chose the wooden chest graphic located below the default red chest set.

- We fade in the screen and announce that the player has found a hidden chest. The rest of the event plays out normally.

With that said and done, here's the promised code:

```
♦Fadeout Screen
♦Text : None, Window, Bottom
:      : You dig under your feet.
♦Set Movement Route : Player (Wait)
:                   : ◊Turn Right
:                   : ◊1 Step Backward
♦Set Movement Route : This Event (Wait)
:                   : ◊Image: !Chest(4)
♦Wait : 30 frames
♦Fadein Screen
♦Text : None, Window, Bottom
:      : You found a hidden chest!
♦Play SE : Chest1 (90, 100, 0)
♦Set Movement Route : This Event (Wait)
:                   : ◊Direction Fix OFF
:                   : ◊Turn Left
:                   : ◊Wait: 3 frames
:                   : ◊Turn Right
:                   : ◊Wait: 3 frames
♦Control Self Switch : A = ON
♦Change Items : [Elixir], + 1
♦Text : None, Window, Bottom
:      : Elixir was found!
```

You can copy-paste that same event for all of your hidden treasure needs.

■ **Note** The Turn Right movement command is used for the player in the previous event because of the nature of the hidden treasure. Since the event doesn't trigger until the player presses the Action Button, they could conceivably turn in a direction before activating the event that will cause the 1 Step Backward command to fail (and thus hang the game). Generally, if your hidden treasure location does not have free space in all four of its adjacent squares, you may be better served by forcing the player to turn in a specific direction before making him/her take the step back. I'll leave it as an exercise to the reader to determine in which of the other four hidden treasure locations such an extra command would be necessary.

The Treasure Hunter

Next, let's head back to Seaside and set up the treasure hunter NPC. We want him to do the following:

- Greet the player when talked to for the first time. He will tell him/her to check the sack on the nearby table.

- Once the player has grabbed the Compass, talking to the NPC again will prompt the character to talk about the shop that he has set up for aspiring treasure hunters. He will sell treasure notes.

- We run a common event to see which treasure notes the player already has. Then, if the player is still missing notes from the shop, the NPC will offer to sell treasure notes.

- If the player says yes, we call the common event for the treasure note shop.

Here's page 1 of the treasure hunter event:

```
◆If : Party has Compass
  ◆Text : None, Window, Bottom
  :     : Neat little instrument, that Compass. Follow it
  :     : and you'll never be lost again.
  ◆Text : None, Window, Bottom
  :     : Okay, fine. You still have to mind your
  :     : surroundings. But, it will help you find hidden
  :     : treasure. Isn't that exciting?
  ◆Show Choices : Yes, No (Window, Right, #1, #2)
  : When Yes
    ◆Text : None, Window, Bottom
    :     : I knew you'd say yes!
    ◆Jump to Label : Continue
    ◆
  : When No
    ◆Text : None, Window, Bottom
    :     : You only say that because you haven't done it before.
    ◆Jump to Label : Continue
    ◆
  : End
  ◆Label : Continue
  ◆Text : None, Window, Bottom
  :     : I'm running a Treasure Note shop. It will tell you
  :     : where to dig for treasure. Use that Compass to find
  :     : out your current location.
  ◆Text : None, Window, Bottom
  :     : Talk to me again if you want to buy Treasure Notes.
  ◆Control Self Switch: A = ON
  ◆
: Else
  ◆Text : None, Window, Bottom
  :     : Hello there! I have never seen you before, traveler.
  :     : Do you wish to embrace the path of the explorer?
  :     : Sure you do! Take a look at the sack over there.
  ◆Control Switches : #0028 THunterTalk = ON
  ◆
 : End
◆
```

As is usually the case for item-based conditionals, I turn "Create Else Branch" on, so that I can use that Else. In this case, we want to see if the player has the Compass in his/her inventory. If the player does not, the text box at the very end of the event will be shown, and a switch is flipped on that we'll use later for the sack that contains the Compass. If the player does have the key item, the treasure hunter will talk a little and give the player a false choice (as in, it doesn't matter what is answered). Then he'll talk about his treasure note shop and urge the player to talk to him again, if he/she wants to buy treasure notes. We flip self-switch A, which allows page 2 of this NPC event to be processed. Page 2 contains a greeting for the player and immediately calls a common event. Because there are a few things to process for the shop we wish to make, it's better to use common events to reduce clutter.

The Treasure Hunter's Treasure Note Shop

For the first common event, we start by checking whether the player has any treasure notes sold by the NPC already. To do that, we create a new variable called TreasureNotesForSale and set it to 5 within the common event (as the NPC will have five notes for sale). Then we create a conditional branch to check if the player has each of the treasure notes. For each note in the player's inventory, the value of TreasureNotesForSale is reduced by 1. If the player has all five treasure notes sold by the NPC, he will say as much via a message: "I don't have any treasure notes for sale!" Otherwise, he will say that he has X treasure notes for sale, where X is equal to the value of TreasureNotesForSale. Then, he will ask the player if he/she wishes to buy a treasure note. If the player says Yes, we call the second common event. If he/she says No, we end the conversation.

Here's the event code for the first common event:

- Name: Treasure Note Check

- Trigger: None

```
♦Control Variables : #0013 TreasureNotesForSale = 5
♦If : Party has Treasure Note 1
   ♦Control Variables : #0013 TreasureNotesForSale -= 1
   ♦
 : End
♦If : Party has Treasure Note 2
   ♦Control Variables : #0013 TreasureNotesForSale -= 1
   ♦
 : End
♦If : Party has Treasure Note 3
   ♦Control Variables : #0013 TreasureNotesForSale -= 1
   ♦
 : End
♦If : Party has Treasure Note 4
   ♦Control Variables : #0013 TreasureNotesForSale -= 1
   ♦
 : End
♦If : Party has Treasure Note 5
   ♦Control Variables : #0013 TreasureNotesForSale -= 1
   ♦
 : End
♦If : TreasureNotesForSale = 0
   ♦Text : None, Window, Bottom
   :     : I don't have any Treasure Notes for sale!
   ♦
 : Else
   ♦Text : None, Window, Bottom
   :     : I have \V[15] Treasure Notes for sale. Would you
   :     : like to purchase one?
```

```
     ♦Show Choices : Yes, No (Window, Right, #1, #2)
     : When Yes
       ♦ Common Event : Treasure Note Purchase
       ♦
     : When No
       ♦Text : None, Window, Bottom
       :     : Take care!
       ♦
     : End
     ♦
  : End
  ♦
```

For the second event, we have the player input a number from 1 to 5. If the NPC has that particular treasure note in stock, he'll give his price and ask if the player wants it. If the player already has that treasure note, the NPC will say as much. Check the following code to see the framework for the second common event:

```
  ♦Text : None, Window, Bottom
  :     : \C[3]Please input the Treasure Note number you would
  :     : like to purchase (1-5 are valid). Input 0 to cancel.
  ♦Input Number : TreasureNoteNumber , 1 digit
  ♦If : TreasureNoteNumber = 0
     ♦
  : End
  ♦If : TreasureNoteNumber = 1
     ♦If : Party has Treasure Note 1
       ♦Text : None, Window, Bottom
       :     : You already own that Treasure Note!
       ♦
     : Else
        ♦Text : None, Window, Bottom
        :      : That'll be 200 Gold, if you will.
       ♦Show Choices : Yes, No (Window, Right, #1, #2)
       : When Yes
         ♦If : Gold ≥ 200
            ♦Change Gold : - 200
            ♦Change Items : Treasure Note 1 + 1
              ♦Text : None, Window, Bottom
              :      : Thank you for your custom!
            ♦Play SE : Item1 (90, 100, 0)
            ♦Text : None, Window, Bottom
            :      : Received \C[2]Treasure Note 1\C[0]!
            ♦
         : Else
            ♦Text : None, Window, Bottom
            :      : You don't have enough gold!
            ♦
            : End
            ♦
```

```
      : When No
        ◆
      :  End
    ◆
  :  End
◆
: End
◆If : TreasureNoteNumber = 2
    ◆
: End
◆If : TreasureNoteNumber = 3
    ◆
: End
◆If : TreasureNoteNumber = 4
    ◆
:  End
◆If : TreasureNoteNumber = 5
    ◆
:  End
◆If : TreasureNoteNumber > 5
    ◆Text : None, Window, Bottom
    :      : I don't have a Treasure Note of so high a number!
    ◆
:  End
◆
```

I left the branches for treasure notes 2 through 5 empty, to save space, but they should also follow the structure laid out for treasure note 1.

■ **Note** \C[n] is one of the various modifiers you can apply to text. It changes the color of text placed after the modifier when used. \C[0] is white. The colors I have used in the preceding event are two of my favorite available in RMMV. (I've already used \C[2] quite a few times in this book.)

Following is a list of the colors I've most used in RMMV:

- \C[2] is orange. I like to use this for important/key items.

- \C[3] is green. I prefer to use this color when I'm writing messages that break the fourth wall, as it were. Because the initial message tells the player directly how to use the input box, it makes sense to differentiate it from what the NPC would say in-game.

- \C[18] is red. If you want to draw the player's attention to a particular word or phrase, you can't get much more emphatic than red.

- Incidentally, \C[32] and above are also white.

Giving the Player the Compass

That, of course, leaves us with creating the sack event that will give the player a Compass and actually add the treasure note items to the Database. Because we need the Compass to access the shop in-game, let's make that event first.

```
◆If : THunterTalk is OFF
    ◆Text : None, Window, Bottom
    :       : Oh, does that sack on the table intrigue you?
    :       : It used to belong to an old treasure hunter, but
    :       : he retired recently. Why don't you take it?
    ◆
:  End
◆If : ThunterTalk is ON
    ◆Text : None, Window, Bottom
    :       : There you go. Take it!
    ◆
:  End
◆Text : None, Window, Bottom
:       : Will you take it?
◆Show Choices : Yes, No (Window, Right, #1, #2)
:  When Yes
    ◆Text : None, Window, Bottom
    :       : Take a look inside. It's not the sack that's
    :       : important!
    ◆Text : None, Window, Bottom
    :       : You open the sack.
    ◆Play SE : Item1 (90, 100, 0)
    ◆Text : None, Window, Bottom
    :       : Harold finds a \C[2]Compass\C[0]!
    ◆Change Items : Compass + 1
    ◆Control Self Switch : A = ON
    ◆
:  When No
    ◆
:  End
◆
```

We check to see if the player has talked to the treasure hunter before. If he/she has, the NPC will urge him/her to take the sack. If not, he will give a little backstory to the sack and then urge the player to take it all the same. When the player does, he/she receives the Compass. As is usual for this type of event, we turn on a self-switch after the player has received the Compass and then have a second blank page that requires it. This will remove the sack graphic from the table once the player has the Compass.

Creating the Treasure Notes

As for the treasure notes, there are two ways to make them. Both ways are easy, but one of them is more efficient than the other.

- We can put the relevant treasure information in the Item description box.

- We can use a short common event to use Show Text commands for the same effect.

One way requires the additional use of common events, while the other requires only the item itself, so we'll be using the first option. See Figure 10-4 for the treasure notes, with their respective descriptions. As they share the same general settings, I copied the settings box once and just have screenshots of the different descriptions.

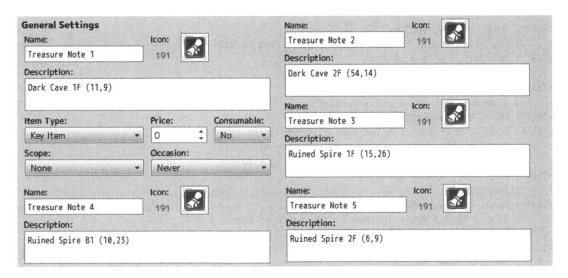

Figure 10-4. *The five treasure notes, with their location descriptions*

That just about sums up hidden treasure chests and how we can have the player find them. Of course, we can hide all sorts of things besides treasure. When the second boss was defeated by Harold and Marsha back in Chapter 6, we had him mention a dark castle far to the north. We have already added a bridge that the player can cross after defeating the first boss. However, to get the player from the second area to the third, let's make a hidden dungeon that the player must have the Compass to find. Instead of using a treasure note to hide the location, we can have an NPC at the arena tell the player about it.

A Hidden Location

We'll have our new NPC require the player to have cleared out Rank C before she'll tell them the exact location of the dungeon. Since different players have different play styles, we have to accommodate both of the following possibilities:

- The player talks to the NPC as soon as he/she notices her on a first visit to the arena.

- The player talks to the NPC for the first time after having cleared out Rank C of the arena.

A Page of Evented Plot

While we're at it, we might as well have her drop some plot tidbits. (Seems like so long ago that we last had something relevant to the main plot, right?) On that note, here's the first part of page 1 of the new NPC's event, full of juicy plot:

```
◆Text : None, Window, Bottom
:     : Oh, hello there. Haven't seen either of you before!
◆Text : Actor1(0), Window, Bottom
:     : My name is Harold.
◆Text : Actor3(7), Window, Bottom
:     : I am Marsha.
◆Text : None, Window, Bottom
:     : Nice to meet you! I'm Therese. I've been here
:     : for the better part of two years, honing my skills
:     : to be able to protect the villagers of Rocksdale.
◆Text : Actor1(0), Window, Bottom
:     : Rocksdale?
◆Text : None, Window, Bottom
:     : It's a hidden mountain town to the north of here.
:     :  Where are you two from, anyway?
◆Text : Actor3(7), Window, Bottom
:     : We hail from Seaside.
◆Text : None, Window, Bottom
:     : Wait, isn't that the port town to the far south?
◆Text : Actor1(0), Window, Bottom
:     : Not THAT far south, but yes.
◆Text : None, Window, Bottom
:     : Therese ponders her choice of words carefully.
◆Text : None, Window, Bottom
:     : I do not wish to call you two liars, but no one has
:     : left the southern continent in over fifteen years.
◆Show Balloon Icon: Player, Exclamation (Wait)
◆Text : Actor3(7), Window, Bottom
:     : Truly?
◆Text : None, Window, Bottom
:     : I'm afraid so.
◆Text : None, Window, Bottom
:     : Marsha thinks on Therese's words.
◆Text : Actor3(7), Window, Bottom
:     : Both continents are connected by a stone bridge.
◆Text : None, Window, Bottom
:     : Which disappeared without a trace around the same time.
◆Text : Actor1(0), Window, Bottom
:     : I think we stopped the source of that.
◆Text : None, Window, Bottom
:     : So it would seem.
```

Not much to say here. Plot is plot. Following are the final parts of page 1.

```
♦If : RankCClear is OFF
   ♦Text : None, Window, Bottom
   :     : Tell you what: If you can clear Rank C of the Arena,
   :     : I'll tell you where the entrance to the forest maze
   :     : lies. You can reach the northern part of this continent
   :     : through there.
   ♦
: End
♦If : RankCClear is ON
   ♦Text : None, Window, Bottom
   :     : You two have already cleared Rank C, so I think
   :     : it's safe to trust you.
   ♦Text : None, Window, Bottom
   :     : Go to (57,76) and examine the area. You should find
   :     : a secret entrance. You'll need a Compass. So, if you
   :     : don't already have one, you'd better find one.
   ♦If : Self Switch B is OFF
      ♦Control Self Switch : B = ON
      ♦Text : Actor1(0), Window, Bottom
      :     : Many thanks!
      ♦Text : Actor3(7), Window, Bottom
      :     : Your assistance is appreciated.
      ♦Text : None, Window, Bottom
      :     : No problem. Just do me a single favor.
      ♦Text : Actor1(0), Window, Bottom
      :     : Sure. What do you need?
      ♦Text : None, Window, Bottom
      :     : Stay safe. A nefarious monster lives in the castle
      :     : past the mountain range.
      ♦
   : End
   ♦
: End
♦Control Self Switch : A = ON
♦
```

Making Sure That the Player Has Progressed in the Arena

Here, we have the NPC confirm that the player has already cleared out Rank C of the arena. If he/she has, then the NPC will give the hidden location on the world map. Harold and Marsha will thank the NPC and self-switch B will be flipped on. Self-switch A is flipped at the end of page 1, regardless of what happens. Page 2 requires that self-switch A be flipped. If the player talked to Therese for the first time before completing Rank C, page 2 is where he/she will land when he/she talks to her again (otherwise, the player will skip to page 3).

```
♦If : RankCClear is  OFF
   ♦Text : None, Window, Bottom
   :     : Oh hi there! Go clear Rank C, would ya?
   ♦
: End
```

```
♦If : RankCClear is ON
   ♦Text : None, Window, Bottom
   :     : Congratulations on clearing Rank C!
   :     : I think it's safe to trust you two.
   ♦Text : None, Window, Bottom
   :     : Go to (57, 76) and examine the area. You should find
   :     : a secret entrance. You'll need a Compass. So, if you
   :     : don't already have one, you'd better find one.
   ♦If : Self Switch B is OFF
      ♦Control Self Switch : B = ON
      ♦Text : Actor1(0), Window, Bottom
      :     : Many thanks!
      ♦Text : Actor3(7), Window, Bottom
      :     : Your assistance is appreciated.
      ♦Text : None, Window, Bottom
      :     : No problem. Just do me a single favor.
      ♦Text : Actor1(0), Window, Bottom
      :     : Sure. What do you need?
      ♦Text : None, Window, Bottom
      :     : Stay safe. A nefarious monster lives in the castle
      :     : past the mountain range.
   ♦
   : End
   ♦
: End
♦
```

If the player has yet to clear Rank C when he/she talks to Therese again, she'll urge him/her to go do so. If the player has cleared Rank C, we have a similar sequence play out, in which Therese tells the player where to press the Action Button to find the hidden dungeon. Page 3 is processed when self-switch B has been turned on and consists of Therese asking if the party needs her to repeat her directions. If they say yes, she will do so.

■ **Note**   Instead of having page 3 work in this manner, you could have Therese give the party a note that repeats her words via calling a common event. In that case, you could just have her say some form of greeting when self-switch B is on instead.

```
♦Text : None, Window, Bottom
:     : Hello there! Do you need me to repeat my directions?
♦Show Choices : Yes, No (Window, Right, #1, #2)
: When Yes
   ♦Text : None, Window, Bottom
   :     : Go to (57,76) and examine the area. You should find
   :     : a secret entrance, so long as you have a Compass.
   ♦
: When No
   ♦Text : None, Window, Bottom
   :     : Ok. Stay safe, you two!
   ♦
: End
♦
```

The player now knows to look at 57, 76 in the world map to find a hidden dungeon.

Creating Our Hidden Location

Using Load, add Swamp to our map list. Then, let's place an event triggered by the Action Button at that location that leads to that new area. We want to make sure the player cannot find the location without having the Compass, so you'll want to set the *Item: Compass* condition on page 1 of the event. As for the transfer event, it looks like this:

```
♦Text : None, Window, Bottom
:     : You found a hidden location!
♦Transfer Player : Swamp (18,37) (Direction: Up)
♦
```

On that map, you'll want to set up the appropriate transfer events. The player arrives at the southern end of the area and must make their way to the northern end as displayed in Figure 10-5. Note how I tweaked the area immediately around the northern cliff to add an entrance that will lead to our game's third dungeon.

Figure 10-5. *The area that connects the world map with our game's third dungeon*

As usual, you'll want a Parallel event to cover the transfer locations for this area. The cave entrance in this area should lead into our third dungeon, where I will take the time to talk about the last type of hidden thing that I will cover in this chapter.

Hidden Passages

For those times when you want players to explore off the beaten path or otherwise flex their minds to figure out how to reach the end of the dungeon, hidden passages do the trick. For this exercise, we will require the following:

1. Go to the Tilesets tab in the Database. Then find the Dungeon tileset and add Dungeon_A4 to slot D. This will allow us to use certain tiles from tileset A for eventing purposes.

2.   Click over to tileset A in Dungeon, making sure that Passage is selected on the right side of the page, and set the Transparent tile to passable. Passable tiles have a circle instead of an x.

3.   Add the Forest of Decay, Ice Cave, and Forest maps to your project. They will make up our third dungeon. Make it so that the cave entrance in the Swamp transfers the player to the Forest of Decay.

I used a screenshot (Figure 10-6) to show the greater extent of the changes that we will be making to the stock dungeon. Mainly, we want to restrict free passage through the dungeon, such that the player has to find and use the secret passages to progress through the floor. I used the Fill tool to replace the Grass Maze roof tiles with Darkness tiles (this allows the secret passages to remain secret) and then painted in the secret passages with Transparent tiles.

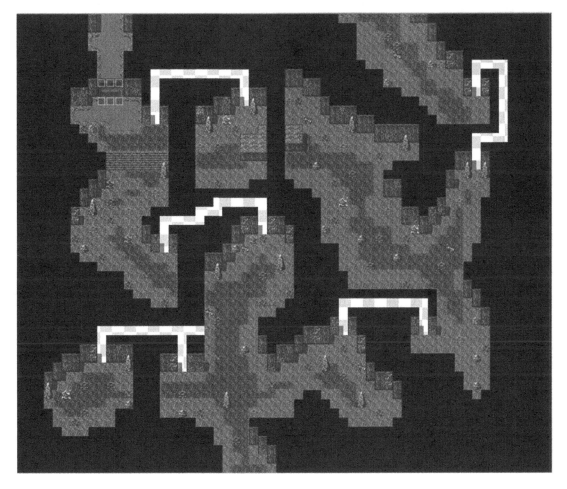

Figure 10-6. *The Forest of Decay, first floor of our third dungeon, tweaked to include various secret passages*

You can easily see each of the secret passages added to the Forest of Decay, given that Transparent tiles display as white in MV's map editor (they used to display as a shade of blue in Ace's map editor, so for screenshot creation, I appreciate the change as it makes the passages easier to see). Of course, if we leave the passages as-is, they won't be too secret. On that note, let's add a few events to hide the passages from plain sight. Figure 10-7 shows how those events would look on one of our secret passages.

Figure 10-7. *One of the secret passages in the first floor of the dungeon*

- Once you have Dungeon_A4 in Dungeon's D tileset, you can use wall and roof tiles to complement your event graphics. Here, we have two individual events.

- The top wall tile is Above Characters.

- The bottom wall tile is Same As Characters. You can have it so that the player effortlessly passes through the tile by checking Through in that event. What I do is ever so slightly more involved.

```
♦Text : None, Window, Bottom
:     : You find a secret entrance!
♦Control Self Switch: A = ON
♦
```

Mainly, I have a two-page event, in which page 1 announces that the player has found a secret entrance. Then, I flip on self-switch A, which causes the tile to disappear, leaving behind a transparent tile (which appears black in-game) that allows the player to continue forth. On that note, you'll want to make sure that there are transparent tiles beneath each of the secret passage events. That will allow the player to actually walk through one side to reach the next. For side-facing secret passages, such as the one in Figure 10-8, you can assign a Same As Characters priority to the tile connecting the passage to the dungeon.

Figure 10-8. *A side-facing secret passage*

When the player clicks the Action Button, we can display the same text message as in the previous event and change that event's priority to Above Characters. In this case, you wouldn't remove the event graphic on page 2, so that the player passes under the event tile.

■ **Note** Of course, given the fact that we filled in the Forest of Decay with Darkness tiles, this would only make the side-facing secret passage stick out like a sore thumb. I'll be leaving it as-is in the source code folder, for illustrative purposes, but feel free to remove the image from that particular passage event in your own project.

In any case, it's also a good time to mention that you will notice small graphical discrepancies, as RMMV won't try to meld the wall event graphics as it would if you had drawn them with the Map Editor. Figure 10-9 is an example of what I mean. Notice the vertical lines on either side of the secret passage and the horizontal line splitting the two events.

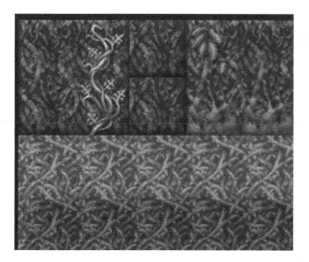

Figure 10-9. *A picture of the visible discrepancy when terrain tiles are used as event graphics*

This can be highly taxing on the map event cap, given that you'll want to use a single event for each tile that needs to be covered up. In our dungeon's case, that would be two events per front-facing wall (you can get away with a single roof tile for the side-facing passage). As a result, it's best to use this type of eventing sparingly.

▪ **Tip**   Another cool use of passable transparent tiles in Darkness is to make areas without illumination. You could just have corridors that disappear into nothingness and start into new areas unexpectedly.

▪ **Note**   We will be adding enemies and equipment to our Database in Chapter 12. The enemies will be used to populate our third dungeon and the region surrounding the hidden location. The equipment will be used to populate an upcoming shop as well as possible treasure for the player to find in chests throughout the dungeon.

Additional Exercises

That just about concludes this chapter. Here are a few exercises to apply your learned knowledge:

1.   Create a new item that can be used to detect secret passages.

   • You could have secret passage events require the player to have the item in his/her inventory to actually find it, much as we had the hidden location require the Compass.

   • In the source code project, you'll find that I created a Lantern item (that happens to be the fourth hidden treasure; the one located in the Lava Cave) that is used to find the secret passages. If the player does not have the Lantern, the passage will not be uncovered.

2. Make it so that the player must learn of the dungeon's location from Therese before he/she can go find it.

   - You would want to do this to stop *sequence breaking* (that is, players doing things out of an intended order). I don't mind sequence breaking at all, but I'm sure there are people out there who do.

   - You would just need a switch that is flipped on when Therese's self-switch B is on. Then, you require the player to have the Compass and to have flipped on that switch to progress.

Summary

This chapter covered hidden things that can be implemented throughout the course of a game, such as treasure and passages. The knowledge of common events gained in Chapter 9 was used to great effect for the hidden treasure. In addition, we have placed the foundation for our third dungeon. In the next chapter, we will discuss puzzles and how to create them within RMMV.

PART 3

■ ■ ■

The Finishing Touches

We have come a long way from the start of the book, wouldn't you agree? In that time, we have done the following with our game:

- Created two dungeons and started working on a third
- Made two fun minigames for our players to distract themselves from the main narrative
- Created a pair of sidequests for much the same purpose
- Created a town and an overarching plot for the player to follow

Our player learned that a great evil lies in a castle to the northeast of the second continent. So he/she set off to the hidden dungeon to find a way to reach the dark castle. This last part of the book will be dedicated to finishing up our game. But, don't fret! I still have some neat things lined up in what's left!

CHAPTER 11

Puzzles

A common mainstay of most RPGs, both new and old, is the puzzle. Defeating monsters and other assorted baddies to get through dungeons can be fun for quite a while, but puzzles break the monotony and make it so that the players have to flex their mental muscles as well as their alter egos' physical muscles. In this chapter, I will present three puzzles that I first devised in my time working with RPG Maker VX Ace, newly adapted for RMMV. Without further ado, let us begin with the first one.

Slippery Floors!

Perhaps the bane of any gamer who has played RPGs for even a short time, slippery floors prevent you from controlling your character until it slams face-first into an obstacle. Creating slippery floors is actually a highly nuanced process in RMMV eventing, as there are many things to take into consideration. For example:

- You must prevent the player from inputting actions as he or she is slipping.

- You must define what constitutes a slippery floor, unless you have an entire floor full of such tiles.

- You want the game to auto-input movement commands in the same direction, until the player gets stuck against an obstacle.

- You have to determine when the player has been stopped by an obstacle, so that he or she can move manually again.

The good news is that, once you understand what you need to do, you only require a single event to handle everything.

Creating Our Staging Area

First, however, I'm going to unveil the tweaked version of the Ice Cave. After all, what else would the player character slip on than ice? Take a look at Figure 11-1 to see the area map. I removed most of the dark ice scattered throughout the level, instead concentrating it into a relatively large part of the northern portion of the map. I also added some rocks (the Lumps of Ice tile in the B tab of the Dungeon tileset, to be precise) to control where the player can slide to at any given time. Besides that, I added a secret passage that provides a shortcut the player can open after completing the sliding puzzle. Basically, this ensures that the player only has to complete the puzzle once; they can bypass it if they ever have to pass through this area again.

© Darrin Perez 2016
D. Perez, *Beginning RPG Maker MV*, DOI 10.1007/978-1-4842-1967-6_11

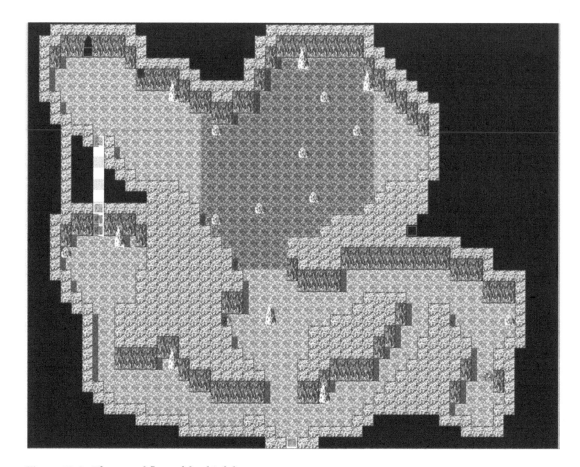

Figure 11-1. *The second floor of the third dungeon*

Before we work on our sliding puzzle, I think this most recent secret passage bears mentioning. Unlike the various passages in the Forest of Decay we added in Chapter 10, we only want this one to be available if the player has already completed the puzzle. In other words, *we only want the entrance to open if the player is approaching from the far end of the passage.* This is surprisingly easy to do. As you can see in Figure 11-1, there are a total of four events. Let's break them down quickly:

- The first event (from top to bottom) functions like the secret entrance events in the Forest of Decay. The event has an initial page that is Same As Characters. Unlike the previous front-facing events, the second page of this event has a priority of Above Characters (recall that we can do this so that the player passes under the tile). We don't want to remove the event's image, as that will give an unintended visual effect.

- The second and third events have a single page with Above Characters priority. These are meant only for the player to pass under, nothing more.

- The last event is where our one-way entrance is. The last page of the event is a blank image over a Transparent tile and Below Characters priority. The page before that has the following event code, with. a priority of Same As Characters and a Trigger of Action Button.

```
♦If : Player is facing Down
   ♦Text : None, Window, Bottom
   :      : You find a weak section of ice and open the way!
   ♦Control Self Switch : A = ON
   ♦
 : End
♦If : Player is facing Up
   ♦Text : None, Window, Bottom
   :      : The ice here appears to be weak. Unfortunately, you'll
   :      : need to strike it from the other end to open the way.
   ♦
 : End
♦
```

Not much to tell, really. We take advantage of the player-facing conditional (which, as you might recall, we used back in Chapter 7 for the dragon statue event) to make sure the player is facing downward when interacting with the event. If they are, they can clear out the ice and create the shortcut. If not, they will be forced to navigate the sliding puzzle to enter through the other side. Now then, I think it's time to slide on ice!

Eventing Our Sliding Puzzle

We'll begin by defining the icy floor as slippery, through the use of terrain tags. You could use regions as well. The particular tile I'm using is Dark Ground G (Ice Cave), located within the A tab of the Dungeon tileset. Once that is done, we can create the event to hold our slippery floor logic. The event in question has three pages. Here's page one of the event. It has a Trigger of Parallel.

```
♦Control Variables : #0002 X = Map X of Player
♦Control Variables : #0003 Y = Map Y of Player
♦Get Location Info : TerrainTag, Terrain Tag, ({X},{Y})
♦If : TerrainTag = 1
   ♦Control Self Switch : A = ON
   ♦
 : End
♦
```

As we do with most of our Parallel events, we have it write the player's current location to a pair of variables and then fetch the location info for the tile that the player character is standing on at that moment. Next, we have a conditional branch that triggers only if the Terrain Tag is equal to 1. If it is, we set the event's self-switch to A in preparation for page 2 of the event. Following, you can see page 2. It has a Trigger of Autorun and a conditional of Self Switch A.

```
♦If : TerrainTag = 1
   ♦Loop
      ♦Set Movement Route : Player (Skip, Wait)
      :                    : ◊Walking Animation OFF
      :                    : ◊ Speed: 5
      :                    : ◊ Frequency: 5
```

```
    ◆Label : Repeat
    ◆Control Switches : #0030 WalkMovement = OFF
    ◆Set Movement Route : Player (Skip, Wait)
    :                    : ◊1 Step Forward
    ◆Control Variables : #0019 X' = Map X of Player
    ◆Control Variables : #0020 Y' = Map Y of Player
    ◆If : X' = X
       ◆If : Y' = Y
           ◆Control Self Switch : B = ON
           ◆Break Loop
           ◆
       : Else
           ◆Control Variables : #0002 X = Map X of Player
           ◆Control Variables : #0003 Y = Map Y of Player
           ◆Jump to Label : Repeat
           ◆
       : End
       ◆
    : Else
        ◆Control Variables : #0002 X = Map X of Player
        ◆Control Variables : #0003 Y = Map Y of Player
        ◆Jump to Label : Repeat
        ◆
    : End
    ◆
  : Repeat Above
  ◆
 : End
◆
```

Page 2 starts with the same Terrain Tag conditional branch that marked the end of page 1. The first event command after the branch is Loop. Event commands within a Loop repeat endlessly until you use a Jump To Label (or the Break Loop event command) to escape the loop. In essence, an Autorun event is a loop (that's why it is so easy to accidentally hang your game using one, if you forget to use a self-switch or some other method to break out of the event page).

The first order of action when the event enters its loop is to make it so that the player appears to be sliding on air. As mentioned in Chapter 2, turning off a character's walking animation will accomplish precisely that. We can increase the speed at which the player slips on ice by using Change Speed and increasing its value. I set it to 5. Change Frequency does nothing in this particular exercise, but I kept it there for testing purposes. You'll see why it does nothing as I reveal more of the event. The last thing I placed in that sample code was Label: Repeat. That was not a coincidence. Everything after that label will be repeated until a certain condition is met (more on that later). As of this time, the player character has no walking animation. We want to have a dedicated switch that is off when the player cannot move and is flipped on when he/she can. (You could invert the states so that the switch is on when the player cannot move. Just make sure you keep track of the fact.) WalkMovement will be that switch. On Page 3, we'll have a conditional branch that checks to see if WalkMovement is off. If it is, we restore the player's walking animation and normalize his/her speed. But, I'm getting ahead of myself.

When the player is found to be on slippery ground, he/she will slip uncontrollably in his/her current direction. It is extremely important that you toggle both the Skip If Cannot Move and Wait For Completion check boxes. If the former is untoggled, the game will hang as soon as the player reaches an obstacle. If the latter is untoggled, the event will not work. (Give it a try and note how the character moves on the icy terrain.) Next, I assign a new pair of variables to store the player's current X and Y coordinates after moving one space. Why? Well, recall the last item in our list of requirements for a sliding puzzle. We need to check to see if the player has been stopped by an obstacle.

We can figure that out by comparing the values of X' and Y' with the values of X and Y. The only time X' and X (and Y' and Y) will be identical is when the player is stationary. How can I guarantee this? It all comes down to the event flow. At the very top of the event, we write the player's location to X and Y. After moving a single space (or failing to, if the character is already adjacent to an obstacle), we write his/her new location to X' and Y'.

We escape the loop if the values of X' and Y' are equal to the values of X and Y; otherwise, we loop back to the top of the sequence.

A Note About Redundant Code

You may have already noticed that we don't actually require that Loop command. That's something really important to learn in programming in general and RMMV specifically: *Don't do in ten lines what you can do in nine or fewer.* In other words, make your events as efficient as possible. As you gain proficiency with RMMV, you'll probably find cases in which you created an event that has some fat that can be trimmed with no negative effects. In this case, the Loop command doesn't take anything away from the slippery floor event, but you can use labels to achieve the same effect.

Eventing Our Sliding Puzzle (Continued)

Here's the last page of the slippery floor event. It has a conditional of Self Switch B and an Autorun Trigger:

```
♦If : WalkMovement is OFF
   ♦Set Movement Route : Player (Skip, Wait)
   :                   : ◊Walking Animation ON
   :                   : ◊Speed: 4
   :                   : ◊Frequency: 3
   ♦Control Switches : #0030 WalkMovement = ON
   ♦Control Self Switch : A = OFF
   ♦Control Self Switch : B = OFF
   ♦
: End
♦
```

This is where we go if the player is stationary after bumping into an obstacle. We check to make sure that WalkMovement is off and restore the player character's walking animation and set its speed back to 4. We set WalkMovement to ON. Similarly, we take both self-switches that have been turned on and toggle them off. Now, we're all set. Think hard about what the event is doing, and see if you can trim it down some more.

Creating the Icy Area

Of course, we've gone through all the trouble of creating this event. It wouldn't be proper to just have it there doing nothing. Hence, let's make a little ice maze. You can already see it in a zoomed-out state in the full-map screenshot, but Figure 11-2 shows a zoomed-in picture of the relevant area.

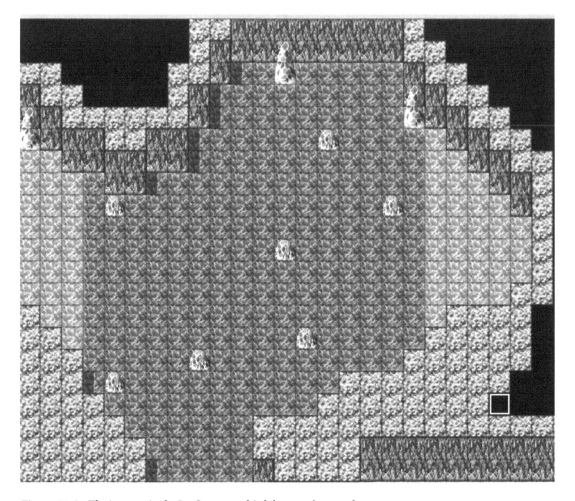

Figure 11-2. *The ice area in the Ice Cave, our third dungeon's second area*

Note the small section to the east of the slippery ground. That would be a good place to put some chests to reward exploration. You can add or remove obstacles, as wanted, to make it easier or harder to reach the eastern niche or the exit to the area.

An Intermission

Now then, let's add the third and final floor to our dungeon, to prepare it for the second puzzle of this chapter (see Figure 11-3).

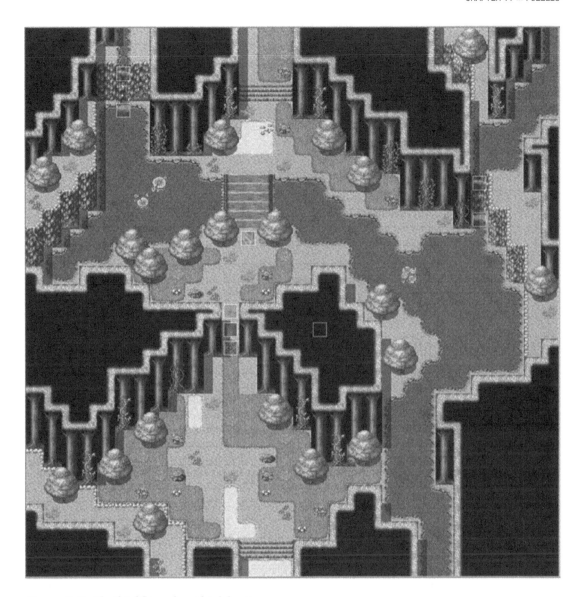

Figure 11-3. *The third floor of our third dungeon*

I didn't really do much for this third floor. As you can see, I added a tree on the left side of the bridge, such that the player needs to pass in between the trees to reach the exit. More immediately, I reduced the size of the gap in the treeline for much the same reason. The door you can see blocking access past the treeline is the protagonist of our next puzzle.

■ **Tip** To add the pair of events above the door, you'll need to add the Outside_A4 tileset to tab D of the Outside tileset.

Riddles!

Riddles are one of my favorite ways of flexing my gray matter. Quite a few RPGs have one quest or another that requires solving a riddle. For this exercise, we'll have that locked door pose a riddle to the player when he/she interacts with it. If the player can answer the riddle correctly, the door will open; otherwise, it will remain shut, patiently waiting.

Overview

How do we begin? We have two ways of handling a riddle.

- We could use Show Choices to display five possible answers and a Cancel option. Alternatively, we could have Show Choices display six answers and set the Cancel option to Disallow (forcing the player to choose an answer) or Branch (and then have a Continue/Cancel branch pop up if the player would rather not try to answer).

- We can use Name Input Processing to have the player write his/her answer to the riddle and then have a conditional branch that triggers if the answer is correct.

I'll be showing off the second method, as its eventing is a little more involved.

Our Riddle of Choice

The first order of business is to figure out what riddle we want the player to solve. I'll be using a classic riddle solved by Oedipus. Here it is (well, one translation of it, anyway): "What is that which has one voice and yet becomes four-footed and two-footed and three-footed?" (The traditional answer for that, by the way, is man. For the purposes of this exercise, we'll make *human* the answer.) As the correct answer has five letters, we want the input box generated by the Name Input Processing command to have a limit of five characters. As you may have already noticed, we are using this event command in quite an unconventional way. It is intended as the means of changing a character's name. For example, you could have a Name Input Processing event that allows the player to change Harold's name to something else. Here, we want to use the command to allow the player to answer a riddle.

Creating Our Riddle Event

To begin, you'll want to make your way to the Actors tab of the Database and increase the maximum number of actors from four to five. Once you do that, you'll get a blank actor on the new slot. That's exactly what we want. You could have a portrait for the riddle giver in this way, if you so desire. Because the player is talking to a door, we'll skip that. Next, we have to write the player's input into a variable. This is where we call upon scripting once again to come to our aid. We need scripting for four small things:

1. Placing the blank actor's name into a variable. We need to find out where RMMV stores actor names.

2. Using a bit of JavaScript to make the player's answer case-insensitive.

3. Using the Script option in the Conditional Branch command to write out the conditional we need.

4. For subsequent attempts, we want to clear out the blank actor's name before the player tries again.

You might wonder why at all we have to do this. After all, Conditional Branch also has an option on page 2 to check for a particular actor's name. Well, let's follow that thought process and work out a simple riddle event. In theory, your riddle event could look as simple as this:

```
♦Text : None, Window, Bottom
:      : What is that which has one voice and yet becomes
:      : four-footed and two-footed and three-footed?
♦Name Input Processing : #0005, 5 characters
♦If : Name of #0005 is human
   ♦Text : None, Window, Bottom
   :      : Correct.
   ♦
: Else
   ♦Text : None, Window, Bottom
   :      : Wrong.
   ♦
: End
♦
```

We have a single text box giving the riddle to be solved, and then a screen comes up, so that the player can write in his/her answer. The screen in question is displayed in Figure 11-4.

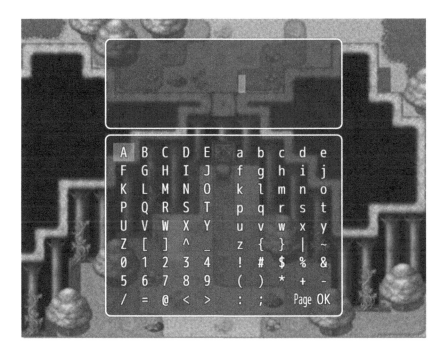

Figure 11-4. *The Name Input Processing event command in action*

However, as you'll quickly find, if you do not write *human* exactly as I did in the relevant sentence, you will receive an error message. After all, the conditional branch is looking for "human," not "hUmAn" or "HUMAN." It also doesn't solve the minor problem that the blank actor's name will not be cleared if the player writes an incorrect answer. So, let us begin with our small snippets of JavaScript.

Finding How RMMV Handles Actor Names Within Its Code

First, we have to find out how RMMV handles actor names within the code. A good place to start our search is the code that governs the Conditional Branch command. After all, one of the possible conditionals involves inputted names. So, open the rpg_objects.js file with your text processor of choice and run a search for "Conditional Branch" The Find function will place you near the end of the file. Scroll down from where you land until you find this part of the code.

```
case 4:  // Actor
    var actor = $gameActors.actor(this._params[1]);
    if (actor) {
        var n = this._params[3];
        switch (this._params[2]) {
        case 0:  // In the Party
            result = $gameParty.members().contains(actor);
            break;
        case 1:  // Name
            result = (actor.name() === n);
            break;
```

From this, we learn that whatever our end result looks like, it has to involve $gameActors in some capacity. As it turns out, that is correct. There *is* a Game_Actors class within MV's code (it's also located within rpg_objects.js), and checking it out reveals two tidbits. The first is in the class description: *The wrapper class for an actor array.* An *array* in programming is a list of items. In this case, Game_Actors combines all of the relevant actor information into a single array. The second tidbit is the actor method within Game_Actors, shown here:

```
Game_Actors.prototype.actor = function(actorId) {
    if ($dataActors[actorId]) {
        if (!this._data[actorId]) {
            this._data[actorId] = new Game_Actor(actorId);
        }
        return this._data[actorId];
    }
    return null;
};
```

In essence, it means that, if we want to get something related to an actor within MV, we need to start the line of code with $gameActors.actor(n), where n is equal to the actor's ID in the Database. In this case, we want a specific actor's name, so let's head on over to Game_Actor, where we're almost immediately greeted by the information following:

```
Game_Actor.prototype.initMembers = function() {
    Game_Battler.prototype.initMembers.call(this);
    this._actorId = 0;
    this._name = '';
```

```
this._nickname = '';
this._classId = 0;
this._level = 0;
this._characterName = '';
this._characterIndex = 0;
this._faceName = '';
this._faceIndex = 0;
this._battlerName = '';
this._exp = {};
this._skills = [];
this._equips = [];
this._actionInputIndex = 0;
this._lastMenuSkill = new Game_Item();
this._lastBattleSkill  = new Game_Item();
this._lastCommandSymbol = '';
```

Quite a few variable assignments, aren't there? For the purposes of this exercise, all you have to know is that the listed attributes are contained within the array created by $gameActors. This is what you would need to write in the Script box of Control Variables to fetch an actor's name: $gameActors.actor(n)._name (note that there's a dot right after the right parenthesis and then an underscore directly after that).

⬛ **Caution**   Make sure that you write _name and not name. Writing the latter will instead try to write the contents of the name function into the variable, which is not at all what we want to do.

⬛ **Note**   Experiment with trying to grab the other attributes in the same way. Just replace _name with the attribute in question and see what happens. Level, in particular, could be pretty useful in creating areas that can only be accessed if a player is of a certain level or higher.

Using the Script Option to Store and Modify Text in a Variable

To be precise, we'll be storing an actor name within the Riddle1 variable, but this can be applied to any other type of text you can think of. While the most common use of variables in RMMV is to store numbers, text can fit in there just fine. In any case, now that we know how to call for a specific actor's name, we can write that value into a variable by using the Script option:

◆Control Variables : #0016 Riddle1 = $gameActors.actor(5)._name

That's what the event command should look like, once you're done (5 is the database ID of the new blank actor for this specific exercise). Next, we have to make sure that the player receives a positive response for a correct answer, no matter how it is written. There is a pair of methods within JavaScript called toLowerCase() and toUpperCase() that can be used to modify text. Suppose the player writes "Human" in the name input screen. If we modified it with .toLowerCase(), it would become "human." On the other hand, .toUpperCase() would turn it into "HUMAN." For this exercise, I'll be using .toLowerCase(). What we want to do is modify the contents of the Riddle1 variable after the previously pictured event command has been processed. It's as simple as doing the following:

- Finding Script on page 3 of the event command list

- Writing in $gameVariables.setValue(16,$gameActors.actor(5)._name.toLowerCase()) (replace 16 with whichever variable ID you are using for your riddle)

■ **Note** setValue is a method that can be used for $gameVariables (and $gameSwitches) to, as the name explicitly says, set the value of a particular variable or switch. For $gameVariables, it is expressed in the form $gameVariables.setValue(x,y) where *x* is the variable ID in the Database and *y* is the value to place within that variable.

Finishing Up Our Riddle Event

Next, we need a conditional branch, to check whether the value of our riddle variable is equal to human (if you used .toUpperCase instead of .toLowerCase, you'll want to check for HUMAN instead). We use the script option and write out $gameVariables.value(16) = "human" (make sure you include the quotation marks). In this particular case, you can either check "Create Else Branch" or have another conditional branch for $gameVariables.value(16) != "human" (!= is "not equal" in programming). In either case, the last thing that requires scripting is emptying out the actor name. To do this, we have another line of script: $gameActors.actor(5)._name = ""

The quotation marks are important here as well. If you leave the method assignment completely empty, the game will crash with an error. Here's what the completed event looks like:

```
♦Text : None, Window, Bottom
:      : What is that which has one voice and yet becomes
:      : four-footed and two-footed and three-footed?
♦Name Input Processing : #0005, 5 characters
♦Control Variables : #0016 Riddle1 = $gameActors.actor(5)._name
♦Script : $gameVariables.setValue(16,$gameActors.actor(5)._name.toLowerCase())
♦If : Script : $gameVariables.value(16) == "human"
   ♦Text : None, Window, Bottom
   :      : Correct.
   ♦
: Else
   ♦Text : None, Window, Bottom
   :      : Wrong.
   ♦
: End
♦Script : $gameActors.actor(5)._name = ""
♦
```

Because we want the door to open on a correct answer, you'll want to flip a self-switch after the door announces "Correct." Next, you display a message stating that the door opens and then switch to a second event page that is completely blank and requires the previously set self-switch to be on. Not much else to it!

One of the beauties of programming (and working with RMMV events) is that there can be multiple correct solutions to a problem. Some may even be equally efficient! I have one more puzzle to discuss in this chapter, so let's get to it!

Remote Statue Manipulation!

I left the most nuanced of the three puzzles for last. Manipulating objects from a distance has been a mechanism used in many video game genres throughout the years. For this exercise, the player will be sent to a distant snowy mountain to move two statues to their respective pedestals. Figure 11-5 is a screenshot of the area in question. The map is 17×17 and uses the Outside tileset.

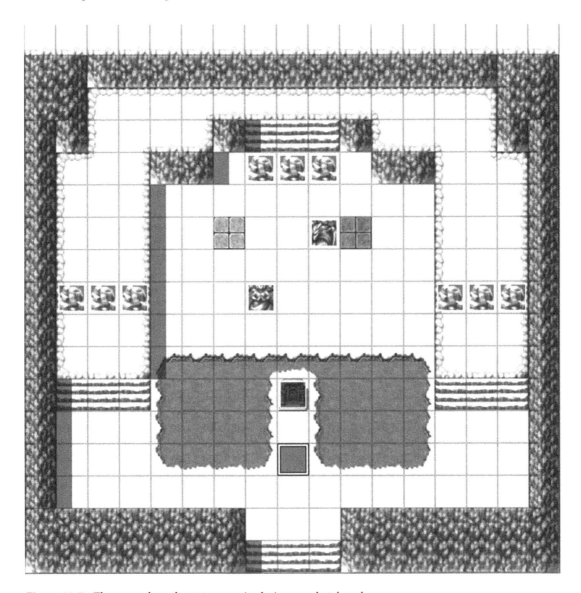

Figure 11-5. *The map where the statue manipulation puzzle takes place*

We have a pair of statues (their graphics are in !Other2) that will be our statues for this exercise. The rocks on either side of the area are actually events that will disappear once the puzzle has been completed. The same goes for the three rocks blocking the staircase at the northern end of the area.

Overview

Here are the things that we need to do, in no particular order:

- Have an event that allows the player to start the puzzle (we'll place it on the gravestone).

- Once the puzzle has started, we freeze the player character in place and scroll the map up a few squares, so that the statues are at the center of the player's vision.

- Set up an event that translates the player's arrow keystrokes into statue movement. This event could also allow the player to press a button to cancel out of the puzzle (if the player would rather go do something else, for example) without completing it.

- Make the extra rocks disappear once the puzzle has been solved.

- After each move, check to see if the statues are on their pedestals. If they are, we flip a switch confirming that the puzzle has been solved. Otherwise, we allow the player to move the statues again.

- Create the two events that will represent the statues.

- Create an invisible event that blocks the player from moving while the puzzle is in progress.

First, place the assorted rocks that will prevent the player from passing to the other side of the area until he/she completes the puzzle. Next, place a golden statue event at (7, 8) and a silver statue event at (9, 6). In both events' Options, untoggle Walking and toggle Direction Fix. This will stop the event images from changing to something unintended when the statues are moved. I specified color to differentiate the two statues. This will be important, as we want the golden statue to go on the left pedestal and the silver statue to go on the right pedestal. The pedestals are at (6, 6) and (10, 6) and are two variations of the cobblestone tiles present in tab A of the Exterior tileset.

Creating the Puzzle Trigger (Interaction) Event

The first event we're going to fill out is the first one that the player will interact with, namely, the gravestone event. When the player interacts with the gravestone, we want a message to be displayed, and then the game will ask if the player wants to touch the gravestone. If he/she does, we scroll the map up to focus the player's vision on the statues. We need to differentiate between when the puzzle is active and when it is not. For that, we can have a switch called StatuePuzzleStart. When it is off, the puzzle is inactive. When it is on, the puzzle is active. Check the following code to see the gravestone event in its entirety and note the extra things it has. Some of it may not make sense currently, but it should by the end of this exercise.

```
◆If : StatuePuzzleDone is OFF
  ◆If : StatuePuzzleStart is OFF
    ◆Text : None, Window, Bottom
    :     : The gravestone says: Place the statues on their
    :     : pedestals to open the way forward.
```

```
    ◆Text : None, Window, Bottom
    :     : Will you touch the gravestone?
    ◆Show Choices : Yes, No (Window, Right, #1, #2)
    : When Yes
        ◆Scroll Map : Up, 5, 4
        ◆Set Movement Route : Player (Wait)
        :                     : ◊Direction Fix ON
        ◆Text : None, Window, Bottom
        :     : \C[3]Press Shift to reset the statues.
        :     : Press a directional key to move the statues.
        ◆Control Switches : #0033 ButtonPressOFF = ON
        ◆Control Switches : #0032 StatuePuzzleStart = ON
        ◆
    : When No
        ◆              .
    : End
    ◆
  : End
◆
: End
◆If : StatuePuzzleDone is ON
  ◆Text : None, Window, Bottom
  :     : This gravestone no longer serves any purpose.
  ◆
: End
◆
```

So, the player has touched the gravestone and is now looking at the statues. We have to make it so that he/she can actually move them. That's a job worthy of a Parallel event. First, however, two squares south of the gravestone, you'll want to place a blank event that requires StatuePuzzleStart to be flipped on and has a Same As Characters priority. This ensures that the player is locked into one location for the duration of the puzzle. Given that we're going to be using arrow key conditionals, we don't want the player's character to suddenly run off mid-puzzle.

Creating the Puzzle Logic Event

The Parallel event will have two pages. The first page will cover button presses, while the second page will check to see if the statues are at their desired destinations. Here's the first part of page 1 of the Parallel event:

```
◆If : Button [Down] is pressed down
  ◆Set Movement Route : LeftStatue (Skip)
  :                     : ◊Move Down
  ◆Set Movement Route : RightStatue (Skip, Wait)
  :                     : ◊Move Down
  ◆Jump to Label : SpotCheck
  ◆
: End
◆If : Button [Left] is pressed down
  ◆Set Movement Route : LeftStatue (Skip)
  :                     : ◊Move Left
```

```
   ♦Set Movement Route : RightStatue (Skip, Wait)
   :                    : ◊Move Right
   ♦Jump to Label : SpotCheck
   ♦
: End
♦If : Button [Right] is pressed down
   ♦Set Movement Route : LeftStatue (Skip)
   :                    : ◊Move Right
   ♦Set Movement Route : RightStatue (Skip, Wait)
   :                    : ◊Move Left
   ♦Jump to Label : SpotCheck
   ♦
: End
♦If : Button [Up] is pressed down
   ♦Set Movement Route : LeftStatue (Skip)
   :                    : ◊Move Up
   ♦Set Movement Route : RightStatue (Skip, Wait)
   :                    : ◊Move Up
   ♦Jump to Label : SpotCheck
   ♦
: End
```

We have a conditional branch for each separate direction. Of course, it wouldn't be much of a puzzle if both statues moved identically, so we make it so that the right statue (the silver one) moves on an inverted horizontal axis. In simpler terms, the silver statue will move left when the player presses right and right when the player presses left. Notice how I only use the Wait command once per branch. There's nothing wrong with having a Wait command on the left statue's movement as well, but it just makes the puzzle take longer. When you set it up as I have, both of the statues will move in response to the keystroke, and the puzzle flows faster. Here's the second half of page 1:

```
♦If : Button [Shift] is pressed down
   ♦Text : None, Window, Bottom
   :     : Reset the statues?
   ♦Show Choices : Yes, No (Window, Right, #1, #2)
   : When Yes
      ♦Set Event Location : LeftStatue, (7,8)
      ♦Set Event Location : RightStatue, (9,6)
      ♦Scroll Map : Down, 5, 4
      ♦Set Movement Route : Player (Wait)
      :                    : ◊Direction Fix OFF
      ♦Control Switches : #0032 StatuePuzzleStart = OFF
      ♦
   : When No
      ♦
   : End
   ♦
: End
♦Label : SpotCheck
♦Control Switches : #0033 ButtonPressOFF = OFF
♦Control Switches : #0034 ButtonPress = ON
♦
```

As mentioned before, we want the player to have a way to stop the puzzle if he or she would rather do something else. So, when the player presses Shift (normally used to dash on the map; the player won't need to move his/her character during the course of this puzzle, so this is the perfect button to use for this exercise) during the puzzle, the game will ask if he or she wishes to reset the statues. Saying No does nothing, but saying Yes returns both statues to their initial positions. We scroll the map down the number of squares that we had moved it up previously and turn off the Direction Fix that we had imposed on the character.

At the very bottom of page 1, we have the SpotCheck label referenced in the quartet of directional conditional branches. The pair of button press switches is used for flow control. In essence, we want the following sequence:

- The player presses one of the arrow keys. The relevant actions are processed and switches are flipped, causing the Parallel page to execute page 2.

- Page 2 of the event checks to see if both statues reached their respective pedestals in that particular button press.

- If they didn't, we toggle switches such that page 1 is now ready to be executed once again.

It is functionally a two-page loop that can be broken by puzzle completion or the player pressing Shift and selecting Yes. With that said, page 1 requires that StatuePuzzleStart and ButtonPressOFF be on. Page 2, on the other hand, requires that StatuePuzzleStart and ButtonPress be on. Don't let the minor switch name differences trip you up! If they do, feel free to differentiate them a little more. Check the following code for the first part of page 2 of the Parallel event.

```
♦Control Variables : #0021 LeftStatueX = Map X of LeftStatue
♦Control Variables : #0022 LeftStatueY = Map Y of LeftStatue
♦Control Variables : #0023 RightStatueX = Map X of RightStatue
♦Control Variables : #0024 RightStatueY = Map Y of Right Statue
♦If : LeftStatueX = 6
  ♦If : LeftStatueY = 6
    ♦If : RightStatueX = 10
      ♦If : RightStatueY = 6
        ♦Text : Actor1(0), Window, Bottom
         :    : About time!
        ♦Fadeout Screen
        ♦Play SE : Push (100, 100, 0)
        ♦Set Event Location : LeftStatue, (6,6)
        ♦Set Event Location : RightStatue, (10,6)
        ♦Control Switches : #0031 StatuePuzzleDone = ON
        ♦Scroll Map : Down, 5, 4
        ♦Fadein Screen
        ♦Control Switches : 0032 StatuePuzzleStart = OFF
        ♦Set Movement Route : Player (Wait)
         :                  : ◊Direction Fix OFF
        ♦
      : Else
        ♦Jump to Label : DirectionCheck
        ♦
      : End
      ♦
```

```
        : Else
          ◆Jump to Label : DirectionCheck
          ◆
        : End
    ◆
: Else
    ◆Jump to Label : DirectionCheck
```

Dissecting the Statue Manipulation Puzzle Logic

Now, don't run off just yet. This might seem a bit overwhelming, but it's actually very simple. Here's a play-by-play of what the preceding event does:

- We create a whopping four new variables to store the values of X and Y for both of the statues.

- Once they are adequately stored, we check those values against the pedestal positions, as defined earlier in this section.

- If *all* four of the variables check out, it means that both statues are in their rightful places. We have Harold say a short remark and then fade out the screen.

- A sound effect is played, and the event locations of both statues are moved to the pedestal location. If you do not do this, the statues will move back to their original locations after the player leaves the map. For our game's purposes, this is actually unimportant (this will be a location visited only once), but it can be, if you want to make puzzles of this type in locations that the player would want to visit multiple times.

- We set StatuePuzzleDone to on, scroll the map back down the same number of steps we scrolled it up before, and fade in.

- The rest of the event has the same logic used when the player presses Shift to cancel out of the puzzle.

- On the other hand, if *any* of the four variables are off, we jump to the DirectionCheck label near the bottom of the page:

```
    ◆
: End
◆Label : DirectionCheck
◆Control Switches : #0034 ButtonPress = OFF
◆Control Switches : #0033 ButtonPressOFF = ON
◆
```

By swapping which of the button-press switches is toggled, we can switch between the two pages of the Parallel Process event as needed. On that note, we have concluded our third and final puzzle of this chapter!

Creating the Second Town

Only three more things remain before finishing this chapter. First, we need to add a relevant event that will lead us to the snowy statue puzzle mountain area. See Figure 11-6 for a zoomed-in screenshot showing the barrier that the player must bring down before being able to make their way out of the last floor of the dungeon and into our game's second town.

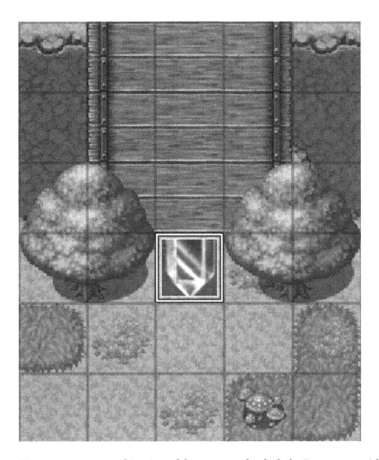

Figure 11-6. *Zoomed-in view of the event used to link the Forest map with our statue puzzle map*

The event image is from the !Crystal graphic set. The event has two pages, a Same As Characters priority, and an Action Button Trigger. When interacted with, the crystal transfers the player to (8, 14) of the statue puzzle map. Page 2 requires the StatuePuzzleDone switch to be on and has a blank image and a Below Characters Priority with no event contents. In other words, the crystal will impede the player's progress until he/she solves the statue puzzle. Second, we must add transfer events in the statue puzzle event that lead back to the Forest (I decided to use individual events for each of the three squares of the bottom staircase). There's nothing special about those transfer events, so I'll leave them as an exercise to you, the reader. Last, but definitely not least, let's add a second town that connects with this final level of the dungeon. Use Load to add Mountain Village to your project's map list. We'll be working on the town in the next chapter. For now, take some time to add transfer events to connect our third dungeon's maps with each other and with our newly added town (see Figure 11-7 for a screenshot of our new town).

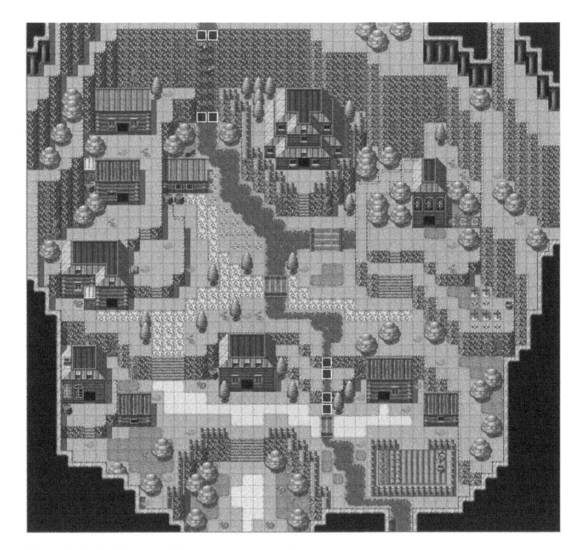

Figure 11-7. *The Mountain Village, our game's second town*

■ **Tip** For the Ice Cave, it may be better to place the transfer events on the map than to use a Parallel event. That way you don't have two Parallel events polling the same data (in this case, writing the player's X and Y values to likewise-named variables). I've noticed that the game stutters a bit when that happens.

Additional Exercises

As usual, I'll close out the chapter by giving you some exercises to work on.

1. Create a crate-pushing puzzle that involves three buttons that need weight to stay pushed down. When all three buttons are pressed, open a door.

   - If you want to have a crate that can be both pushed and pulled, you could have a Show Choices command that disallows being canceled. Then, the player could choose whether to push or pull the crate.

   - Be mindful of the order of your movement events. You want the crate to move first when pushed, but you want the player to move first when it is pulled. Doing it backward is self-defeating at best and can hang your game at worst (if you don't set the relevant move commands to skip, if they cannot be executed).

2. Make a snowball that slides in one direction until it collides with an obstacle.

   - This is as simple as applying the same sliding logic to the snowball that we assign to the player.

   - The snowball can have an Action Button trigger. Given that it can be pushed from all directions, you could use a conditional branch for each of the player's facings, to handle the block's movement.

░ **Note** You can find example events for both extra exercises in the map named Ch.11 Extra Exercises.

Summary

This chapter covered three puzzles that I created originally for RPG Maker VX Ace and updated appropriately for MV. We made a door that could only be opened by correctly answering a riddle, a movement puzzle involving slippery ice, and a manipulation puzzle involving a pair of dragon statues. In the next chapter, we'll be populating our newly added town.

CHAPTER 12

■ ■ ■

Final Preparations

We are fast approaching the end of this book. Our game, short as it may be, is nearly complete. All that is left is to populate the mountain town of Rocksdale, connect it with the world map, and create the game's final dungeon. Well, all that and filling out the random encounter tables for our third dungeon and the final world map areas, adding appropriate equipment for Rocksdale's shop and some of the treasure chests to be made for the third dungeon. We also want to finish the dragon statue event we started back in Chapter 6. I'll be covering the final dungeon in Chapter 13. When last we saw our heroes, they had just arrived at Rocksdale. Let's get started!

Populating Rocksdale

A town isn't much of one without nonplayer characters (NPCs) and building interiors. As with Seaside, here's some setting flavor for Rocksdale:

> *The quiet town of Rocksdale has always been a favorite destination for travelers seeking to settle down and otherwise retire from the outside world. In recent times, monsters have started to threaten the townsfolk's safety, prompting a few of the villagers to leave their seclusion and train themselves for the day when the foul creatures decide to do more than just harass. The village elder is a wise man who knows of a secret passage that leads to the other side of the mountain ridge, where a solitary castle and its dark master await the chosen one of legend . . .*

Riveting, I know! Compared to the Fishing Village sample map, that for the Mountain Village is more spacious and has more buildings. As in Seaside, we'll want an inn, an equipment shop, and an item shop. The largest house will be home to a rather important NPC, while the temple will be home to a transfer event that will take the player to the outskirts of the Dark Master's castle. The two houses at the top-left end of the village will be locked, See Figure 12-1 for a screenshot of Rocksdale with suggested edits.

© Darrin Perez 2016
D. Perez, *Beginning RPG Maker MV*, DOI 10.1007/978-1-4842-1967-6_12

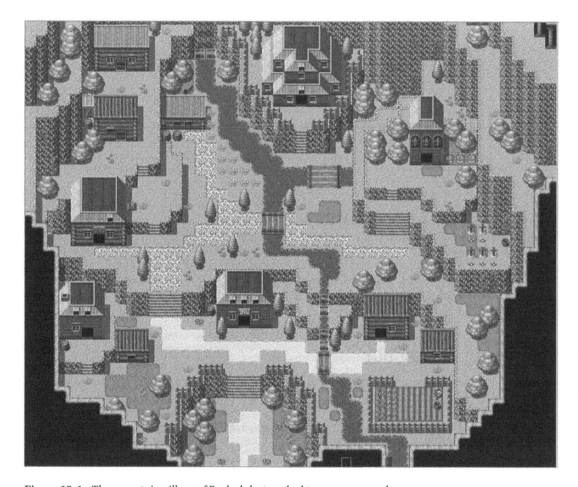

Figure 12-1. *The mountain village of Rocksdale, tweaked to serve our needs*

Here's a list of the main plot events that I will be covering within Rocksdale:

- When the player goes up the steps into the village, the town greeter will inform the player that he/she should make his/her way to the large house in the northeastern part of the village.

- The player reaches the dwelling and finds the village elder, named Wren. Wren has been waiting for Harold's arrival for nearly two decades. He speaks of a malevolent being that lives within a castle in the middle of a dark swamp and of the orb that could weaken the being's power.

- Wren tells the player that a secret passage exists within the village. He further explains that it leads to the far side of the mountain ridge. More important, the passage puts the adventuring party within reach of the villain's castle.

The Town Greeter

Our first order of business will be to place the town greeter on the map. Let's place our relevant NPC at (19, 34). While I'm going to have the greeter give the bulk of his conversation via an Autorun, I'll still have him say a few words when talked to a second time.

```
♦Text : None, Window, Bottom
:     : Welcome to Rocksdale, adventurers. We don't have
:     : much, but I hope you enjoy your stay.
```

First, here's the Parallel event that we'll use to flip the switch for the Autorun to trigger.

```
♦Control Variables : #0002 X = Map X of Player
♦Control Variables : #0003 Y = Map Y of Player
♦If : Y = 36
  ♦If : X ≥ 18
    ♦If : X ≤ 20
      ♦Control Switches : #0039 MountainArrival = ON
```

There's nothing in that code that we haven't already performed many times before. We want to trigger the Autorun in this way to prevent the game from hanging. Check the following code to see the Autorun event in all of its glory.

```
♦Show Balloon Icon : TownGreeter, Exclamation (Wait)
♦Text : None, Window, Bottom
:     : Did you two reach this place through the forest pass?
♦Text : Actor3(7), Window, Bottom
:     : We did.
♦Text : None, Window, Bottom
:     : The villager's eyes widen in disbelief.
♦Text : None, Window, Bottom
:     : You must go visit Wren. He lives in the large
:     : dwelling at the northern part of town. He has
:     : been waiting for a long time.
♦Text : Actor1(0), Window, Bottom
:     : For us?
♦Text : None, Window, Bottom
:     : I believe it would be best for him to speak of it
:     : himself.
♦Text : Actor3(7), Bottom
:     : Very well.
♦Control Self Switch : A = ON
♦
```

An exclamation balloon will be displayed over the villager's head when the Autorun starts. After the short conversation, we switch on self-switch A. We give page 2 of the event a non-Autorun trigger, and that completes our first task of the chapter.

Creating the Village Elder and His Home

Next, we need a worthy interior for the village elder. We'll use the Mansion sample map for our purposes. I left the map mostly intact, as you can see in Figure 12-2.

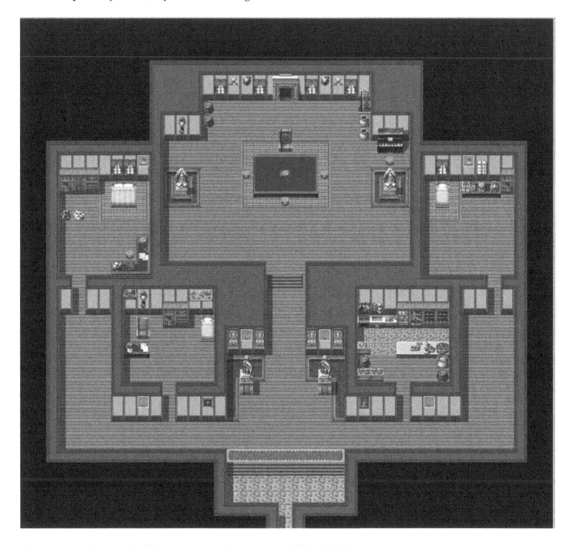

Figure 12-2. *The tweaked Mansion sample map available in RMMV*

We'll place the village elder himself at (20, 11). This event is essentially plot exposition for the player. He or she gets to learn a little more about the game world and then receives his/her next main objective. Take a look at the following for the event code:

```
♦Show Balloon Icon : This Event, Exclamation (Wait)
♦Text : Actor1(0), Window, Bottom
:     : I'm Harold.
♦Text : Actor3(7), Window, Bottom
:     : And I am Marsha.
```

```
♦Text : None, Window, Bottom
:      : I am Wren, the leader of this small village. It
:      : was the father of my father's father, king of the
:      : western lands, who said that you would return.
♦Text : Actor1(0), Window, Bottom
:      : You're not making any sense, Wren.
♦Text : None, Window, Bottom
:      : Marsha clears her throat.
♦Text : Actor3(7), Window, Bottom
:      : Perhaps it would be best to allow him to
:      : speak.
♦Text : None, Window, Bottom
:      : My ancestor claimed that the chosen one would return
:      : to the world in its time of greatest need. I beseech
:      : your aid to defeat the dark master.
♦Text : Actor1(0), Window, Bottom
:      : It is what we're here for.
♦Show Balloon Icon : This Event, Music Note (Wait)
♦Text : None, Window, Bottom
:      : Wonderful! There is an orb of power that will aid
:      : you in your quest. My ancestor claimed that it
:      : is hidden within the lowest level of the castle.
♦Text : Actor3(7), Window, Bottom
:      : How did he know that?
♦Wait : 30 frames
♦Show Balloon Icon : This Event, Silence (Wait)
♦Text : None, Window, Bottom
:      : Isn't it obvious? The castle where the evil
:      : enveloping our land resides was the king's home
:      : in times past.
♦Text : Actor3(7), Window, Bottom
:      : In hindsight, it all makes sense. How do
:      : we get there?
♦Text : None, Window, Bottom
:      : There is a secret passage inside of the village
:      : temple. Tap the wall three paces north of the
:      : northeastern pillar.
♦Text : Actor1(0), Window, Bottom
:      : Thank you, Wren!
♦Text : None, Window, Bottom
:      : On the contrary, thank you.
♦Control Switches : #0040 ElderTalk = ON
♦Control Self Switch : A = ON
```

Like most plot-advancing events, this one is important not for what it does internally, but for the information it gives the player. Thanks to the village elder, the player learns that the castle inhabited by the mysterious Dark Master used to be home to the king of the western lands. At the end of the conversation, we flip on the ElderTalk switch, which allows the player to find the secret passage within the temple.

The Temple of Rocksdale

RPG Maker VX Ace had a Temple sample map that I used in the first edition of this book for this section. While no such equivalent exists in MV, I decided to recreate that map within MV, as it's perfect for what we want it for. The new map is 17×22 and uses the Inside tileset. The BGM is set to Town2. The secret passage is visible in Figure 12-3, but there's another event that may not be as easy to see. I placed a Same As Characters/Action Button event on the statue's lower half. If the player interacts with the statue, he/she will be teleported to Seaside. Where exactly? Take a look at Figure 12-4 to see.

Figure 12-3. *A screenshot of the temple*

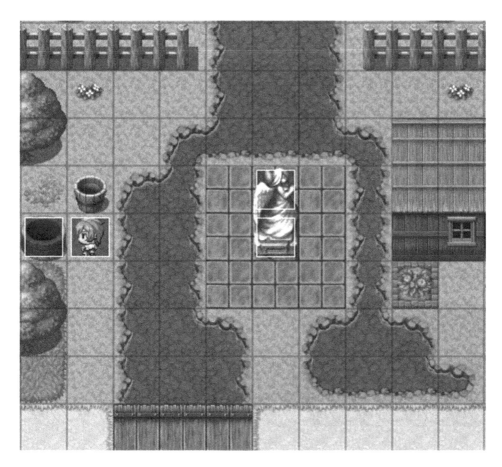

Figure 12-4. *Where the player lands if he or she touches Rocksdale's statue*

Because this statue is two squares tall, we need a pair of events to draw it. The top half has a priority of Above Characters and no commands. The lower half has a priority of Same As Characters and returns the player to the mountain village if he/she touches it.

■ **Tip** If you want to make it so that the statue at Seaside is only visible after the player has used Rocksdale's statue, you can add an appropriate condition to both of the events. ElderTalk will work, as will creating a new switch that is flipped the first time that the player uses Rocksdale's statue.

Leaving Rocksdale

The secret passage event is three pages long. To use the appropriate wall graphic for the first two pages of the event, you'll need to add Inside_A4 to tab D of the Inside tileset in the Database. Because we don't want the player to find the passage ahead of time, the first page will have no conditionals and no event commands.

The only thing the first page will have is the wall graphic. Page 2 will require that ElderTalk is switched on and shares the same graphic as page 1. However, if the player interacts with the wall using the Action Button, the event in the following code is triggered:

```
♦Text : Actor1(0), Window, Bottom
:      : This should be the place.
♦Text : None, Window, Bottom
:      : Harold taps the wall with his knuckles.
♦Wait : 60 frames
♦Fadeout Screen
♦Play SE : Push (100, 100, 0)
♦Text : None, Window, Bottom
:      : You have found a secret staircase!
♦Control Self Switch : A = ON
♦Fadein Screen
```

The use of Fadeout/Fadein Screen in page 2 allows us to switch to page 3's event graphic off-camera via the usual self-switch toggle. Figure 12-5 shows what it looks like in-game.

Figure 12-5. *Harold finds himself staring at a staircase*

Page 3 of the secret passage event has a Below Characters priority and a Player Touch trigger. It requires self-switch A to be on. The first time the player takes this passage, we want to display some extra text. Thus, we start page 3 with a conditional branch requiring self-switch B to be off. If it is, we display the additional text; otherwise, we skip straight to the transfer event.

```
♦If : Self Switch B is OFF
   ♦Control Self Switch : B = ON
   ♦Fadeout Screen
   ♦Text : None, Window, Bottom
   :      : Harold and Marsha walk down the steps and find
   :      : themselves in a rocky passage.
```

```
    ♦Text : None, Window, Bottom
    :     : Several minutes later, they find themselves at a
    :     : new location…
    ♦Play SE : Move1 (90, 100, 0)
    ♦Wait : 60 frames
    ♦
  : End
♦Transfer Player : World 1 (49,69) (Direction: Down)
```

If you were to play-test the game after adding that specific event, you would find a considerable lack of screen after being transferred back to the world map. We could add in the Fadein Screen command directly before Transfer Player, but that would look somewhat sloppy in execution. Instead, go to the world map's Parallel transfer event and add the following to it:

```
♦If : X = 49
  ♦If : Y = 69
    ♦If : Self Switch A is OFF
      ♦Fadein Screen
      ♦Control Self Switch : A = ON
      ♦
    : End
    ♦
  : End
  ♦
 : End
♦
```

We use a self-switch conditional branch within the coordinate conditional, as we only require this to trigger once (to match the fading-out sequence caused at Rocksdale's temple).

■ **Caution** Be very careful with the preceding example when applying it to your own games. In a more open world map, your players might cross your declared coordinate(s) prematurely during their adventures. When they get around to triggering the area transition, the fade-in is functionally nonexistent, and the game will hang.

With all that done, Harold and Marsha will find themselves near the Dark Master's castle, as shown in Figure 12-6.

Figure 12-6. *Surrounded by a forest of dead trees, the final dungeon awaits!*

New Items and Equipment

Back in Chapter 10 I said that I would discuss adding new stuff to the Database in this chapter. Since we want to have new shops in Rocksdale, it's more immediately pertinent to discuss items and equipment first. I'll leave enemies for the next section. We want Rocksdale to sell equipment that will prepare the player to siege the final dungeon. In fact, that equipment will be the second-highest tier present within our game (the final dungeon will have several chests containing even better equipment, but more on that in the next chapter). See Table 12-1 for a list of the new armors that will be sold at Rocksdale.

Table 12-1. *A List of the New Armors to Be Added to the Database*

Name	Stats / Traits	Price
Light Plate	+30 Defense, +6 M. Defense	4000
Full Plate	+35 Defense, +7 M. Defense	5500
Arcane Vestment	+20 Defense, +20 M. Defense / +7 Evasion	6000
Arcane Cap	+7 Defense, +7 M. Defense / +7 Evasion	2000
Fury Ring	+25 Attack, -10 Defense	2000
Overflow Ring	+25 M. Attack, -10 M. Defense	2000
Plated Barbute	+15 Defense	3000

The Light Plate, Full Plate, and Plated Barbute (a barbute is basically a type of helmet) should be of the Light Armor type, the Arcane Vestment and Arcane Cap should be of the Magic Armor type, and the two rings should have the General Armor type. Note how the rings take away Defense and Magic Defense, respectively, when worn. This provides a sort of trade-off for the player, which requires them to decide whether to accept the penalty in question. Now, take a look at Table 12-2 for an overview of the new weapons to be added to Rocksdale's equipment shop.

Table 12-2. *A List of the New Weapons to Be Added to the Database*

Name	Stats / Traits	Price
Mythril Blade	+30 Attack / +10 Attack Speed	4000
Mythril Claymore	+45 Attack / +5 Attack Speed, Seal Equip: Shield	8000
Golden Bow	+35 Attack / Seal Equip: Shield	5000
Mythril Bow	+42 Attack / Seal Equip: Shield	7000
Arcane Wand	+15 Attack, +35 M. Attack	16000

This table has two swords, two bows, and a single wand for Marsha should she ever manage to save up 16000 Gold (as playtests should show, she probably doesn't need the extra magical damage). Now, before I give you a list of the equipment that you should include in the third dungeon's chests, see Table 12-3 for three new items to be added to the Database.

Table 12-3. *A List of New Items to Be Added to the Database*

Name	Effects	Price
Energy Dew	Restores 500 HP and 200 MP to all allies.	600
Life Dew	Restores 1500 HP to all allies.	750
Magic Dew	Restores 500 MP to all allies.	1500

There isn't much to say about the new items. They are basically the mass versions of Energy Potions, Life Potions, and Magic Potions respectively. They cost three times the Gold that their single target counterparts do, so they're only particularly useful in battle, where every action counts. Outside of battle, the player will probably prefer using the cheaper versions. Take some time to create the Item and Equipment shops for Rocksdale, using Tables 12-1 and 12-2 for the equipment shop and the list in Figure 12-7 for the item shop.

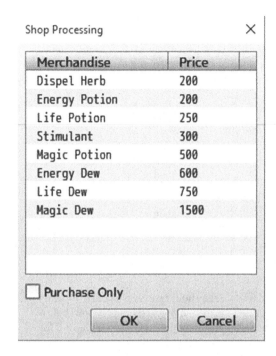

Figure 12-7. *A list of items to be sold at Rocksdale's item shop*

If you're so inclined, you could have Rocksdale's item shop sell only the three Dew items, given that we give the player a way to travel instantly between both towns via the statues. Before we move on to the next section, add eight chests to our third dungeon; four in the first level (Forest of Decay), four in the second level (Ice Cave), and none in the third level. Among the chests, let's give the player some equipment. Fill four of the eight chests with the following: Golden Bow, Light Plate, Fury Ring, and Magic Turban. Fill the other four chests with items of your own choosing. Next, we should populate the world map's Regions and the third dungeon with enemies.

Enemies of the World

To be fair, I could have covered this earlier in the book, but I figured it'd be better to clump them all here, away from the central ideas they would have otherwise cluttered. After all, I also have the dragon statue event back at the Ruined Spire that I still have to complete. It's as good a time as any to go off on this tangent. First, we need to create our new enemies. Take a peek at Table 12-4 for details.

Table 12-4. *A List of the New Enemies That Will Populate the Third Dungeon, Surrounding Areas, and the Final Dungeon*

Name	HP	MP	ATK	DEF	MAT	MDF	AGI	LUK	EXP	G
Ghost	500	100	20	120	100	60	50	50	368	440
Rogue	900	0	75	50	75	50	75	75	368	500
Zombie	1200	0	70	40	40	70	20	20	415	440
Frost Viper	600	150	100	60	70	40	100	100	415	500
Liquid Gold	4	0	10	999	10	999	255	255	256	4096

Of particular note is the final enemy in the table, who is an homage to a classic Japanese RPG monster archetype: that of the nearly unkillable and cowardly enemy that grants a massive reward if somehow defeated. Here's a more detailed breakdown of each new enemy type. New skills will be listed in Table 12-5 after the breakdown.

- Ghosts have low HP and Magic Defense, but immense physical Defense. This means that magical attacks will be preferred in battles with Ghosts. They use two skills: Magic Attack with a Condition of *Always* and a Rating of 5, and Icebolt with a Condition of Turn 2+2*X and a Rating of 9. Ghosts are weak to Light (Element Rate: Light * 200%), resistant to Thunder (50%), and immune to Ice (0%). They have a 1/5 chance to drop a Smoke Bomb and a 1/10 chance to drop a Stimulant.

- Rogues are fairly balanced enemies with a slight bent toward damage-dealing at the expense of defensive stats. They use Attack and Cleave *Always* with a Rating of 5. Rogues also have Toxic Gas, which they use first on Turn 2 and then every 3 turns thereafter (Rating of 9). They have a 1/5 chance to drop Eye Drops and a 1/10 chance to drop a Dispel Herb. This enemy has 10% Evasion and 10% Critical Rate, along with one instance of Action Times + 20%. Each instance of Action Times+ allows an extra action at X%, where X is the percentage probability of using the extra action on any given turn. So, if an enemy has three Action Times+ entries, it can potentially act four times each turn.

Note This is not to be confused with Atk Times+, which influences how many extra times the enemy attacks when it uses the normal Attack skill.

- Zombies have a large amount of HP and a decent amount of Attack and Magical Defense. What makes them dangerous is their 30% chance to inflict Poison on Attack (via `Attack State: Poison + 30%`) along with their special Attack variant, Drain Attack, which is their only used skill. Zombies are weak to Fire (200%) and strong against Thunder (50%). They have a 1/5 chance to drop a Life Potion and a 1/10 chance to drop a Life Dew on defeat.

Note The three enemies already listed use their same-named battler graphics.

- Frost Vipers are highly agile enemies that pack a punch with their physical attacks. They use Attack Always with a Rating of 5 and Icebolt every three turns starting on Turn 2 (Rating of 9) They inflict Poison half of the time that they use Attack, and they are weak to Fire (150%) and resistant to Ice (50%). This enemy has a 1/7 chance of dropping a Big Bomb when defeated. Frost Vipers use the Snake battler graphic with a Hue of 240.

- As already mentioned before, Liquid Golds are a special enemy. Rather than fight the player, they seek to escape at the first possible opportunity. Their immense defensive stats pretty much eliminate the ability to damage them through conventional means, and their 70% Evasion and Magic Evasion rating makes it so most attacks won't stick, either. Their Action Pattern consists of Attack and Escape, both with a Condition of Always. Attack has a Rating of 5, while Escape has a Rating of 4. If the Liquid Gold is still in combat with the player by turn 3, it is guaranteed to use Escape (Rating of 9) to flee battle. This enemy has a 1/10 chance to drop a Bat's Brew (incidentally, they will be the only enemy in the game that can drop this rare beverage). Liquid Golds use the Slime battler graphic with a Hue of 240.

As promised, see Table 12-5 for a list of the new skills to be added to the Database.

Table 12-5. *A List of New Skills to Be Added to the Database*

Name	Scope	MP Cost	Damage Type / Element Type / Damage Formula / Effects and Other Notes	Animation
Magic Attack	1 Enemy	0	HP Damage / Normal Attack / a.mat * 4 – b.mdf * 2 / Add State: Normal Attack 100%	Normal Attack
Toxic Gas	All Enemies	0	HP Damage / Physical / (b.mhp/8) / Add State: Blind 40%, Add State: Confusion 20%, Hit Type: Certain Hit	Pollen
Drain Attack	1 Enemy	0	HP Drain / Normal Attack / a.atk * 4 – b.def * 2 / Add State: Normal Attack 100%	Normal Attack

With the greater details now written in stone, you can take a bit of time to add these new enemies and their associated skills to the Database. Add single-unit and two-unit Troops for each of our newly added enemies. Then take a look at Figure 12-8 for the full encounter list that we'll be using for the world map.

Troop	Weight	Range
Bat	25	1
Bat*2	20	1
Slime	20	1, 2
Slime*2	10	1, 2
Orc	15	2
Orc*2	10	2
War Orc	5	3
Minotaur	5	3
Snake*2	10	3
Forest Rat*3	10	4
Forest Rat*5	10	4
Troll	5	4, 5
Ruffian	5	4, 5
Ruffian*2	5	4, 5
Ghost	10	7, 8, 9
Ghost*2	20	7, 8, 9
Rogue	10	6, 7, 8
Rogue*2	20	6, 7, 8
Spirit Essence	10	8
Zombie	10	6, 7, 9
Zombie*2	20	6, 7, 9
Frost Viper	20	8
Frost Viper*2	30	8
Liquid Gold	9	8, 9
Liquid Gold*2	1	8, 9

Figure 12-8. *The encounter list for our game's world map*

We'll use Regions 6–8 for the rest of the second landmass and 9 for the area surrounding the final dungeon. Check Figure 12-9 to see just how I laid out the relevant regions.

Figure 12-9. *The world map, now updated with regions. Not pictured is part of the Region 9 layout.*

■ **Reminder**   Don't forget to set new battlebacks for each newly added region in the appropriate Parallel event! I'll leave that as an exercise for you.

Next, we need some encounters for our third dungeon, which we'll formally call the Hidden Pass. Much like the Dark Spire, the last floor will be left encounter-free. That said, see Figure 12-10 for the encounter list for the first floor of our dungeon (the Forest of Decay map). Then check out Figure 12-11 for the encounter list for floor 2 (the Ice Cave).

Troop	Weight	Range
Ghost	10	Entire Map
Ghost*2	20	Entire Map
Rogue	10	Entire Map
Rogue*2	20	Entire Map
Zombie	10	Entire Map
Zombie*2	20	Entire Map
Spirit Essence	10	Entire Map
Liquid Gold	10	Entire Map

Figure 12-10. *Random encounter list for the Forest of Decay area of our third dungeon*

Troop	Weight	Range
Ghost	10	Entire Map
Ghost*2	20	Entire Map
Rogue	10	Entire Map
Rogue*2	20	Entire Map
Spirit Essence	15	Entire Map
Frost Viper	15	Entire Map
Frost Viper*2	30	Entire Map
Liquid Gold	5	Entire Map
Liquid Gold*2	5	Entire Map

Figure 12-11. Random encounter list for the Ice Cave area of our third dungeon

That will do it for this section. Before closing it out, here are some ideas to flesh out Rocksdale:

- Have one of the villagers give the player a sidequest involving the scarecrow in town. You could have it attack the player, when examined. When it is defeated, the player is attacked by a puppet-master. Defeating the mini-boss completes the sidequest.

- Add several NPC, to liven up the village. The locals should talk mostly about the monsters threatening to attack. Have one of them make reference to Therese.

With both the Hidden Pass and the world map fully populated, let's turn our attention to the dragon statue in the Dark Spire. I had originally left the event incomplete in Chapter 6, because I wanted to make an optional boss fight—a superboss fight, to be exact.

A Discussion of Superbosses

The general flow of an RPG involves defeating bosses, until you reach a final boss. Superbosses are located outside of that continuity and exist solely as a form of challenge for the player. If the player can beat a superboss, he/she is more than ready to beat the final boss and, by extension, the game itself. The monster that I created for this precise purpose can be seen in Figure 12-12.

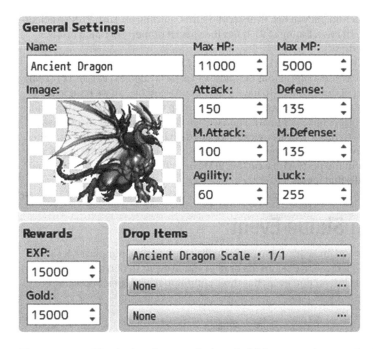

General Settings

Name: Ancient Dragon

Max HP: 11000

Max MP: 5000

Image:

Attack: 150

Defense: 135

M.Attack: 100

M.Defense: 135

Agility: 60

Luck: 255

Rewards

EXP: 15000

Gold: 15000

Drop Items

Ancient Dragon Scale : 1/1

None

None

Figure 12-12. *The Ancient Dragon. It gives the highest experience and gold gains of any monster in the game.*

The Ancient Dragon boasts higher stats than the game's final boss. Harold and Marsha will most likely not be ready to take this beast on until they have gotten the gear from the final dungeon and perhaps some extra level-ups as well. Defeating the Ancient Dragon gives the player a whopping 15,000 experience and gold. More important, it gives the player the best accessory in our game. The Ancient Dragon Scale is a new accessory that grants +10 to all eight of a character's main stats, +5 Evasion, +5 Critical Rate, and 10 Attack Speed (AGI only applied during attacks). The Ancient Dragon resists Fire, Ice, and Thunder (taking only 50% damage from all three sources) and also has a Critical Rate of 20%. You can see the Ancient Dragon's Action Pattern list in Figure 12-13.

Action Patterns

Skill	Condition	R
Attack	Always	1
Firebolt	Always	1
Icebolt	Always	1
Dual Attack	HP 26% ~ 75%	4
Spark Storm	HP 26% ~ 75%	4
Ruin	HP 26% ~ 75%	4
Triple Attack	HP 0% ~ 25%	7
Fireblast	HP 0% ~ 25%	7
Iceblast	HP 0% ~ 25%	7

Figure 12-13. *The Ancient Dragon's action pattern list*

Not pictured is the final skill in the action pattern list. Every seven turns, starting on Turn 7, the Ancient Dragon uses a new skill called Devastate (it has a Rating of 9). It has the special property of doing more damage the later in the fight that it is used.

Devastate's damage formula is [(a.mat * $gameVariables.value(17)) - b.mdf * 5] with an Attack Element of None, and it hits All Enemies. We set it up so that the value of $gameVariables.value(17) (I call it TurnCount) is factored into the first part of the formula. To have a turn-count variable, all we have to do is go into the Ancient Dragon's troop (after creating it, of course) and add a troop event page with a Turn End conditional that has a Turn span (so it triggers once per turn). Then we use Control Variables to increase the value of TurnCount by 1. So, every seven turns, Devastate causes extra damage equal to seven times the Ancient Dragon's MAT (so, 700) minus five times the target's Magic Defense. Basically, the battle is a race to defeat the superboss before it can wipe out the party with a casting of Devastate. Of course, the less HP the Ancient Dragon has, the stronger the skills that it uses.

Completing the Dragon Statue Event

Now that we have created our superboss and given it a robust set of skills to use against our player, let's complete the dragon statue event. As you'll recall, we set up the dragon statue event so that the player could inspect it from different angles. The interaction event has three conditional branches. Following is a refresher for part of the event:

```
◆If : Player is facing Right
   ◆If : X = 32
      ◆Jump to Label : Text
      ◆
    : End
   ◆
 : End
```

Recall that we use a Jump to Label command so as to not have to write the same text three times in the same event. The other two directional branches work in the same way. The following code is located after the three branches:

```
◆Label: Text
◆Text : None, Window, Bottom
:      : You see a majestic dragon statue. It hums with
:      : power.
◆Text : Actor3(7), Window, Bottom
:      : I sense immense power emanating from this
:      : statue. Be mindful. It would be best to
:      : return at a later time.
◆Text : None, Window, Bottom
:      : Touch the statue?
◆Show Choices : Yes, No (Window, Right, #1, #2)
: When Yes
  ◆Jump to Label : DragonStatue
  ◆
: When No
  ◆
: End
◆
```

At the Yes present within the interaction event, you'll want to place the Jump to Label event command as just shown. Then, at the very end of the event, you'll want to add the following:

```
♦If : #0100 is ON
    ♦Label : DragonStatue
    ♦Text : None, Window, Bottom
    :       : You place a hand on the statue.
    ♦Text : None, Window, Bottom
    :       : You feel yourself being whisked away!
    ♦Change Battle BGM : Battle3 (90, 100, 0)
    ♦Control Self Switch : A = ON
    ♦Battle Processing : Ancient Dragon
    ♦
: End
♦
```

That is a dummy switch, a strategy we've used in previous chapters to make sure this part of the event can only execute when jumped into. When the player decides to touch the statue, we change the battle BGM and set self-switch A to on. Then, we send the player into the superboss battle. If the player triumphs, the interaction event flips to a second page that displays only the first bit of descriptive text. Look at the following code:

```
♦If : Player is facing Right
    ♦If : X = 32
        ♦Text : None, Window, Bottom
        :       : You see a majestic dragon statue. It hums with power.
        ♦
    : End
```

With that said, we have one thing left to do.

Setting Up the Use of the Exit Skill/Item Inside a Dungeon with Two Exits

We have set up all of our relevant transfer events for the third dungeon, but we have yet to update them with appropriate changes to the DungeonLocation variable. More important, we also need to update the common event that is tied to our Exit Scroll. The third dungeon is peculiar in that it has two exits. There is the cave entrance hidden within the forest, and there is the entrance in Rocksdale. So we need to have one value of DungeonLocation for each of the two entrances. We'll set them in the order that the player finds them, so that the entrance to the third dungeon from the hidden location will set DungeonLocation to 3, while the entrance in Rocksdale will set its value to 4. Let's get started.

```
♦Control Variables : #0002 X = Map X of Player
♦Control Variables : #0003 Y = Map Y of Player
♦If : Y = 6
    ♦Control Variables : #0011 DungeonLocation = 3
    ♦Transfer Player: Forest of Decay (24,47) (Direction: Up)
    ♦
: End
```

We have this event on the cave entrance map. Directly inside, at the Forest of Decay, we tweak that event, so that DungeonLocation will become 0 if the player steps back out.

■ **Note**   In what is another difference between this dungeon exit and the two previous locales, you can set DungeonLocation to 0 when the player leaves the mines, or when he/she steps back into the world map. I decided to set the value back to 0 as soon as the player breaks free of the mines, as the cave entrance is not part of the dungeon.

```
◆Control Variables : #0002 X = Map X of Player
◆Control Variables : #0003 Y = Map Y of Player
◆If : Y = 49
   ◆Control Variables : #0011 DungeonLocation = 0
   ◆Transfer Player : Swamp (21,7) (Direction: Down)
   ◆
: End
◆
```

Next, we must handle the other possible dungeon exit. The following code belongs to the transfer event in Rocksdale:

```
◆Control Variables : #0002 X = Map X of Player
◆Control Variables : #0003 Y = Map Y of Player
◆If : Y = 43
   ◆Control Variables : #0011 DungeonLocation = 4
   ◆Transfer Player : Forest (13,4) (Direction: Down)
   ◆
: End
```

Note that we set DungeonLocation to 4 here instead of 3. The last transfer event to be tweaked is the one that leads from the Forest to the mountain village.

```
◆Control Variables : #0002 X = Map X of Player
◆Control Variables : #0003 Y = Map Y of Player
◆If : Y = 0
   ◆Control Variables : #0011 DungeonLocation = 0
   ◆Transfer Player : Mountain Village (19,41) (Direction: Up)
   ◆
: End
```

With that done, we have only to tweak the common event that governs our exit code, and we're all set, like so:

```
◆If : DungeonLocation = 3
   ◆Change Items : Exit Scroll - 1
   ◆Control Variables : #0011 DungeonLocation = 0
   ◆Transfer Player : World 1 (57,76) (Direction: Down)
   ◆
: End
```

```
♦If : DungeonLocation = 4
   ♦Change Items : Exit Scroll - 1
   ♦Control Variables : #0011 DungeonLocation = 0
   ♦Transfer Player : Mountain Village (19,41) (Direction: Up)
   ♦
: End
♦
```

You'll want to update the spell variant of the common event as well, if you assigned the spell to Harold and/or Marsha. With all that done, you can put another notch on your belt. This chapter is complete!

Summary

Over this chapter, I covered our preparations leading up to the final dungeon of the game. We populated Rocksdale with a few essential NPCs that drive the main narrative forward. Adding other buildings and NPCs to the town was left as an exercise for you. In addition, we completed the dragon statue event that had been started all the way back in Chapter 6, introducing our game's superboss in that way. Last but not least, we updated the transfer events of our latest dungeon to include the DungeonLocation variable and did the same for the common event that governs our Exit skill/item. In the next chapter, we will create and populate our game's final dungeon.

CHAPTER 13

The Final Dungeon

It has been 12 chapters, and I hope you have enjoyed the journey up to now. While I will be covering a few more things before I conclude this book, this will be the last chapter that's directly related to the game we've been developing together. The final dungeon is perhaps the most important part of a role-playing game. The player has gone through countless tribulations and obstacles, and he/she is finally at the doorstep of whoever, or whatever, is causing the game's central conflict. In our game, Harold and Marsha find themselves in front of an ancient castle that used to house the kings of the western lands. It has been corrupted by a malevolent being known by many names but who we'll call the Dark Master. During the course of this chapter, we will be developing our game's final dungeon.

The Beginning of the End—the Exterior and the First Floor

For our game's final dungeon, I will use the Demon Castle series of sample maps, along with the Cursed Cave map, for a total of five new maps (but the dungeon itself has four floors). The first order of business is to add Demon Castle to our project (this is the map that houses the Demon Castle exterior). Then right-click on the Demon Castle map and Load the Demon Castle 1F map (the first floor of the castle interior). Once that has been done, you'll want to use transfer events to connect the Demon Castle map with the world map and Demon Castle 1F.

Note The DungeonLocation value of the final dungeon should be 5. Keep in mind that the castle we placed on the world map has two tiles that are considered passable (namely, the two bottom tiles).

The Teleportation Puzzle

Once we have our first floor added, we are going to create a little puzzle. It's only logical that a final boss is going to do everything in his power to stop the player from reaching it. Similarly, a final dungeon isn't much of one if the player can just walk up to the final boss as easy as saying it. What I'm going to add is a teleportation puzzle. To build this puzzle, we'll need the following:

- The use of Region mode, to paint in the areas that will teleport the unwary player when he/she steps on them.

- A Parallel event to handle the transfer events when the player steps on a Region.

- A crystal that can be destroyed to flip on a switch. When the switch is flipped on, the Parallel event is skipped, allowing the player to progress in the dungeon.

© Darrin Perez 2016
D. Perez, *Beginning RPG Maker MV*, DOI 10.1007/978-1-4842-1967-6_13

For the sake of convenience, I painted the destination of each teleport Region trap on the map, using the same Region number. For example, the line made up of Region 63 will teleport the player to the square marked as 63. Check Figure 13-1 for the area involved in the teleportation puzzle.

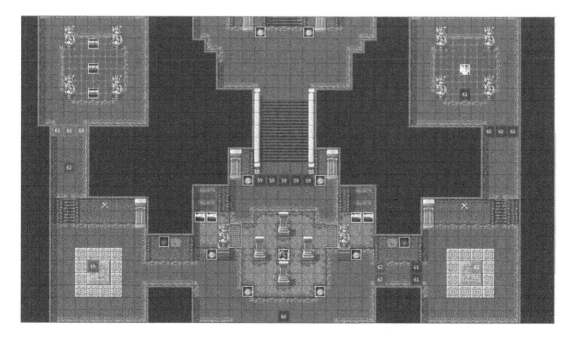

Figure 13-1. *The Regions that will be used to create our teleportation puzzle. The player needs to step on the area marked 61 to reach the crystal that will destroy the traps.*

▪ **Note**   Don't forget to erase the Regions at your intended destination. The reason for this will become obvious when we work on the Parallel event.

As intended, the path to the next floor is blocked by teleportation Regions. Region 61 leads to the crystal that the player needs to destroy to remove the teleportation traps.

▪ **Note**   This map comes with quite a few preset events, mostly for torches that add an appropriately eerie ambience to this dungeon. Included are two crystals. I left the right one intact for this exercise, while I removed the left one, replacing it with some chests we'll be populating later in the chapter.

Creating the Puzzle Logic

We have defined where each Region leads within the floor, so let's work on the Parallel event now. The first part of our Parallel event will check the player's X and Y coordinates and then use the Get Location Info event command to get the Region ID from his/her current location. Whenever the player steps into a Region, he/she is teleported to the appropriate destination. Once the player shatters the crystal powering the teleportation traps, he/she can advance.

```
♦Control Variables : #0002 X = Map X of Player
♦Control Variables : #0003 Y = Map Y of Player
♦Get Location Info : TeleportLocation, Region ID, ({X},{Y})
♦If : TeleportTrapOFF is ON
   ♦Jump to Label : Skip
   ♦
: End
♦If : TeleportLocation = 63
   ♦Transfer Player : Demon Castle 1F (40,38)
   ♦
: End
♦If : TeleportLocation = 62
   ♦Transfer Player : Demon Castle 1F (6,30)
   ♦
: End
♦If : TeleportLocation = 61
   ♦Transfer Player : Demon Castle 1F (39,24)
   ♦
: End
♦If : TeleportLocation = 60
   ♦Transfer Player : Demon Castle 1F (24,42)
   ♦
: End
♦If : TeleportLocation = 59
   ♦Transfer Player : Demon Castle 1F (8,38)
   ♦
: End
♦Label : Skip
```

Here you can see why you need to erase the Region squares I used to mark each destination. The event is set up so that the player will be moved if he/she steps upon a Region.

■ **Caution**   If you didn't heed my previous warning, you'll trap the player in an infinite loop, once he/she is teleported, given that his/her destination also contains the same Region ID used to get there in the first place!

Creating the Crystal That Controls the Puzzle

The last thing left to do for this puzzle is to set up the crystal event, which will have two pages. Page 1 will contain the lion's share of the code, and page 2 will exist solely to inform the player that the crystal has been shattered. As mentioned previously, I'm using one of the preset crystals as the graphic for this event.

```
♦Text : None, Window, Bottom
:     : A glowing crystal floats in place.
♦Text : Actor3(7), Window, Bottom
:     : This crystal is probably what is stopping
:     : us from getting anywhere. We should
:     : shatter it.
```

```
♦Text : None, Window, Bottom
:      : Will you destroy it?
♦Show Choices : Yes, No (Window, Right, #1, #2)
: When Yes
   ♦Fadeout Screen
   ♦Play SE : Crash (90, 100, 0)
   ♦Text : None, Window, Bottom
   :      : The crystal shatters!
   ♦Control Switches : #0041 TeleportTrapOFF = ON
   ♦Control Self Switch : A = ON
   ♦Fadein Screen
   ♦
: When No
   ♦
: End
♦
```

When the player decides to shatter the crystal, we fade out the screen, play an appropriate sound effect, and display a message. We flip on a self-switch and then fade the screen back in, allowing the event to process page 2. Page 2 of the crystal event uses the gray Rubble tile (located in tileset B) as its graphic, requires self-switch A to be on, and displays a single message. The message is: "Where once the glowing crystal stood, only rubble remains." Before we finish working on the first floor of our final dungeon, it's time for one more intermission to add stuff to our project's Database!

Populating the Demon Castle

Our game's final dungeon deserves new enemies and new equipment. We started last chapter's intermission with equipment, so let's start this chapter's intermission with enemies.

The Enemies of the Demon Castle

Since we are working with a final dungeon, its enemies should be at their strongest. Without further ado, take a look at Table 13-1.

Table 13-1. *A List of New Enemies to Be Added to the Database*

Name	HP	MP	ATK	DEF	MAT	MDF	AGI	LUK	EXP	G
Centurion	1000	100	70	90	70	90	50	90	570	625
Soldier	500	0	100	50	100	50	45	90	350	400
Vampire	1000	600	90	60	90	60	90	60	626	675
Werewolf	1200	0	80	80	80	80	80	80	626	675
Dragon	3000	1000	90	90	65	90	60	100	1500	1500
Mimic	400	0	110	110	110	110	110	110	0	1000

I'm sure you know what comes next by now. Incidentally, it's the last time in this book that we'll have such a breakdown, so have at it!

- Centurions use the Captain battler graphic at Hue: 60. They use Attack and Cleave *Always* (both with a Rating of 5) and Fortify every three turns starting at Turn 3 (Rating of 9). Centurions have a 1/10 drop chance for three items: Full Plate, Mythril Blade, and Large Shield.

- Soldiers use Attack and Dual Attack *Always* with a Rating of 5, and have a 1/20 chance of dropping Light Plate. Centurions and Soldiers are noteworthy in that they are part of a special troop, but more on that shortly.

- Vampires resist Ice (50%) and are weak to Light (200%). They use Attack *Always* with a Rating of 5, Drain Attack every two turns starting on turn 1 (Rating of 6) and Ruin every three turns starting on turn three (Rating of 9). Vampires have a 1/5 chance of dropping a Stimulant and a 1/10 chance of dropping a Life Dew on defeat.

- Werewolves are resistant to Physical (50%), have 10% Evasion Rate, and have one instance of Action Times + 100%. They use only the basic Attack skill but use it twice per turn. Werewolves have a 1/5 chance of dropping a Big Bomb.

- Dragons stand head and shoulders above every other regular enemy type, dwarfed only by our game's final boss (whom we'll discuss at length later in the chapter) and its superboss. They use Attack, Firebolt, and Icebolt (Rating of 5) while their HP is over 25%; once their HP is down to 25% or less, they use Double Attack, Fireblast, and Iceblast (Rating of 9). You might recognize this action pattern as a trimmed-down version of the one we used for the Ancient Dragon in the previous chapter. It only seemed appropriate that a weaker version of our game's superboss would use similar skills. For Traits, they slightly resist Fire, Ice, and Thunder (75% for all three elements) and have a Critical Rate of 10%. They drop no items.

- Mimics are our game's final regular (non-boss) enemy, and they represent an interesting monster archetype: That of the false object. In MV's case, Mimics are monsters that pose as chests, waiting for a foolish adventurer to try to open them so they can pounce. Historically, Japanese RPGs have also had fake doors and even fake walls (notably, the Demon Wall from *Final Fantasy 4*) that are actually monsters. Our game's Mimic has one instance of Action Times + 100% and the Attack and Magic Attack skills (with a Condition of Always and a Rating of 5). It is guaranteed to drop a Big Bomb when defeated (1/1 chance).

Now that we have our dungeon's enemies, you should take a moment to create the various troops that will contain them: Vampire*2, Werewolf*2, Dragon, Mimic.

But, wait! Where are the first two enemy types in that troop list? As it turns out, the Mimic isn't the only enemy type that belongs to a new archetype. Take a look at Figure 13-2 for how this special troop should look.

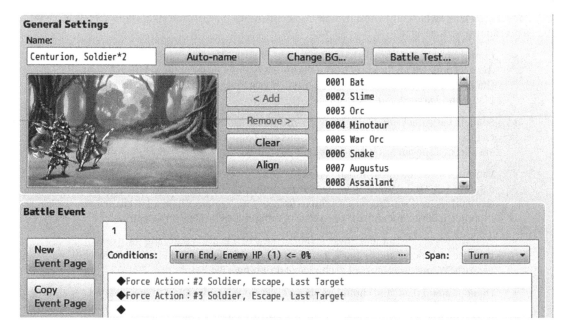

Figure 13-2. *The associated troop page for our first two enemy types*

As you can see, this troop has one Centurion and two Soldiers. Of particular note is the associated troop event. If the Centurion falls, the two Soldiers will flee combat at the end of that turn, having lost their leader. That said, the Soldiers inflict enough damage and are frail enough to merit being defeated first, lest they overwhelm Marsha's meager physical defenses if left uncontested.

The Ancient Armaments

Now that the Demon Castle has appropriately difficult enemies to challenge the player in his/her last leg of the adventure, we want to create new equipment that can allow the player to meet that challenge. Recall back in Chapter 6 when we created the pair of artifacts for the Ruined Spire. Our final dungeon will have a whopping eight pieces of unique equipment for the player to find. See Table 13-2 for a detailed list of what they will be.

Table 13-2. *A List of the Weapons, Armors, and Accessories That Make Up the Ancient Armaments*

Name	Stats / Traits	Weapon or Armor Type / Equipment Type (if applicable)
Ancient Sword	+40 Attack / +20 Attack Speed	Sword
Ancient Bow	+60 Attack / +10 Attack Speed, Seal Equip: Shield	Bow
Ancient Wand	+25 Attack, +40 M. Attack	Cane
Ancient Robe	+35 Defense, +35 M. Defense / Seal Equip: Head	Magic Armor / Body
Ancient Shield	+20 Defense / Element Rate: Physical * 75%	Shield / Shield
Ancient Armor	+50 Defense, +15 M. Defense / Seal Equip: Head	Light Armor / Body
Ancient Ruby Brooch	+15 Defense, +15 M. Defense, +150 Max HP / Max HP * 115%, State Rate: Poison * 0%	General Armor / Accessory
Ancient Onyx Brooch	Max HP * 80%, Element Rate: (Physical, Fire, Ice, Thunder, Darkness) * 70%	General Armor / Accessory

I placed a grand total of 17 (!) chests throughout the game's final dungeon, six of which will contain items from this set. The location of the other two items is a secret I will unveil later in the chapter. Now we can resume where we previously left off.

Encounters of the First Floor

We can now add a list of encounters that the player will be forced to face in the first floor of the Demon Castle. You can see the list in Figure 13-3.

Troop	Weight	Range
Centurion, Soldier*2	3	Entire Map
Vampire*2	1	Entire Map

Figure 13-3. *The encounter list for the first floor of the Demon Castle*

There's not much to it. The player has a 3 in 4 chance of encountering the Centurion-led troop and a 1 in 4 chance of facing two Vampires. The first floor will ease the player into the final dungeon a bit, before unleashing its fury in the later floors. Speaking of which, we're almost done with the first floor.

Wrapping up the First Floor

We created a neat teleportation puzzle for the player to solve, which pretty much covered the lower half of the first floor. But what about the top half? There's quite a bit of space. The staircase leading to the next floor is obvious, but we want to add a few more things. First, make your way to the top-left corner of Demon Castle 1F. It appears to be a cell of some sort. Let's edit that area so that it contains two chests, a staircase that leads down to the Cursed Cave, and a way for the player to open the cell from the inside. See Figure 13-4 for the end result.

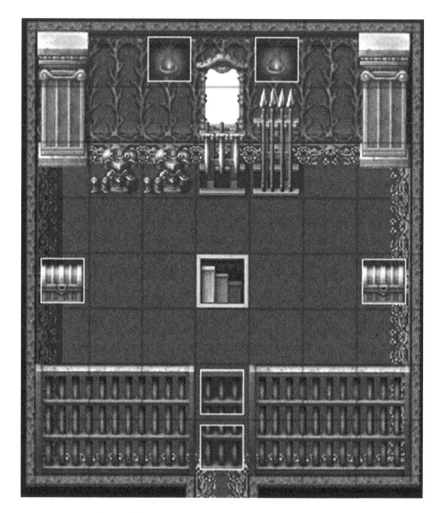

Figure 13-4. *The top-left corner of the first floor, with added tweaks*

There's not much to this. First we remove the premade cell door graphic and then create a pair of events where they once stood. We then set up the cell door so that it opens only when interacted with from above (recall that we did this for the secret passage in the Ice Cave back in Chapter 11). The top event for the cell door has two pages; the first has no condition with a priority of Above Characters, while the second page has no event graphic, a priority of Below Characters, and a switch condition of *DemonCastleCell*. The bottom event contains the facing conditionals. When the player is facing down, the cell door opens and the DemonCastleCell switch is turned on, erasing both cell door events and allowing the player free passage to and from this part of the floor. I won't write out the event per se, but you should be able to figure it out with the information I have given you and by applying what you learned the last time we created such an event. That said, if you find yourself stumped, don't hesitate to check the source code to see how I did it.

With that done, make your way to the upper-right corner of the floor and add another staircase leading down into the otherwise completely empty section. That covers the extent of the tweaks we will make to this first floor of the final dungeon. Now we need only fill the five chests present on this floor. I want this area to have three pieces of the Ancient Armaments, so fill two of the three chests in the lower part of the level with the Ancient Ruby Brooch and the Ancient Robe and the third with an item of your choice (or gold if you would rather). Then, fill one of the chests behind the cell door with the Ancient Shield and the other one with another item of your choice. I differentiate the Ancient Armament chests by making them golden (you'll recall that I did that back in Chapter 6 for the chest containing the Dragontooth Blade as well). Of course, what self-respecting final boss allows the would-be heroes to just get such strong equipment without a fight? Not this one, that's for sure! On that note, let's add a Mimic encounter to each of the three Ancient Armament chests present on this floor. To do that (assuming that you're using the Quick Treasure Event), you need only add the following lines of code between the Set Movement Route and Control Self Switch event commands.

```
♦Text : None, Window, Bottom
:      : The chest was a Mimic!
♦Battle Processing : Mimic
```

As it turns out, the first line isn't strictly necessary, but it's good to let the player know that something different is happening with the chest they have just opened.

■ **Note**   You can insert that code into any part of the default treasure chest event's first page, and the end result will be the same. The game interrupts event processing to do battle processing, so that the event will functionally "freeze in place" until the player defeats the forced encounter.

Once the player defeats the Mimic, they will be awarded the treasure within the chest as normal. If you haven't done so already, take a moment to add both the Demon Castle 2 (not a typo on my end; the second and third floors of the Demon Castle sample map lack the F in their default name that Demon Castle 1F has), and Cursed Cave sample maps to your project. We'll be working on our dungeon's basement next.

The Basement

We had the village elder of Rocksdale tell Harold and Marsha that an orb of great power was hidden beneath the castle. More important, the orb will be necessary to defeat the final boss. This makes the basement the most important floor for the player to visit during his/her time in the final dungeon. I tweaked the Cursed Cave a bit in preparation for what we want to do. You can see the tweaked layout in Figure 13-5.

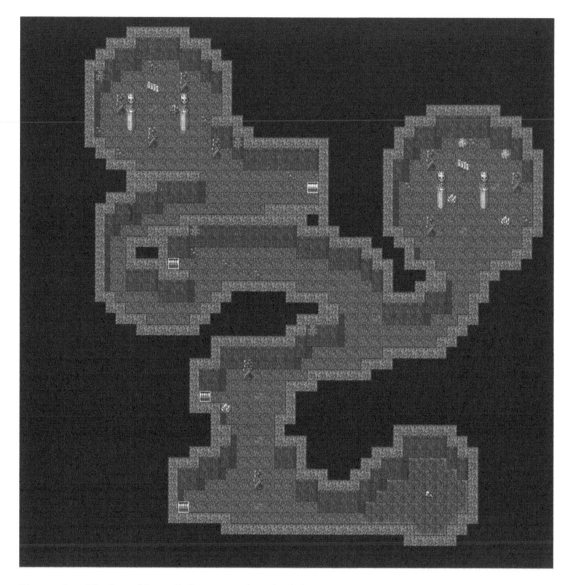

Figure 13-5. *The Cursed Cave, the basement of our final dungeon*

You're probably thinking that one of the chests contains the orb. You'd be wrong. The orb is in the hands of the skeleton at the lower-right corner of the area. One of the four chests contains the Ancient Sword, guarded by a Mimic. Fill the other three chests with whatever you'd like.

Here's the code for the event related to the skeleton:

```
♦Text : None, Window, Bottom
:     : The skeleton lets off a faint glow. Will you touch it?
♦Show Choices : Yes, No (Window, Right, #1, #2)
: When Yes
```

```
◆Text : None, Window, Bottom
:      : Light envelops your body!
◆Change Items : Orb of Light + 1
◆Play ME : 'Fanfare1', 100, 100
◆Text : None, Window, Bottom
:      : You have found the \C[2]Orb of Light\C[0]!
◆Text : Actor3(7), Window, Bottom
:      : Such power! Keep it safe, Harold.
◆Control Self Switch : A = ON
◆
: When No
 ◆
: End
◆
```

The skeleton event is blank, with a Same As Characters priority and an Action Button trigger. If the player touches the skeleton, he/she will receive the Orb of Light, the item needed in order to have a fighting chance against the final boss.

■ **Note**   Alternatively, you could remove the skeleton graphic from the map and add it to the event itself. The overall result is the same.

The Orb of Light is a Key Item in the same vein as the Old Key we created in Chapter 5. That is to say, it cannot be used from the inventory at any time. It will be automatically used by Harold when the party faces down the final boss. Use transfer events to connect the western stairs in the Cursed Cave with the staircase on 1F at (8, 6) on the first floor. In addition, couple the eastern staircase at (41, 13) with the first floor stairs at (39, 6). With that set up, take a look at Figure 13-6 containing the basement's encounter list, before moving on to the next section.

Troop	Weight	Range
Vampire*2	2	Entire Map
Werewolf*2	2	Entire Map
Dragon	1	Entire Map

Figure 13-6. *The list of encounters for the Demon Castle's basement*

The Second Floor

Two floors down and two more floors to go! The second floor of our dungeon is the third location our player should visit, and it's the last floor before reaching the boss. We had a teleportation puzzle for the first floor of our dungeon, and the player received an important item in the basement. Comparatively speaking, the second floor will be more mundane. That said, it also happens to be the floor that will receive the most changes to better fit the overall flow of the dungeon. A look at the northern end of the exterior Demon Castle map will show several entrances that lead into the castle (Figure 13-7).

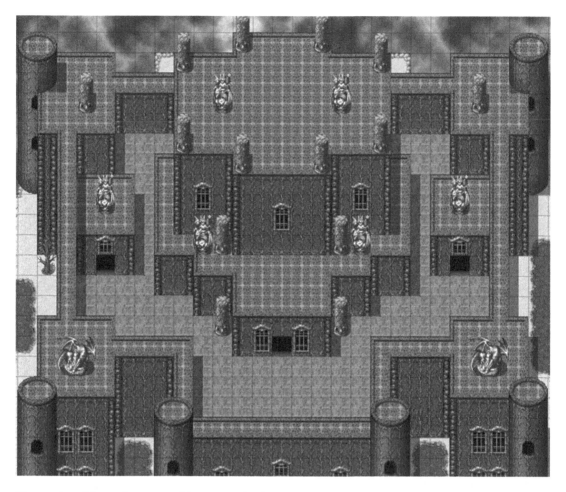

Figure 13-7. *The northern part of the Demon Castle map*

As you can see, there are three entrances that lead into the castle. A look at the sample maps provided for this area reveals that the side entrances don't really get used for much of anything. Conversely, both the second and third floors of the castle have an exit that could lead out into the central entrance. Thus, I decided to redesign the second floor so we can use those extra entrances. See Figure 13-8 for the end result.

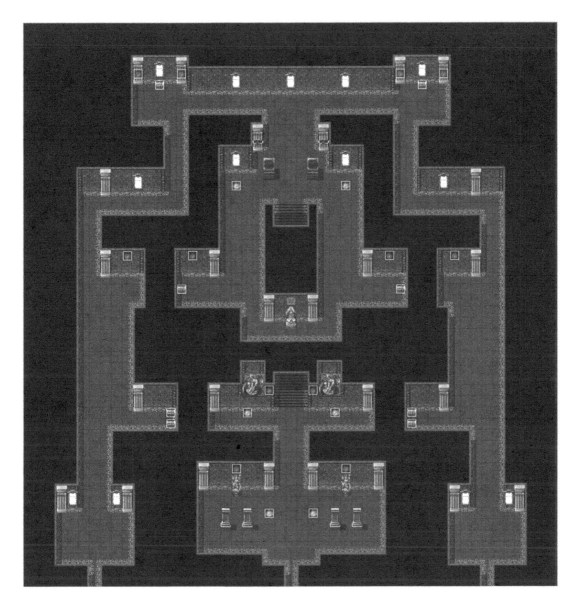

Figure 13-8. *The tweaked Demon Castle 2 map*

Our game's last eight treasure chests are present on this floor. If you are reading a color version of this book (or are following along with the source code project open), you'll notice that all of the chests are blue. Two of the chests will contain the Ancient Bow and Ancient Onyx Brooch respectively while the other six will contain miscellaneous items. However, as you may have already inferred, we're going to be devious about it. Four of the eight chests will contain a monster in a box; namely, a Dragon.

■ **Tip**   To accomplish this, you need only edit the previous Mimic chest event so that the text mentions a Dragon appearing and the Battle Processing event calls the Dragon troop instead.

Both of the chests containing Ancient items will have a Dragon. You can set two of the regular item chests to spawn a Dragon as well, just to keep the player on their toes. Before we go about linking our various exits together via transfer events, let's talk a bit about the statue that's a few spaces below the stairs down to the first floor. See Figure 13-9 for a zoomed-in version of the area surrounding the statue.

Figure 13-9. *The goddess statue placed a few squares below the stairs leading down to the first floor*

On the lower half of the statue, I placed an event with Same As Characters priority and an Action Button trigger. This statue will heal Harold and Marsha when they touch it.

```
◆Text : None, Window, Bottom
:     : A single statue stands defiant in the dreary darkness.
:     : Will you touch it?
◆Show Choices : Yes, No (Window, Right, #1, #2)
: When Yes
   ◆Play SE : Heal1 (90, 100, 0)
   ◆Recover All : Entire Party
   ◆Text : None, Window, Bottom
   :     : The party's HP and MP are restored!
   ◆
: When No
   ◆
: End
◆
```

If you decide to make the final dungeon a point of no return (as in, the player cannot leave the dungeon once he/she enters), you'll want the player to have some way of recovering his/her HP and MP. Otherwise, a prolonged stay will drain his/her recovery items to the point that he/she may not be able to finish the game. Providing for recovery also allows the player to gain levels safely by defeating the enemies in the area and staying near the statue. There are five exits on the second floor, so here's a list of where each one should lead.

- The three-space section of the staircase that encompasses (23, 17), (24, 17), and (25, 17) leads to the three-space section of the staircase on the first floor that encompasses (23, 18), (24, 18), and (25, 18).

- The southwestern exit at (6, 49) connects with the Demon Castle exterior entrance at (12, 12).

- The central exit at (24, 49) connects with the Demon Castle exterior entrance at (21, 16).

- The southeastern exit at (42, 49) connects with the Demon Castle exterior entrance at (30, 12).

- Finally, the three-space section of the staircase that encompasses (23, 31), (24, 31), and (25, 31) leads to the three-space section of the staircase on the third floor that encompasses (18, 28), (19, 28), and (20, 28). While you're at it, take a moment and add the Demon Castle 3 sample map to your project if you haven't already.

■ **Caution**   As with the teleportation puzzle back on the first floor, be careful you don't create a situation in which you trap your player in an infinite loop! The single-space transfer events should land adjacent to the destination, not *on* them.

The last thing to do for this floor is to reveal the encounter list (Figure 13-10).

Troop	Weight	Range
Vampire*2	1	Entire Map
Werewolf*2	1	Entire Map
Dragon	3	Entire Map

Figure 13-10. *The encounter list for the second floor of the Demon Castle*

The general idea behind my encounter lists for this dungeon is that the player will have a greater chance of encountering harder enemies the farther away he/she gets from the entrance. This approach ramps up the tension in anticipation of the fated encounter with the final boss. The player will have a 60% chance of encountering a Dragon and a 40% chance to encounter one of the other two enemy types.

The Final Floor

After fighting through two floors and a basement's worth of enemies, and collecting the Ancient Armaments, the player has finally reached the final dungeon's top floor. While there will be no random encounters on this floor, a final boss does not merely allow itself to be challenged so easily! A seemingly impenetrable barrier will prevent the player from walking up to the final boss. How can the player breach this obstacle? I think it's appropriate at this time that we honor one of the most classic RPG conventions. Let's have a boss rush!

A Boss Rush Overview

In some RPGs (and games of other genres, for that matter), the push toward the final boss is punctuated by having to re-fight all of the bosses that were previously battled. In our game, the player only has to fight two bosses (Augustus, at the Dark Cave, and the Dark General, at the Ruined Spire), so our boss rush will be two enemies long. You could loosely classify boss rushes into two broad categories:

1. Consecutive boss rush. The player has to fight each of the bosses without having a chance to recuperate, rest, or otherwise replenish his/her resources.

2. Nonconsecutive boss rush. The player gets a chance to restore him-/herself after each of the individual boss fights.

We'll be making a boss rush of the second type.

Layout of the Final Floor

I made only minor tweaks to the final floor. To be fair, the third floor of the Demon Castle is rather nondescript. A pair of alcoves on either side of the throne room will serve us for our boss rush. Until the player has defeated both returning bosses, he/she will be unable to pass through the center of the room (marked by Region 66) into the throne room where the final boss awaits. See Figure 13-11 for a look at the tweaked final floor.

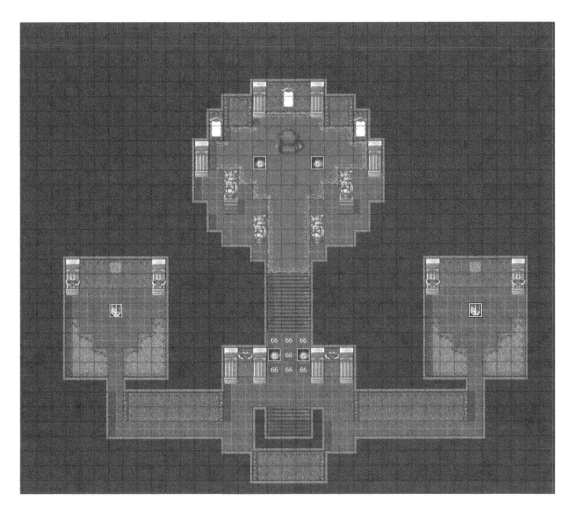

Figure 13-11. *Our final dungeon's top floor*

Creating the Blocking Event

Until the player completes the boss rush, he/she will be pushed back every time an attempt is made to pass through one of the squares marked with Region 66. Here's the barrier event that requires the player to complete the boss rush:

```
♦Control Variables : #0002 X = Map X of Player
♦Control Variables : #0003 Y = Map Y of Player
♦Get Location Info : TeleportLocation, Region ID, ({X},{Y})
♦If : BossBarrierOFF is ON
   ♦Jump to Label : Skip
   ♦
:  End
```

```
♦If : TeleportLocation = 66
   ♦Text : None, Window, Bottom
   :     : A strange force blocks the way!
   ♦Set Movement Route : Player (Wait)
   :                    : ♢1 Step Backward
   ♦If : Self Switch A is OFF
      ♦Text : Actor3(7), Window, Bottom
      :     : It appears we are blocked by another
      :     : sort of power, much like the one back
      :     : at the first floor. Let's try to find
      :     : the source.
      ♦Control Self Switch : A = ON
      ♦
   : End
   ♦
: End
♦Label : Skip
```

As you can see, we can copy-paste the teleportation puzzle event to the point where we can even have the same variable to handle both. The first time the player triggers this event, we have Marsha mention that the situation is similar to what has happened once already and urge the player to find the source of the barrier. As you may have already inferred, the switch that will be flipped on after the player destroys the two crystals is BossBarrierOFF. So, the player cannot progress past that point and is forced to explore the side areas. Where does the player end up?

The Boss Rush

The player will be staring at one of two gray crystals. Depending on the crystal in question, they will either be forced to have a rematch with a stronger version of Augustus (the left crystal) or the Dark General (the right crystal).

The crystal event will have three pages, as we want to cover the following:

- On Page 1, we want to tell the player that the crystal is emanating some sort of power and should be destroyed. If the player tries to destroy it, he/she is attacked by a stronger version of one the game's bosses. A self-switch is flipped, and page 2 becomes active.

- If the player defeats the stronger boss, he/she can interact with the crystal again and destroy it for real.

- Once the crystal is destroyed, the player receives a similar message about "rubble being all that remains of the crystal."

Here's the first part of the first page of the crystal event. It is the same for both bosses.

```
♦Text : None, Window, Bottom
   :     : A dark crystal floats in place.
♦Text : Actor3(7), Window, Bottom
   :     : I feel a terrible power coming from this
   :     : crystal. We should destroy it.
♦Text : None, Window, Bottom
   :     : Will you destroy it?
```

```
◆Show Choices : Yes, No (Window, Right, #1, #2)
: When Yes
  ◆Text : None, Window, Bottom
  :     : You will do no such thing!
  ◆Text : None, Window, Bottom
  :     : The party is interrupted by an enemy!
```

What follows from this point depends on the boss the player is about to face.

- If Augustus:

```
◆Text : Actor3(7), Window, Bottom
:     : Uncle?
◆Text : None, Window, Bottom
:     : Yes, Marsha. I have been resurrected by the will of
:     : the Dark Master. He decrees that none shall reach
:     : his inner sanctum! Fall before my power!
◆Change Battle BGM : Battle2 (90, 100, 0)
◆Battle Processing : Neo Augustus
◆Control Self Switch : A = ON
◆
```

- If Dark General:

```
  ◆Change Battle BGM : Battle2 (90, 100, 0)
  ◆Battle Processing : Forgotten General
  ◆Control Self Switch : A = ON
  ◆
```

Basically, if Augustus is the boss to face, then Marsha recognizes him, he makes a brief villainous speech, and the battle begins (after an appropriate change in music). But if the party is to face the stronger version of the Dark General, no words are traded. This is because the new version of the second boss is a different entity and not the same Dark General the player battled back at the second dungeon. In either case, here's the final part of the first page of the crystal event, which is also identical regardless of the boss fought:

```
: When No
  ◆
: End
◆
```

Before I show the second page of the crystal event, take a look at Figures 13-12 and 13-13, to see of the settings for Neo Augustus and the Forgotten General, stronger versions of the bosses the player had to face earlier in the game.

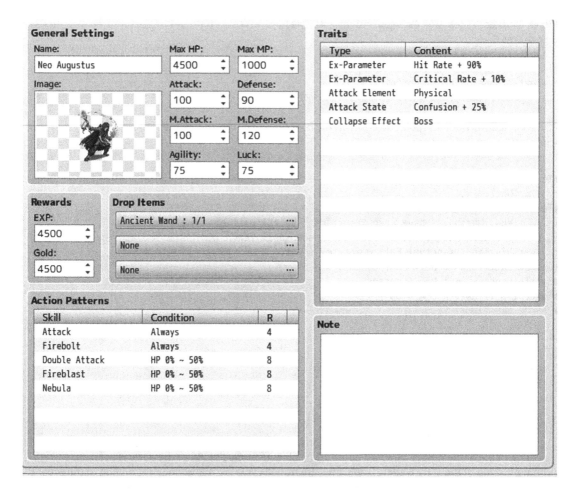

Figure 13-12. *Neo Augustus, the stronger version of our game's first boss*

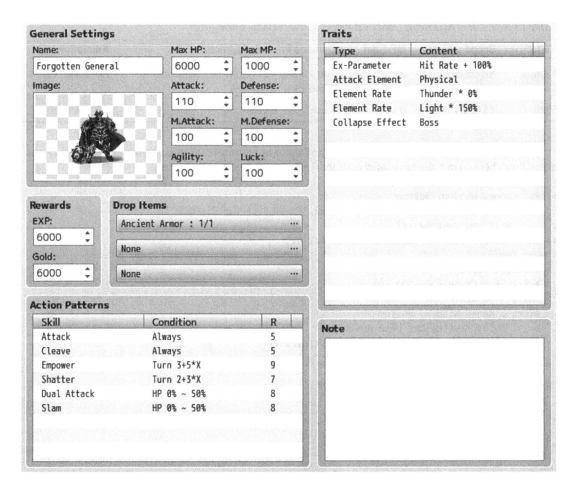

Figure 13-13. *The Forgotten General, the stronger version of our game's second boss*

Neo Augustus gets a fairly strong power boost in the form of higher stats, his added attack state with normal attacks being Confusion instead of Poison, and the addition of Nebula, a stronger version of the Ruin spell first used by the Dark General. He holds the Ancient Wand, which Marsha will appreciate getting once he is defeated.

The Forgotten General doesn't get as much of a power-up (relatively speaking) as Neo Augustus did, but that's mainly because Harold and Marsha encounter the Dark General later on. Thus, the difference in the player's overall power is lower in this case than it was for Augustus. This boss drops the Ancient Armor, which is body armor that Harold can wear. Slam is another new skill. This one deals slightly more physical damage than a normal attack and ignores part of its target's defense. Before continuing with the crystal event, Table 13-3 lists the two new skills created for the boss rush. As you may imagine, the final boss will get some skills of his own, but those will be a surprise for later.

Table 13-3. *A List of New Skills Used by the Bosses of Our Game's Boss Rush*

Name	Scope	MP Cost	Damage Formula / Effects	Animation
Nebula	All Enemies	32	400 + a.mat * 3 - b.mdf * 4 / Poison 20%, Blind 15%, Sleep 12%	Darkness All 2
Slam	1 Enemy	0	a.atk * 4.5 – b.def * 1.5	Hit Physical

After you add the new bosses and skills to the Database, it's time to move on. Here's page 2 of the crystal event. From here on out, the associated code for this event applies to both crystals.

```
◆Text : None, Window, Bottom
:     : The shadow crystal floats in place.
:     : Will you destroy it?
◆Show Choices : Yes, No (Window, Right, #1, #2)
: When Yes
    ◆Fadeout Screen
    ◆Play SE : Crash (90, 100, 0)
    ◆Wait : 60 frames
    ◆Text : None, Window, Bottom
    :     : The crystal has been destroyed!
    ◆Control Variables : #0025 CrystalsDestroyed += 1
    ◆Control Self Switch : B = ON
    ◆Fadein Screen
    ◆
: When No
    ◆
: End
◆
```

Once the player defeats either boss, he/she can interact with their crystal again and destroy it for real. The last page of both crystal events is identical to the second page of the teleportation puzzle crystal. It would require self-switch B to be flipped on. In the page itself, you would replace the crystal graphic with the rubble tile from Tileset B and give a message to the effect that the crystal is no more. Once both crystals have been destroyed, we'll want to flip on the BossBarrierOFF switch, allowing the player to get past the barrier blocking his/her way to the Dark Master's location. We can do this via a simple two-page Autorun event when the CrystalsDestroyed variable is equal to 2. Page 1 of the Autorun would have the conditional of CrystalsDestroyed > 2 and would look like this.

```
◆Text : None, Window, Bottom
:     : The barrier blocking the way to the Dark Master has
:     : been destroyed!
◆Control Switches : #0043 BossBarrierOFF = ON
◆Control Self Switch : A = ON
◆
```

As I said, simple! We give a message telling the player that the barrier is down and turn on the BossBarrierOFF switch, which will allow the player to ascend the staircase into the final boss's throne room.

■ **Note**   I glossed over changing the battle BGM back to normal after the boss fights. The easiest way to do this is with the tried-and-true strategy of granting Immortal status to the boss on Turn 0 of the battle and then revoking it when they drop to 0 HP or less. You would change the battle BGM right before removing the state at the end of the battle.

The Final Boss

The player has fought tooth and nail through the entirety of the final dungeon to reach his/her foe. As is standard in RPGs, the final boss in our game is in the last possible place that Harold and Marsha would think of looking. Thus, the Dark Master is at the castle's third floor, in the throne room that is unlocked by clearing the boss rush.

Creating the Pre-Battle Autorun Event

When the player reaches the top of the staircase past the area marked by Region 66 successfully, an Autorun event will take over, tinting the screen. The player will walk toward the final boss as the tint slowly fades. Once there, the final boss will exchange some banter with the player's party before starting combat. Before we can start work on the Autorun event, we need to use a conditional branch within a Parallel event (you can place the following code below the Skip label in the Parallel event we used to block the passage off in the first place) that detects whether the player has reached the top of the staircase.

```
◆If : Y = 18
  ◆If : Self Switch B is OFF
    ◆Control Switches  : #0044 FinalBossEncounter = ON
    ◆Control Self Switch : B = ON
    ◆
  : End
  ◆
 : End
◆
```

Naturally, our pre-battle Autorun event will require FinalBossEncounter to be switched on before starting. Speaking of which, here's the relevant code for the Autorun event.

```
◆Tint Screen : (-68,-68,-68,0), 60 frames (Wait)
◆Text : None, Window, Bottom
:     : Oho! So, you two have finally made it. Pity that
:     : this is where your quest ends.
◆Set Movement Route : Player (Wait)
:                   : ◊1 Step Forward
:                   : ◊1 Step Forward
◆Tint Screen : (-51,-51,-51,0), 60 frames
◆Text : None, Window, Bottom
:     : It's truly fascinating what humans will do for the
:     : sake of such petty things like justice and hope.
◆Set Movement Route : Player (Wait)
:                   : ◊1 Step Forward
:                   : ◊1 Step Forward
```

303

```
♦Tint Screen : (-34,-34,-34,0), 60 frames
♦Text : None, Window, Bottom
     :     : So, what would you like your gravestones to read?
♦Set Movement Route : Player (Wait)
     :                  : ◊1 Step Forward
     :                  : ◊1 Step Forward
♦Tint Screen : (-17,-17,-17,0), 60 frames
♦Set Movement Route : Player (Wait)
     :                  : ◊1 Step Forward
♦Tint Screen : (0,0,0,0), 60 frames
♦Text : Actor1(0), Window, Bottom
     :     : The only one who's going to need a
     :     : gravestone here is you!
```

■ **Caution**   If you overestimate the number of movement commands needed, the lack of a Skip at the end of the movement sequence will cause the game to hang.

```
♦Text : Actor3(7), Window, Bottom
     :     : I concur. It is past time that you be
     :     : dethroned!
♦Text : None, Window, Bottom
     :     : Ah, Augustus's niece. You already know the truth of
     :     : the world. Or, at the least, you suspect it. So
     :     : foolish are you that you would subject the people
     :     : of the west to the truth?
♦Text : Actor3(7), Window, Bottom
     :     : It serves no one to live in lies!
♦Text : Actor1(0), Window, Bottom
     :     : What are you talking about, Marsha?
♦Text : None, Window, Bottom
     :     : Ohoho! You haven't even told your traveling
     :     : companion. Riveting! That'll be something to talk
     :     : about. For sure. In the afterlife!
♦Change Battle BGM : Battle3 (90, 100, 0)
♦Control Self Switch : A = ON
♦Battle Processing : Dark Master
```

At the end of it all, the player realizes that Marsha knows something he/she does not. However, there's a boss to defeat!

The Dark Master and the Final Battle

We want to use a troop event that triggers as soon as the battle starts to check and see if the player has the Orb of Light in his/her inventory. If the player does, we apply a state to the Dark Master that lowers all of his stats except AGI, MHP, and MMP by 50%. If he/she doesn't, the player has the unenviable task of somehow beating an enemy even stronger than the game's superboss. See Figure 13-14 for the Dark Master's relevant information.

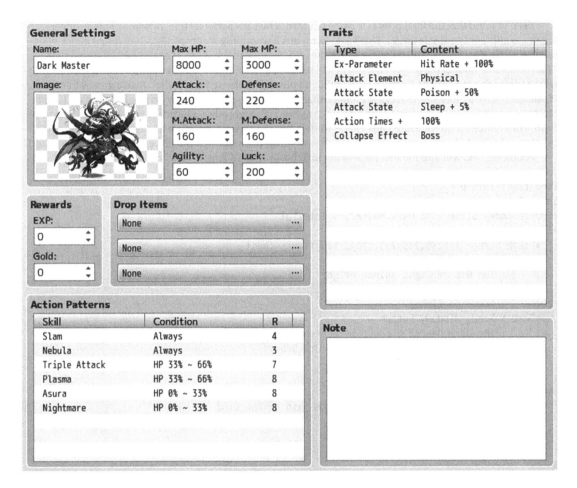

Figure 13-14. *The Dark Master's relevant information*

You will notice that defeating the Dark Master awards no experience, gold, or items. Given that the game will end after defeating the final boss, there isn't much of a point in the player earning any of that. Table 13-4 lists the new skills that our final boss will use.

Table 13-4. *A List of the Skills Used Exclusively by Our Game's Final Boss*

Name	Scope	MP Cost	Damage Formula / Effects	Animation
Asura	3 Random Enemies	0	50 + a.atk * 2 – b.def * 2, 5% Variance / Invocation: Repeat: 2	Slash Physical
Plasma	1 Enemy	25	Attack Element: Physical, (150 + a.mat * 2 - b.mdf) + (150 + a.atk * 2 - b.def)	Neutral One 1
Nightmare	1 Enemy	32	300 + a.mat * 2 - b.mdf * 4 / Poison 55%, Blind 35%, Sleep 30%, Confusion 25%	Darkness One 1

Keep in mind that the final boss acts twice per turn. Thus, it's perfectly fine for some of his stronger attacks to affect only a single target. That said, Asura hits a whopping six times. Each individual attack does relatively little damage, so it all balances out in the end. Plasma attacks both of its target's defensive stats. This means that both of the player characters will suffer the brunt of the attack's damage through their weaker defensive stat (Magic Defense for Harold and physical Defense for Marsha). It also means that Plasma will have a more stable average damage than most other spells that only do magical damage (which Marsha trivially resists, but inflicts severe damage to Harold). Nightmare is basically an improved version of Ruin. The chance for the various status effects to stick has improved. Confusion has also been added to the list of possible maladies. If nothing else, this fight will surely burn through the player's Dispel Herb supplies!

Following, you will find the first page of the final boss's troop event:

```
Condition: Turn 0
Span: Battle
◆Change Enemy State : #1 Dark Master, + Immortal
◆If : Party has Orb of Light
   ◆Flash Screen : (255,255,255,170), 120 frames (Wait)
   ◆Text : None, Window, Bottom
   :     : The Orb of Light shines bright!
   ◆Text : None, Window, Top
   :     : Accursed light!
   ◆Text : None, Window, Bottom
   :     : The Dark Master's power is weakened!
   ◆Change Enemy State : Entire Troop, + Orb Debuff
   ◆
: Else
   ◆Text : None, Window, Top
   :     : You dared to face me without the aid of the Orb?
   :     : Hahaha!
   ◆
: End
◆
```

We make the Dark Master immortal at the start of the fight, so that we can trigger a troop event when he drops to 0% HP or less. Orb Debuff is the name of the negative state applied to the Dark Master. When the player manages to defeat the Dark Master, the other troop event page is triggered.

```
Condition: Enemy HP (1) <= 0%
Span: Battle
◆Text : None, Window, Top
:     : Guh! Impressive...
◆Control Switches : #0045 FinalBossDefeated = ON
◆Change Enemy State : #1 Dark Master, - Immortal
```

After the player defeats the final boss, we should have an Autorun event that leads into the credits. However, let's entertain a "What if?" situation first. Mainly, what if the final boss had a second form?

Transform!

A hallmark of many classic RPGs is a final boss with multiple forms. Let's give our Dark Master a second form (you can see its information in Figure 13-15). We'll use the Darklord-final battle sprite. The final form of the final boss deserves a special attack. So, I took Plasma as the base and made a new spell called Nihil Break. It costs 80 MP and has a damage formula of $[(200 + a.mat * 3 - b.mdf) + (200 + a.atk * 3 - b.def)]$ with no Variance. Much like Plasma, it is a Physical element spell. Now, how do we switch our final boss to his second form? We can use the Enemy Transform command on page 3 of the event command list. In this case, when the player drops the Dark Master to 0 HP, we want him to transform into his second form. You can also use Enemy Transform for several other neat enemy archetypes, such as an unhatched egg that could turn into a dragon if you don't destroy it fast enough, or a jack-in-a-box-type monster that randomly morphs into one of several others when a certain condition is met.

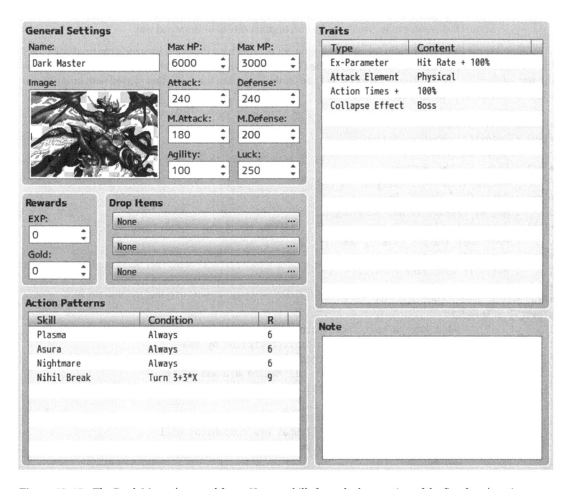

Figure 13-15. *The Dark Master's second form. He uses skills from the last section of the first form's action patterns and his signature Nihil Break every third turn starting on Turn 3.*

■ **Note** You can find an example troop for this variation on our final boss battle in troop slot #49.

The End (of the Game)

After a journey spanning four dungeons, three area bosses, two towns, and one Dark Master, this RPG has been completed! Of course, that only refers to the scope of this book concerning the subject. There is no reason that you have to stop working on the game. After all, we left a lot of things in the air. For example:

- What is the truth that the Dark Master (and the Dark General, for that matter) hinted at? Marsha seems to have known what was going on, but she kept her companion in the dark.

- What happens next, plot-wise? Perhaps there is more than one Dark Master. Therese ended up a loose end, in terms of characterization. Maybe she joins Harold and Marsha after they defeat the Dark Master.

- No one had been able to leave Seaside and return for the past few years. The defeat of the Dark Master may give the player an opportunity to understand why.

There's some food for thought for you. As for me, let me finish up the event involving the final boss. The FinalBossDefeated switch is flipped on when the Dark Master is finally defeated. (You could also flip it on at the start of the fight, as the player cannot escape the battle.) Page 3 of the event that started with an Autorun will end with an Autorun as well.

```
♦Fadeout BGM: 5 sec.
♦Text : Actor1(0), Window, Bottom
:     : It is over!
♦Text : None, Window, Bottom
:     : Marsha smiles wistfully at Harold.
♦Text : Actor3(7), Window, Bottom
:     : No, my friend. It has only begun.
♦Text : Actor1(0), Window, Bottom
:     : Huh? What are you talking about?
♦Text : Actor3(7), Window, Bottom
:     : Well, it goes like this...
♦Fadeout Screen
♦Play BGM : Theme1 (90, 100, 0)
♦Text(S) : Speed 2
:              : What Marsha next tells Harold leaves the young hero in
:              : disbelief. A world in ruins...controlled by two
:              : other Dark Masters. Why had the west alone been
:              : spared? To that question, all Marsha did was smile
:              : and point at Harold cryptically.
:              :
:              : So many questions unanswered. What path will our
:              : heroes' journey take next? What new companions will
:              : they find? Does humanity yet live in the rest of the
:              : world?
```

We fade out the background music in preparation for the ending. After a small chat between the two party members, the screen is faded out, we play some different background music, and some scrolling text is displayed. Unlike Show Text, Show Scrolling Text should only be used on a black screen (this event command displays only text, no text boxes).

```
♦Fadeout BGM : 2 sec.
♦Wait : 120 frames
♦Play BGM : Theme6 (90, 100, 0)
♦Text(S) : Speed 2
:                 : CREDITS:
:                 :
:                 : Me - For making this game.
:                 :
:                 : You - For playing it.
:                 :
:                 : KADOKAWA Games - For making RPG Maker MV.
:                 : Without it, this game would not exist.
:                 :
:                 : THANKS FOR PLAYING!!!
♦Return to Title Screen
```

Once we have displayed the epilogue text, we fade out the BGM once again and then start the music that's played by default at the title screen. Some short credits later, we send the player back to the title screen.

More Tips and Tricks for Final Dungeons

While this chapter is as good as done, there are so many more things that you can do with a final dungeon. RPGs have had all types of final dungeons, ranging from the one-room final dungeon (justified by the difficulty of getting into that one room; the player usually needs a series of keys or artifacts to open the path) to a sprawling mega-fortress that dwarfs the Demon Castle many times over. Here's a list of other things you can add to the final dungeons of your future games.

- *Uncontrollable movement puzzle*: You could either use the ice puzzle we created before or make a new type of puzzle in which the player is forced in a certain direction, based on where he/she has stepped. Much like the teleportation puzzle we used on the first floor, this can be used to force the player to figure out how exactly he/she can get past that particular area.

- *The escape*: Once the player defeats the final boss, instead of ending the game right then and there, you can make it so that a countdown begins. (You can use the *Control Timer* event command for this purpose.) If the player has not escaped the castle when the timer hits zero, you can either give him/her a Game Over (probably a jerk move, considering that the player had to defeat the final boss even to get that far and probably has not even saved) or send him/her back to the throne room to try to escape again. On a related note, you might make it so that the timer doesn't start until the player starts trying to escape, so that he/she has a chance to save the game beforehand.

- *An alternate take on the boss rush*: Besides creating a boss rush as we have, you can also stagger its appearance. For example, if your game has four main bosses and you want them to reappear in the final dungeon that also has four floors, you can block each floor with a single boss. The player has to defeat the boss to advance upward (or downward).

- *An alternative to the final boss fight*: Perhaps the final boss gets its power from a crystal nexus or some other arcane artifact. Destroying the artifact could provide the player another way of winning the game while avoiding confrontation. It didn't seem appropriate for our game, but an RPG that wants to reward differing play styles could benefit from such an approach.

- Make it so that the final boss is weakened according to the number of sidequests the player has carried out. This is a neat way of rewarding the player for taking the time to explore beyond the beaten path.

Summary

Over the course of this chapter, we created our game's final dungeon and populated it. We used a teleportation puzzle on the dungeon's first floor that would stop the player from progressing until he/she had destroyed the crystal powering the traps. Additionally, we had chests that were actually monsters and attacked the player when opened. In the basement, we had the player find an artifact of power that could be used to weaken the final boss. On the second floor, we had chests guarded by Dragons and a healing statue. The way to our final boss in the third floor was blocked by an invisible barrier that required our player to defeat stronger versions of bosses already faced. Finally, we created a final boss (with a second alternate form) that, when defeated, triggered the end credits. In the next chapter, we will tackle some basic scripting exercises in RMMV.

CHAPTER 14

Basic Scripting Exercises in RMMV

We have now finished our game. All that is left is to cover a few things that I didn't cover in earlier chapters. Although an in-depth look into JavaScript scripting within RMMV is outside the scope of this book, it is still a good idea for this chapter to cover the basics through a series of exercises. Chapter 15 will cover other miscellanea that did not fit within the overall narrative of our game and the book so far.

What Is JavaScript?

JavaScript is a prototype-based object-oriented programming language that was designed by Brendan Eich in 1995 while he was working at Netscape. It is used for the entirety of RMMV's code base. Learning how to use JavaScript will help you greatly whenever you decide to start customizing your games with plugins.

What Is Object-Oriented Programming?

In a sentence: it is programming that uses code organized into *objects* as the building blocks for a desired result. In the case of JavaScript, prototypes are used to create master copies of code that can then be cloned for use as needed throughout any given program. This is in contrast to Ruby and other object-oriented programming languages where classes are used instead.

Note You'll see MV's documentation refer to its various main functions as *classes*. That term provides more clarity for RPG Maker veterans accustomed to working with Ruby, but it is not strictly correct when talking about JavaScript. All you need to know if you're new to JavaScript is that what the MV developers call a class is a function that contains other functions (those contained functions are called *methods*; a method is a function stored as an object property).

As you may have inferred, a function is an object. In fact, when talking about object-oriented programming in general and JavaScript specifically, it's probably easier to list what *isn't* considered an object. In any case, we've been seeing examples of how JavaScript (and thus object-oriented programming) works, in the few scripting exercises we tackled for our game. Here's what we've touched upon already:

- The character $ is used to represent global variables within RPG Maker MV's code. This is a holdover from Ace and other earlier RPG Maker iterations, where Ruby was the scripting language and $ the sign to mark a variable as global. That means a value denoted with $ can be used anywhere within a project (such as our game).

- An underscore before a variable (such as _name in the next bullet) designates that variable as private. In other words, such a variable is only meant to be accessed from specifically designated functions and methods. Note that this is a JavaScript naming convention and not actually enforced by the underscore symbol (which JavaScript treats as just another symbol).

- $gameActors.actor(n) (where *n* is the actor ID) is an array that contains several defining aspects of Actors in RMMV, such as name, level, and nickname. In Chapter 11, we used $gameActors.actor(n)._name for one of our project's puzzles.

- An array is an ordered collection of objects.

As you can see, there are quite a few things we already know. During the course of this chapter, we'll be tackling other simple things that we can do with only the most basic of JavaScript experience. Of course, there are two things we need to do before we start work on this chapter proper. The first order of business is getting a better text editor. While Notepad has served us well up to now, we could benefit from having a few extra programming-specific features. So, let's get Atom!

What is Atom?

Atom is a free, open source text and source code editor for Windows, OS X (Mac), and Linux that can also be used as an IDE (integrated development environment). We just want it for two features:

- **Line numbers.** Instead of having to say: "*Find the code line in rpg_objects.js that reads this that there*", I can just say: "*go to line 7852 in rpg_objects.js*". Doesn't seem like much of a difference, but it's definitely a lot neater to read. Of course, I'll generally list a little of what is to be found at that line number, so you can use the Find function to better effect.

- **Code coloring.** When you open a code file within Atom, it tries to auto-detect what language the code is written in (from a fairly large list of preset programming languages). After detecting the language (or, alternately, the user manually defining which language it is within the software, by changing the detected language in the lower-right corner of the Atom interface), the program automatically colors the various commands appropriately. If nothing else, it can help you get a better idea of how JavaScript code flows within RMMV's js files.

Downloading Atom

To be able to use Atom, we need to *download* the software. Make your way to https://atom.io.

If You're On Windows

You'll want to click the button Download Windows Installer, where you will be prompted to save the file (85.1 MB in size) to your computer.

If You're on Mac

You can click Other Platforms, find the atom_mac.zip file, and left-click it. You'll get a prompt to save the file to your computer.

Installing and Running Atom

In either case, you now have the Atom file on your computer. Take a few minutes to install it as per your operating system. Once Atom is installed, it will instantly launch, leaving you at a screen much like that in Figure 14-1.

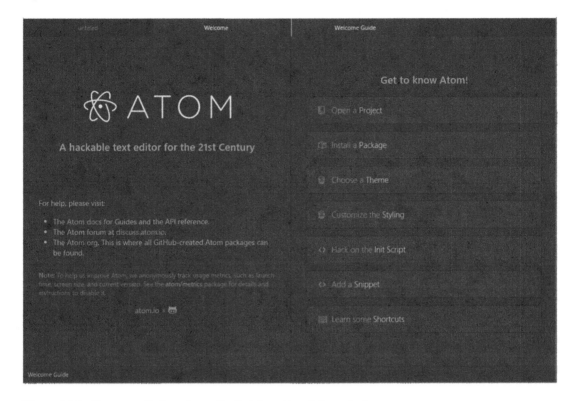

Figure 14-1. *The screen that greets you the first time Atom is launched*

Move the mouse cursor to the Welcome Guide tab (that's the currently active tab). You should see a small x appear while your cursor is anywhere in the tab area. Click that x to close the Welcome Guide. Then do the same for the Welcome tab, which will leave you with a single tab, titled *untitled*. We are ready to do the second thing I wanted to do before starting the chapter's JavaScript coverage.

Scripted Damage Formulas—RMMV Edition

Did you think I forgot about what we discussed back in Chapter 3? Okay, maybe I did. Just for a bit. Seriously though, it's high time we adapt that module I created for Ace into a plugin for use in MV. For reference, here's the Ace module copy-pasted from its first appearance earlier in the book.

```
module Winter
  module_function

  def phys(p, a, b, v = $game_variables)
    if a.atk > b.def
      return (a.atk*p*(1.00+(1.00-(b.def*1.00/a.atk*1.00))))
```

```
      else
          return (a.atk*p*(a.atk*1.00/b.def*1.00))
    end
end

#Express in the form Winter.phys(p, a, b)
#p is the power multiplier for the ATK stat of the caster.

def sitva(bd, p, a, b, v = $game_variables)
    return ((bd + a.mat*p)*(a.mat*1.00/b.mdf*1.00))
end

#Express in the form Winter.sitva(bd, p, a, b)
#bd is the base damage of the Sitva
#p is the power multiplier for the MAT stat of the caster.
end
```

Without further ado, here's the adaptation of the Ace module for custom damage formulas, rewritten for MV:

```
//=========================================================================
// CustomDamageFormulas.js
//=========================================================================

/*:
 * @plugindesc A Beginning RPG Maker VX Ace Module adapted for RPG Maker MV
 * @author Darrin Perez
 * @help
 * Allows custom damage formulas to be expressed in the form Winter.module,
 * where module is equal to one of the variable properties in the js file.
 *
 * phys: Used for physical skills. Express in the form Winter.phys(p,a,b)
 * p is the power multiplier for the ATK stat of the attacker.
 *
 * magic: Used for magical skills. Express in the form Winter.magic(bd,p,a,b)
 * bd is the base damage of the spell
 * p is the power multiplier for the MAT stat of the attacker.
 */

var Winter = Winter || {};

Winter.phys = function (p, a, b) {
  if (a.atk > b.def) {
    return (a.atk*p)*(1.00-(b.def*1.00/a.atk*1.00));
    } else {
    return (a.atk*p)*(a.atk*1.00/b.def*1.00);
    }
};

Winter.magic = function(bd, p, a, b) {
return ((bd + a.mat*p)*(a.mat*1.00/b.mdf*1.00));
};
```

As you might have noticed, the single greatest change to this Ace module turned MV plugin is all of the text *before* the code. In Ruby, you would use the pound sign (#) to denote a comment. In any language, comments in code are ignored by the program when the file is executed. In JavaScript, you can use // to comment out a single line or the combination of /* and */ to comment out everything between those two symbols. You can see examples of both in this code file. You can find a copy of this plugin (and the other plugin created for this chapter, for that matter) within the source code project's plugin folder (located within the js folder we've been to a few times already mainly to look at rpg_objects.js). Take some time to write out the plugin within Atom, for the sake of practice. Then let's go ahead and dissect this newly-created plugin together:

- CustomDamageFormulas.js is the filename of the plugin written out within the js itself (pretty much every script/plugin I've ever seen does this, so I just followed suit). @plugindesc, @author, and @help are three metatags that you can place within comments in your plugin so that potential users can see what your plugin does at a glance. I'll show them off in action a bit later.

- After the explanation contained within @help, we have our actual plugin. It starts with

  ```
  var Winter = Winter || {};
  ```

In JavaScript, every variable needs to be defined before initial use. Here we're defining the Winter variable as Winter *or* new object (the ‖ symbol is the or operator in JavaScript, while the curly braces denote the creation of a new object). Throughout this book, we have seen that variables can hold characters (numbers, letters, and symbols). As it turns out, variables can hold entire functions as well! This is possible because a variable is an object, and objects in JavaScript can hold multiple values.

Note If you recall the note I wrote back in Chapter 11 about using _name and not name for our riddle puzzle, using the latter instead references the function MV uses to get a determined actor's name. Now you have the exact reason this can happen at all.

- Once we define Winter, we can then proceed to add methods to it via the use of variable properties.

- In the case of Winter.phys, Winter is the variable name, and phys is the variable property. As the previous note implies, this form is textually equivalent to stating that Winter is the object and phys is the method. The declared function can hold three parameters (or arguments; again, both terms are correct) called p, a, and b. p is the power multiplier as applied to the attacker's Attack Stat, while a and b represent the attack user and its target respectively. The rest of the function should be self-explanatory. We have the code check to see if the attacker has greater ATK than the defender has DEF. If that is the case, then we execute the first formula in the function. Otherwise (if the attacker has equal or less ATK than the defender's DEF), the code will execute the second formula.

- After Winter.phys, we have Winter.magic, which is a simpler method that holds four parameters instead of phys's three. Rather than have two formulas based on the interplay between the attacker's Attack stat and the defender's Defense stat, we instead have a single formula that is used regardless of the relationship between the user's Magic Attack and target's Magic Defense. The value bd is the base damage of the spell, before any other calculations (for example, the stock Thunder spell in MV does 100 base damage), while p is the power multiplier applied to the attacker's MAT, and a and b have the same meanings as in the phys function.

■ **Caution** The curly braces and semicolons used throughout the plugin are critical to its proper functioning. A single removal can be enough to prevent the plugin from working at all. Code can be pesky like that.

■ **Note** You can find two example skills in Skill slots #245 and #246. You can find an enemy that uses both of the example skills in Enemy slot #251. Last, you can also find the troop containing that enemy for Battle Test purposes in Troop slot #251.

There you go! Feel free to add to or remove from it as you see fit for your own game projects. Make sure you save your completed plugin in the plugins folder of your game project and then start up MV if you haven't already. Once your project has loaded, go to the Tools section of the main menu and find the Plugin Manager (or press F10). Then double-click the first slot in the completely empty list to open a window much like the one in Figure 14-2.

Figure 14-2. *The Plugin Manager window used to add or remove plugins from an MV project. Note the effects of using @plugindesc and @author within our new plugin*

Setting which plugin you wish to add to your project is as easy as clicking the button below Name and selecting it from the dropdown that appears. By the way, the dropdown menu looks *only* at the plugins folder of your project, which happens to be why you don't see any of the core code files for MV (such as our often-referenced rpg_objects) in that list. With all of that done, go to Atom and create a new file. You'll notice that the filename at the top of the program stays the same. Close the tab for the plugin we already created, and then close the project folder with the same name by right-clicking it and selecting Remove Project Folder (you can find it directly to the left of the individual file tabs, under the first few menu options such as File and Edit). Then you will be left with your single, untitled document. But wait! I haven't shown how the information written within the @help metatag looks in the Plugin Manager (see Figure 14-3).

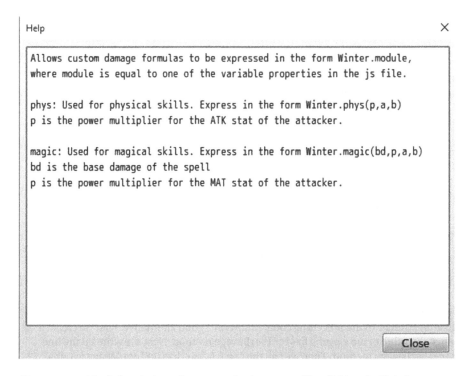

Figure 14-3. *The help window of our new plugin, accessed by clicking the Help button*

Much better! Now then, I do think that it's time to start work on our chapter's material—tweaking MV's functionality using basic JavaScript. The first exercise will be to move our modified floor damage code over to a new plugin. This new plugin, incidentally, will contain all of the code for the rest of this chapter. I'll call it Snippets.js (and you can find it within the chapter source code plugins folder as such), but you can name it as you like.

Damage Floors Revisited

I covered damage floors all the way back in Chapter 4. There, I discussed that you can change the damage that such terrain causes, based on Regions. Terrain tags work even better, and you can differentiate between types of floor damage in that way as well. Recall that we used the *switch* statement to return differing amounts of floor damage based on the value of a certain variable. First, we'll want to revert the changes made to the code in rpg_objects. The end result should look like the following:

```
Game_Actor.prototype.basicFloorDamage = function() {
    return 10;
};
```

After reverting the rpg_objects method, you'll want to write the following in our new file:

```
var _Game_Actor_basicFloorDamage = Game_Actor.prototype.basicFloorDamage;
Game_Actor.prototype.basicFloorDamage = function() {
_Game_Actor_basicFloorDamage.call(this);
switch ($gameVariables.value(4)) {
    case 0:
    default:
        return 10;
    case 1:
        return 20;
    case 2:
        return 35;
    case 3:
        return 60;
  }
};
```

When I introduced the code for variable damage floor damage, I noted that directly altering a function isn't the best way to go about things. In the preceding code, I show off a good alternative. First we create a new variable and assign it the value of the existing basicFloorDamage method. Next, we write up the line that starts out the basicFloorDamage method. Then we call the Game_Actor_basicFloorDamage variable we created, and pass this as a parameter, causing the contents of the existing basicFloorDamage method (contained within _Game_Actor_basicFloorDamage) to be added to our new, altered, function.

The notation this is used in JavaScript to mark instances. For example, you'll typically see variables inside of functions expressed within RMMV's code as this.varname or this._varname (where, naturally, varname is the actual name of the variable). Such a variable is used within that particular instance of the function at hand; once the function is finished executing, that variable instance ceases to exist, only to be replaced by another one when the function is called again. Don't worry if that didn't make too much sense; this is notorious for tripping up even veteran JavaScript programmers. For the purposes of this text, just know that the preceding code uses this in a correct way.

Anyway, the last part of the function (the new code for the basicFloorDamage method) is nothing we haven't seen before, so I'll just leave you with the reminder that values of $gameVariables.value(4) that are not covered within the cases just shown (under 0 or over 3) will return a default value of 10.

Before we move on to the next section, recall that we have another snippet that can be transferred to our new plugin file. Here's the code we want to move over (it is from Chapter 9 and is located in rpg_managers.js):

```
BattleManager.setEscape = function(bool) {
    this._canEscape = bool;
};
```

Once you have copied over the code to the Snippets plugin, you can go ahead and erase it from rpg_managers.js. The second exercise will involve changing how critical hits are calculated, so that they are influenced by the Luck stat of the attacker and the defender.

Critically Coded

As robust as RMMV is right out of the box, it has a few quirks that bug me. Ironically, some of those quirks were also present back in Ace. Thankfully, you can tweak such things with the power of JavaScript. This exercise is very nearly a one-liner. All we need to do is find the code that governs critical hit rates. Open up rpg_objects.js in Atom and run a search for "critical" (use the Find in Buffer option from the Find submenu; alternately press Ctrl+F). Among the 11 results that should pop up, we're interested in the very first one (it's on line 1640 of rpg_objects). Once there, you should be able to see the following code:

```
Game_Action.prototype.itemCri = function(target) {
    return this.item().damage.critical ? this.subject().cri * (1 - target.cev) : 0;
};
```

What we see here is a method (`Game_Action.prototype.itemCri`) that accepts a single parameter when run. As you may recall from earlier in the book, what we're looking at right now is a ternary expression. It is equivalent to the following code, as the question mark takes the place of the `then`, while the colon does the same for the `else`.

```
if this.item().damage.critical
then this.subject().cri * (1- target.cev)
else 0
```

That's the extent of this particular method. Basically, if the skill or item is capable of landing criticals, then the chance of landing a critical is equal to the user's critical hit chance, multiplied by 1 minus the enemy's critical evasion rate (the result is a percentage). Let's add a new section to our Snippets plugin to hold the altered version of our `itemCri` method. Here's the altered result:

```
var _Game_Action_itemCri = Game_Action.prototype.itemCri;
Game_Action.prototype.itemCri = function(target) {
_Game_Action_itemCri.call(this,target);
return this.item().damage.critical ?
  (this.subject().cri + (this.subject().luk * 0.002)) -
  (target.luk * 0.002) * (1 - target.cev) : 0;
};
```

In my version, I made it so that the luck of both the user and the target influence the ability to land a critical hit.

■ **Note** You'll see that I split what would have otherwise been a humongous `return` line. As a general rule, you should only split a line in a way that doesn't break an expression in half. So, I make a new line after the question mark from the ternary expression and another one directly after the minus sign. Since JavaScript looks for semicolons to signify line ends, this doesn't affect our method negatively. Just make sure not to accidentally insert extra semicolons.

For every 5 Luck that the user has, he/she gains 1% to his/her Critical Rate. For every 5 Luck that the target has, the user loses 1% of his/her Critical Rate. How can I be so certain that we are working with percentages? There are two good ways to prove it:

1. Change the multiplier on `this.subject().luk` to 1. You will notice that the attacker always lands critical hits, no matter how low its Luck is. If we were working with whole numbers, the attacker's Critical Rate would be equal to its Luck and not a guaranteed 100%.

2. Note that Critical Evasion is expressed in the Database as a percentage, yet it is subtracted from 1 here. If we were working with whole numbers, you would have to subtract from 100 instead. 10% Critical Evasion will result in (1 - 0.10) and not (1 - 10), for example.

To be honest, it also helps that while initially testing this, I noticed that the attacker would land guaranteed critical hits when I had whole numbers for multipliers within the formula. So another thing I wanted to fix within RMMV was the way that battle messages were expressed. Mainly, the ones that appear when damage is dealt or healing is performed. You've probably noticed that the default messages are a bit clunky. How do we go about improving this? Make some space at the bottom of your Snippets plugin file. Then, allow me to welcome you to the next section!

Coded Messages (in a Bottle)

What I seek to change is the messages that are displayed after an actor or an enemy performs a skill that has a damaging or healing effect. In MV, there is now an entire section of the Terms tab in the Database that covers precisely that. However, a cursory look at the messages in question won't be much help. For example, the Actor Gain message reads: "%1 gained %2 %3!" So what can we do? In RPG Maker Ace, the text handling for such messages was done within the `Game_ActionResult` class. However, in MV, they are somewhat less intuitively contained within `Window_BattleLog` (which isn't even part of the rpg_objects.js file). `Window_BattleLog` starts on line 4726 of the rpg_windows.js file, so go ahead and use Find in Buffer in Atom to get there a bit faster. I took a bit of time to playtest six messages, so here's a bullet list of what each one is about:

- **Enemy Damage.** Displayed when an actor deals HP damage to an enemy. By default it reads "EnemyName took *x* damage" (where *x* is the damage value the enemy has been inflicted).

- **Actor Damage.** Displayed when an enemy deals HP damage to an actor. By default, it reads "ActorName took *x* damage."

- **Enemy Drain**. Displayed when an actor drains an enemy. By default, it reads "EnemyName was drained of P *x*" (where P is equal to HP, MP or TP, as relevant to the game context).

- **Actor Drain.** Displayed when an enemy drains an actor. By default, it reads "ActorName was drained of P *x*."

- **Enemy Recovery.** Displayed when an enemy recovers HP or MP. By default, it reads "EnemyName recovered P *x*."

- **Actor Recovery.** Displayed when an actor recovers HP or MP. By default, it reads: "ActorName recovered P *x*."

As you can see, and to the credit of MV's developers, those messages are almost perfect. The operative word here is *almost*. The two damage messages don't need altering, but the drain and recovery messages do. The easy way to fix the relevant messages is by swapping the parameters in the relevant messages.

For example, the default Enemy Drain message is: "%1 was drained of %2 %3!" By swapping the %3 with the %2, we get a correctly fixed message. But since this is the scripting chapter and all, let's take some time to fix it internally. That way, we can leave the messages as-is within the Database, and they will display correctly all the same. We have a total of three methods to modify, so let's get started. Head over to line 5254 of rpg_windows.js, where you'll find the Window_BattleLog.prototype.makeHpDamageText method, listed here:

```
Window_BattleLog.prototype.makeHpDamageText = function(target) {
    var result = target.result();
    var damage = result.hpDamage;
    var isActor = target.isActor();
    var fmt;
    if (damage > 0 && result.drain) {
        fmt = isActor ? TextManager.actorDrain : TextManager.enemyDrain;
        return fmt.format(target.name(), TextManager.hp, damage);
    } else if (damage > 0) {
        fmt = isActor ? TextManager.actorDamage : TextManager.enemyDamage;
        return fmt.format(target.name(), damage);
    } else if (damage < 0) {
        fmt = isActor ? TextManager.actorRecovery : TextManager.enemyRecovery;
        return fmt.format(target.name(), TextManager.hp, -damage);
    } else {
        fmt = isActor ? TextManager.actorNoDamage : TextManager.enemyNoDamage;
        return fmt.format(target.name());
    }
};
```

Dissecting the makeHpDamageText Method

In a nutshell, we can divide this method into two parts.

- The first four lines after the method assignment are all variable declarations. Those variables are used in the second part of the method.

- Everything else, starting with the if statement, covers a total of four scenarios:

  1. The initial if statement displays a message when the attacker uses a skill that drains HP. A draining attack heals the user for the same amount of HP that it deals to its target.

  2. The first else if statement is called when the attacker uses a skill that does HP damage.

  3. The second else if statement is relevant when the character uses a skill that heals HP.

  4. The else statement is used for the niche case in which the attacker uses a skill that does no damage to its target.

With that established, let's dissect the first statement. It is three lines long and says the following:

```
if (damage > 0 && result.drain) {
    fmt = isActor ? TextManager.actorDrain : TextManager.enemyDrain;
    return fmt.format(target.name(), TextManager.hp, damage);
```

Our variable assignment in the first line (fmt) is a perfect example of a local variable. As its name implies, a local variable is used only wherever it is called. Thus, whatever is plugged into fmt is used only for this particular statement and then scrapped. The isActor? variable returns true if the battler is an Actor. If he/she is an enemy, it will return false. If isActor? is true, the TextManager.actorDrain text will be displayed; otherwise, the TextManager.enemyDrain text will be displayed. The second line uses the format method to create the appropriate text message.

The format method used on fmt accepts a certain number of parameters. Pertinently, it accepts parameters equal to the number of % symbols in the target message. In the case of both the Actor Drain and Enemy Drain messages, that number is 3, and format plugs in the value of its parameters accordingly, from left to right. So, %1 would be equal to target.name(), %2 would be equal to TextManager.hp, and %3 would be equal to damage. I pointed out earlier that the damage messages were fine as-is, so we can skip the first else if statement. Here's the second:

```
} else if (damage < 0) {
    fmt = isActor ? TextManager.actorRecovery : TextManager.enemyRecovery;
    return fmt.format(target.name(), TextManager.hp, -damage);
```

This statement covers what happens when an actor or enemy uses a recovery spell that restores HP. Notice that the -damage parameter is used instead of damage. Except for that difference, everything else is the same as in the if statement. Now we have all the information we need to fix this method to our heart's delight, as the last (else) statement also prints a correctly phrased message when called.

Tweaking the makeHpDamageText Method

Without further ado, let's tweak this method. Here is what the code for the makeHpDamageText method should look like when properly tweaked.

■ **Caution**   Make sure to write this out in your Snippets js file and not the rpg_windows.js file! It's all too easy to get distracted and accidentally change the core method when you're basically looking at two almost identical sets of code separated only by a single tab within Atom.

```
var _Window_BattleLog_makeHpDamageText = Window_BattleLog.prototype.makeHpDamageText;
Window_BattleLog.prototype.makeHpDamageText = function(target) {
_Window_BattleLog_makeHpDamageText.call(this,target);
    var result = target.result();
    var damage = result.hpDamage;
    var isActor = target.isActor();
    var fmt;
    if (damage > 0 && result.drain) {
        fmt = isActor ? TextManager.actorDrain : TextManager.enemyDrain;
        return fmt.format(target.name(), TextManager.hp, damage);
    } else if (damage > 0) {
        fmt = isActor ? TextManager.actorDamage : TextManager.enemyDamage;
        return fmt.format(target.name(), damage);
    } else if (damage < 0) {
        fmt = isActor ? TextManager.actorRecovery : TextManager.enemyRecovery;
        return fmt.format(target.name(), TextManager.hp, -damage);
```

```
    } else {
        fmt = isActor ? TextManager.actorNoDamage : TextManager.enemyNoDamage;
        return fmt.format(target.name());
    }
};
```

I bolded each of the changes and additions made to the makeHpDamageText method. They can easily be summarized:

- The first three lines of the tweaked method are nothing we haven't seen before. We assign the basic method to a variable and then use the call method to declare the instance of the method contained within the variable as the one to be used, allowing us to make changes without worrying about messing something up.

- We swap the damage (and -damage respectively) in both the if statement and the second else if statement such that they are expressed as the second parameter within the format method instead of the third.

One down, two more to go!

Dissecting the makeMpDamageText Method

The second of the three action-result display methods is makeMpDamageText, located in line 5274 of rpg_windows.js. This time, let's go backwards. Instead of listing the messages, I'm going to show off the method itself first. Based on what we saw for the HP text method, try to predict how each message will print within the game.

▪ **Tip** Finding patterns in code will help you understand how things in RMMV work. The entirety of MV's code is transparent and available within any given project's folder, so you should be able to poke around and get a handle on just about anything, once you have some more JavaScript experience.

```
Window_BattleLog.prototype.makeMpDamageText = function(target) {
    var result = target.result();
    var damage = result.mpDamage;
    var isActor = target.isActor();
    var fmt;
    if (damage > 0 && result.drain) {
        fmt = isActor ? TextManager.actorDrain : TextManager.enemyDrain;
        return fmt.format(target.name(), TextManager.mp, damage);
    } else if (damage > 0) {
        fmt = isActor ? TextManager.actorLoss : TextManager.enemyLoss;
        return fmt.format(target.name(), TextManager.mp, damage);
    } else if (damage < 0) {
        fmt = isActor ? TextManager.actorRecovery : TextManager.enemyRecovery;
        return fmt.format(target.name(), TextManager.mp, -damage);
    } else {
        return '';
    }
};
```

The only real difference between this method and the previous one, besides using TextManager.mp instead of TextManager.hp and the addition of the TextManager.actorLoss and TextManager.enemyLoss messages, is the fact that the else statement has a pair of quotation marks instead of actual content. The reasoning behind this is actually very simple: makeHpDamageText already covers the text displayed when a skill or item does no damage. Writing it out a second time in this method would be redundant. Have you figured out how each message will print out in-game? As it turns out, all of the messages will display the MP abbreviation before the number value (whether it is caused by drain, damage, or recovery). For the sake of limiting redundancy, I will only describe the Enemy Loss and Actor Loss messages, which are completely new.

- **Enemy Loss.** Displayed when an actor inflicts MP damage on an enemy. By default, it reads: "EnemyName lost MP x" (where x is the damage value the enemy has been inflicted).

- **Actor Loss.** Displayed when an enemy inflicts MP or TP damage to an actor. By default, it reads: "ActorName lost P x."

■ **Note** Curiously, there appears to be no way to inflict TP damage via the use of skills or items in MV. However, as you'll see in a few sections, there is code for a message to be displayed when a character loses TP. As I have pretty much already telegraphed, the message that would be used is the Actor Loss message also used for MP damage.

Tweaking the makeMpDamageText Method

Take a stab at tweaking this method, given what we have discussed up to now. Whenever you're ready, check the following code to see the tweaked version.

```
var _Window_BattleLog_makeMpDamageText = Window_BattleLog.prototype.makeMpDamageText;
Window_BattleLog.prototype.makeMpDamageText = function(target) {
_Window_BattleLog_makeMpDamageText.call(this,target);
    var result = target.result();
    var damage = result.mpDamage;
    var isActor = target.isActor();
    var fmt;
    if (damage > 0 && result.drain) {
        fmt = isActor ? TextManager.actorDrain : TextManager.enemyDrain;
        return fmt.format(target.name(), damage, TextManager.mp);
    } else if (damage > 0) {
        fmt = isActor ? TextManager.actorLoss : TextManager.enemyLoss;
        return fmt.format(target.name(), damage, TextManager.mp);
    } else if (damage < 0) {
        fmt = isActor ? TextManager.actorRecovery : TextManager.enemyRecovery;
        return fmt.format(target.name(), -damage, TextManager.mp);
    } else {
        return '';
    }
};
```

As before, all necessary changes are in bold. Not much to it, right?

The makeTpDamageText Method

The final method is makeTpDamageText (located in line 5293 of rpg_windows.js), which covers what happens when a skill or item lowers or increases the TP of an actor or enemy (although, as I noted previously, there seems to be no way to lower TP via skill or item usage). All we have to do here is flip the two latter parameters once again. I'll skip listing the unmodified method, since it's more of the same, and just go ahead and list the tweaked method. As usual, changes are in bold.

```
var _Window_BattleLog_makeTpDamageText = Window_BattleLog.prototype.makeTpDamageText;
Window_BattleLog.prototype.makeTpDamageText = function(target) {
_Window_BattleLog_makeTpDamageText.call(this,target);
    var result = target.result();
    var damage = result.tpDamage;
    var isActor = target.isActor();
    var fmt;
    if (damage > 0) {
        fmt = isActor ? TextManager.actorLoss : TextManager.enemyLoss;
        return fmt.format(target.name(), damage, TextManager.tp);
    } else if (damage < 0) {
        fmt = isActor ? TextManager.actorGain : TextManager.enemyGain;
        return fmt.format(target.name(), -damage, TextManager.tp);
    } else {
        return '';
    }
};
```

Again, the else statement contains quotation marks, as the no-damage situation is handled in makeHpDamageText. Once you have all three of the tweaked methods set up within your Snippets js file, you are done! Before moving on to the next exercise, here's a brief aside to write out the Enemy Gain and Actor Gain messages, which are new to this method:

- **Enemy Gain.** Displayed when an enemy gains TP. By default, it reads: "EnemyName gained TP *x*" (where *x* is the recovery value). As adjusted, it will more properly read: "EnemyName gained *x* TP."

- **Actor Gain.** Displayed when an actor gains TP. By default, it reads: "ActorName gained TP *x*." As adjusted, it will more properly read:" ActorName gained *x* TP."

Let's work on a much simpler exercise now.

Of TP and Their Preservation

TP, or Tactical Points as they're referred to within MV's code, are another resource that actors can use to power their skills, much as spellcasters use MP to cast Magic. Naturally, there wouldn't be much of a point to the distinction if they were identical, so here's a short bullet list of the ways that TP differs from MP:

- Each party member starts each battle with between 0 and 25 TP.
- A character can gain TP from taking damage and skills that grant TP.
- After each battle, the party's TP is reset.
- TP as a stat is not displayed anywhere in the default RMMV game menu, only in battle. You would have to use a plugin to add a visible TP stat to the game's menu.

But what if you want TP in your game to act like the Limit Break bar in *Final Fantasy VII*? Making TP a persistent resource is actually extremely easy but requires code tweaking, so it's a perfect exercise for this chapter. As usual, we have to find where and how RMMV handles TP. We know that TP is set at the start of battle and reset at its end.

Searching for TP

Let's run a search in Atom for TP using Find in Buffer as we always do. We will direct our search to the rpg_objects.js file. Writing out **TP** and clicking Find within the Find in Buffer interface will return a whopping 87 results. This occurs because Atom defaults to case insensitivity, which means that a search for TP is actually looking for tp, tP, Tp, *and* TP. To solve this problem, you need only click the second button to the right of Find (which has the Aa symbol). As soon as you do, you'll see the 87 results drop down to a much more reasonable 6. Of particular interest is Game_BattlerBase.FLAG_ID_PRESERVE_TP (located in line 2111), where we can see that Preserve TP is a special flag that can be set. Where? In weapons and armor. You can create pieces of equipment that grant their users the ability to carry over their TP values from battle to battle. Of course, that's not what we came here for, so let's click that Find button some more.

The next item of interest is also part of the Game_BattlerBase class (line 2572). Here's the relevant snippet.

```
Game_BattlerBase.prototype.isPreserveTp = function() {
    return this.specialFlag(Game_BattlerBase.FLAG_ID_PRESERVE_TP);
};
```

This is a method that allows us to set the flag to preserve TP. If you get the sudden urge to search for isPreserveTp, I applaud you. That is definitely the right way to go. Running a search for the term returns a mere three results. The latter two are in Game_Battler and are exactly what we're looking for. The first of them is the onBattleStart method (line 3252), which initializes a player's TP at the start of each battle, unless the flag has been set:

```
Game_Battler.prototype.onBattleStart = function() {
    this.setActionState('undecided');
    this.clearMotion();
    if (!this.isPreserveTp()) {
        this.initTp();
    }
};
```

The other result is the onBattleEnd method, which covers things that are resolved at the end of a battle, such as states that expire on battle end:

```
Game_Battler.prototype.onBattleEnd = function() {
    this.clearResult();
    this.removeBattleStates();
    this.removeAllBuffs();
    this.clearActions();
    if (!this.isPreserveTp()) {
        this.clearTp();
    }
    this.appear();
};
```

■ **Note**   This process of tracking down code may seem inefficient, but it's an awesome way to figure out how RMMV handles the many things that make it tick.

Tweaking the TP Preserve Methods

Now take a look at the following code for the tweaked methods that should be present within our snippets plugin.

```
//Modified onBattleStart method
var _Game_Battler_onBattleStart = Game_Battler.prototype.onBattleStart;
Game_Battler.prototype.onBattleStart = function() {
_Game_Battler_onBattleStart.call(this);
    this.setActionState('undecided');
    this.clearMotion();
};
//Modified onBattleEnd method
var _Game_Battler_onBattleEnd = Game_Battler.prototype.onBattleEnd;
Game_Battler.prototype.onBattleEnd = function() {
_Game_Battler_onBattleEnd.call(this);
    this.clearResult();
    this.removeBattleStates();
    this.removeAllBuffs();
    this.clearActions();
    this.appear();
};
```

Play-test the game afterward and you'll realize that there have been no real changes to how TP works. Use // to comment out the line in each method that calls the original versions of the methods and then play-test again. Now it should work fine. Take note of the following:

- Your party members start their first battle with 0 TP (initTp() handles the randomization of TP, but we removed it from on_battle_start).

- More important, your party members should now be able to carry over their TP from battle to battle (because we removed clearTp(), which handles the removal of TP at the end of battle).

Pretty awesome, isn't it? As for why the methods only work when those particular lines are commented out, it's actually quite simple. Throughout this chapter, we've either created entirely new functions (the code for the custom damage formulas) or modified parts of existing functions (everything else). As it turns out, this happens to be the very first time in the chapter where we have needed to *remove* parts of a function. As stated at the start of the chapter, what we're doing with lines such as _Game_Battler_onBattleStart.call(this) is calling the *original* function. So here's what that modified function looks like with the call:

```
var _Game_Battler_onBattleStart = Game_Battler.prototype.onBattleStart;
Game_Battler.prototype.onBattleStart = function() {
    this.setActionState('undecided');
    this.clearMotion();
```

```
    if (!this.isPreserveTp()) {
        this.initTp();
    }
    this.setActionState('undecided');
    this.clearMotion();
};
```

As you can see when it is explicitly written out, our attempt to modify the function is rather pointless in this case, as we want to remove that if statement, and that won't happen unless we directly modify the function. So remove the

```
_Game_Battler_onBattleStart.call(this);
```

and

```
_Game_Battler_onBattleEnd.call(this);
```

lines from the appropriate methods and you're all set!

■ **Note**   You can also remove the variable declarations immediately before both of the modified methods, but that's not strictly necessary. Their existence won't really affect anything.

Other TP Considerations

While we're on the subject of TP, we also have the maxTp method in line 2596 of Game_BattlerBase. You can increase or decrease the maximum amount of TP that a player can stockpile. You could have skills that require more than 100 TP to use, in theory. In practice, the Database enforces the cap on TP cost of skills and TP gain from skills.

■ **Note**   Play-testing an altered TP cap will promptly reveal that the bar still fills up as if the party member had a cap of 100 TP. To correct this graphical hiccup, take a look at tpRate (line 2623) and change the denominator in the expression to the same value as your maximum TP cap.

Also, if you increase the TP cap and then try to use the TP Gain effect, you'll find that you still get the same amount of TP, even though the amount should change based on the new cap. It's beyond the scope of this book to fix that particular problem, but if you'd like to try your hand at it, you might be well-served by starting your search in rpg_objects.js for EFFECT_GAIN_TP and seeing what pops up. In any case, here are the modified methods for maxTp and tpRate. As you can see, I set the new TP maximum to 500 and modified the tpRate method to match.

```
//Modified max TP method
var _Game_BattlerBase_maxTp = Game_BattlerBase.prototype.maxTp;
Game_BattlerBase.prototype.maxTp = function() {
_Game_BattlerBase_maxTp.call(this);
    return 500;
};
```

```
//Modified tpRate method
var _Game_BattlerBase_tpRate = Game_BattlerBase.prototype.tpRate;
Game_BattlerBase.prototype.tpRate = function() {
_Game_BattlerBase_tpRate.call(this);
    return this.tp / 500;
};
```

Without further ado, let's move on to another interesting scripting opportunity.

```
};
```

Game Over by Incapacitation

By default, the only way that a player will receive a game over is if his/her entire party is dead. However, not every RPG throughout the years has followed such a system. Take the *Final Fantasy* games, for example. If the entire party is unable to act, that will result in a game over, even if the party is otherwise still alive. Petrification and Paralysis are two of the most common status effects that can cause this alternate game over. A look at the States tab reveals that none of the default movement-blocking states has infinite duration. Perhaps it was something that the designers thought of but decided against implementing. In any case, all we have to do is find the code that governs game overs and work from there. Running a search in rpg_objects.js for "game over" returns a single result:

```
Game_Interpreter.prototype.command353 = function() {
    SceneManager.goto(Scene_Gameover);
    return true;
};
```

It's a good start but, as it turns out, we're digging in the wrong spot (as you'll see in a bit, that's not entirely true, but just humor me for a bit, would you?). However, this method tells us where we should continue our search. Open trpg_scenes.js and run a search for "game over" there. Amusingly, this will only return a single result as well. The critical difference here is where that result leads. When you click Find, you will find yourself looking at MV's Scene_Gameover class (it starts on line 2416 of rpg_scenes), which, as the description itself states, is "the scene class of the game over screen." We know that Scene_Gameover is used for the game over screen, but where is the code that determines when to call it up? A search for Scene_Gameover in rpg_scenes.js returns 18 results, but the one we want is on line 121 of rpg_scenes (this is part of the Scene_Base class). This code, as it turns out, has great promise for this exercise.

```
Scene_Base.prototype.checkGameover = function() {
    if ($gameParty.isAllDead()) {
        SceneManager.goto(Scene_Gameover);
    }
};
```

We already started down this rabbit hole, but the checkGameover method is where we really start getting into the meat of how this works. Our next step is to find the isAllDead() method in Game_Party and see what that entails. Go back to rpg_objects.js (or reopen it if you happened to close it after opening rpg_scenes.js) and run a search for isAllDead. Running a search for that method turns up a rather curious result.

Namely, isAllDead is defined in two places. Actually, that's not strictly true, as I'll promptly explain. Here's the Game_Unit method:

```
Game_Unit.prototype.isAllDead = function() {
    return this.aliveMembers().length === 0;
};
```

Now let's take a look at the Game_Party equivalent.

```
Game_Party.prototype.isAllDead = function() {
    if (Game_Unit.prototype.isAllDead.call(this)) {
        return this.inBattle() || !this.isEmpty();
    } else {
        return false;
    }
};
```

Why are they different? The Game_Party version of the isAllDead method builds upon the isAllDead method in Game_Unit. For an analogy, think of it as a parent and a child. Game_Unit is the parent of Game_Party. The Game_Unit version of the method provides a return value (this.aliveMembers().length === 0) that can then be used in Game_Party to determine whether the entire player's party is dead. If it is, the method tries to determine if the player is currently in battle. If they are not, a game over can still result if the isEmpty method returns false (the exclamation mark to the left of the method denotes opposition; so it checks for the method to be *false* rather than *true*). Since the isEmpty method holds a value of 0 (line 4757 of rpg_objects), it will return false if the size method (located a few lines earlier, at 4753) happens to return a length of 0. Of course, this should generally be impossible during the course of a conventional playthrough, as you need at least one party member to do just about anything. In any case, if neither of the two conditions applies, then the method returns a value of false (which means at least one party member is still alive). Our next task is to find aliveMembers. As we want the method definition, what we're looking for is on line 4586 of rpg_objects.

```
Game_Unit.prototype.aliveMembers = function() {
    return this.members().filter(function(member) {
        return member.isAlive();
    });
};
```

The expression contained within aliveMembers contains a new method, as it were: .filter is a Javascript array method that tests an array and creates a new one with all elements that pass a true/false test. In the case of the aliveMembers method, .filter is testing to see if the members() array contains living party members. It then returns the list of living party members via member.isAlive(). Being alive is defined by the isAlive method, which can be found in line 2647 of rpg_objects.

```
Game_BattlerBase.prototype.isAlive = function() {
    return this.isAppeared() && !this.isDeathStateAffected();
};
```

■ **Note** The && in this method is the logical operator for *and*. We have also already seen the || operator, which is the logical *or*, and the exclamation mark (!) which is the logical operator for *not*.

We have nearly reached the bottom of this rabbit hole. isAppeared() is only used to determine whether a certain battler is hidden or not (and, thus, only really applies to enemies, as Actors in battle always exist). So, let's just search for isDeathStateAffected (note the absence of the exclamation mark). Here's the isDeathStateAffected method, located in line 2215.

```
Game_BattlerBase.prototype.isDeathStateAffected = function() {
    return this.isStateAffected(this.deathStateId());
};
```

This method contains a single return statement. After quite a few searches, we have found what we are looking for. An isDeathStateAffected() is used to check for the KO state in an actor or enemy. As it happens, the deathStateId method definition is located directly below the isDeathStateAffected method definition.

```
Game_BattlerBase.prototype.deathStateId = function() {
    return 1;
};
```

■ **Note** This one-line method returns the state ID (as located in the Database) of Knockout, which is the only state recognized by default in RMMV as incapacitating.

So, suppose you wanted to make it so that Sleep (state #10 in the default state list in RMMV) counts as an incapacitating state. Here is how I did it:

```
//Modified isDeathStateAffected state
var _Game_BattlerBase_isDeathStateAffected = Game_BattlerBase.prototype.
isDeathStateAffected;
Game_BattlerBase.prototype.isDeathStateAffected = function() {
_Game_BattlerBase_isDeathStateAffected.call(this);
    return this.isStateAffected(this.deathStateId()) ||
    this.isStateAffected(this.incapStateId());
};

//New function for Game_BattlerBase
Game_BattlerBase.prototype.incapStateId = function() {
    return 10;
};
```

■ **Note** In this code, you could also replace this.incapStateId() with the ID value of the state you want to evaluate (10, in this case). My way allows you to switch the ID within the new function, so it's just a tad neater. For an even more elegant solution, you might want to take a look at Tsukihime's Custom Death States script, located at his Himeworks website: http://himeworks.com/files/rmmv/scripts/HIME_CustomDeathStates.js.

To test whether the change is working, you can give one of the existing enemies a Sleep-inducing skill (or give their normal attacks a 100% Sleep State Rate) and then run a Battle Test. If you get a Game Over screen after being afflicted by Sleep, you'll know that it is working correctly. Speaking of game overs, I have one last exercise to work through.

Adding a Menu to the Game Over Screen

This last exercise is going to involve some copy-pasting. Mainly, we're going to copy the RMMV code that handles the Title screen's menu and integrate that into the class that governs the Game Over screen. The first order of business is finding the two classes. As it so happens, both the Title screen and the Game Over screen are governed by classes with the Scene prefix. Let's open rpg_scenes.js and copy all of the code contained in Scene_Gameover to the Snippets file. Next, take a look at Scene_Gameover and analyze what is going on.

- Scene_Gameover executes several methods that create the background that says "game over," handle the fade-out after the party is defeated and the subsequent fade-in to the Game Over screen, and play the appropriate music.

- What we're interested in is the transition-to-Title-screen method (gotoTitle).

Because we want the game to pop up a menu at the Game Over screen, instead of just cutting to the Title, we might as well go ahead and excise what we won't be using. Delete the gotoTitle method and then erase the entire if statement from Scene_Gameover's update method. With that done, find Scene_Title in rpg_scenes.js (starts on line 233). Our objective at the Scene_Title class is to figure out what methods are used to call up the Title screen's menu. If we take a look at the create method for Scene_Title, we see that four methods are called up. Our method of interest is createCommandWindow. A closer look at it shows the following code:

```
Scene_Title.prototype.createCommandWindow = function() {
    this._commandWindow = new Window_TitleCommand();
    this._commandWindow.setHandler('newGame',  this.commandNewGame.bind(this));
    this._commandWindow.setHandler('continue', this.commandContinue.bind(this));
    this._commandWindow.setHandler('options',  this.commandOptions.bind(this));
    this.addWindow(this._commandWindow);
};
```

The first expression in the method draws a new window on the screen. Then each of the next three expressions handles a menu option via the setHandler method (located in Window_Selectable; starts on line 710 of the rpg_windows.js file). setHandler accepts two parameters. The first is the *symbol* and the second is the *method*. For example, the first setHandler expression in create_command_window calls the commandNewGame method when the 'newGame' symbol is invoked. This will become relevant in the next section. For now, the result, as you've almost certainly seen countless times during play-testing, is that the Title menu has three options. So we know that we want to draw the Title menu into the Game Over screen. The next question becomes: *How* is this method drawing the window to the screen? If we compare the start methods of Scene_Title and Scene_Gameover, we see that the game over method doesn't draw a command window (createCommandWindow). Here's what we need to do, in order:

- From Scene_Title: Copy the createCommandWindow (lines 310 to 316 of rpg_scenes), commandNewGame (lines 318 to 323), commandContinue (lines 325 to 328), and commandOptions (lines 330 to 333) methods to the Snippets file.

- In each of the four copied methods, change their class definition from Scene_Title to Scene_Gameover.

- From Scene_Gameover: Copy the create (lines 2427 to 2431 of rpg_scenes) and update (lines 2438 to 2443) methods to the Snippets file. Place these two methods above the other four previously copied methods.

Finally, we need to make a few modifications to the two methods we copied last. Take a look at the following tweaked version of the code for this exercise. All changes from the original methods are bolded.

```
Scene_Gameover.prototype.create = function() {
    Scene_Base.prototype.create.call(this);
    this.playGameoverMusic();
    this.createBackground();
    this.createWindowLayer();
    this.createCommandWindow();
};

Scene_Gameover.prototype.update = function() {
  if (!this.isBusy()) {
      this._commandWindow.open();
  }
    Scene_Base.prototype.update.call(this);
};

Scene_Gameover.prototype.createCommandWindow = function() {
    this._commandWindow = new Window_TitleCommand();
    this._commandWindow.setHandler('newGame',  this.commandNewGame.bind(this));
    this._commandWindow.setHandler('continue', this.commandContinue.bind(this));
    this._commandWindow.setHandler('options',  this.commandOptions.bind(this));
    this.addWindow(this._commandWindow);
};

Scene_Gameover.prototype.commandNewGame = function() {
    DataManager.setupNewGame();
    this._commandWindow.close();
    this.fadeOutAll();
    SceneManager.goto(Scene_Map);
};

Scene_Gameover.prototype.commandContinue = function() {
    this._commandWindow.close();
    SceneManager.push(Scene_Load);
};

Scene_Gameover.prototype.commandOptions = function() {
    this._commandWindow.close();
    SceneManager.push(Scene_Options);
};
```

With that out of the way, you're done! Now, play-test your game and get into a situation that causes a game over. (It might be quicker to create an event that calls up the Game Over screen when you interact with it.) If you have followed these instructions, your Game Over screen should look like Figure 14-4.

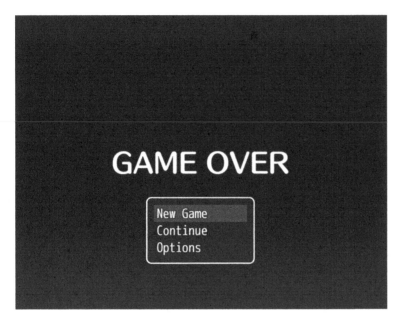

Figure 14-4. *The Game Over screen, menu now included*

If you just wanted to have the Title screen menu in your game over, you are done.

Tweaking the Game Over Menu

However, what if you wanted to tweak the menu? As mentioned before, the menu window and options are handled in createCommandWindow. You may be thinking that removing an option from this method is all you would have to do. That is actually not true. If you do that, you'll still see the option in the Game Over menu. When you try to press the action button to get the option to do something, it will do nothing. Clearly, we must look elsewhere for the solution to this problem. The window itself is created and populated in Window_TitleCommand. However, altering that method will change the Title menu as well. Thus, you'll want to do the following:

1. Copy Window_TitleCommand to your Snippets plugin.

2. Click on Find in Buffer and write **Window_TitleCommand** in the top entry box (the one used to Find text). Then type **Window_GameoverCommand** in the bottom text box. See Figure 14-5 for a visual aid. Then, click Replace until Atom returns no results in the Snippet file for Window_TitleCommand.

Figure 14-5. *The Find in Buffer interface for Atom*

3. Hop over to your altered Scene_Gameover method and switch this._ commandWindow = new Window_TitleCommand(); to this._commandWindow = new Window_GameoverCommand();

4. Back at Window_GameoverCommand, find the makeCommandList method (it's near the bottom of the method), which looks like this:

```
Window_GameoverCommand.prototype.makeCommandList = function() {
    this.addCommand(TextManager.newGame,    'newGame');
    this.addCommand(TextManager.continue_, 'continue', this.isContinueEnabled());
    this.addCommand(TextManager.options,    'options');
};
```

As you can see, this method is responsible for the three options that we see in the Title menu. To make the point, comment out (by typing in // before the line of code) the newGame command. If you have followed my instructions correctly, the Game Over menu should now look like Figure 14-6.

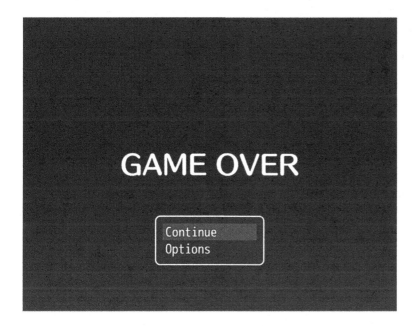

Figure 14-6. *The Game Over menu after the changes*

On the other hand, if you wanted to add a menu option to that list (for example, the ability to go back to the Title screen), you would be best served by finding the addCommand method, to see how it works. Your search should be directed at Window_Command (that would be rpg_windows.js). Once there, you should quickly find the addCommand method (it's on line 1327 of rpg_windows)

```
Window_Command.prototype.addCommand = function(name, symbol, enabled, ext) {
    if (enabled === undefined) {
        enabled = true;
    }
}
```

```
    if (ext === undefined) {
        ext = null;
    }
    this._list.push({ name: name, symbol: symbol, enabled: enabled, ext: ext});
};
```

> ⬛ **Note** The triple equal signs here are a strict comparison operator. They signify "equality without type coercion." What does that mean? Well, for a single example, 1 == "1" would return true, but 1 === "1" would return false (as they have the same value, but different type; the left 1 is a number, while the right 1 is a string). Basically, == looks for the value to be the same, but === *also* wants the type to be the same.

For most menu options, you'll only be using the first two parameters. The command name is defined in the TextManager Object starting on line 1454 of the rpg_managers.js file. The symbol used in the addCommand method is the handle defined within setHandler. The Continue option also uses the third parameter, which determines whether or not you can select it from the menu. (When the player has no save files for the game, Continue will be grayed out.) .push is a JavaScript array method. As the method name implies, .push sends an object to the end of an array (the array, in this case, being _list). Going back to Window_GameoverCommand, we can see the format of an addCommand object that accepts two parameters:

```
this.addCommand(TextManager.options,    'options');
```

> ⬛ **Note** To summarize the menu logic: addCommand adds options to menus, while setHandler gives those options their functionality. As demonstrated already, you need both to create a new menu option.

The Title screen option is called in the form toTitle. So you would write the following in makeCommandList to add that command to Window_GameoverCommand:

```
this.addCommand(TextManager.toTitle,    'toTitle');
```

Place that between the two existing addCommand expressions. Then you would add the following line to createCommandWindow in Scene_Gameover, so that the option actually does something when the player interacts with it. I placed it between the Continue and Option commands.

```
this._commandWindow.setHandler('toTitle', this.commandToTitle.bind(this));
```

Last, you need to add the commandToTitle method itself, or the game will return an error telling you that the method is undefined.

> ⬛ **Note** I named the method commandToTitle, to keep with the naming conventions used for this command in RMMV. As it turns out, there *is* a preexisting method of the same name.

As noted, there's an existing method called `commandToTitle`. In fact, running a search for the method in rpg_scenes.js will return only two results. The second result (line 1614) contains what we're looking for. Here's the method:

```
Scene_GameEnd.prototype.commandToTitle = function() {
    this.fadeOutAll();
    SceneManager.goto(Scene_Title);
};
```

Copy-paste that method to the `Scene_Gameover` class you have tweaked, change the class definition from `Scene_GameEnd` to `Scene_Gameover`, and we're done! Play-test your game and cause a game over. If you have done everything correctly, the screen should look like Figure 14-7.

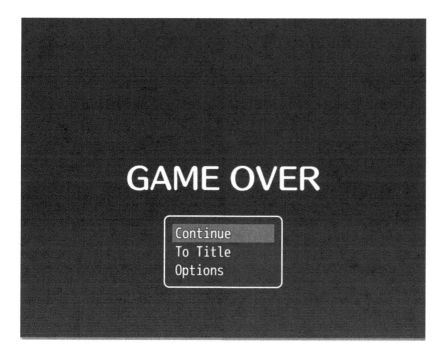

Figure 14-7. *The changed Game Over menu*

Now, before we bid this chapter farewell, I need to at least mention *plugin commands*. They are a new type of event command that can be used for your plugins should they need the additional functionality. We never had a need to use them for our Snippets plugin or our Custom Damage Formulas plugin, but I'll steer you toward MV's Help documentation (specifically the "Using Official Plugins" section), where you can read up on how some of Kadokawa's plugins implement Plugin Commands. In closing, I humbly urge you to continue exploring the depths of RMMV's codebase. Appendix B has a link to a list of plugins that can be used for RMMV. If you want to investigate how something can be done, check to see if a script already exists for that functionality. There's nothing wrong with picking the brains of those who have more experience than you.

Summary

During the course of this chapter, we performed several basic scripting exercises that involved tweaking parts of MV's code to achieve things that aren't possible via eventing. Among them were causing a game over if the player's entire party is incapacitated by another status effect that isn't Knockout, tweaking the TP cap, and making sure that those tweaks were reflected properly within the game. In the final chapter of this book, I will cover some miscellaneous concepts.

CHAPTER 15

More Tips and Tricks for RMMV

I'd like to congratulate you for making it this far. This is the final chapter of the book. It has been an awesome journey, full of learning experiences! Of course, this book is just a taste of the full potential of RMMV. I urge you to continue reading and learning more about what makes this game-development engine tick. What better for a final chapter than a melting pot of tips and tricks that you can apply to your own games? The exercises in this chapter will use variable amounts of scripting, depending on what is needed. Without further ado, let's walk this final leg of our journey together.

Note You can find examples for each of this chapter's exercises nested within the Chapter 15 Material map of this chapter's source code project.

Forcing Certain Party Members to Participate in a Battle

Our first exercise for this final chapter is inspired by a common RPG convention: forced party compositions. If you have ever wanted to create a boss fight in which a certain party member must be present in the active party, this should be relevant to your interests. In RMMV, the maximum active party size is four. A possible fifth (or more) party member is placed into the party reserves.

Tip The first four spots of your party represent your active party members. You can tell who is in the party reserves, based on the appearance of their status. The status of reserve party members is slightly transparent.

You can use the Formation option in the in-game menu to switch between your party members. Party members that are in the reserves gain a share of the experience gained in battle *if* (and only if) the EXP for Reserve Members check box is toggled in the System tab of the Database. In any case, here's our hypothetical situation:

> *In an alternate reality of our game, Harold starts with a full party of four members. The party arrives at Seaside as usual and eventually recruits Marsha. As the fifth party member, Marsha is placed at the bottom of the roster. That makes her a reserve member. Fast-forward to the encounter with Augustus. Marsha will want to face off against her uncle. If anyone is to stop her kin, she's reasoned, she should be the one. If Marsha happens to be in the active party, the battle starts as usual; otherwise, Marsha will demand to be in the active party.*

Overview

For this exercise, you'll need the following:

- A new test map (the tileset and the size do not matter). Then, copy-paste the Augustus event from the first dungeon to our test map.

- An Autorun event that is active only when a switch is flipped. This event will use a scripted conditional branch to determine whether Marsha is in the active party. If she is, we process the battle against Augustus. If she isn't, we have Marsha say some words and use the Open Menu command to allow the player to change his/her active lineup.

- The Autorun will keep running until Marsha is in the active party.

This is a rather easy event. The only thing that should give you even a second of pause by now is the single line that we have to use as a conditional branch. To find it, we must figure out how RMMV handles party members internally.

Finding Out How RMMV Handles Party Members

A good place to start figuring that out is the conveniently named Game_Party. Open rpg_objects.js with Atom and run a search for Game_Party. You needn't go far from the start of the class at line 4718, as there is some promising code starting from line 4771. Specifically, I'm talking about the code shown here:

```
Game_Party.prototype.battleMembers = function() {
    return this.allMembers().slice(0, this.maxBattleMembers()).filter(function(actor) {
        return actor.isAppeared();
    });
};

Game_Party.prototype.maxBattleMembers = function() {
    return 4;
};
```

In fact, the method we need happens to be battleMembers. In essence, what that method does is find every available party member and then take the first one to four of them and place them into an array. This array is named $gameParty.battleMembers().

■ **Note** We use battleMembers, as only the active party members can participate in battle. We want to see if Marsha is part of that array or not.

Now, the next question is: How do we use that array? Recall that we've seen the .contains method at least once before for use in determining whether an array contains a certain value. As it so happens, our answer is in the isBattleMember method for Game_Actor (line 3763):

```
Game_Actor.prototype.isBattleMember = function() {
    return $gameParty.battleMembers().contains(this);
};
```

That means our expression currently looks like this: `$gameParty.battleMembers.contains(this)`. So close, yet so far. We need to replace `this`. But with what? We have to know if Marsha is in the active party, so we must check for her actor ID. Recall from Chapter 11 (and the previous chapter) that actor information arrays are called in RMMV in the form `$gameActors.actor(n)`. Thus, Marsha's array would be `$gameActors.actor(3)`. That is the value we need to check for.

Creating the Forced Party Member Event

Following, I have placed the event commands belonging to the second half of page 1 of Augustus's event. It has been tweaked so that instead of calling a Battle Processing command, it flips on a switch that will trigger our Autorun event:

```
♦Text : Evil(3), Window, Bottom
:     : Heh, think you can surpass the power
:     : that has been granted to me? Prepare to
:     : suffer!
♦Change Battle BGM : Battle2 (90, 100, 0)
♦Control Switches : #0046 ActivePartyMember = ON
♦
```

When the `ActivePartyMember` switch has been flipped on, this activates the Autorun event on the map, which will check to see if Marsha is in the active party:

```
♦If : Script : $gameParty.battleMembers().contains($gameActors.actor(3));
  ♦Battle Processing : Augustus
  ♦
: Else
  ♦Text : Actor3(7), Window, Bottom
  :     : I wish to participate in this battle.
  ♦Text : None, Window, Bottom
  :     : Use the Formation option from the menu to add
  :     : Marsha to your active party.
  ♦Open Menu Screen
  ♦
: End
♦
```

The conditional branch uses the Script option and reads as follows:

```
$gameParty.battleMembers().contains($gameActors.actor(3));
```

We can toggle "Create Else Branch" to get the `else` statement to work with when Marsha is not included in `battleMembers`. Alternatively, we can have another conditional branch that reads: `$gameParty.battleMembers().contains($gameActors.actor(3)); == false`. In either case, when Marsha is not in the player's active party, she expresses a wish to participate in the battle at hand, and then a system message is displayed. You can add a color change command to that text (`\C[n]`; *n* is the value of color you wish to use). I'm partial to green for system messages (that would be `n = 3`), but you can use the color of your preference. After the message is displayed, we have the in-game menu pop up, allowing the player to bring in Marsha from the reserves.

■ **Caution**   If Marsha is not in the player's party at all, this event will infinitely loop, as it recognizes that Marsha is not in `battleMembers` but has no way of checking if she is in the party at all. You can use an *Actor in the Party* conditional branch to handle such an exception.

To test this event properly, you'll want to have an event that gives the player a full party and then adds Marsha to the end of the party as a reserve. You'll need to create a fifth actor beforehand. I created a new Mage called Corvus in Actor slot 6. Then, check the following code for a sample event:

```
♦Change Party Member : Add Therese
♦Change Party Member : Add Lucius
♦Change Party Member : Add Corvus
♦Change Party Member : Add Marsha
♦
```

You can place an NPC with these commands anywhere on the test map. You can talk with that NPC first, to fill up your party, and then test the rest of the events at leisure.

■ **Note**   Don't forget to set the player's starting position on your test map!

With all that said and done, this is the final chapter, and I have not yet discussed play-testing features. This is as good a time as any to do so.

Play-Testing Features

RMMV has a pair of convenient and helpful features that are available only during play-testing. The first is known as the debugger. During play-testing, pressing F9 will bring up a screen similar to the one shown in Figure 15-1.

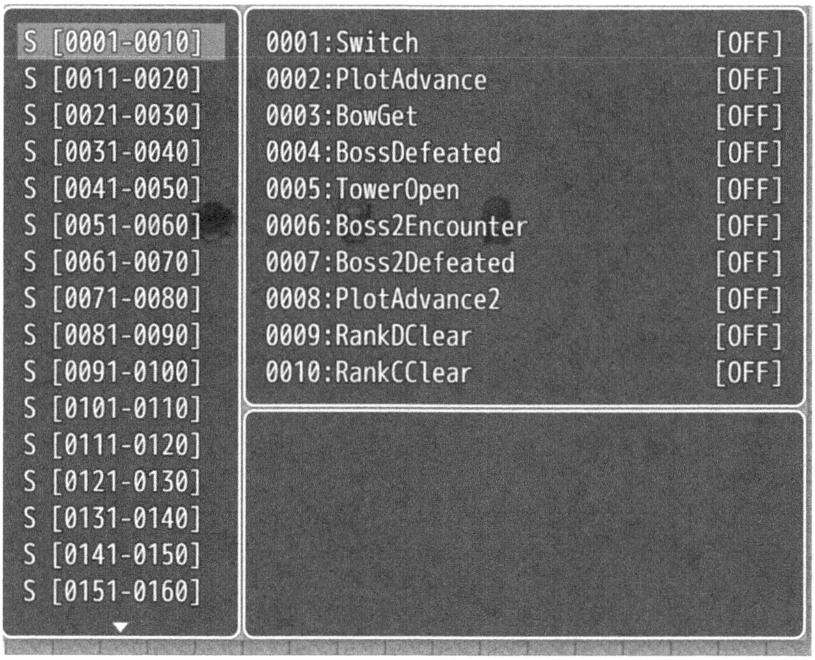

```
S [0001-0010]        0001:Switch                [OFF]
S [0011-0020]        0002:PlotAdvance           [OFF]
S [0021-0030]        0003:BowGet                [OFF]
S [0031-0040]        0004:BossDefeated          [OFF]
S [0041-0050]        0005:TowerOpen             [OFF]
S [0051-0060]        0006:Boss2Encounter        [OFF]
S [0061-0070]        0007:Boss2Defeated         [OFF]
S [0071-0080]        0008:PlotAdvance2          [OFF]
S [0081-0090]        0009:RankDClear            [OFF]
S [0091-0100]        0010:RankCClear            [OFF]
S [0101-0110]
S [0111-0120]
S [0121-0130]
S [0131-0140]
S [0141-0150]
S [0151-0160]
       ▼
```

Figure 15-1. *The debugger in RMMV*

The debugger contains a complete list of switches and variables present in your project. More important, you can see the state of each switch and variable and even tweak it for testing purposes. Perhaps you want to set Tree to 5 in our game off the bat, to see if the Autorun event triggers correctly. Maybe you want to see if Therese acts appropriately once the player has beaten the appropriate rank of the arena. Instead of having to play through all of that, you can use the debugger to flip switches or change the value of variables. It is also a helpful reference when things go wrong in eventing, and you want to see what isn't setting itself properly. The other feature, while not as flashy, is useful all the same. By holding down the Ctrl key, you can clip through otherwise impassable terrain. My favorite use of ignoring passability is when I have accidentally made certain squares impassable when they should be passable. I can keep the squares in mind and just use Ctrl to bypass the accidental obstacles, instead of having to fix them then and there. Depending on what you are play-testing, this can be quite a time-saver.

It's time for another exercise! If you want to make a desert that requires precise movement to get through successfully, you're going to love this one.

Of Deserts and Ghostly Locations

Deserts are a video game constant, particularly deserts that penalize the player who does not know the correct route to traverse them. You might be surprised to know that we can recycle events used in previous chapters to pull this off without a hitch. Don't believe me? Take a look at Figure 15-2 to see the 25×25 map I'll be using for this exercise.

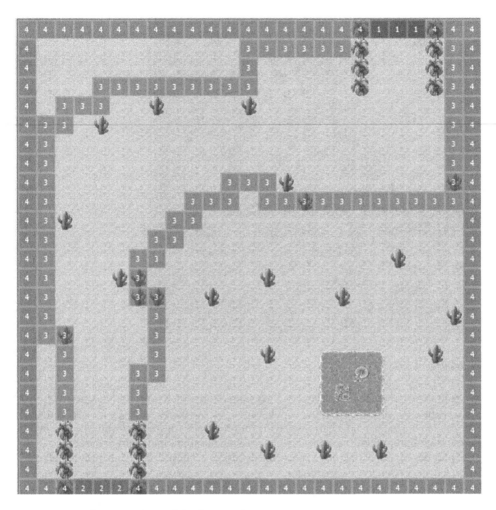

Figure 15-2. *The map to be used for this exercise*

The Desert Event

We need the following things to complete this exercise:

- A Region ID (I'm using 3) that will trace an invisible border around the map. Crossing that border will send the player back to the start of the area.

- A pair of Regions (1 and 2) that will transfer the player out of the desert area.

- Some doodads to dot the map. I use cacti.

- A Parallel event that will handle all of the Region-based shenanigans.

Because everything else is already established in the screenshot of the map, let's skip ahead to our Parallel event. It isn't anything that we haven't done before, as you'll quickly see.

```
♦Control Variables : #0002 X = Map X of Player
♦Control Variables : #0003 Y = Map Y of Player
♦Get Location Info : Region, Region ID, ({X},{Y})
♦If : Region = 3
   ♦Text : None, Window, Bottom
   :     : You get lost in the desert!
   ♦Transfer Player : The Desert Event (4,21) (Direction: Up)
   ♦
:  End
♦If : Region = 2
   ♦Comment : Insert transfer event here.
   ♦
:  End
♦If : Region = 1
   ♦Comment : Insert transfer event here.
   ♦
:  End
♦
```

If you can make teleportation puzzles, you can make deserts that cause the player to get lost and send him/her back to the start of the area as well! You may have noticed that I didn't use Region 4 at all. You could have a desert nomad sell the player some goggles or breathing apparatus that allows him/her to explore the inner parts of the desert. In that case, Region 3 would no longer warp the player back to the start of the area. That task would be transferred to Region 4, as it were. The player could then explore the oasis, among other things. Let's move on to a similar exercise.

Forest Event Overview

Suppose you wanted to make an area like the Lost Woods in some of the *Legend of Zelda* games. That is to say, one in which you can move in several directions, only one of them correct. Going the wrong way will send you back to the start of the area. We can use Regions for that as well. However, what if I told you that we could pull this off using a single 17×13 map? Seems crazy, right? Let's get started!

For this exercise, we'll need the following:

- The aforementioned 17×13 map, using the Dungeon tileset (Figure 15-3). It should have one Region for each cardinal direction, as in the screenshot.

- A Parallel event that handles what happens when the player steps on a certain Region at a specific time.

- A variable to quantify the player's progress, given that we're only using one area.

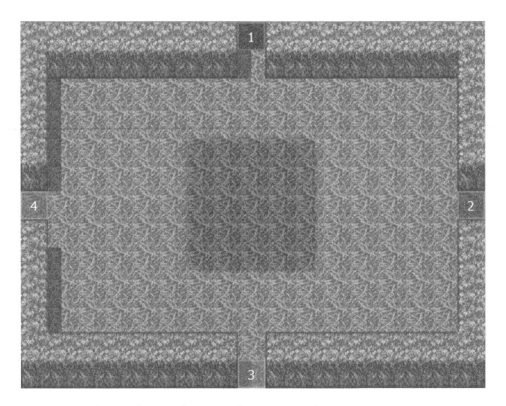

Figure 15-3. *The map that must be traversed in a certain order*

That does it for needs, although we'll also probably want some graphics that appear, based on the player's progress into the labyrinth. We'll call the variable WoodsLocation. If the player goes in the correct direction, we increase the variable's value by one; otherwise, we zero it out. If the player can successfully get through five areas in a row, then he/she will have cleared the labyrinth. The reward can be reaching the inner part of the area or a treasure chest filled with a rare item. You'll want the Parallel event to have five pages. Each one will require that the WoodsLocation variable be at a value one higher than the page before. In other words, page 1 is unconditional, while page 2 requires the variable to be equal to 1. Page 3 requires the variable to be at 2, and so forth, up to page 5, which needs the variable at a value of 4. With all that said, we need to figure out in what order the player has to walk through the labyrinth to clear it. I personally decided on right, right, left, down, up. Region-wise, that is 2, 2, 4, 3, 1.

Creating the Forest Event

Now that we know what we want our mysterious forest to do, all that's left is to write out the appropriate events.

■ **Tip** If you add this area to your own game, you'll want to come up with a way for the player to figure out in what direction he/she should go next. It could be a helpful NPC that gives the exact course to take or plants that appear as the player gets deeper into the labyrinth.

Following is the template for what each page of the Parallel event should look like:

```
♦Control Variables : #0002 X = Map X of Player
♦Control Variables : #0003 Y = Map Y of Player
♦Get Location Info : Region, Region ID, ({X},{Y})
♦If : Region = 1
   ♦Transfer Player : The Forest Event (8,6)
   ♦Control Variables : #0026 WoodsLocation = 0
   ♦
:  End
♦If : Region = 2
   ♦Transfer Player : The Forest Event (8,6)
   ♦Control Variables : #0026 WoodsLocation += 1
   ♦
:  End
♦If : Region = 3
   ♦Transfer Player : The Forest Event (8,6)
   ♦Control Variables : #0026 WoodsLocation = 0
   ♦
:  End
♦If: Region = 4
   ♦Transfer Player : The Forest Event (8,6)
   ♦Control Variables : #0026 WoodsLocation = 0
   ♦
:  End
♦
```

When the player walks to the eastern exit (Region 2), the value of WoodsLocation is increased by 1. Otherwise, the variable is zeroed out. In either case, the player is transferred back to the center of the area. For each page, the correct entrance should be the one that increases the value of WoodsLocation.

■ **Caution**   Because we are working with a Parallel event, you want the player to be transferred *before* you change the value of WoodsLocation; otherwise, you'll run into weird interactions, such as the screen fading out twice in a row and WoodsLocation being reset, even if the player has stepped through the right area.

I added several plant events (using the Small Sprouts graphic in tab B of the Dungeon tileset) that are visible only when the value of WoodsLocation is at a certain number or higher. This will give a visual representation to the player that he/she is progressing. Figure 15-4 shows what the labyrinth looks like when WoodsLocation is equal to 5.

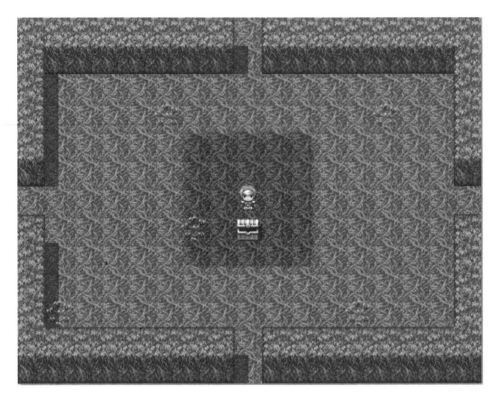

Figure 15-4. *The labyrinth state when* WoodsLocation *is equal to 5. I reward the player with a chest containing a powerful weapon*

That concludes this pair of exercises. A little information about vehicles follows, before we perform our next exercise.

Vehicles

I never covered vehicles during the course of creating our game, as we never had occasion to use them. Quite a few RPGs make do without a single vehicle, and others have vehicles that are not player-controlled. So don't feel like you *must* have vehicles in your game. RMMV has three types of vehicles, the graphics of which can be changed in the System tab of the Database. Each can be used to navigate different types of terrain. In order of freedom of movement, they are as follows:

- *Boat*: To be honest, the default graphic is more of a canoe. In any case, the boat can cross shallow water (Pond and Sea in the Overworld tileset).

- *Ship*: A full-fledged vessel, such as in all of those pirate movies! The ship can cross shallow water and deep water.

- *Airship*: The default airship is more of a blimp or dirigible. The airship can travel over any terrain but can only land on solid ground. Additionally, an airship can fly over events. Airships are on a higher layer than even Above Characters events, so you'll want to use Parallel events for events involving them.

If you want to experiment with tweaking the passability of boats and ships, the relevant vehicle logic is handled in the Game_Map class. Figure 15-5 shows a test map that I created for the purpose of displaying each of RMMV's vehicles.

Figure 15-5. *The test map I created to show off the three vehicles. From left to right, the different terrain tiles are Grassland A, Pond, Sea, and Deep Sea*

You can set the starting position of a vehicle much as you can the player characters themselves. In addition, you can move a vehicle from one location to another instantly, by using the Set Vehicle Location event command. This is useful when you have the plot move the player from one part of the world to another instantly. It would only make sense that his/her ship would be docked at the new town and not stranded at the previous port (assuming, of course, that your player took the ship to the new port in the first place). The other vehicle-related event command is Get on/off Vehicle, which does as the name implies.

■ **Note** In a rare exception to event commands that will crash your game if used incorrectly, you can use the Get on/off Vehicle command just about anywhere and get away with it. It won't actually do anything, unless your player can leave the vehicle correctly. (It won't strand you in the middle of the ocean, for example.)

Next, let's touch upon an enemy-related exercise. Namely, making a battle in which there are two enemies, both of whom must be defeated on the same turn; otherwise, the survivor will revive his/her comrade.

Two of a Kind

In RPGs, this type of battle falls under the broad umbrella of what are considered to be gimmick battles. Basically, a gimmick battle is one in which only a certain strategy (or a limited number of strategies) can bring the player victory. A fight with a pair of twins, in which one revives the other, dissuades unfocused attacks and promotes a calculated approach to the task at hand. For this exercise, we'll use a pair of zombies. For the sake of differentiation, copy the Zombie entry in the Database into an empty slot and use the hue setting to change the graphic's colors a little. Then change the new enemy's name to something else (such as Zombie Lord or Zombie Knight). Last, increase the new enemy's stats a bit. For reference, you can see a screenshot of the Zombie Lord in Figure 15-6.

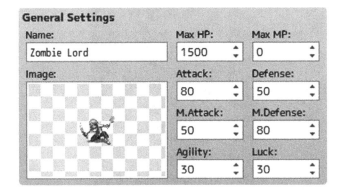

Figure 15-6. The Zombie Lord enemy that will accompany his lesser ally into battle

Next, let's create a troop that has one Zombie Lord and one Zombie. In the troop event, you'll want to have a pair of event pages, one for each of the enemies. We will use double conditionals for the events themselves (see Figure 15-7).

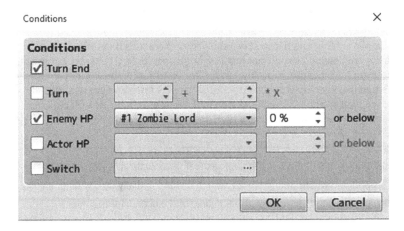

Figure 15-7. The conditions for page 1 of the troop event. Page 2 requires that the other enemy (#2 Zombie) be at 0% HP or below, instead

With that set up, we can fill out the pages themselves. Both of the pages will have a Span of Turn (so that they trigger once every turn) and a single Force Action event command.

Page 1's Force Action command is #2 Zombie, Reanimate, Index 1.

Meanwhile, Page 2's Force Action command is #1 Zombie Lord, Reanimate, Index 2.

To create Reanimate, I added a new spell (you can see it in slot #43 of with a Scope of 1 Ally (Dead)) with the Remove State: Knockout 100% and Recover HP 100% Effects. That concludes this exercise! Let me end this section with a few interesting notes about Force Action.

- A skill used with Force Action can be executed even if the user doesn't have the MP to cast it.

- Similarly, the user doesn't even need to *have* the skill in his/her list to be forced into using it. I confirmed this by having Harold throw Fire spells (remember that Harold doesn't have access to the basic Fire spell) around with Force Action.

- You can have a skill force the user to use another skill. If you're not careful, you could create a loop of skills that keep triggering infinitely until the battle is done or otherwise unwinnable (depending on what the skill in question does).

A Full House

While we're on the subject of troops and enemies, there's one other thing I've neglected to mention up to now. If you right-click a specific enemy's graphic within a troop, you get a single option named Appear Halfway. Clicking it causes the enemy to appear translucent in the troop display at the Database. If you begin a battle with some of the enemies in that state, they will not initially appear in the encounter. As the name of the option pretty much blurts out, you can use this to create enemies that appear during the course of a battle. This is useful in situations such as the following:

- A battle in which enemy reinforcements arrive at regular intervals.

- An enemy that has a skill that causes allies to appear.

- A battle with multiple waves of enemies. Defeat one wave to cause the next one to appear.

For this exercise, we will create a troop containing five Assailants. The first, third, and fifth Assailants will be present from the start of the battle. The second and fourth Assailants will appear in response to their defeated allies. Take a look at Figure 15-8.

Figure 15-8. *A zoomed-in screenshot of our horde of Assailants. Note how the second and fourth Assailants are nearly transparent, compared to their allies*

The first troop event page should execute at the start of the battle. It gives the first and fifth Assailants the Immortal state. The second page is triggered when the first Assailant drops to 0% HP or less, causing the second Assailant to appear and the first one to be defeated. The last page is triggered when the fifth Assailant drops to 0% HP or less, causing the fourth Assailant to appear and the fifth one to be defeated. I will let you translate this into the relevant events. Just keep in mind that your event pages should have a span of Battle, as you don't want them to trigger more than once during the battle. Also, keeping in mind that death is prioritized over every other battle event in RMMV, you want the new enemy to appear before the old one loses its immortality; otherwise, a clever player could use a skill that hits all enemies, bypassing the reinforcements completely by defeating all of them at the same time.

Amusingly, that used to happen all the time with older RPGs, given the limitations of programming. Players would just find sneaky ways to prevent reinforcement waves from appearing, by overtaxing the battle logic or employing any other such shenanigans.

Ye Olde RPG—A Treatise on Quest Experience

Japanese RPGs (with most of the exceptions being relatively recent titles) tend to give the player characters most, if not all, of their experience via combat. That was part of the reason older Japanese RPGs were notorious for their grinding (repeatedly fighting monsters in the same area to get gold, experience, and items) and overall difficulty. Can't defeat any of the monsters outside of town? Don't have the gold to get items? Tough luck! Classic Western RPGs, such as *Wasteland* and the *Ultima* series, were actually somewhat better about that. Usually. That leads to my next topic.

Think back to the Bat Wing sidequest we created in the fishing village of Seaside for our players to complete. The player got gold out of it, but what if we wanted to offer experience as well? We could use the *Change EXP* event command to accomplish that task. Change EXP allows you to give experience points to (or take away from) a certain party member or the entire party (you can designate a specific actor ID using a variable as well). The value of EXP given or taken can be a fixed value or that of a variable. Last, you can toggle the "Show Level Up" check box, which will prompt the game to display the level-up box, if the experience gained from the command is enough to bump the character up one or more levels.

■ **Note**   *Change Level* can be used to much the same effect. In that event command, you are declaring how many levels you wish to add or subtract from the chosen character.

Using those two event commands, you give the player even more incentive to complete sidequests and also a way to progress in the game without having to battle monsters ceaselessly.

The Other Actor Event Commands

As it turns out, I've covered most of the event commands contained in the Actor section of the list. With that said, I haven't covered *all* of them. Here's a bulleted list of the ones I have glossed over until now.

- I didn't really mention *Change HP* or *Change MP*, as our only instances of out-of-combat healing were covered neatly by *Recover All*. However, those two commands are more versatile, as they allow you to increase *or* decrease the relevant stat. You could have a poisoned well that injures the party when it drinks from it, or a floating fairy that recovers the entire party's MP. The one thing to note is that you can make it so that damage inflicted with Change HP can't knock out its victim (by not toggling the "Allow Knockout" check box).

- *Change TP* is even more situational than the previous two event commands. With the changes we made to the code in the previous chapter, you would be able to change an actor's TP outside of battle. Otherwise, any such change would be wiped out thanks to the initTp method executed at the start of every battle.

- *Change State*: This is something that you probably won't be using constantly. Most instances of adding or removing states from an actor are covered by skills and items on both sides of a battle. This could be useful for a damage floor that additionally inflicts a status effect, however.

- *Change Parameter*: In addition to experience and states, you can also permanently change an actor's stats, for better or worse. *The minimum for any stat except MP is 1. MP can be zeroed out.* An interesting use of this event command could be for a dungeon that disallows magic. Just make it so that the MP of every party member is set to 0 (ensuring that you write the value of each party member's MP to a specific variable beforehand), and you're set. *It would probably be easier to just make a Silence state and inflict it on the party when it enters the dungeon, to be fair.*

- *Change Skill*: These allow you to give or take away skills from a party member. For an actual video game example of this happening, see Garnet from *Final Fantasy IX*. She starts the game with, quite frankly, a ridiculous number of Eidolons (entities that can be summoned for powerful effects). The plot takes them away from her until a time when she regains them. You could have a similar thing happen in your game. Maybe your party's mage gets amnesia from witnessing a horrible event and forgets how to cast anything save the simplest cantrips. Or perhaps the game's villain seals away the knowledge of the one spell that could defeat him, forcing the party to find a way to unseal it, so that the party's magician can learn it once again.

- *Change Equipment*: This is perhaps the Actor event command I use least. It has its situational uses, but I'm not a huge fan. Essentially, it allows you to change an actor's current equipment. This is good to use when a member of your party is going to leave it permanently or semipermanently (in which case, losing the items it had equipped would be bad). Just use Change Equipment commands to remove all of its gear and you're set. Note that this doesn't make items appear out of thin air. If you want to use this command to equip an actor with a new weapon he/she has found, it must actually be in his/her inventory (by use of Change Weapons), before you call for it to be equipped.

- In hindsight, we could have used *Change Name* instead of the script equivalent for our riddles back in Chapter 11. Basically, you choose the actor whose name you want to change and choose their new name. It's Name Input Processing, but without giving the player a chance to decide on the new name. *Change Nickname* is the same thing, but for nicknames instead of names.

- *Change Class* allows you to change an actor's class. Version 1.1 of MV added a Save Level checkbox to this command that, as it states, will preserve the character's level after the class change. Otherwise, this command will drop your actor's level back to 1 (with the respective drop to parameters that this would cause), but it won't cause him/her to forget any skills. This could be pretty neat for a class system like that of *Dragon Warrior III*. Imagine if Harold could learn every skill available to every class in the game!

- Last, *Change Profile* allows you to change a character's biographic profile. This is good if a particularly important plot event has occurred and you want to reflect the fact in a given character's description.

The Bridge

As an interesting hypothetical situation, say that you want to make a bridge that meets both of the following conditions:

- It allows the player to walk under it.

- It allows the player to cross it.

If you were to place your bridge using map tiles, you would meet the second condition but not the first. If you were to use events to create your bridge, you'd run into a different problem. Namely, you would have to check for two different conditions. How do we solve this problem? We'll need the following items:

- A Parallel event that checks the player's location

- An event that has a graphic that will serve as our bridge tile

The first order of business is to figure out how the player will interact with the map containing the bridge. For example, take a look at Figure 15-9, to see the map I'm using for this exercise. The player's starting position is at the top of a staircase. While the player is atop this ledge, he/she should be able to walk on the bridge tiles. While the player is on the lower part of the area, he/she should be able to walk under the bridge. We need the bridge tile events to have two pages. Page 1 will have no conditions and will have a Below Characters priority. The second page will require that a certain switch be flipped on and have an Above Characters priority. The Parallel event will flip the switch on when the player walks down to the ground level and turn it back off when the player ascends to the ledge.

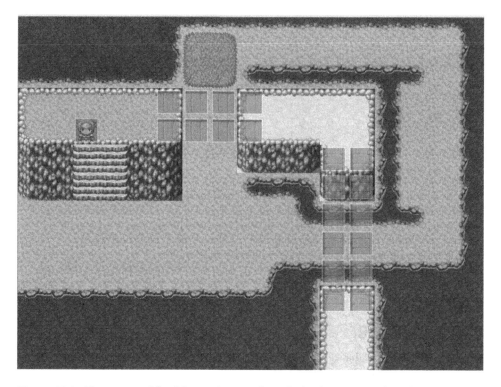

Figure 15-9. *The map used for this exercise. Note how the bridges connect directly with the ledges*

The first bridge uses the horizontal stone bridge tiles, while the second bridge uses the vertical stone bridge tiles. You can find both of the tiles in tab B of the Outside tileset.

■ **Note** Interestingly enough, it appears that the bridge tiles in MV do not share the selective passability of their Ace counterparts. You can fix this by going to the Tilesets tab and clicking Passage (4 dir). Then make your way to tab B of the Outside tileset and set the passability appropriately. The horizontal stone bridge tile should only have left and right arrows for passability, while the vertical stone bridge tile should only have north and south arrows.

```
◆Control Variables : #0002 X = Map X of Player
◆Control Variables : #0003 Y = Map Y of Player
◆If : Y = 4
  ◆If : X ≥ 2
    ◆If : X ≤ 3
      ◆Control Switches : #0047 BridgeAbove = OFF
      ◆
    : End
  ◆
  : End
◆
: End
```

```
♦If : Y = 5
   ♦If : X ≥ 2
      ♦If : X ≤ 3
         ♦Control Switches : #0047 BridgeAbove = ON
         ♦
      : End
      ♦
   : End
   ♦
: End
♦
```

BridgeAbove is the switch that must be flipped on for the bridge tiles to allow the player to pass under them. You could also have a dungeon in which the player has to pull a lever, press a button, or otherwise cause a switch to be flipped. Once the switch is flipped, a bridge to advance deeper into the dungeon appears. All you would need in that case are the bridge tiles with a Below Characters priority and a requirement for a switch to be flipped, and the event that would flip that switch.

Before we move on to the final exercise of our book, a small aside is called for to discuss the Resource Manager, which I glossed over back in the very first chapter.

The Resource Manager

The Resource Manager is a helpful tool that can be used, as its name states, to manage your MV project's resources. See Figure 15-10 for a screenshot of the Resource Manager.

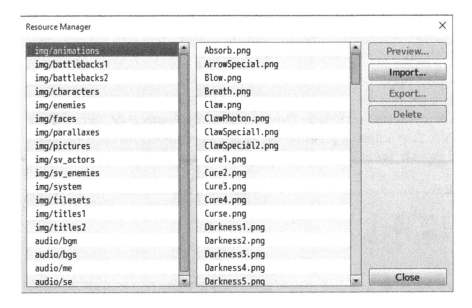

Figure 15-10. *The Resource Manager in RMMV*

The various audio and image folders of the project are listed on the left, while the contents of the currently selected folder are on the right. You can click Preview after selecting an image file to see it in full detail. Audio cannot be previewed from the Resource Manager, but you have the Sound Test for that anyway. I'm going to make it a point to use the Resource Manager for our final exercise, but more on that when it's relevant.

The Town Map

This is the end of the end. After this exercise, I will close out this chapter with the summary, and we will be done with the book. (You'll want to check Appendix A for information about exporting your game to various platforms and Appendix B for helpful resources related to RMMV and other such things.) How better to end a book about an RPG development engine than by explaining how to create a map? To complete this exercise, we'll need the following:

- A screenshot of the area for which we wish to have a map
- A picture of a symbol/marker denoting the player's location on the map
- A pair of common events governing the map logic
- An item to execute the map logic

I will be using the Fishing Village exterior for this exercise.

Preparing Our Map Pictures

The first order of business is figuring out how big the map has to be. Taking a screenshot of the game while you are play-testing will give you a fairly close estimate (I got 818×624). Next, right-click on the map name in the lower-left corner of the editor and select Save as Image. Save the resulting png file to a folder of your choice. If you open it with the image editor or photo viewer of your choice, you'll realize that the fishing village buildings are missing their doors!

■ **Note** This occurs because the Save as Image option only saves the map graphics. Events are not considered graphics, so they don't appear at all.

If not having doors displayed in the image is unacceptable to you, there is a workaround.

1. Go into the Resource Manager and find the img/characters folder.

2. From there, scroll down to the !Door1 graphic set.

3. Click it and export it to the location of your choice. Make sure that your name includes the .png extension (you could name it door.png, for example)

4. Then, click img/tilesets.

5. Click Import and then find the !Door1 graphic set that you exported.

6. Last, go to the Tileset tab of the Database and assign the new graphic (which will carry the filename you gave it without the .png extension; I called it door1) to the E tab of the Outside tileset.

Now you can place doors to cover the entrances, for your screenshot needs. Just make sure to erase the graphics afterward! Use your image-editing software of choice (any will work, including Windows' own Paint application) to resize the map image you saved previously to 818×624. Next, you'll want to make a picture that can be used as a marker for the player's current location. It should be small enough not to take up excessive space on the map, yet big enough to be seen. The marker that I created is 30×30 in size. Once we have both of our pictures, we need to add them to our Resource Manager. Find the img/pictures folder in the manager (curiously, RMMV comes with no stock pictures) and import your two images to that folder accordingly.

Using the Show Picture Event Command

With that set up, it's time to use the *Show Picture* event command. Take a look at Figure 15-11 to see a screenshot of the event command, as displayed within RMMV.

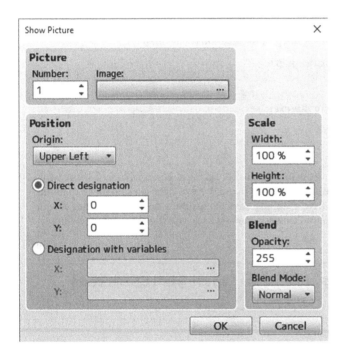

Figure 15-11. *The Show Picture event command*

You can assign a picture a control number (Number). As the tool tip in RMMV states: "Control number of the picture. The larger [the] number, the higher priority." Think of it like a stack of papers. The lower a picture's number, the deeper it is located within the stack. So if we want our marker to be placed on top of the map, it must have a higher control number. With that said, you can pick any number from 1 to 100. The map could be 99, and the marker could be 100. To keep it simple, I'll give the map a 1 and the marker a 2. We can set which graphic is shown by selecting it with Image. If you hadn't imported the two images to img/pictures accordingly, the browser window would be empty. For *Display Position*, we'll want the automap to be positioned at 0, 0, with an Upper Left origin. *Origin* determines how the image is placed on the screen. If you choose Center, it will be the map's center that is placed at 0, 0. We don't want that. For our map marker, we will also use an Upper Left origin, but it will be positioned with the use of variables. Last, you can set *Blending* options. The lower the opacity of your picture, the more translucent it will appear.

Creating Our Town Map Common Events

This is where it gets interesting. The general idea for our common events is the following:

- When the player uses the Map item, we want to determine the player's X and Y coordinates. After that, we apply a multiplier to the X and Y variables.

- Afterward, we use a pair of Show Picture commands to display the map and the map marker.

What multiplier do we need? We have to correlate the pixel size of the map picture (818×624) with the tile size of the map in the map editor (40×40). This is as easy as dividing the first value by the second for both X and Y. The multiplier for X is (818/40 = 20.45), and the multiplier for Y is (624/40 = 15.6). Here's the first common event:

```
◆Control Switches  : #0048 TurnOffMap = ON
◆Control Variables : #0002 X = Map X of Player
◆Control Variables : #0003 Y = Map Y of Player
◆Control Variables : #0002 X *= 20.45
◆Control Variables : #0003 Y *= 15.6
◆Show Picture : #1, Map, Upper Left (0,0), (100%,100%), 255, Normal
◆Show Picture : #2, Marker, Upper Left ({X},{Y}), (50%,50%), 255, Normal
◆
```

■ **Note**   You can use the Script option in Control Variables to write in decimal numbers. The Constant option allows only whole numbers.

I used a 50% zoom for the map marker because, when displayed, 30×30 looks clunky on the map. As it stands, you can create a suitable item to hold the Map common event and then start up the game. However, you'll find that using the Map event will cause the screen to display the area map and map marker without a way to remove the pictures. That is what the TurnOffMap switch is for. When the switch is on, the second common event is processed. I give it a Parallel trigger, so that it is running concurrently until needed. The only role that the second common event has is to erase the pictures that have been created and flip off the TurnOffMap switch until it is needed once again.

```
◆If : Button [Shift] is pressed down
  ◆Erase Picture : #1
  ◆Erase Picture : #2
  ◆Control Switches : #0048 TurnOffMap = OFF
  ◆
: End
◆
```

■ **Reminder**   The Shift key is normally used when you want your character to run (or *dash*, as it's formally called within MV).

Erase Picture asks for a control number and erases the displayed image that has the number. That concludes this exercise. Give the player a Map item and test it out!

Variants on the Map Exercise

What we have is good and all, but following are some possible variants for you to think about as well.

1. Make it so that the map marker moves as the player does.

    - As you have almost certainly noticed, you can still control the character when the map is displayed.

    - To pull this off, all you need to do is copy-paste the part of the first common event that handles the X and Y variables and add a *Move Picture* event command directly below that.

    ```
    ◆Control Variables : #0002 X = Map X of Player
    ◆Control Variables : #0003 Y = Map Y of Player
    ◆Control Variables : #0002 X *= 20.45
    ◆Control Variables : #0003 Y *= 15.6
    ◆Move Picture : #2, Upper Left ({X},{Y}), (50%,50%), 255, Normal, 15 frames
    ```

2. Make a minimap of the area.

    - I'm thinking in a manner similar to that of the *Grinsia* minimap, where you have a semitransparent map in the upper-left corner.

    - This is actually relatively simple. We render the same map picture with the Upper Left origin but set the Zoom to 25% (which will shrink it to a quarter of its size). This drops it down to roughly 205×156. Additionally, we set its Opacity to 128, as we want the minimap to be somewhat see-through.

    - Then, we quarter the multipliers, which would become 5.11 (approximately) and 3.9 (exactly) for X and Y, respectively, for the map marker as well. I also dropped the marker's Zoom down to 25%, to keep it in line with the smaller map.

    - You could make an item that reveals an area's map to the player for a certain number of steps.

    - Keep in mind that you'll need a picture for each individual area in which you plan to have a minimap. How would you handle an area like our interior structure map for the port town, where there are multiple different areas on the same map? That's an exercise for you.

Summary

This chapter covered a range of miscellaneous topics that were not covered in the book's previous chapters. Among them were creating a battle that requires a certain party member to participate, having encounters in which some of the enemies appear during the battle rather than at the start, and creating mazes within a single map, with the use of variables and Regions.

APPENDIX A

Exporting Your RMMV Game

This appendix covers the process of project deployment—exporting your RPG Maker MV game as an executable package for people to play on various platforms.

Overview

In the Ace version of this book, I didn't cover project deployment at all, given that games created in RPG Maker VX Ace could only be played on Windows PCs, making the process rather more straightforward. However, I think it bears mentioning in this second edition, as games created with this version of the engine can be played on PCs, Macs, and even mobile/tablet operating systems (iOS and Android). So, without further ado, see Figure A-1 for a screenshot of the Deployment screen (which you can reach by clicking File and then Deployment; it has no associated hotkey).

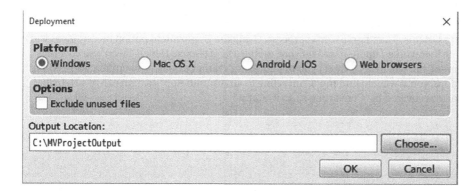

Figure A-1. A screenshot of the Deployment menu. Note the various platform options for your game project's deployment

Version 1.1 of MV added the option to exclude unused files, which is extremely useful for cutting down the size of your game's project. Here's how you would go about deploying the game project for each platform.

For Windows

After selecting "Exclude unused files" and choosing your output location, click OK. Then a pop-up will say that MV is "Creating a distribution package." Once the package is ready, you will get a pop-up with a checkmark saying "Succeeded to create a distribution package." You can run the game if you're using Windows by opening the package folder and clicking Game.exe.

For Mac OS X

Make sure that "Exclude unused files" is toggled and that your output location is correct; then click OK. The distribution package will be created and you will get the same pop-up as with Windows when MV has finished the process. If you're using a Mac, you can run the Game.app file by clicking on it. On Windows, Game.app will appear as a folder which, curiously, can be explored much like any other folder. You can actually play the game on your default browser (if it meets the minimum processing requirements for MV) by finding and clicking on the index.html file.

For Web Browsers

Of course, MV 1.1 also has an option to make a game directly for web browsers as well (1.0 had no such option). After creating the distribution package you can (according to Kadokawa's MV Help file) "run your game on a web browser by uploading your exported project folder to a web server."

For Android/iOS

You'll notice that I left this deployment option for last. As it so happens, creating a complete package for one of the mobile operating systems is a rather involved process. Using the Deployment option merely gives you the project files to be further worked upon, based on your mobile OS of choice. Hence, I won't be covering how to do the deployment, but will instead direct you to Kadokawa's rather extensive documentation on the subject. For Android apps, you'll want to find the "Converting to an Android App" section of MV's Help file. For iOS apps, the process is covered in "Converting to an iOS App."

Useful Resources for RPG Maker MV

This appendix is a compilation of helpful resources for just about anything related to your RMMV games. Do you need help with a certain idea that you have stuck in your head? Perhaps you could seek aid from one of the links listed under "Tutorials and General Help." Are you thinking of hiring someone to help you create your very own commercial game? Some of the other links should cover that. On that note, let us begin.

Tutorials and General Help for RMMV

Game design, like most things in life, is a constant process of renewal and learning new ways to tackle old (and not-so-old) problems. Following are some links to sites that contain tutorials and/or communities of people willing to help out aspiring role-playing game (RPG) designers.

> `http://forums.rpgmakerweb.com`: The official forum for Enterbrain's video game development engines, including RMMV.

> `http://forums.rpgmakerweb.com/index.php?/forum/130-rpg-maker-mv-tutorials/`: Also part of the official site. As the web link suggests, this subforum offers tutorials for many topics concerning RPG Maker MV.

> `http://www.rpgmakervxace.net/forum/146-rpgmaker-mv/`: One of the most populated unofficial forums related to RPG Maker VX Ace on the Internet. This link leads to their new MV subforum. If you can't find the answer you're looking for on the official site, this should be your next destination.

> `https://rpgmakermv.co/`: A relatively new unofficial forum that, as the web site name states, is dedicated to talking about RPG Maker MV.

Note Search engines will steer you toward `rpgmakerweb.com` whenever they get a chance. Degica has done a fairly good job of positioning itself as the universal destination for all things RPG Maker (which, given that it's the publisher, is fair play). You can buy resource packs (music, art, and so on) from them, as well as a few other items of interest.

© Darrin Perez 2016
D. Perez, *Beginning RPG Maker MV*, DOI 10.1007/978-1-4842-1967-6

Art and Spriting

Need art for your RMMV game? Want to learn how to create it yourself? I have you covered with a pair of links. To be fair, art is easily my weakest asset when it comes to game design. However, a wise man once told me: "You need not know everything . . . only the people who *do*."

http://rpg-maker-artists.deviantart.com: A community on deviantART for RPG Maker artists. As a general statement, deviantART is an incredibly useful site for all things art. If you have an artistic inclination, you could join the community; otherwise, it is probably a good place to look for people who can create unique sprites and/or other pieces of art for your RMMV games.

http://finalbossblues.com/pixel-tutorials: Offers a variety of cool tutorials for making your own pixel art. The tutorials are specifically targeted at RPG Maker XP, VX, and VX Ace users but should have relevance outside the RPG Maker series as well. After all, art is art.

Tutorials and References for JavaScript

A veritable treasure trove of resources for JavaScript exists on and off the Internet. Following are but some of the sites available:

https://www.codecademy.com/learn/javascript: Codecademy's mission, as stated, is "Teaching the world how to code." It does an exemplary job at it, if I may be so bold as to offer an endorsement. It has course plans for several of the most popular programming languages, including JavaScript.

http://www.w3schools.com/js/: This site has a helpful and easy-to-understand reference to many of JavaScript's internal workings.

https://developer.mozilla.org/en-US/Learn/JavaScript: A very comprehensive guide on JavaScript for both beginners and programmers with a little more experience.

Sounds and Music

No game is truly complete without an awesome soundtrack. Here are some links to music that can spruce up your project accordingly.

http://www.scythuzmusic.com/: The site of Benjamin Carr, alias Scythuz. I have had the pleasure of purchasing some of his tracks in the past. He delivers high-quality work at competitive rates. There is a contact page on his site, if you would like to commission some music tracks from him.

http://rpgmaker.net/resources/music/: Links to a list of music resources for RPG Maker.

http://videogamecaster.com/royalty-free-music-and-sounds/: Has a large list of sites that provide music and sounds for free and commercial use.

Video Game Writing Tutorials

The story and general flow of an RPG are two of its most important elements. Here are some links to sites that discuss video game writing:

> `www.paladinstudios.com/2012/08/06/how-to-write-a-good-game-story-and-get-filthy-rich/`

The article in question is from 2012, but it has a good treatise on writing a good story for your games.

> `http://blog.rpgmakerweb.com/tutorials/design-by-layer-1/`

> `http://blog.rpgmakerweb.com/tutorials/design-by-layer-ii/`

Nick Palmer wrote up a pair of helpful tutorials for writing an RPG story on the official RPG Maker blog.

Note   If you require someone (or a group of someones) with whom to collaborate on a project, posting a thread in the official forums is never a bad idea. It may well be that you find like-minded individuals with design strengths to offset your weaknesses.

Plugins

These are perhaps the best way to add or change the functionality of your game. If you decide to cut your teeth on JavaScript within RPG Maker MV, looking at other people's work is probably the best way to begin. Seeing what others before you have done is a great way to discover exactly what is and isn't possible within RMMV.

> `http://mvplugins.com/`: *Provides a large list of RPG Maker MV plugins for use. As of the time of this writing, there are 407 plugins available.*

> *Himeworks MV Plugins* (`http://himeworks.com/mv-plugins/`): Tsukihime, or just Hime for short, is an experienced RPG Maker scripter. In fact, I used his Change Currency script to solve the arena token currency text problem in Chapter 7 of the first edition of this book. He has since turned his eye toward MV and making plugins for it. I highly recommend checking out his work!

> *Galv's Scripts* (`http://galvs-scripts.com/rpgmaker/mv-plugins/`): Galv is but one of many skilled scripters within the RPG Maker community. As of the time of writing, he has 22 plugins for RPG Maker MV on his site, covering a variety of things you might need for your own game.

Note   If you are planning on releasing a commercial game, make sure that the scripts you are using are permitted in such a game. Most scripts list such licensing details in the comments section, but, when in doubt, don't hesitate to ask the scripter directly.

RMMV Games

There's no shame in taking a look at the games created by your fellow RMMV users and seeing what can be done with the engine. It may well be that you figure out how to do something new after seeing other games in action! On that note, following is a link to a list of some of the RMMV games that are available:

> http://rpgmaker.net/games/?engine=37: A list of completed RMMV games on rpgmaker.net. Given the large number of games on the list, I did not check to see whether any of them are commercial (cost money). It is still very much worth a look.

Closing Notes

In closing, I'd like to emphasize that the RPG Maker community is filled with many talented and wonderful people. If you ever need help with anything related to RMMV, don't hesitate to ask them for help. Just treat them with a modicum of respect (this is probably good advice relating to anybody, in the real world as on the Internet), and everything will be fine. Good luck with your endeavors, and may your games be awesome!

Index

▨ T, U

■ V

■ W, X, Y, Z

Get the eBook for only $5!

Why limit yourself?

Now you can take the weightless companion with you wherever you go and access your content on your PC, phone, tablet, or reader.

Since you've purchased this print book, we're happy to offer you the eBook in all 3 formats for just $5.

Convenient and fully searchable, the PDF version enables you to easily find and copy code—or perform examples by quickly toggling between instructions and applications. The MOBI format is ideal for your Kindle, while the ePUB can be utilized on a variety of mobile devices.

To learn more, go to www.apress.com/companion or contact support@apress.com.